National First Edition

The

LEGAL GUIDE

for

STARTING & RUNNING

A SMALL BUSINESS

By Attorney Fred Steingold
Edited by Mary Randolph and Ralph Warner

NOLO PRESS   BERKELEY

YOUR RESPONSIBILITY WHEN USING A SELF-HELP LAW BOOK

We've done our best to give you useful and accurate information in this book. But laws and procedures change frequently and are subject to differing interpretations. If you want legal advice backed by a guarantee, see a lawyer. If you use this book, it's your responsibility to make sure that the facts and general advice contained in it are applicable to your situation.

KEEPING UP-TO-DATE

To keep its books up-to-date, Nolo Press issues new printings and new editions periodically. New printings reflect minor legal changes and technical corrections. New editions contain major legal changes, major text additions or major reorganizations. To find out if a later printing or edition of any Nolo book is available, call Nolo Press at (510) 549-1976 or check the catalog in the *Nolo News*, our quarterly newspaper.

To stay current, follow the "Update" service in the *Nolo News*. You can get the paper free by sending us the registration card in the back of the book. In another effort to help you use Nolo's latest materials, we offer a 25% discount off the purchase of any new Nolo book if you turn in any earlier printing or edition. (Turn the page to see our "Recycle Offer.")

FIRST EDITION	July 1992
Second Printing	January 1993
EDITORS	Ralph Warner and Mary Randolph
ILLUSTRATION	Mari Stein
BOOK DESIGN	Jackie Mancuso and Amy Ihara
COVER DESIGN	Toni Ihara
INDEX	Jane Meyerhofer
PRINTING	Delta Lithograph

Steingold, Fred.

The legal guide for starting and running a small business / by Fred S. Steingold ; edited by Ralph Warner and Mary Randolph. -- 1st national ed.

p. cm.

Includes index

ISBN 0-87337-174-7 : $19.95

1. Small business--Law and legislation--United States__Popular works. I. Warner, Ralph E. II. Randolph, Mary. III Title.
KF169.Z9S84 1992

346.73' 0652--dc20

[347.306652]   92-14279

CIP

ACKNOWLEDGMENTS

Special thanks to Nolo Publisher Jake Warner—the cheerful perfectionist whose ideas infuse every page of this book—and to Nolo Editor Mary Randolph, who deftly whipped the manuscript into final shape.

Thanks, too, to the rest of the remarkable Nolo family for their invaluable contribution—especially Steve Elias, Robin Leonard, Barbara Hodovan, Jackie Mancuso, Tony Mancuso and Barbara Kate Repa.

In addition to the folks at Nolo, these other professionals generously shared their expertise to make this book possible:

- Attorneys Charles Borgsdorf, Larry Ferguson, Peter Long, Michael Malley, Robert Stevenson, Nancy Welber and Warren Widmayer.

- Certified Public Accountants Mark Hartley and Lonnie Loy.

- Insurance Specialists James Libs, Mike Mansel and Dave Tiedgen.

Finally, thanks to my small business clients, who are a constant source of knowledge and inspiration.

RECYCLE YOUR OUT-OF-DATE BOOKS
AND GET 25% OFF YOUR NEXT PURCHASE

OUT-O F-DATE = DANGEROUS

Using an old edition can be dangerous if information in it is wrong. Unfortunately, laws and legal procedures change often. Generally speaking, any book more than two years old is of questionable value. Books more than four or five years old are a menace.

To help you keep up-to-date, we extend this offer:

If you cut out and deliver to us the title portion of the cover of any old Nolo book, we'll give you a 25% discount off the retail price of any new Nolo book. For example, if you have a copy of *Tenants' Rights*, 4th edition, and want to trade it for the latest *California Marriage and Divorce Law*, send us the *Tenants' Rights* cover and a check for the current price of *California Marriage and Divorce*, less a 25% discount.

Information on current prices and editions is listed in the back of this book and in the catalog in the *Nolo News* (see offer at the back of this book).

This offer is to individuals only.

A Legal Guide To Starting and Running a Small Business

INTRODUCTION

APPENDIX

INTRODUCTION

The law increasingly affects every aspect of a small business operation, from relationships with landlords, customers and suppliers to dealings with governmental agencies over taxes, licenses and zoning. Being surrounded by legal issues places most small business owners in an unhappy dilemma—either buy expensive legal help from a lawyer or go without.

Here is another alternative: a self-help book designed to answer most of the legal questions you're likely to ask in starting and running your business.

Fortunately, understanding and coping with most small business legal issues isn't akin to doing your own brain surgery. In truth, it's more like taking an aspirin when you feel a headache coming on.

No self-help law book, no matter how good, can eliminate the need to consult an attorney once in a while. But armed with the practical legal information you'll find here, you'll be able to make most day-to-day decisions on your own, seeking professional advice only when you truly need it.

If you understand basic legal issues, you can avoid basic legal problems. But staying out of trouble shouldn't be your only goal. Whether you're a retailer, professional, craftsperson, distributor or small manufacturer, a good understanding of the law can help you fashion policies and strategies that will pay off.

For example, suppose you want to lease a building. Typically, you'll have two worries. If you sign a long lease and your business doesn't succeed, you'll be stuck with an unneeded space. On the other hand, if you choose a very short lease and your

business is the big hit you hope it will be, the landlord may jack up the rent.

Fortunately for the legally knowledgeable, there is an easy detour around this dilemma. It's called the lease option contract. Typically, for a small payment or a slightly increased rent, you can start with a short lease that gives you one, or even several, options to renew at an agreed-upon rental amount (often, the original rent plus an adjustment for inflation) if your business does well.

Dealing with customers is much the same. If you know the law that regulates advertising, refunds and warranties, you have a strong basis to establish policies that tell your customers you really do put their interests first. Seen this way, legal rules do not define how you'll treat customers. Instead, they form the foundation on which you build a more generous relationship, which will convert one-time customers into regulars and regular customers into advocates for your business.

Finally, a personal note. I'm a small business lawyer and legal writer based in Ann Arbor, Michigan. I advise many people with dreams and aspirations much like yours. Much of what I tell them day to day is in this book.

There is one thing I'd like to emphasize right here at the beginning. You're about to take charge of your legal decision-making in an exciting new way. In fact, you'll begin to look at law differently—not as an enemy to be feared but as a fact of business life that you can grasp and be comfortable with. In business, as elsewhere, knowledge is power, and this book helps you put the power of law in your hands.

Icons

Throughout the book, we use icons to alert you to certain information.

Fast Track

We use this icon to let you know when you can skip information that may not be relevant to your case.

Warning

This icon alerts you to potential problems..

Recommended Reading

When you see this icon, a list of additional resources that can assist you follows.

Cross-Reference

This icon refers you to a further discussion of the topic elsewhere in this book.

Sole Proprietorship, Partnership or Corporation: Which Legal Form Is Best for Your Business?

1

When you start a business, you'll have to decide whether you want to structure it as a sole proprietorship, general partnership, limited partnership or corporation. There's no right or wrong choice that fits everyone. Your job is to understand how each legal structure works and then pick the one that best meets your needs. The best choice isn't always obvious. You may, after reading this chapter, decide to seek some guidance from a lawyer or an accountant.

For many small businesses, the best initial choice is either a sole proprietorship or—if more than one owner is involved—a partnership. These forms of business are relatively simple and inexpensive to establish and maintain.

Forming and operating a corporation is more complicated and costly, but it's worth it for some small businesses. One factor that may tilt you toward incorporating is the desire to take advantage of a corporation's ability to limit your personal liability for business debts and judgments. Another might be a more favorable tax rate structure that, in certain circumstances, enables a corporation to stash away earnings for future use at a relatively low tax rate. In addition, a corporation can provide a wide range of fringe benefits to its employees (including the owners) and deduct the cost as a business expense.

Keep in mind that your initial choice of a business form doesn't have to be permanent. You can start out as a sole proprietorship or partnership and later, if your business grows or the risks of personal liability increase, convert your business into a corporation.

What About Cooperatives?

Some idealistic people dream of forming a business of true equals—an organization owned and controlled democratically by its members. The organizers of these enterprises may be interested in consumer "co-ops" that run food buying clubs or small stores. They may be looking into housing co-ops to provide housing for members and perhaps others. Or they may want to create a workers' co-op to manufacture and sell arts and crafts.

These grass-roots business organizers often refer to their businesses as a group, collective or co-op. These are usually informal rather than legal labels. Except for certain types of mostly agricultural co-ops, everyone who starts a business with others—even a business that embraces lofty principles of egalitarianism and cooperation—needs to select a legal structure for the business. Generally, this means picking one the of the traditional formats described in this chapter: partnership, corporation or, perhaps, a nonprofit corporation.

To learn more about cooperative-type organizations and how to start one, I recommend *We Own It: Starting and Managing Cooperatives and Employee Owned Ventures* by Peter Jan Honigsberg, Bernard Kamoroff and Jim Beatty (Bell Springs Publishing). It's available from Nolo Press.

WAYS TO ORGANIZE YOUR BUSINESS

TYPE OF ENTITY	MAIN ADVANTAGES	MAIN DRAWBACKS
Sole Proprietorship (Section A)	Simple and inexpensive to create and operate Owner reports profit or loss on his or her personal tax return	Owner personally liable for business debts
General Partnership (Section B)	Simple and inexpensive to create and operate Owners (partners) report their share of profit or loss on their personal tax returns	Owners (partners) personally liable for business debts
Limited Partnership (Section C)	Limited partners have limited personal liability for business debts as long as they don't participate in management General partners can raise cash without involving outside investors in management of business	General partners personally liable for business debts More expensive to create than general partnership Suitable mainly for companies that invest in real estate
Regular Corporation (Section D)	Owners have limited personal liability for business debts Fringe benefits can be deducted as business expense Owners can split corporate profit among owners and corporation, paying lower overall tax rate	More expensive to create than partnership or sole proprietorship Owners must meet legal requirements for stock registration and paperwork Separate taxable entity
S Corporation (Section D)	Owners have limited personal liability for business debts Owners report their share of corporate profit or loss on their personal tax returns Owners can use corporate loss to offset income from other sources	More expensive to create than partnership or sole proprietorship Owners must meet legal requirements for registration and paperwork Income must be allocated to owners according to their ownership interests Fringe benefits limited for owners who own more than 2% of shares
Professional Corporation (Section E)	Owners have no personal liability for malpractice of other owners	More expensive to create than partnership or sole proprietorship Owners must meet legal requirements for registration
Nonprofit Corporation (Section E)	Corporation doesn't pay income taxes Contributions to charitable corporation are tax-deductible Fringe benefits can be deducted as business expense	Full tax advantages available only to groups organized for charitable, scientific, educational, literary or religious purposes Property transferred to corporation stays there; if corporation ends, property must go to another nonprofit
Limited Liability Company (Section F)	Owners have limited personal liability for business debts even if they participate in management Profit and loss can be allocated differently than ownership interests	A new hybrid, available in only some states Tax treatment (as a partnership) still a little uncertain despite a recent favorable IRS ruling

A. Sole Proprietorships

The simplest form of business entity is the sole proprietorship. If you choose this legal structure, then legally speaking you and the business are the same. You can continue operating as a sole proprietor as long as you're the only owner of the business.

Establishing a sole proprietorship is cheap and relatively uncomplicated. If you're going to conduct your business under a trade name such as Smith Furniture Store rather than John Smith, you'll have to file an assumed name or fictitious name certificate at a local or state public office. This is so people who deal with your business will know who the real owner is. (See Chapter 4 for more on business names.) In addition, you may have to obtain a business license to do business under state laws or local ordinances.

States differ on the amount of licensing required. In California, for example, almost all businesses need a business license, which is available to anyone for a small fee. In other states, business licenses are the exception rather than the rule. But most states require a sales tax license or permit for all retail businesses. Dealing with these routine licensing requirements generally involves little time or expense. However, many specialized businesses—such as an asbestos removal service or a restaurant that serves liquor—require additional licenses which may be harder to qualify for. (See Chapter 5 for more on this subject.)

From an income tax standpoint, a sole proprietorship and its owner are treated as a single entity. Business income and business losses are reported on your own federal tax return (Form 1040, Schedule C). If you have a business loss, you may be able to use it to offset income that you receive from other sources. (For more tax basics, see Chapter 6.)

1. Personal Liability

A potential disadvantage of doing business as a sole proprietor is that you have unlimited personal liability.

Example 1: Lester is the sole proprietor of a small manufacturing business. When business prospects look good, he orders $50,000 worth of supplies and uses them up. Unfortunately, there's a sudden drop in demand for his products, and Lester can't sell the items he's produced. When the company that sold Lester the supplies demands payment, he can't pay the bill.

As sole proprietor, Lester is personally liable for this business obligation. This means that the creditor can sue him and go after not only Lester's business assets, but his other property as well. This can include his house, his car and his personal bank account.

Example 2: Shirley is the sole proprietor of a flower shop. One day Roger, one of Shirley's employees, is delivering flowers using a truck owned by Shirley's business. Roger strikes and seriously injures a pedestrian. The injured pedestrian sues Roger, claiming that he drove carelessly and caused the accident. The lawsuit names Shirley as a co-defendant. After a trial, the jury returns a large verdict against Roger—and Shirley as owner of the business. Shirley is personally liable to the injured pedestrian. This means the pedestrian can go after all of Shirley's assets, business and personal.

One of the major reasons to incorporate a business is that, in theory at least, incorporation allows you to avoid most personal liability. (See Section D.1 for a discussion of why you may not need to incorporate for this reason.)

2. Income Taxes

As a sole proprietor, you and your business are one entity for income tax purposes. The income of your business is taxed to you in the year that the business receives it, whether or not you remove the money from the business. By contrast, a corporation is a separate entity for income tax purposes. As a shareholder in a corporation, you don't pay tax on money earned by the corporation until you receive payments as compensation for services or as dividends. The corporation pays its own taxes.

Special S Corporation Rules

There's a different rule for corporations which have elected S corporation status under federal tax regulations. Basically, an S corporation is taxed like a sole proprietorship or partnership: The owners report their share of corporate profits on their own tax returns, whether or not the money has been distributed to them. See Section D.2.a below for more.

Compared to a sole proprietorship, a corporation can offer some tax advantages if you're able to leave some income in the business as "retained earnings" (See Section D.2.b below for an explanation of how this works.) For example, suppose you wanted to build up a reserve to buy new equipment or your small label manufacturing company accumulated valuable inventory as it expanded. In either case, you might want to leave $50,000 of corporate profits or assets in the business at the end of a year. If you operated as a sole proprietor, those "retained" profits would be taxed at your marginal tax rates. But if you incorporated, the rate would almost surely be lower. (Again, see Section D.2.6.)

3. Fringe Benefits

If you operate your business as a sole proprietorship, tax-sheltered retirement programs are available. A Keogh plan, for example, allows a sole proprietor to salt away a substantial amount

of income free of current taxes. You can't really do any better by setting up a corporation.

A corporation does have an advantage when it comes to medical expenses, which a corporation can deduct as a business expense. (See Section D.2.b.2 below.) As a sole proprietor, your ability to deduct health insurance premiums is quite limited. You can deduct such premiums as an itemized deduction on Schedule A, but only to the extent that the premiums—plus other uncovered medical expenses—exceed 7.5% of your adjusted gross income for the year.

4. Routine Business Expenses

Day-to-day business expenses can be deducted in the same way for a sole proprietorship and a corporation. Whether it's car expenses, meals, travel or entertainment, the same rules apply to both types of business entity.

You'll need to keep accurate books for your business that are clearly separate from your records of personal expenditures. The IRS has strict rules for tax-deductible business expenses, and you need to be able to document those expenses if challenged. One good approach is to keep separate checkbooks for your business and personal expenses—and pay for all of your business expenses out of the business checking account. But whatever your system, please pay attention to this basic advice: It's simple to keep track of business income and expenses if you keep them separate from the start—and murder if you don't.

B. Partnerships

If two or more people are going to own and operate your business, you must choose between establishing a partnership or a corporation.

You'll find more on partnerships in Chapter 2. For a full treatment of partnerships, see *The Partnership Book* by Denis Clifford and Ralph Warner (Nolo Press). This section looks at general partnerships and not limited partnerships, which are covered in Section C.

The best way to form a partnership is to draw up and sign a partnership agreement. Legally, you can have a partnership without a written agreement, in which case you'd be governed entirely by a law called the Uniform Partnership Act (explained in Chapter 2). Beyond a written agreement, the paperwork for setting up a partnership is minimal—about on a par with a sole proprietorship. You may have to file a partnership certificate with a public office to register your partnership name, and you may have to obtain a business license or two. The income tax paperwork for a partnership is marginally more complex than that for a sole proprietorship.

1. Personal Liability

As a partner in a general partnership, you face personal liability similar to that of the owner of a sole proprietorship. Your personal assets are at risk in addition to all assets of the partnership.

In a partnership, any partner can take actions that legally bind the partnership entity. That means, for example, that if one partner signs a contract on behalf of the partnership, it will be fully enforceable against the partnership and each individual partner, even if the other partners weren't consulted in advance and didn't approve the contract. Also, the partnership is liable, as is each individual partner, for injuries caused by any partner while on partnership business.

Example 1: Ted, a partner in Argon Associates, signs a contract on behalf of the partnership which obligates the partnership to pay $50,000 for certain goods and services. Esther and Helen, the other partners, think Ted made a terrible deal. Nevertheless, Argon Associates is bound by Ted's contract even though Esther and Helen didn't sign it.

Example 2: Juan is a partner in Universal Contractors. Elroy, one of his partners, causes an accident while using a partnership vehicle. Juan and all the other partners will be financially liable to people injured in the accident if the car isn't covered by adequate insurance. The same would be true if Elroy used his own car while on partnership business.

In both of these situations, the personal assets (home, car and bank accounts) of each partner will be at stake, in addition to partnership assets. But remember that a partnership can protect against many risks by carrying adequate insurance.

2. Partners' Rights and Responsibilities

Unless agreed otherwise, a person can't become a partner without the consent of all the other partners. However, in larger partnerships, it's common for partners to provide in the partnership agreement that new partners can be admitted with the consent of a certain percentage of the existing partners—75%, for example.

Under the laws controlling partnerships, a partnership is automatically dissolved if one of the partners dies or withdraws as a partner, unless the partners have provided in advance for this situation. Partnership agreements often contain provisions that do allow the partnership to continue. A partnership agreement, for instance, may provide for a buy-out if one of the partners wants to leave the partnership, avoiding a forced liquidation of the business.

Example: Tom, Dick and Mary are equal partners. They agree in writing that if one of them dies, the other two will buy the deceased partner's interest in the partnership so that the business will continue. To fund this arrangement, the partnership buys life insurance covering each partner. If Tom dies first,

under the terms of the agreement, his wife and children will receive $50,000 to compensate them for the value of Tom's interest in the business.

Each partner is entitled to full information—financial and otherwise—about the affairs of the partnership. Also, the partners have a "fiduciary" relationship to one another. This means that each partner owes the others the highest legal duty of good faith, loyalty and fairness in everything having to do with the partnership.

Example: Wheels & Deals, a partnership, is in the business of selling used cars. No partner is free to open a competing used-car business without the consent of the other partners. This would be an obvious conflict of interest and, as such, would violate the fiduciary duty the partners legally owe to one another.

3. Income Taxes

In terms of income and losses, the tax picture for a partnership is basically the same as that of a sole proprietorship. A partnership doesn't pay income taxes. It must, however, file an informational return that tells the government how much money the partnership earned or lost during the tax year. It also tells what share of the income or loss belongs to each partner. Each partner then pays income tax on his or her share, whether or not this income was actually distributed during the tax year. If the partnership loses money, each partner can deduct his or her share for that year from income earned from other sources.

Investment Partnerships

This analysis assumes that the partner actively participates in the business. If, instead, a partner is a passive investor (as is often the case in partnerships designed to invest in real estate), any loss from the partnership business is treated as a passive loss for that partner. That means that for federal income tax purposes it can be deducted only from passive income—not from ordinary income.

When it comes to retained earnings, tax-sheltered retirement plans and fringe benefits, a partnership is like a sole proprietorship, and the discussion at the end of Section A applies to partnerships as well.

 Put it in writing. If you go the partnership route, I strongly recommend that the partners sign a written partnership agreement, even though an oral partnership agreement is legal. The human memory is far too fallible to rely on for the details of important business decisions. Chapter 2 contains basic information on how to write a partnership agreement.

C. Limited Partnerships

The kind of partnership you've been reading about so far is a "general partnership." It's very different than another form of partnership known as a "limited partnership." This legal animal, in certain circumstances, combines the best attributes of a partnership and a corporation.

Most limited partnerships are formed to invest in real estate. For most other small businesses with more than one owner, chances are that you'll be better able to meet your needs by forming either a general partnership or a corporation.

A limited partnership works like this. There must be one or more general partners with the same basic rights and responsibilities (including unlimited liability) as in any general partnership, and one or more limited partners who are usually passive investors. The big difference between a general partner and a limited partner is that the limited partner isn't personally liable for debts of the partnership. The most a limited partner can lose is the amount that he or she:

- paid or agreed to pay into the partnership as a capital contribution; or

- received from the partnership after it became insolvent.

To keep this limited liability, a limited partner may not participate in the management of the business, with a very few exceptions. A limited partner who does get actively involved in the management of the business risks losing immunity from personal liability and having the same legal exposure as a general partner.

The advantage of a limited partnership as a business structure is that it provides a way for business owners to raise money— from the limited partners—without having to either take in new partners who will be active in the business or engage in the intricacies of creating a corporation and issuing stock.

Example: Anthony and Janice hope to buy run-down houses, renovate them and then sell them at a good profit. All they lack is the cash to make the initial purchases. To solve this problem, they first create a partnership consisting of the two of them. Then they establish a limited partnership, with their own partnership as the general partner, and seek others who are willing to invest for a defined interest in the venture. Anthony and Janice figure that they need $100,000 to get started. They sell ten limited partnership interests at $10,000 each. The limited partners are given the right to a percentage of the profits for a specified number of years.

A general partnership that's been operating for years can also create a limited partnership to finance expansion.

Example: Judith and Aretha are partners in a small picture frame shop for two years. They want to expand into a bigger store in a much better location, where they can stock a large selection of fine art prints as well as frames. To raise money, they create a limited partnership, offering a $20,000 investor an 8% interest in the total net profits of the store for the next three years as well as the return of the invested capital at the end of that period. They sell four limited partnership interests, raising $80,000.

Doing business as a limited partnership can be at least as costly and complicated as doing business as a corporation. State laws typically require that a limited partnership file registration information about the general and limited partners. Most limited partnerships specialize in real estate investments because of tax advantages for those who are passive investors; the investor is often able to personally write off depreciation and other real estate deductions.

D. Corporations

This book deals primarily with the small, privately owned corporation. I'll assume that all of the corporate stock is owned by one person or a few people, and that all shareholders are actively involved in the management of the business—with the possible exception of friends and relatives who have provided seed money in exchange for stock. Because there are many complexities involved in selling stock to the public, I don't discuss public corporations.

The most important feature of a corporation is that, legally, it's a separate entity from the individuals who own or operate it. You may own all the stock of your corporation, and you may be its only employee, but—if you follow sensible

organizational and operating procedures—you and your corporation are separate legal entities.

All states but Arizona have adopted legislation that permits a corporation to be formed by a single incorporator. All states permit a corporate board that has a single director, although the ability to set up a one-person board may depend on the number of shareholders (see Chapter 3 for more details). In addition, many states have streamlined the procedures for operating a small corporation to permit decisions to be made quickly and without needless formalities. For example, in most states, shareholders and directors can take action by unanimous written consent rather than by holding formal meetings, and directors' meetings can be held by telephone.

1. Limited Personal Liability

One of the main advantages of incorporating is that, in most circumstances, it limits your personal liability. If a court judgment is entered against the corporation, you stand to lose only the money that you've invested. Generally, as long as you've acted in your corporate capacity (as an employee, officer or director) and without the intent to defraud creditors, your home, personal bank accounts and other valuable property can't be touched by a creditor who has won a lawsuit against the corporation.

Example 1: Andrea is the sole shareholder, director and officer of Market Basket Corporation, which runs a food store. Ronald, a Market Basket employee, drops a case of canned food on a customer's foot. The customer sues and wins a judgment against the business. Only corporate assets are available to pay the damages. Andrea is not personally liable.

 Liability for your own acts. If Andrea herself had dropped the case of cans, the fact that she is a shareholder, officer and director of the corporation wouldn't protect her from personal liability. She would still be personally liable for the wrongs (called torts, in legal lingo) that she personally commits.

So much for theory. In practice, incorporating may not actually give you broad legal protection. In the real world, banks and some major corporate creditors often require the personal guarantee of individuals within the corporation. So the limited liability gained from incorporating isn't always as valuable a legal shield as it first seems.

Example 2: Market Basket Corporation borrows $75,000 from a bank. Andrea signs the promissory note as president of the corporation, but the bank also requires her to guarantee the note personally. The corporation runs into financial difficulties and can't repay the debt. The bank sues and wins a judgment against the business for the unpaid principal plus interest. In collecting on the judgment, the bank can go after Andrea's assets as well as the corporation's property. Incorporation offers no advantage over a sole proprietorship.

Liability insurance can protect against many of the risks of doing business. But if you operate a high-risk business—child care center, chemical supply house, asbestos removal service or college town bar—and you can't get (or can't afford) liability insurance for some risks that you're concerned about, incorporation may be the wisest choice.

Example: Loren is afraid that a clerk at his After Hours beverage store might inadvertently sell liquor to an under-aged customer or one who has had too much to drink. If that customer got drunk and hurt someone in a car accident, there might be a lawsuit against the business.

Loren contacts his insurance agent to arrange for coverage, but learns that his liquor store can afford only $50,000 worth of liability insurance. Loren buys the $50,000 worth of insurance, but also forms a corporation—After Hours Inc.—to run the business. Now if an injured person wins a large verdict, at least Loren won't be personally liable for the portion not covered by his insurance.

The lesson of these examples is clear: Before you decide to incorporate your business primarily to limit your personal liability, analyze what your exposure will be if you simply do business as a sole proprietor (or partner). Chapter 3 contains further examples of businesses where incorporating makes sense because of unusual risks that you'd otherwise be exposed to.

The limited liability feature of corporations can be valuable, protecting you from personal liability for:

- Debts that you haven't personally guaranteed, including most routine bills for supplies and small items of equipment.

- Injuries suffered by people who are injured by business activities not covered adequately by insurance.

Also, for a business with more than one owner, incorporating can offer a great deal of protection from the misdeeds or bad judgment of your co-owners. In a partnership, as noted above, each partner is personally liable for the business-related activities of the other partners.

Example: Ted, Mona and Maureen are partners in Mercury Enterprises. Mona writes a nasty letter about Harold, a former employee, which causes Harold to lose the chance of a good new job. Harold sues for defamation and wins a $60,000 judgment against the partnership. Ted and Maureen are each personally liable to pay the judgment even though Mona wrote the letter.

If Mercury Enterprises had been a corporation, Mona and the corporation would have been liable for the judgment, but Ted and Maureen would not. Ted and Maureen would lose money if the assets of the corporation were seized to pay the judgment, but their own personal assets would be safe.

LAW IN THE REAL WORLD

Going With Your Gut

Several years ago, John took over his dad's rug cleaning business as a sole proprietor. He didn't expect the business to ever grow beyond its status as a small local facility with six employees and $400,000 in annual sales. But grow it did—first to ten, then to 25 employees, operating in four suburban cities and taking in $3.5 million a year.

About this time, John and his wife bought a nice house, put a few dollars in the bank and finished paying off the promissory note to his dad for the purchase of the business. Things were going so well that John began to worry about what would happen to his personal assets if the business was sued for big bucks. He reviewed his insurance coverage and sensibly increased some of it. He reviewed his operations and improved several systems, including the one for storing, handling and disposing of toxics. Still he felt vaguely disquieted.

Finally, even though he couldn't identify any risks likely to result in a successful lawsuit against his company, John decided to incorporate, to limit his personal liability for the business's debts. He tried to explain his gut feelings of worry to his father, but felt he wasn't quite making sense. The older man interrupted and said, "I think you're trying to say that things have been going so well lately that something is bound to mess up soon. And if they do, you want as much of a legal shield between your personal assets and those of the business as possible."

"Precisely," John said, "But I've already protected myself against all obvious risks, so I can't logically justify a decision to incorporate."

His father replied, "C'mon, son, business decisions are like any other—if your gut tells you to be a little extra careful, go with it. Running a small business means being ready to trust your own intuition."

 Payroll taxes. Limited liability doesn't protect you if you fail to deposit taxes withheld from employees' wages—especially if you have anything to do with making decisions about what bills the corporation pays first. Because this debt isn't dischargeable in bankruptcy (most others are), you want to pay it first.

2. Income Taxes

Federal taxation of corporations is a very complicated topic. Here I deal only with basic concepts.

The federal tax laws distinguish between two types of corporations. A regular corporation (sometimes called a "C corporation") is treated as a tax-paying entity separate from its investors and must pay corporate federal income tax. By contrast, a corporation that chooses "S corporation" status doesn't pay federal income tax; instead, income taxes are paid by the corporation's owners.

a. S CORPORATIONS

Electing to do business as an S corporation lets you have the limited liability of a corporate shareholder but pay income taxes on the same basis as a sole proprietor or a partner. Among other things, this means that as long as you actively participate in the business of the S corporation, business losses can be used as an offset against your other income—reducing, maybe even eliminating, your tax burden. The corporation itself doesn't pay taxes, but files an informational tax return telling what each shareholder's portion of the corporate income is.

Example: Paul decides to start an environmental clean-up business. Because insurance isn't available to cover all of the risks of this business, he forms a corporation called Ecology Action Inc. This limits

Paul's personal liability if there's a lawsuit against the corporation for an act not covered by insurance.

Paul is also concerned about taxes. He expects his company to lose money during its first few years; he'd like to claim those losses on his personal tax return to offset income he'll be receiving from consulting and teaching work. He registers with the IRS as an S corporation. Unless he changes that tax status later, his corporation won't pay any federal income tax. Paul will report the corporation's income loss on his own Form 1040 and will be able to use it as an offset against income from other sources.

Should You Elect S Corporation Status?

For federal tax purposes, it's normally best to elect to be an S corporation rather than a regular corporation—although to be sure that this assumption is correct, you need to discuss the subject with a knowledgeable accountant or other tax advisor.

Starting as an S corporation is wise for several reasons. For one, your business may have an operating loss the first year. With an S corporation, you can pass that loss through to your personal income tax return, using it to offset income that you (and your spouse, if you're married) may have from other sources. In later tax years, if there are tax advantages to being a regular corporation, you can easily drop your S corporation status.

Limits on deductions. You can deduct S corporation losses on your personal return only to the extent of their "basis"—the IRS term for the money you put into the corporation and the corporate debts that you personally guarantee. Also, if you don't work actively in the S corporation, there are potential problems with claiming losses from passive activities. For the most part, you can only use losses from passive activities to offset

income from passive activities. See your tax advisor for technical details.

To be treated as an S corporation, all shareholders must sign and file IRS Form 2553. (See Chapter 6, Section B.) Shareholders pay income tax on their share of the corporation's income regardless of whether they actually received the money or not. If the corporation suffered a loss, shareholders can claim their share of that loss.

Example: Assume the same facts as above except that there are two other shareholders in Ecology Action Inc. Paul owns 50% of the stock, and Ellen and Ted each own 25%. Paul would report 50% of the corporation's income or loss on his personal tax return, and Ellen and Ted would each report 25% on theirs.

Most states follow the federal pattern in taxing S corporations: they don't impose a corporate tax, choosing instead to tax the shareholders for corporate income. About half a dozen states, however, do tax an S corporation the same as a regular corporation. The tax division of your state treasury department can tell you how S corporations are taxed in your state.

b. REGULAR CORPORATIONS

Under federal income tax laws, a regular corporation is a separate entity from its shareholders. This means that the corporation pays taxes on any income that's left after business expenses have been paid.

As you saw earlier in this chapter, a sole proprietorship doesn't pay federal income tax as a separate entity; the owner simply reports the business's income or loss on Schedule C and adds it to (or, in the case of a loss, subtracts it from) the owner's other income. Similarly, a partnership doesn't pay federal income tax; rather, the partnership annually files a form with the IRS to report each partner's share of yearly profit or loss from the partnership business. Each partner then adds his or her share of partnership income to other income reported on his or her personal tax return (the familiar Form 1040) or deducts his or her share of loss. And an S corporation is treated as a sole proprietorship or partnership for federal income tax purposes.

A regular corporation is different. It reports its income on Form 1120 and pays tax on that income. In addition, if the income is distributed to shareholders in the form of dividends, the shareholders pay tax on the dividends they receive.

In practice, however, a regular corporation may not have to pay any income tax even though it is a separate taxable entity. In most incorporated small businesses, the owners are also employees. They receive salaries and bonuses as compensation for the services they perform for the corporation. The corporation then deducts this "reasonable" compensation as a business expense. In many small corporations, compensation to owner-employees eats up all the corporate profits, so there's no taxable income left for the corporation to pay taxes on.

Example: Jody forms a one-person catering corporation, Jody Enterprises Ltd. She owns all the stock and is the main person running the business. The corporation hires her as an employee, with the title of president. The corporation pays her a salary plus bonuses that consume all of the corporation's profits. Jody's salary and bonuses are tax-deductible as a corporate business expense. There are no corporate profits to tax. Jody simply pays tax on the income that she receives from the corporation, the same as any other corporate employee.

(1) Tax Savings Through Income-Splitting

As an alternative to drawing out all the corporate profits for salary and bonuses, you may want to leave some corporate income in the corporation to finance growth of your business. You can often save tax dollars this way because, for the first $75,000 of taxable corporate income, the tax rate and actual taxes paid will generally be lower than what you'd pay as an individual. The federal government taxes the first $50,000 of taxable corporate income at 15%, the next $25,000 at 25%, and all taxable income over $75,000 at 34%. To make larger corporations pay back the benefits of these lower graduated tax rates, corporate taxable incomes between $100,000 and $335,000 are subject to an additional 5% tax.

Here's an example of how, with proper planning, a small incorporated business can split income between the corporation and its owners, retain money in the corporation for expenses, and lower the corporation's tax liability to an amount that's actually less than what would have to be paid by the principals of the same business if it were not incorporated.

Example 1: Sally and Randolph run their own incorporated lumber supply company, S & R Wood Inc. Their sales increase to $1.2 million a year. After the close of the third quarter, Sally and Randolph learn that S & R Wood is likely to make $110,000 net profit (net taxable corporate income) for the year. They decide to reward themselves and other key employees with moderate raises in pay, give a small year-end bonus to other workers and buy some needed equipment.

This reduces the company's net taxable income to $40,000—an amount that Sally and Randolph feel is prudent to retain in the corporation for expansion or in case next year's operations are less profitable. Taxes on the retained earnings are paid at the lowest corporate rate, 15%. If Sally and Randy had wanted to take home more money, they could have increased their salaries, at a tax cost of 28% or 31%. The salaries would have been a tax-deductible business expense.

Sally and Randy could have also declared a stock dividend. But because this would have subjected them to a double tax of 15% at the corporate level plus 15% or (more likely) 28% or 31% personally, depending on their tax bracket, it would have been a poor choice.

Example 2: Assume S & R Wood is not incorporated but instead is operated as a partnership. Now the entire net profits of the business ($110,000 minus the bonuses to workers and deductible expenditures for equipment) are taxed to Sally and Randolph. The result is that the $40,000 (which was retained by the corporation in the above example) is taxed at their individual rate of 28% or 31% rather than the 15% corporate rate.

For a more detailed explanation of how income-splitting can be an advantage to owners of small corporations, see *How To Form Your Own Corporation* (California, Florida, New York and Texas editions) by Anthony Mancuso (Nolo Press).

The main point to remember is that once a business becomes profitable, doing business as a regular corporation allows a degree of flexibility in planning and controlling your federal income taxes unavailable to partnerships and sole proprietorships. To determine whether or not favorable corporate tax rates are a compelling reason for your business to incorporate, you'll need to study IRS regulations or go through an analysis with your accountant or other tax advisor.

Tax savings may be largely a theoretical advantage concern for the person just starting out. If your business is like many start-ups, your main concern will be generating enough income from the business to pay yourself a reasonable wage. Retaining profits in the business will come later. In this situation, the tax advantages of incorporating are illusory.

Example: In its first year of operation, Maria's store, The Bookworm, has a profit of $25,000. As the sole proprietor, Maria withdraws the entire $25,000 for her personal expenses, which places her in the 15% tax bracket after she subtracts her deductions and personal exemption. She anticipates similar profits the second year. If she can get by on $20,000 a year, it doesn't make sense for Maria to incorporate to take advantage of income-splitting techniques. If she leaves $5,000 in the corporation, it will be taxed at 15%, so her total tax bill will be the same.

S Corporations and Personal Service Corporations

The lower tax rates for retained earnings don't apply to S corporations or to certain personal service corporations. As discussed in Section D.2.a, individual shareholders in an S corporation pay taxes on their portion of corporate earnings whether or not those earnings are distributed to them.

Personal service corporations are defined under federal tax laws and have two basic characteristics: (1) the professional employees of the corporation own the stock; and (2) the corporation performs its services in the fields of health, law, engineering, architecture, accounting, actuarial science, performing arts or consulting. In these cases there's a flat corporate rate of 34%. This means that with a personal service corporation there's no tax advantage in retaining earnings in the corporation. Many professional corporations (discussed in Section E.1) are classified as personal service corporations.

---

(2) Fringe Benefits

Another tax-related consideration that often amounts to an incorporation advantage is that a corporation can treat as tax-deductible business expenses the cost of fringe benefits it gives employees, including owner-employees like yourself. No similar deductions are allowed for the owner of a sole proprietorship. These benefits include:

- deferred compensation plans
- group term life insurance
- reimbursement of employee medical expenses that are not covered by insurance
- health and disability insurance
- death benefit payments up to $5,000.

A regular corporation can deduct these benefits for all owner-employees. For example, a corporation can provide medical insurance for its employees and deduct these payments as a business expense—including the portion paid for the employee-owners of the corporation. An S corporation cannot deduct these benefits for an owner-employee who owns 2% or more of the corporate stock.

Because a sole proprietor or partner can't write off similar benefits as a tax deduction, qualifying for benefits would seem to be a powerful reason to incorporate and not to elect S corporation status. Not so fast. Obviously there's no benefit unless your business provides these benefits to employees in the first place. And that may be to be too expensive for some new businesses—especially because many types of employee benefits must be provided on a nondiscriminatory basis to a wide range of employees and not designed to primarily aid the business owner. If you put together a fringe benefit package that favors you and other owner-employees, the IRS will deny your corporate tax deduction. Few new businesses can afford the cost of carrying these programs—a cost that typically more than offsets any tax advantage to you as owner of an incorporated small business.

Here are some of the IRS ground rules for fringe benefit plans:

- *Medical Reimbursement Plans.* If your business promises to pay employees' medical expenses that are not covered by health insurance, your plan can also include the spouse and dependents of each employee. Usually you'll set a limit on the total amount which can be reimbursed during the year. Employees are not taxed on reimbursements they receive. At least 70% of your employees must be eligible to benefit under the plan. Also, the plan must make equal dollar amounts of benefits available to all eligible employees. You can exclude employees who are under 25, work less than 35 hours per week or have been employed less than three years. All other employees must be covered. If you violate these rules, an owner may have to pay tax on all or part the reimbursements that he or she receives under the plan.

- *Group Life Insurance.* Your business can provide up to $50,000 of group term life insurance tax-free to employees if you meet certain conditions. To deduct the cost of the insurance, your plan must benefit at least 70% of all employees, cover a "fair cross section" of all employees or limit the number of key employee participants to 15%. (A key employee is an officer, one of the top ten owners, or an owner of least 5% of the company.) All benefits available to participating key employees must be available to all other participating employees as well. You can provide different dollar amounts of life insurance to different employees without being "discriminatory" if the amount of coverage is uniformly related to compensation.

Clearly, this is technical stuff. If you open a video store and hire a bunch of students to work part-time during peak periods, and contract out for bookkeeping services, you can set up a medical reimbursement plan without having to worry about covering a whole slew of employees. You could exclude the students because they're under 25 and work less than 35 hours a week. Your bookkeeper, being an independent contractor, wouldn't be an employee and wouldn't have to be covered. So perhaps your plan would cover only yourself and your few full-time employees, plus the families of all covered employees.

(3) Retirement Plans

It used to be that by incorporating you could set up a better tax-sheltered retirement plan than you could get as a sole proprietor, a partner or a shareholder-employee in an S corporation. The differences are no longer significant. Through a Keogh retirement plan that is available to sole proprietors and partners, you can shelter retirement funds to practically the same extent as you can with a corporate retirement plan.

The few differences that remain between corporate and individual plans run the gamut from the arcane to the inconsequential. Consider the most significant remaining difference: If you're a participant in the retirement plan of a regular corporation, you can borrow up to $50,000 from your account if you meet various tax requirements. Try to do the same thing with your Keogh plan funds or the funds you put into an S corporation retirement plan and you'll have to pay an excise tax on the money you borrow. Is that a compelling reason to incorporate? For most people, the answer is no.

3. Illusory Incorporation Advantages

What, in addition to limited liability and some marginal tax advantages, can you gain by incorporating? In drumming up enthusiasm for incorporating, lawyers and accountants often point to additional supposed benefits—but these advantages are rarely all they're cracked up to be.

Il'usory Benefit: Easy Transfer of Corporate Stock If You Sell the Business. The sales pitch is that if you want to sell your interest in the corporation (which may be as much as 100% if you own all of the stock), you simply endorse your stock certificate on the back and turn over the certificate to the new owner. The corporation then issues a new stock certificate in the new owner's name to replace the one that you endorsed.

Reality: There's no market for a small company's stock. And most small business owners go to great lengths to restrict the transferability of their stock. Moreover, in most sales of a corporate business, the corporate assets are transferred rather than the stock. (See Chapter 7.)

Illusory Benefit: Continuity of Business. A corporation continues even if an owner dies or withdraws. Or there may be a buy-sell agreement—perhaps funded by insurance—in which co-owners of the corporation have the right to buy out your inheritors. Either way, the corpora-

tion stays alive, in contrast to a sole proprietorship or partnership, which is automatically dissolved when the owner or a partner dies.

Reality: You don't need to incorporate to ensure that your business will continue after your death. A sole proprietor can use a living trust or will to transfer the business to her heirs. Partners frequently have insurance-funded buy-sell agreements that allow the remaining partners to continue the business. The death of a principal is traumatic whether you're a sole proprietorship, a partnership or a corporation. Usually the factors that allow a business to survive are personal and have nothing to do with its formal legal structure.

Illusory Benefit: Centralized Management. In corporations with a number of shareholders, management is typically centralized under a board of directors. With a partnership consisting of many partners, management can become fragmented.

Reality: With a business consisting of one, two or three owners, it doesn't take a board of directors to centralize the management; chances are you and the other owners will make all decisions over a cup of coffee.

In weighing pros and cons of incorporation, concentrate on whether you believe you have a real need to limit your personal liability and also on whether you can get substantial tax benefits by retaining some earnings in the corporation and setting up fringe benefit plans. For many—perhaps most—new businesses, a sole proprietorship or partnership is perfectly adequate. And remember that if you start out as a sole proprietorship or partnership, you can always incorporate the business later.

E. Special Kinds of Corporations

If you decide to operate your small business as a corporation, chances are you'll form either a regular corporation or an S corporation. But you should be aware of two other kinds of corporations: professional corporations and nonprofits. These less common corporate varieties may be just what you're looking for.

1. Professional Corporations

Laws in every state permit certain professionals to form corporations known as "professional corporations" or "professional service corporations." In many states, people in certain occupations (for example, doctors, lawyers or accountants) who want to incorporate their practice can do so only through a professional corporation. In some states, some professionals have a choice of incorporating as either a professional corporation or a regular corporation (which can elect to be an S corporation).

The list of professionals eligible to incorporate is different in each state. Usually, though, mandatory professional incorporation requirements apply to these professionals:

- accountants
- engineers
- health care professionals such as audiologists, dentists, nurses, opticians, optometrists, pharmacists, physical therapists, physicians and speech pathologists
- lawyers
- psychologists
- social workers
- veterinarians.

Call your state's corporate filing office (usually the secretary of state or corporation commissioner) to see who is covered in your own state. Typically, a professional corporation must be organized for the sole purpose of rendering professional services. All shareholders must be licensed to render that service. For example, in a medical corporation, all of the shareholders must be licensed physicians.

Professional corporations aren't as popular as they used to be. The main reason for professionals to incorporate—favorable corporate taxation rules—has disappeared. Before 1986, professionals who incorporated could shelter more money from taxes than sole proprietors or partners could. This has all changed. Most professional corporations are classified as "personal service corporations" by the IRS, which means that their corporate income is taxed at a flat 34%. So there's no longer any advantage to be gained by the two-tiered tax structure that allows ordinary corporations to save taxes on some retained earnings.

Are there any reasons left for professionals to incorporate? Perhaps. Tax laws still give favorable treatment to fringe benefits for corporate employees. (See Section D above.)

The other reason to consider incorporation is the limitation on personal liability. It's no secret that malpractice verdicts against professionals continue to climb. Incorporating can't protect a professional against liability for his or her negligence, but it can protect against liability for the negligence of an associate.

Example 1: Dr. Anton and Dr. Bartolo are surgeons who practice as partners. Dr. Bartolo leaves an instrument inside a patient, who bleeds to death. The jury returns a $2 million verdict against Dr. Bartolo and the partnership. There is only $1 million in malpractice insurance to cover the judgment. Dr. Anton (along with Dr. Bartolo) would be personally liable for the $1 million not covered by insurance.

Example 2: Drs. Anton and Bartolo create a professional corporation. Dr. Bartolo commits the malpractice described in Example 1. Dr. Anton, a corporate employee, would not be personally liable for the portion of the verdict not covered by insurance. Dr. Bartolo, however, would still be personally responsible for the $1 million excess, because he was the one guilty of malpractice. (In some states,

Dr. Anton would be free from personal liability only if the professional corporation carried at least the minimum amount of insurance mandated by state law.)

Insurance is a better alternative for most professionals than is the limited liability offered by incorporation. But with malpractice rates soaring for many professionals, it's often hard to afford all you could possibly need, and forming a professional corporation can be a useful back-up.

2. Nonprofit Corporations

Each state permits people to form nonprofit corporations, also known as not-for-profit corporations. The main reason people form these corporations is to get tax-exempt status under the Internal Revenue Code (Section 501(c)(3)). If a corporation is tax-exempt, not only is it free from paying taxes on its income, but people and organizations who contribute to the nonprofit corporation can take a tax deduction for their contributions. Because many nonprofit organizations rely heavily on grants from public agencies and private foundations to fund their operations, attaining 501(c)(3) status is critical to success.

Tax-exempt status isn't the only benefit available to a nonprofit corporation. An organization that plans to do some heavy mailing may be attracted by the cheaper postal rates charged nonprofits. And the nonprofit label seems to create an altruistic aura around the organization and the people running it. The message is, "We're not in this for the money—we really do love kids (or music or animals)."

The legal standard for tax-exempt status is that the corporation has been formed for religious, charitable, literary, scientific or educational purposes.

What kinds of groups should consider becoming nonprofit corporations? Here's a partial list:

- child care centers
- shelters for the homeless
- community health care clinics
- museums
- hospitals
- churches, synagogues, mosques and other places of worship
- schools
- performing arts groups
- conservation groups.

Most nonprofit corporations are run by a board of directors or trustees who are actively involved in the work of the corporation. Officers and employees (some of whom may also serve on the board) carry out the day-to-day business of the corporation and receive salaries. Because both profit and nonprofit corporations can take a tax deduction for the reasonable salaries of their employees, there may not be too much difference in the operation of the two types of corporations.

Keep in mind that if you put assets into a nonprofit corporation, you give up any ownership or proprietary interest in those assets. They must be irrevocably dedicated to the specified nonprofit purposes. If you want to get out of the business, you can't just sell it and pocket the cash. The nonprofit corporation goes on; if it ends, any remaining assets must go to another nonprofit.

This book is addressed primarily to people starting and running business for profit, so you'll find little here on the peculiarities of nonprofit corporations. If you want to learn about such corporations in greater depth, see *How To Form Your Own Nonprofit Corporation* by Anthony Mancuso (Nolo Press). That book provides step-by-step instructions for forming a nonprofit corporation in all states.

F. A New Hybrid: The Limited Liability Company

You'd think that with the sole proprietorship, two types of partnerships and two types of corporations to choose from, you'd have plenty of legal structures available for your business—and indeed you do. But there's a new kid on the block that you should at least become acquainted with: the limited liability company (LLC). This hybrid is available in a few states, but likely will become available more widely.

It's best to think of an LLC as a partnership whose partners enjoy freedom from personal liability—like shareholders of a corporation. Can't you accomplish that by setting up a limited partnership? Or an S corporation? Well, yes—to an extent. But some limitations may be bothersome.

Example 1. Andy, Beatrice, Carlos and Dina form a limited partnership. Because every limited partnership needs at least one general partner, Andy becomes the general partner; Beatrice, Carlos and Dina are limited partners. This arrangement has two problems. First, as the general partner, Andy remains personally liable for partnership debts. Second, while Beatrice, Carlos and Dina (the limited partners) are protected from personal liability, they enjoy this protection only if they play no active part in managing the business. These problems may discourage the four from forming a limited partnership.

Example 2. Andy, Beatrice, Carlos and Dina form an S corporation. As shareholders of the S corporation, all four enjoy freedom from personal liability even if they actively take part in managing the business. But the tax laws restrict them. If they're equal shareholders (25% each), each must report 25% of the corporation's profit or loss on his or her tax return—no more and no less. Partners and owners of an LLC have more flexibility in allocating profit and loss. Also, a corporation can't own stock in an S corporation; this isn't true of a partnership or LLC.

The LLC avoids the problems raised in these two examples. First, all the owners enjoy freedom from personal liability. Second, for tax purposes, profit and loss can be allocated differently than ownership interests; for example, the owners of the LLC can agree to allocate 40% of the business's profit to a person who owns a 25% interest. Third, a corporation can own an interest in an LLC.

These advantages aren't important for well over 90% of small and mid-sized businesses. But for a handful of enterprises, the LLC opens up some interesting new possibilities. Some lawyers and accountants feel that the LLC fills a niche—but how wide a niche remains to be seen. State legislatures are continuing to pass laws permitting businesses to be formed as limited liability companies. These laws are scrutinized on a state-by-state basis by the IRS—which gave its first tax clearance in 1988. It's expected that by 1994, as many as half the states will have laws permitting formation of an LLC.

STRUCTURING A PARTNERSHIP AGREEMENT

2

There are two kinds of partnership: the general partnership and the limited partnership. This chapter discusses forming the more common kind, general partnerships. See Chapter 1, Section C, for basic information about limited partnerships.

Features of the General Partnership

Main advantages

    Simple and inexpensive to create and operate

    Owners (partners) report their share of profit or loss on their personal tax returns

Main disadvantage

    Owners (partners) personally liable for business debts

A. Why You Need a Written Agreement

When you form a partnership to run a small business, your partners will be family members, close friends or business associates. You may think it's unnecessary to sign a document with people you know quite well. Experience proves otherwise. No matter how rosy things are at the beginning, every partnership inevitably faces problems over the years. A well-thought-out written agreement will help you preserve the business, as well as your friendship.

You can, however, have a legally valid partnership even without a written partnership agreement. If you don't sign an agreement, the laws of your state will dictate how the partnership is run. That isn't all bad. Every state except Louisiana has adopted the Uniform Partnership Act (UPA), sometimes with slight variations. This law solves many common partnership problems in a sensible way. For example, the UPA says that if you don't have an agreement, each partner shares equally in the profits and has an equal voice in management of the business. The UPA goes on to say that partners are not entitled to

receive compensation for services they provide to the partnership.

While it's conceivable that the provisions of the Uniform Partnership Act are exactly what you and your partners want, partners usually prefer to modify at least some of them. For example, if one partner contributes far more assets than others, that partner may deserve a greater share of the profits. Or you may not want each partner to have an equal voice in running the business. Similarly, you may want to include customized provisions on how to value a partner's interest in the business if a partner dies or leaves. In that situation, many partners want to assign some value to the good will of the business—something that does not happen automatically under the Uniform Partnership Act. With a written partnership agreement, you can tailor your partnership to fit your needs.

There are other benefits to working out the details in a written partnership agreement. You'll focus on issues you might not have thought of—issues about which you and your partners may have different opinions. For example, what if one partner wants special compensation above and beyond her share of the profits if she frequently works evenings or weekends on partnership business? By getting issues out into the open early, you can nip problems in the bud.

Most Partnership Information Is Confidential

The terms of a partnership agreement for a general partnership don't have to be made public. In some states, you must file a certificate, stating the names of the partners, with a county official (such as the county clerk) or state official (such as the secretary of state). (See Chapter 4.)

B. An Overview of Your Partnership Agreement

It's up to you and your partners to decide what shape the partnership will take. A lawyer can help you focus on issues and suggest possible solutions, but you and your partners—not the lawyer—must make the basic choices.

This section goes through the clauses that are usually included in a partnership agreement for a small business.

Where To Find Help With Partnership Agreements

For the most part, the clauses in this chapter are taken from *The Partnership Book* by Denis Clifford and Ralph Warner (Nolo Press). See that book for many additional clauses.

Also watch for *Nolo's Partnership Maker,* a software package scheduled for release in Fall 1992. If you have an IBM or compatible computer, you can use this software to easily assemble a customized partnership agreement.

---

1. Name and Term

Although many partnerships do business using the last names of the partners, it's both legal and com-

mon for a partnership to have one name and to do business under another name. For example, the partnership of Jones, Gold and Sanchez could decide to do business as Seafood Express. The name Seafood Express would be an assumed name or fictitious name, which you'd have to register with the appropriate state or county office.

 Chapter 4 contains a thorough discussion of business and product names.

Another issue is how long the partnership will last. If you want it to go on indefinitely, include a clause like this:

> The partnership shall last until it is dissolved by all the partners or a partner leaves, for any reason, including death.

On the other hand, if you plan to develop a particular piece of real estate or do some other finite task, you might want a clause with a definite date, such as one of the following:

> The partnership shall commence as of the date of this agreement and shall continue for a period of _____ years, at which time it shall be dissolved and its affairs wound up.

> or

> The partnership shall continue until ____ [specify an event such as "the completion and sale of The Commercial Office Plaza"], at which time the partnership shall be dissolved and its affairs wound up.

2. Purpose

The purpose of the partnership should be broadly stated in plain English. The advantage of a broad statement of partnership purposes is that you have flexibility if the business evolves. Here are two typical purpose clauses:

> The purpose of the partnership is to operate one or more stores for the sale of records, tapes, compact discs or other related merchandise.

> or

> The purpose of the partnership is to operate a bookkeeping and tax preparation service for individual clients and small businesses.

On the other hand, if you're sure you're creating your partnership for a short-term, specific purpose, such as presenting one trade show, it would be appropriate to use a more limited purpose clause, such as this one:

> The purpose of the partnership is to organize and present this year's Builders and Home Improvement Show at the Municipal Convention Center.

3. Contributions

Your partnership agreement should describe the initial contributions that you and your partners will make. Often, each partner contributes cash only. The amounts of contributions may be equal, but don't have to be. For example, one partner might contribute $5,000 while another contributes $1,000 and a third contributes a pick-up truck. If a partner contributes property such as a vehicle, tools, a building, a patent or a copyright, you need to agree on the value of that property. You can also provide that one of the partners will contribute personal services (perhaps painting the business headquarters) in return for a partnership interest. Keep in mind that a partner can sell, loan, lease or rent property to the partnership too.

a. CASH CONTRIBUTIONS

It's logically neat if each partner contributes an equal amount of cash to a new business. Otherwise, partners who invest more money than the others may feel entitled to a larger voice in making partnership decisions. But in the real world, often not all partners can make equal contributions of cash. One way to handle this is to have the partner who contributes more loan the extra amount to the business rather than contribute it outright.

Example: Ricardo and Alberta are opening a martial arts training center. Ricardo has just left a job at a corporation and received a handsome severance package. He's willing to put $40,000 into the business. Alberta, on the other hand, is a single mother who wants to start a business precisely because she is short of money. She can raise $10,000. Alberta could contribute $10,000 and Ricardo $40,000 with Ricardo having more say in partnership decisions than Alberta. An easier and more democratic approach would be for each to contribute $10,000 in cash, with Ricardo loaning the partnership the additional $30,000, to be repaid over three years at 10% annual interest.

A basic clause for equal cash contributions reads as follows:

> The initial capital of the partnership shall be a total of $_____. Each partner shall contribute an equal share amounting to $_____ no later than _____ 19____. Each partner shall own an equal share of the business.

If a partner can't initially contribute the desired amount of cash, another way to handle this problem is to agree that he or she will make payments over time. Here's a sample clause.

> Arthur Feldman shall be a partner upon making an initial contribution of $1,000 to the capital of the partnership. He will subsequently contribute to the partnership capital, and his capital account shall be credited, in the amount of $100 per month beginning July 1, 1992, until he has contributed the sum of $5,000 (including the initial $1,000 payment).

Interest on Partnership Investment: Should partners receive interest on their contributions of capital? Generally, no—after all, the money is already at work building a jointly owned business. But either way you decide this issue, cover it with a specific clause in the partnership agreement.

b. CONTRIBUTIONS OF SERVICES

Sometimes, a partner's contribution consists wholly or in part of services. In the above example concerning Alberta's contribution to the martial arts training center, another way to handle the disparity in available cash would be for Alberta to agree to work a certain number of hours more than Ricardo at a fixed rate (say $20 per hour) until the contributions were equalized. After that, the partners would work an equal amount of hours each week. If a partner is going to contribute services in return for an interest in the business, this should be spelled out in the partnership agreement.

> **Example:** Margaret and Alice form a 50/50 partnership for catering parties. Each will spend equal time on preparing the food and delivering it. Margaret contributes $10,000 to get the business going. Alice agrees to contribute unpaid labor as a bookkeeper and business manager for one year over and above the amount of time she spends on parties. Their intention is to equalize the contributions of the parties.

c. CONTRIBUTIONS OF PROPERTY

Some or all of the partners may contribute property as well as, or instead of, cash. A clause covering this possibility might look like this:

> _____ shall contribute property valued at $_____ consisting of _____ _____by _____ 19____. [If the property is difficult to describe, describe it in detail on a separate sheet of paper marked "Exhibit A" and add here "and more particularly described in Exhibit A, attached to this agreement."]

⚠ Getting expert help. If you're transferring property to your partnership, you may need the assistance of a tax expert. Such contributions raise questions about what tax basis (value) will be assigned to the property being transferred. The IRS looks at tax basis in determining how much profit you've gained when the property is later transferred or sold. The tax details are beyond the scope of this book.

4. Profits, Losses, Draws and Salaries

How will partners be compensated? The first issue is how you'll divide profits once a year or at the end of some other fixed period. You should also determine if any partners can receive a monthly draw against their share of the profits—that is, be paid a portion of profits sooner than other partners. This might be appropriate if one partner is coming into the partnership with less savings than the others and is counting on partnership income for living expenses.

You'll also need to decide if any partners will receive a salary for work done in the business in addition to their share of profits. If equal partners will all work a roughly equal number of hours, there's no need to pay salaries; an equal division of profits with or without a draw should be adequate. But if one partner will work more hours than the others, paying that partner a salary may be sensible. Or you could give the harder working partner a larger share of the profits. If salaries are paid, they're a normal business expense and don't come out of profits.

If profits are shared equally, the following clause would be appropriate:

> The partners will share all profits equally, and they will be distributed [monthly? yearly?]. All losses of the partnership will also be shared equally.

On the other hand, if profits and losses will be shared unequally, here are some sample clauses to consider:

Partnership profits and losses will be shared among the partners as follows:

Name   Percentage

_____   _____

_____   _____

_____   _____

_____   _____

or

Partnership profits and losses shall be shared among the partners as follows:

Name	% of Profits	% of Losses
_____	_____	_____
_____	_____	_____
_____	_____	_____

or

Partnership profits and losses shall be shared by the partners in the same proportion as their initial contributions of capital bear to each other.

A draw is an advance of anticipated profits paid to a partner or partners. It's easiest if draws are to be made by all partners. But if you want to authorize draws for only certain partners, a clause like the following is appropriate:

Partners _____ and _____ are entitled to draws from expected partnership profits. The amount of each draw will be determined by a vote of the partners. The draws shall be _____ [monthly or on any other kind of schedule that you agree to].

You may also want to provide for the partnership to retain some profits in the business for new equipment, expansion or employee bonuses. Here's a sample clause:

In determining the amount of profits available for distribution, allowance will be made for the fact that some money must remain undistributed and available as working capital as determined by _____ [for example, "all partners" or "a majority of partners"].

Even though profits are reinvested, you and the other partners are taxed on your shares of them at your individual rates. (Chapter 1, Section B.3, discusses how a regular corporation may afford tax advantages over a partnership when a business has retained earnings.)

The Authority of Partners

Do you want each partner to be able to make decisions that bind the partnership in the normal operation of its business? Or do you want some limitations—for example, that large contracts or purchases must be approved in advance by a majority of the partners? You can address this issue in your partnership agreement. But remember that while a limitation on a partner's authority is binding among the partners themselves, it doesn't necessarily limit liability to outsiders who deal with the partner.

Example: Peggy, Roger and Lisa run a bookkeeping and billing service for several doctors, dentists and clinics. Peggy, who is a computer whiz, believes that there's no such thing as too much electronic equipment. So in the partnership agreement, a clause provides that any purchase of equipment requires the approval of at least two of the partners. Peggy buys three notebook computers, two laser printers and assorted modems and fax machines for the partnership, without approval. The partnership and each partner are liable for the $12,000 bill, even though the partners limited liability among themselves. When Peggy purchased the equipment, the computer store didn't know what was in the partnership agreement—the usual case. And Peggy appeared to have authority to bind the partnership. The other partners, however, will have a legal claim against Peggy because she exceeded her authority under the partnership agreement.

LAW IN THE REAL WORLD

A Profitable Experience

Jan and Mike discussed forming a partnership to open a desktop publishing service aimed at helping small businesses design brochures, flyers and other promotional material. The idea of sharing the work and profits 50-50 appealed to both of them. There was only one major hang-up: The form partnership agreement they looked at provided for profits to be divided at the end of the year. This was okay with Mike, who had received a generous severance package from a former job, but not for Jan, who was trying to put her daughter through college and had no financial cushion.

Recognizing their different circumstances, Jan and Mike agreed Jan would be allowed to take a monthly draw against her share of anticipated partnership profits of $3,000. And because they realized a new business needs all the cash it can get its hands on, Mike would wait and take the same amount at the end of the year. Then Mike and Jan would split any additional profits.

To guard against the possibility that Jan's draw would use up more than half of the profits and short-change Mike, the partners also agreed that any amount Jan received over her 50% would be considered a personal loan from the partnership, to be repaid out of future years' profits.

5. Management Responsibilities

It's wise to pin down the basic way you'll operate the business. Commonly, in small business partnerships, all partners are involved in management and supervision, justifying a clause like the following:

All partners shall be actively involved and materially participate in the management of operation of the partnership business.

You can go further if you want every partner to have a veto power:

All partnership decisions must be made by the unanimous agreement of all partners.

Some small business partnerships distinguish between major and minor decisions, allowing a single partner to make a minor decision but requiring unanimity for major ones. If you decide to go down this road, you have to figure out how to define a major decision. The distinction between major and minor decisions—especially purchases or the undertaking of obligations—is often based on a dollar amount. A clause like this one would be appropriate:

All major decisions of the partnership business must be made by a unanimous decision of all partners. Minor business decisions may be made by an individual partner. Major decisions are defined as all purchases and contracts over $5,000 [or other definition of major decisions].

If you want to provide for unequal management powers, here are some clauses to consider:

Each partner shall participate in the management of the business. In exercising the powers of management, each partner's vote shall be in proportion to his or her interest in the partnership's capital.

or

In the management, control and direction of the business, the partners shall have the following percentages of voting power:

Name	Percentage
_____	_____
_____	_____
_____	_____
_____	_____

If the partners are going to contribute different types of skills, you may also want to state that in your partnership agreement. And while it may seem unnecessary to list the hours to be worked, you may avoid possible problems through a clause such as the following:

> Except for vacations, holidays and times of illness, each partner will work _____ hours per week on partnership business.

Consider a clause on leaves of absence or sabbaticals. How much time off is allowed? And what happens to a partner's right to receive pay or profits while on leave?

Other financial matters to be dealt with in the partnership agreement may include the following:

- May partners borrow money on behalf of the partnership? Is there a dollar limit on how much a partner can borrow on behalf of the partnership without the prior consent of all partners?

- Are expense accounts authorized? If so, is there a limit on the amount?

- How many signatures are required on partnership checks and to withdraw money from the partnership bank account?

- How many weeks of paid or unpaid vacation each year are partners entitled to?

6. Partners' Outside Business Activities

A key partnership question is whether or not any partner can engage in outside business. In some instances, they must, at least at first, because the partnership business income isn't enough to live on. If a partner can engage in outside business, what types are permitted? You wouldn't want a partner to directly compete with the partnership. That would be a conflict of interest. But how do you define direct competition? If the partners are running a restaurant, can one of the partners own a catering business? Or work in a delicatessen? There are at least four different approaches to this issue. You can:

- Allow partners to engage in one or more other businesses except for those that directly compete with the partnership business.

- Allow partners to engage in other businesses without any other restrictions.

- List permitted activities.

- Prohibit partners from participating in any other business.

Here's an example of the first approach:

Any partner may engage in one or more other businesses as well as the business of the partnership, but only to the extent that this activity does not directly and materially interfere with the business of the partnership and does not conflict with the time commitments or other obligations of that partner to the partnership under this agreement. Neither the partnership nor any other partner shall have any right to any income or profit derived from a partner from any outside business activity permitted under this section.

LAW IN THE REAL WORLD

Outside Interests

When Ted M. and Ted Y. formed a partnership and opened a bookstore (yup, they called it Two Teds), they didn't expect to make much, if any, money right away. According to their business plan, it would take two to three years for the store to be solidly profitable. In the meantime, both men would have to hold down second jobs. This led to a serious problem. Both men already worked in the book business (Ted M. managed a secondhand book shop, and Ted Y. was a sales rep for a large publisher) and wanted to avoid any hint of a conflict of interest between their personal and partnership interests.

Ted Y. explained his store plans to the publisher he worked for, who agreed to reduce his sales territory and let him work three days per week. (Ted Y. also promised to work 30 hours at Two Teds). Because selling books to stores and selling them to the public aren't competitive operations, it was easy for the Teds to agree in writing as part of their partnership agreement that Ted Y.'s job didn't amount to a conflict of interest with the partnership.

Ted M.'s situation was tougher. No matter how much they thought about it, managing one store while owning part of another in the same city reeked of possible conflicts of interest. To solve this, it was decided that Ted M. would quit managing the other store. Initially, at least, he would work 55 hours per week at Two Teds and be paid a reasonable salary for the 25 hours per week he worked more than Ted Y.

7. Departure of a Partner—Buy-outs

Now we're getting into one of the most essential—but complicated—areas of a partnership agreement: what you'll do if one of the partners voluntarily leaves, becomes disabled or dies. These things are not easy to think about when you're caught up in the excitement of starting a new business. Still, it's risky to postpone facing them. Sooner or later the partnership will change and fundamental issues will come up. A partner may want to leave for any number of reasons—such as to start another business or to move to another part of the country. Or maybe a partner will retire or die. Can the departing partner sell his or her interest? Do the remaining partners or partner have the right to buy it? How is the purchase price determined?

If one partner quits or dies, most partnership agreements very sensibly require a departing partner to give the remaining partners the chance to buy out his or her share and continue the business before selling or transferring it to outsiders. Here's a sample "right of first refusal" clause designed to accomplish this:

> If any partner leaves the partnership, for whatever reason, whether he or she quits, withdraws, is expelled, retires or dies, or becomes mentally or physically incapacitated or unable to fully function as a partner, he or she, or (in the case of a deceased partner) his or her estate, shall be obligated to sell his or her interest in the partnership to the remaining partners, who may buy that interest under the terms and conditions set forth in this agreement.

This option protects the remaining partners. But what if the departing partner has found a buyer who is willing to pay a hefty price for that partnership interest? Some partnerships don't compel a departing partner to take a lower price (as pre-determined in the partnership agreement) than he or she would get from a bona fide outside buyer; their partnership agreements provide that the existing partners must pay the market price for the departing partner's share. Either way you resolve this issue, you should spell out your solution in the partnership agreement.

Here's a different approach:

> If the remaining partners do not purchase the departing partner's share of the business under the terms provided in this agreement within _____ days after the departing partner leaves, the entire business of the partnership shall be put up for sale and listed with an appropriate sales agent or broker.

a. VALUING A PARTNER'S SHARE

One major issue in a buy-out clause is how you'll set the worth of the business—and the value of a partner's share. Let's look at some specific valuation methods.

The **asset valuation method** is based on the current net worth of the business (assets minus liabilities). As of the date the departing partner leaves, the net worth of all partnership assets is calculated and all outstanding business debts are deducted to determine net worth. Because good will isn't a tangible asset, it's not counted. The departing partner receives his or her ownership percentage of this amount, under whatever pay-out terms you agreed on.

The **book valuation method** is a variation of the asset valuation method. You calculate the value of all partnership assets and liabilities as they're set forth in the partnership accounting books, which basically means the acquisition cost. Because book value doesn't cover good will, in a successful business it has little relation to what the business is really worth. Furthermore, the acquisition cost of property is unlikely to be its current worth.

The **set-dollar method** involves an agreement by the partners in advance that if one partner departs from the partnership, the others will buy out his or her share for a pre-established price. Before adopting this method, be aware that the price selected may be arbitrary. Even if accurate for the present time, the worth of the business may fluctuate, making a predetermined value out-of-date. You might consider having the partners unanimously establish a value in writing for the partnership each year.

A **post-departure appraisal** means that you agree to have an independent appraiser determine the worth of the partnership when a partner departs. It sounds good in principle, but because many small businesses aren't amenable to precise valuation, even in the hands of an expert appraiser, it can lead to bitter arguments later.

The **capitalization of earnings method** determines what the business is worth based on what it earns. Unless there's an open market to set a price, the best estimate of what a business is worth often depends on its earning capacity. This method works best with a business that's been around for several years. First you need to measure the earnings of the business for a year or more. Then you must agree on a multiplier (often two to five) which, in effect, takes into consideration the fact that a buyer hopes to reap profits in future years. Finally, you multiply the earnings by your multiplier to arrive at a value. But how do you establish the multiplier? Often one is already loosely established in a particular industry. A consultant or trade magazine may tell you that profitable dry cleaning businesses are often sold on the basis of multiplying profits by a certain number. Be aware that this sort of information is at best an estimate which can change by industry, individual business and year. If you decide to use this method of valuing your business, you'll need expert advice.

You may want to have a different buy-out price depending on when or why a partner departs. For example, a partner who leaves during the initial stages of a business (say, the first one or two years) may only be entitled to the balance in his or her capital account. After that initial period, the departing partner's interest could be calculated by a method that more accurately reflects the actual operation and success of the business.

You could also have varying formulas depending on why the partner leaves. For example, there might be one formula if the partner becomes disabled, retires over age 65 or dies, and another formula if the partner leaves under other circumstances.

b. PAYMENTS TO DEPARTING PARTNERS

Your partnership agreement should provide for a payment schedule if there's a buy-out. Otherwise, the departing partner would have the right to collect for the full value of his or her interest promptly. This could become a serious problem if a partner dies, since the deceased partner's family would likely insist on exercising this right.

Your decision has a close relationship to the method you use for determining the buy-out price. If the remaining partners can pay the price over a number of years, they're usually willing to pay a higher buy-out price than if they must pay all the cash the day a partner leaves.

One of the best ways to finance the buy-out of a partner's interest is through insurance. If a partner dies, the proceeds from the partnership-financed insurance policy are used to pay off his or her share, and partnership operating income doesn't have to be used. Many profitable partnerships buy insurance against each partner's serious illness, incapacity or death. This can be a sensible way of obtaining money to pay off a deceased partner's interest; a term policy, which is relatively cheap, is especially good.

8. Continuity of the Partnership

If a partnership has more than two members, the remaining partners usually want to continue the business as a partnership when a partner leaves. Here's a clause that you can use to assure the continuation of a partnership:

> In the case of a partner's death, permanent disability, retirement, voluntary withdrawal or expulsion from a partnership, the partnership shall not dissolve or terminate, but its business shall continue without interruption and without any break in continuity. On the disability, retirement, withdrawal, expulsion or death of any partner, the others shall not liquidate or wind up the affairs of the partnership, but shall continue to conduct the partnership under the terms of this agreement.

9. Non-Competition of Departing Partner

Another issue relating to a partner who leaves the partnership is future competition. You may want to prohibit the departing partner from competing against your firm. This may include the protection of your trade secrets and customer lists.

Legally, this is a touchy area. Forbidding a partner from engaging in his or her usual way of earning a living is a drastic act, and courts often refuse to enforce unfairly restrictive terms. To be legal, a non-competition agreement normally must be reasonably limited in both time and geographical area and be otherwise fair. State laws vary in regard to non-competition clauses, and it's not always possible to tell whether or not a judge will enforce one. If you're determined to include a non-competition clause in your agreement, it makes sense to see a lawyer familiar with small business concerns.

This sample clause will give you an idea of how these clauses are often drafted:

> On the voluntary withdrawal, permanent disability, retirement or expulsion of any partner, that partner shall not carry on a business the same as or similar to the business of the partnership within the
>
> _____
>
> _____ [describe area] for a
>
> period of _____ [time period you've agreed on].

10. Control of Partnership Name

A business name can be valuable. The partnership agreement should spell out what happens to it if a partner leaves. There are a number of ways to handle this, including a clause stating that the partnership continues to own the name, that one partner owns the name, that control of the name will be decided on at a later date or, finally, that in the event of dissolution, the partnership business name will be owned by a majority of the former partners.

11. Resolving Partnership Disputes

Suppose there's a serious disagreement between the partners and you can't resolve it by personal discussions and negotiations. You may find yourself in court, which is a costly, time-consuming and emotionally draining way to deal with the dispute. Fortunately, there's a way around litigation as a means of resolving disputes. You can provide in your partnership agreement for mediation or arbitration or both. These subjects are treated in more depth in Chapter 18. Please read that discussion if you're not fully familiar with these methods.

Here's an example of a mediation clause:

> Any dispute arising out of this agreement or the partnership business will be resolved by mediation, if possible. The partners pledge to cooperate fully and fairly with the mediator in an attempt to reach a mutually satisfactory compromise to a dispute. The mediator will be _____. If any partner to a dispute feels it cannot be resolved by the partners themselves, he or she shall so notify the other partners and the mediator in writing. Mediation will commence within ___ days of the Notice of Request for Mediation. The cost of mediation will be shared equally by all partners to the dispute.

To protect yourselves should mediation fail, you can follow up with an arbitration clause that takes over if a dispute can't be mediated to the satisfaction of the parties. The partners are bound by the arbitrator's decision, which can be enforced in court.

If you include both mediation and arbitration clauses in your partnership agreement, you need to decide whether the mediator and arbitrator should be the same person. If you have the same person playing both roles, you don't run the risk of having to present the case twice—first to the mediator and then, if mediation fails, to the arbitrator. On the other hand, the person who has ultimate power to make a decision as an arbitrator may be less effective as a mediator.

C. Changes in Your Partnership

As your business changes, your partnership agreement will have to change, too. For example, the addition of a new partner requires revision of at least the clauses listing the partners' names and those covering contributions and distribution of profits. Even if you admit no new partners, the growth of your business may require you to change your agreement. You and your partners may decide to run your expanded business differently than the original business. Or maybe more cash is required, and the partners decide that their contributions should be in proportions different from those originally agreed to. Any time you make a significant change in the structure or operation of your business, you should change the partnership agreement to reflect it.

The owners of most small partnerships specify that the partnership agreement may be amended only by the written consent of all partners. But you can create any amendment clause you choose. For example, you could specify that the agreement can be amended by vote of 51% of the partners or by 51% of the capital accounts.

At some point, your partnership may well decide to add another partner. You may need a new partner's contribution of cash or skills, or you may want to retain a key employee by making him or her a partner. Because a partnership technically is dissolved when a new partner joins it, it's helpful to include a clause in your partnership agreement such as the following one:

> Admission of a new partner shall not cause dissolution of the underlying partnership business, which will be continued by the new partnership entity.

CREATING A CORPORATION

3

Chapter 1 introduced the basic business entities—the sole proprietorship, the partnership and the corporation. This chapter tells you more about setting up a corporation. We'll start with the structure of a corporation, including the roles of the key players: the incorporators, shareholders, directors, officers and employees. Then we'll look at corporate finance—how you get money into the corporation and how you take it out. Next we'll walk step by step through the procedures for setting up a corporation. Finally, we'll examine some sound corporate business practices.

The material in this chapter applies to most, but not all, new corporations. Generally, this material will apply to you if your proposed corporation fits the following profile:

- A relatively small number of people—about ten or fewer—will own the corporate stock.

- All or most of the owners will participate directly in managing and running the business; investors who don't directly participate will generally be limited to friends or family members.

- All of the owners will live in the state in which you form your corporation and conduct your business.

Lawyers often call a small corporation that fits this profile a "closely held corporation." We'll borrow this term in its most general, nontechnical sense.

Classifying your corporation at the outset is important because if you're a closely held corporation and sell stock only to a few friends or family members, normally you'll be exempt from all but the most routine requirements of federal and state securities laws.

But if you sell stock in your corporation to outside investors—people who won't help run the business or aren't closely tied to people who are—you must comply with those laws. So if you want to sell stock to a wider range of people, especially if any of them live in a different state, you'll need to learn more about the requirements of the securities laws. In many states, there are generous exemptions that allow sales of stock to as many as 35 investors with-

out complicated paperwork. But because this is such a technical area and laws vary from state to state, you should seek legal advice from a lawyer knowledgeable about securities laws before you offer stock to outsiders.

A. The Structure of a Corporation

Corporations are controlled primarily by state, not federal, law. This means that 50 different sets of rules cover how corporations are created. Terminology differs from state to state. For example, most states use the term "articles of incorporation" to refer to the basic document creating the corporation, but some states (including Connecticut, Delaware, New Jersey, New York and Oklahoma) use the term "certificate of incorporation." Tennessee calls it a "charter," and Vermont uses the term "articles of association." Fortunately, the similarities in corporate procedure outweigh the differences, so most of what you find in this chapter will apply to your own situation. Nevertheless, watch out for the differences.

People involved in a corporation traditionally play different legal roles: incorporator, shareholder, director, officer, employee. We'll look at those roles here. But, in virtually every state, there's a way that you can set up a corporation in which one or two people play all roles.

LAW IN THE REAL WORLD

Keeping a Hand in the Business

Anne opened a small business providing customized bookkeeping software for manicurists. For several years she struggled financially as she tried to convince small nail shops that buying her computerized system would ultimately be far cheaper than keeping records in a shoe box. Finally, when a trade magazine gave her system a rave review, business took off. Suddenly Anne found herself hiring employees, upgrading and customizing her software and greatly increasing her marketing activities.

It quickly became apparent to Anne that she couldn't do it all herself. Her key employees were increasingly critical to her success. To help ensure their loyalty and hard work, Anne realized it would be wise to give them an ownership interest in the business. She accomplished this by forming a closely held corporation, Digital Nail Inc. Initially Anne owned 100% of the stock, but under the terms of a shareholders' agreement, half a dozen or so key employees receive stock each year.

Although Ann will always remain the majority owner, over time, each longtime employee will gain a significant share. If an employee leaves the company, his or her stock will have to be sold back to Digital Nail at its book (asset) value—considerably less than its market value (assuming the business continued to prosper and was sold or went public). In short, not only does Anne's plan give key employees a stake in the success of the company, it provides a powerful incentive for them to stick with Digital Nail.

1. Incorporators

The incorporators (called the promoters in some states) do the preparatory work. This may include bringing together the people and the money to create the corporation. It always includes preparing and filing the articles of incorporation—the formal incorporation document that is filed with a state office such as the secretary of state. Although several peo-ple can serve as incorporators and sign the articles of incorporation, only one incorporator is required by law, except in Arizona where two is the minimum. Once the articles of incorporation are filed, the incorporator's job is nearly done. The only things that remain to be done are to select the first board of directors and to adopt the corporate bylaws (although, in some states, bylaws may be adopted by the directors).

2. Shareholders

The shareholders own the stock of the corporation. One person can own 100% of the stock. Among the things that only shareholders can do are these:

- Elect directors although the initial board of directors is usually selected by the incorporator or promoter).

- Amend bylaws.

- Approve the sale of all or substantially all of the corporate assets.

- Approve mergers and reorganizations.

- Amend the articles of incorporation.

- Remove directors.

- Dissolve the corporation.

State laws typically require that the shareholders hold an annual meeting. However, in many states, a "consent action" or "consent resolution"—a document signed by all of the shareholders—can be used in place of a formal meeting.

For the corporation to elect S corporation status under federal tax laws, all shareholders must sign the election form that's filed with the IRS. For more on this, see Section F, Step 12.

3. Directors

The directors manage the corporation and make major policy decisions. Among other things, the directors authorize the issuance of stock; decide on whether to mortgage, sell or lease real estate; and elect the corporate officers. Directors may hold regular or special meetings (or both). However, in many states, it's simpler and just as effective for the directors to take actions by signing a document called a "consent resolution" or "consent action."

The incorporators or shareholders decide how many directors the corporation will have. The number of directors is usually stated in the articles of incorporation or in the corporate bylaws. Most states specifically permit corporations to have just one director. In the remaining states, the requirement is that there be at least three directors, but there's an exception for corporations with fewer than three shareholders. If there are only two shareholders, the corporation can operate with two directors; if there's only one shareholder, the corporation needs only one director.

Example 1: Anita, Barry and Clint create a corporation in Michigan. They choose Anita to be the sole director. They can do this because the law in Michigan—as in many other states—permits a corporation to function with a single director regardless of the number of shareholders.

Example 2: Dustin, Erwin and Faye create a corporation in California. They would like Dustin to be the sole director, but California law requires them to have at least three directors if there are three or more shareholders; they can have a single director only if the corporation has a single shareholder. Therefore, Dustin, Erwin and Faye create a three-person board of directors and appoint themselves to those positions.

4. Officers

The officers are normally responsible for the day-to-day operation of the corporation. State laws usually require that the corporation have at least a president, a secretary and a treasurer. The president is usually the chief operating officer of the corporation. The secretary is responsible for the corporate records. The treasurer, of course, is responsible for the corporate finances, although it's common to hand day-to-day duties to a bookkeeper. The corporation can have

other officers—such as a vice-president—as well. In most states, one person can hold all of the required offices.

Example: Abdul forms a Texas corporation. He provides for the two corporate offices—president and secretary—that are required by Texas law. He appoints himself to both offices. This is legal in Texas and in most other states.

5. Employees

Employees work for the corporation in return for compensation. In the small corporations we're considering in this chapter, the owners (shareholders) are usually also employees of the corporation. It's through your salary and other compensation as a corporate employee that you'll receive most of your financial benefits from the business. Often the person who runs the business day-to-day gets the most compensation. This may or may not be the president.

6. How It All Fits Together

If you're new to all of this, the numerous components of a corporation may seem unduly complicated for a small business. Fortunately, it all fits together quite smoothly and easily.

Example: Al, Bev and Carla decide to form a corporation to run a fitness center. Their plan is to invest $10,000 apiece and be equal owners. Since state law requires only one person to sign the papers setting up the corporation, Bev signs the Articles of Incorporation for ABC Fitness Center Inc. and sends them to the Secretary of State's office along with the filing fee. Bev is the *incorporator*.

Next, Bev adopts bylaws for the corporation calling for a three-person Board of Directors. She elects herself, Al and Carla to serve as the first *directors*. The three of them then elect Bev to be the president, Al to be the secretary and Carla to be the treasurer—so the three of them are then the *officers* of the corporation.

When Al, Bev and Carla each pay $10,000 into the corporate bank account, they each receive a stock certificate for 10,000 shares of corporate stock; at that moment, they become *shareholders*.

All three are active in running the business, working 50 hours a week and receiving a salary. Al and Bev, who have experience as personal trainers, take charge of training customers and supervising a small staff of other workers. Carla, who studied business in college, looks after the finances—billing customers, marketing, ordering supplies. So in addition to their other roles in the corporation, Al, Bev and Carla are *employees*.

B. Financing Your Corporation

It doesn't take an MBA degree to grasp the fundamentals of corporate finance as they apply to funding the typical small business. Assets come into the corporation in two forms: equity and debt. Let's look at each.

1. Funding Your Corporation With Equity

Basically, equity means shareholders contribute cash, valuable property or services to the company in exchange for stock in the company. The number of shares issued is somewhat arbitrary, but the customary practice in some places is for new corporations to issue one share for each dollar invested.

The most common way to pay for stock is with cash. For example, you may put $5,000 into the company in return for 5,000 shares of corporate stock. But money isn't the only thing that you can invest in a company in return for stock. You may also transfer physical assets, such as real estate or equipment, or a copyright, patent or trademark. Or you may receive stock in return for past services to the corporation.

 Check before you transfer property for stock Before you transfer property to your corporation in exchange for stock, check

with your tax advisor. If you receive stock for property that has increased in value since you bought it, you may owe taxes.

In some states, you can receive stock in return for promising to perform services to the corporation, or in return for a promissory note. In other words, you might receive 5,000 shares of stock in return for your promise to work for the corporation for 200 hours or to pay the corporation $5,000 six months later. Not all states, however, permit stock to be issued based on a promise of future services or money, so check the rules of your state.

2. Funding Your Corporation With Debt

The other major way to fund a corporation is through debt—that is, by borrowing money. But you should know that if your corporation borrows from a bank or other outside lender, the lender will probably expect you to personally guarantee to repay the debt should the business be unable to.

 Lending money to the corporation. Until fairly recently, it was quite common for shareholders in some new corporations to lend money to the corporation or transfer assets from an existing sole proprietorship in exchange for a promissory note from the corporation. Shareholders gained tax benefits by dividing their initial investment between debt (represented by promissory notes) and equity (represented by stock certificates).[1] Changes in the tax laws, however, have eliminated the shareholder loan as a viable option for purchasing equity in a new corporation.

---

[1]For tax and other reasons, it was easier for a shareholder to withdraw his or her investment if it was in the form of a loan rather than equity. And when the corporation repaid the shareholder for a loan, the shareholder was taxed only on the interest portion—not the principal—which meant that as the business succeeded, the shareholder could withdraw some of his or her investment tax free.

3. Leasing Property to the Corporation

Sometimes you'll want to retain ownership of property being used by the corporation. For example, maybe you own a garage or other small building your company will occupy. With real estate, it's usually better, from a tax standpoint, to have your corporation lease the property from you rather than to transfer the property to the corporation.

Example Nino forms New Age Innovators Inc. to develop some practical new technologies for the plumbing industry. He plans to work out of his garage. He leases the garage to his corporation for $500 a month. On his own personal Form 1040, Nino will report the rent as income and will deduct interest expense (for the mortgage on the building) and depreciation. On its corporate tax return, New Age Innovators Inc. will deduct its rent payments and operating expenses for the garage.

If you lease property to the corporation, have the directors adopt a board resolution approving a lease. Then have the corporation sign the lease as tenant with you, of course, as the landlord. This will be helpful in establishing the existence of a lease if the arrangements are questioned by the IRS.

C. Compensating Yourself

I've just discussed how you put money into the corporation. Now let's get to the fun part—how you take it out.

1. Salary and Bonuses

As a corporate employee, you can receive a reasonable salary plus bonuses which, for tax purposes, are lumped in with salary. (Many corporate owners prefer to pay themselves conservative salaries and then to reward themselves with a year-end bonus if it makes sense economically.) Salaries and bonuses are treated as business expenses of the corporation, which means that the corporation owes no tax on what it pays you. You, in turn, report what you

receive as income on your personal income tax return just as you would if you worked for any other employer. The IRS has rules on how much salary is appropriate—the primary one is that the salary must be reasonable. This is a pretty loose standard and, as a practical matter, doesn't affect most small business people, because their businesses can't afford to pay them the sort of stratospheric salaries the IRS might consider unreasonable.

2. Interest on Loans to the Corporation

If you loan money or property to the corporation when it's underway in exchange for a promissory note, you'll receive interest on your loans. Hopefully, the corporation will repay you the principal amount of the loans as well. But you'll have to pay tax only on the interest you receive—not on the principal portion.

 Minimum interest. Any loan between a corporation and an employee or stockholder for more than $10,000 must carry a minimum interest rate. The rate is based on U.S. Treasury Bill rates. The loan type also determines whether other requirements must be met. Check with your tax advisor for details.

3. Fringe Benefits

Another way to profit from your investment in the corporation is through fringe benefits. For example, your corporation may purchase health insurance for employees and set up a plan under which the corporation reimburses employees for medical expenses not covered by insurance. Health insurance premiums and medical reimbursements paid by the corporation are tax-deductible business expenses for the corporation—and aren't taxable to the employee as personal income. By contrast, if you were to pay for medical expenses with no corporate help, only a limited amount would be tax-deductible on your personal income tax return.

S Corporations Note: S corporations are treated differently under the tax laws. Fringe benefits for an owner-employee who owns more than 2% of the stock of an S corporation are not given this favorable tax treatment.

4. Dividends

You've probably heard about corporate dividends paid to shareholders. This is another way that funds can be removed from a corporation for the benefit of its owners. Perhaps surprisingly, it is rarely done in a small corporation. Because the corporation can't deduct dividends as a business expense, dividends add up to double taxation. (This doesn't apply to S corporations; see Chapter 1, Section D.) The corporation is subject to tax on money paid as dividends, and then the shareholder is taxed a second time. To avoid this double taxation, it's much better to take money out of the corporation through the means previously discussed.

D. Do You Need a Lawyer To Incorporate?

It's possible to form your own corporation without professional help. Every day, many entrepreneurs do exactly that by using an incorporation kit. If you're inclined to go this route, check out *How To Form Your Own Corporation* (California, Florida, New York and Texas editions), by Anthony Mancuso (Nolo Press). If you live in one of the states covered by these excellent books, you'll receive a lot of valuable information about incorporating, even if you decide not to do it yourself.

The obvious motivating factor for setting up a corporation on your own is to save on legal fees, which can range from $1,000 to $2,000 or more, depending on where you live. But be aware that there's a tradeoff: you're subjecting yourself to bureaucratic hassles and, unless you do your homework carefully, possible errors. The paper-filing

phase, by itself, isn't all that difficult. But tax and legal liability problems may not be obvious to the do-it-yourselfer. And if you plan to issue stock to other than a few people who will work in the business or are close friends and relatives, securities laws can be troublesome. Still, dollars are often precious to people just starting out in business, and you may decide that it's worthwhile to attempt to form your corporation by yourself. If you choose that route, it's a good idea to have a lawyer experienced with small businesses look over the final documents before you file them. (Chapter 20 discusses finding, hiring and working with a lawyer.) You should be able to find a lawyer willing to do this at a fraction of the cost of having the lawyer handle the matter from beginning to end.

 Beware of securities law. If you'll have a number of shareholders—especially people who won't be working in the business and who are not close relatives living in your state—consult a lawyer to see that you're in compliance with federal and state securities regulations. (See Section E below.) While most small businesses are considered to be closely held corporations and exempt from these potentially complicated regulations, it's worth spending a few bucks to find out for sure. Anthony Mancuso's how-to-incorporate books, mentioned above discuss this issue in detail.

E. Overview of Incorporation Procedures

While there are differences from state to state, the basic procedures that you or your lawyer will follow in creating a corporation are these:

- Prepare and file the articles of incorporation.
- Select a board of directors.
- Adopt bylaws.
- Elect officers.
- Issue stock.

- Decide whether or not you want to elect S corporation tax status.

In a moment, we'll walk through the incorporation process. Before we do, let's look at one additional step to consider before starting to incorporate: a pre-incorporation agreement. It may be unnecessary if you're planning a one-person corporation or if your corporation consists only of family members. Similarly, a pre-incorporation agreement is less necessary if you and your associates are incorporating an existing business or if you've done business together before. However, if you're going into business with relative strangers, putting your agreement in written form will help you avoid disputes later or, if an argument does arise, will provide a basis for resolving it through arbitration or litigation. (See Chapter 18.) Your written agreement should include these key points:

- the name of the corporation
- its purpose
- how much stock each person will buy and how he or she will pay for it
- what loans each person will make to the corporation and the terms of repayment
- what offices (president, vice-president, secretary, treasurer) each person will hold
- what compensation each of you will receive
- what expense accounts each of you will have
- what fringe benefits will be available.

If the corporation is going to lease real estate or other property from one of the owners, the agreement can also outline the terms of that transaction.

 Where to incorporate—beware the Delaware myth. Many people are sold on the notion that there's something magical about incorporating in Delaware. The reality is that the best state to incorporate in is the state where your headquarters is located. For the vast majority of small business corporations, that means the state where you live. If you incorporate in Delaware you'll still have to register as an out-of-state corporation to do business in your own state.

F. 12 Basic Steps To Incorporate

The following outline will help understand how to go about forming a corporation for your small business. The procedure for incorporating is similar—but not identical—in every state.

Step 1. Choose a Name

In Chapter 4, you'll find more detail about selecting a business name. But here are a few basics about naming a corporation.

In most states, to alert the public to your corporate status you must include certain words in your corporate name, such as *Incorporated*, *Corporation*, *Company* or *Limited*, or the abbreviations *Inc.*, *Corp.*, *Co.* or *Ltd.* And there are certain words you can't use in your name; for example, in California, the words *National*, *United States* and *Federal* are prohibited. In New York, you need the approval of a department of state government to use the words *Benefit*, *Council*, *Educational* or *Housing* in your corporate name. The quickest way to learn what words are required or prohibited in your state is to call or write to the office where you file the articles of incorporation—usually the secretary of state or corporation commissioner's office. In the few states where they're unwilling to help you, the best approach (short of calling your lawyer) is to go to a law library and check the state statute ("code") sections dealing with corporations. For more on law libraries, see Chapter 20, Section D Because you'll probably want to consult these laws frequently, you may want to buy a set from the state or a private publisher.

Most states will reject a corporation name that's the same as one already on file or one that's confusingly similar to the name of an existing corporation. But even if the secretary of state accepts your corporate name (or tells you it's available in a pre-filing name reservation procedure), this doesn't guarantee your legal right to use it. An unincorporated business may already be using it as its trade name, or a business may be using it as a trademark or service mark to identify products or services. In short, as is discussed in Chapter 4, there is a good deal more to do to check out the availability of a particular name.

In many states, a corporation can do business under an assumed or fictitious name. For example, if you incorporate as Miller Manufacturing Company but want to market some of your products under a more specific business name, you can simply file an assumed name certificate for Miller Appliances. Some states require that you file this paper at the same state office where you filed the articles of incorporation (such as the secretary of state's office). In other states, you file your fictitious or assumed name certificate in the counties where your company does business. And some states require that you also publish notice of your assumed or fictitious name in a newspaper.

Before you file your corporate papers, check with your state's corporate filing office. Generally they can make a preliminary check and tell you if the name is available. If you expect some delay before the papers are actually filed, find out whether your state permits you to reserve a name. Many will do so for a month or more.

What happens if you've got your heart set on a name but find that it's too similar to one already in use? One approach is to change it slightly. Most state's name records are computerized, and often a fairly small modification will turn rejection to approval. Or you can ask the owners of the other business to let you use the similar name. In many states you can use such a name if you get the written consent of the corporation that was established earlier.

Using your corporate name as a trademark. If you plan to use your corporate name as a trademark or service mark for products or services, you won't want a name that's very similar to someone else's. As explained further in Chapter 4, even if your name were approved by your corporate filing office, it might infringe the other user's trademark or service mark.

Step 2. Prepare and File Articles of Incorporation

As noted above, in some states articles of incorporation are called certificates of incorporation, charters or articles of association. Here I'll stick with the term articles of incorporation.

In many states, the secretary of state can give you a printed form for the articles of incorporation; all you have to do is fill in some blank spaces. In other states, you must prepare the articles of incorporation from scratch.

Below is an example of articles of incorporation for a California corporation.

SAMPLE ARTICLES OF INCORPORATION

ARTICLES OF INCORPORATION
OF

_____

ONE: The name of this corporation is _____.

TWO: The purpose of this corporation is to engage in any lawful act or activity for which a corporation may be organized under the General Corporation Law of California other than the banking business, the trust company business or the practice of a profession permitted to be incorporated by the California Corporation Code.

THREE: The name and address in this state of the corporation's initial agent for the service of process is:

_____

_____.

FOUR: This corporation is authorized to issue only one class of shares of stock which shall be designated common stock. The total number of shares it is authorized to issue is _____ shares.

FIVE: The names and address of the persons who are appointed to act as the initial directors of this corporation are:

Name   Address

_____   _____

_____   _____

_____   _____

_____   _____

_____   _____

SIX: The liability of the directors of the corporation for monetary damages shall be eliminated to the fullest extent permissible under California law.

SEVEN: The corporation is authorized to indemnify the directors and officers of the corporation to the fullest extent permissible under California law.

IN WITNESS WHEREOF, the undersigned, being all the persons named above as the initial directors, have executed these Articles of Incorporation.

Dated: _____   _____

                                 _____

                                 _____

                                 _____

                                 _____

The undersigned, being all the persons named above as the initial directors, declare that they are the persons who executed the foregoing Articles of Incorporation, which execution is their act and deed.

Dated: _____   _____

                                 _____

                                 _____

                                 _____

                                 _____

While details vary from state to state, the typical articles of incorporation include:

- the corporation's name
- its purpose
- the name of the initial agent for service of process (sometimes called a registered agent or resident agent)
- the number of shares authorized
- the names and addresses of the incorporators.

The purpose clause may seem confusing—it's as if you're being asked to define what your business will do until the end of time. Fortunately, this isn't necessary, because the statutes in many states allow you to use very general language, such as: "The purposes of this corporation shall be to engage in any lawful act or activity for which corporations may be organized under the business corporation law." If such a statement is permitted in your state, it's usually best not to be any more specific. This leaves you free to change the nature of your business without amending the articles of incorporation. It also helps you avoid questions of whether you're acting beyond the scope of your stated purpose if you go into a new business.

Most states require you to designate somebody as a resident agent or registered agent in the articles of incorporation. This is the person who is authorized to receive official notices and lawsuit papers. Normally, you designate the corporate president as this person. If you change the person named or there's a new address, you need to notify the secretary of state's office by filing a proper form.

It may take a few weeks for your articles of incorporation to be processed by the secretary of state's office. If you need quicker action, check to see if expedited handling is available. In some states, you can file your articles of incorporation in person and have the filing process completed within a day. Sometimes, articles of incorporation sent by UPS, Federal Express or other overnight means are treated as in-person filings and given expedited treatment.

If you need to sign contracts, such as a lease, even before the corporation has been formed, it's a good idea to state in the contract that you're acting on behalf of a corporation to be formed and that the contract is subject to ratification by the board of directors of the new corporation. Then, if for some reason the corporation is never formed or if the directors fail to ratify the document, you're free from personal liability. Here is sample language for such a lease.

TYPICAL INCORPORATION FEES

California	$100 plus an $800 initial tax.
Florida	$35 filing fee plus $35 for designating a registered agent, for a total of $70. For a certified copy of your articles, add $52.50.
Michigan	$10 for filing the articles of incorporation plus a franchise fee of $50 for the first 60,000 authorized shares. The minimum combined fee is $60. (There is a fee of $30 for each additional 20,000 authorized shares.)
New York	$100 for filing the certificate of incorporation plus an organization tax of five cents per share for each authorized share with no par value. The minimum organization tax is $10, so total fees are at least $110.
Texas	$200 filing fee plus $100 initial franchise tax prepayment (to be applied toward first-year corporate franchise taxes).

These fees change frequently, so check before you file.

If this approach is not acceptable to the person with whom you're contracting, another possibility is to sign the contract in your own name—thereby assuming personal liability temporarily—but to specifically reserve the right to assign it to the corporation later.

> Landlord grants to Martin Green the right to assign this lease to XYZ Corporation, a corporation to be formed. Upon Landlord's receipt of written notice that such assignment has been made, Martin Green will automatically be released from any personal liability under this lease.

Landlord acknowledges that Martin Green is signing this lease on behalf of XYZ Corporation (a corporation to be formed) and that this lease is subject to ratification by the corporation's Board of Directors. If the corporation is not formed or if the Board of Directors fails to ratify this lease within 30 days of the present date, this lease will be void. In no event will Martin Green have any personal liability under this lease.

Step 3. Elect the First Board of Directors

In some states, initial directors are designated in the articles of incorporation. In other states, the incorporator or incorporators choose the first board of directors. If this is the practice in your state, be sure to document the appointment of directors with a statement or certificate signed by the incorporators. This statement or certificate, which will be inserted into your corporate record book, may look something like the one below.

SAMPLE DESIGNATION OF DIRECTORS BY INCORPORATOR

**ACTION BY INCORPORATOR
OF XYZ CORPORATION**

The Incorporator of XYZ Corporation, a Pennsylvania corporation, designates the following people to serve as the initial Board of Directors of the Corporation:

> Joyce Barker
> Lloyd Epstein
> Norton Phillips

Dated:_____   _____
                                                          Joyce Barker, Incorporator

---

Step 4. Adopt Bylaws

The corporate bylaws contain much more detail than the articles of incorporation. They spell out the rights and powers of the shareholders, directors and officers of the corporation. Typically the bylaws state the time and place for the annual meeting of shareholders, how much notice of the meeting is given and what constitutes a quorum. There are also provisions for special meetings to consider issues so important they can't wait for the next annual meeting and a statement about what actions the shareholders can take by written consent without a formal meeting. Bylaws provide how many directors there are, how they're elected, what their powers are, and if and how they're compensated. Titles of the corporate officers (generally, a president, secretary and treasurer) are listed in the bylaws.

The bylaws may also cover such matters as who is authorized to sign contracts, who has the right to inspect corporate books and records (and under what conditions), the fiscal year of the corporation and how the bylaws can be amended.

In a few states the incorporators must adopt the bylaws; in others, the directors must adopt them.

And in still other states, you can choose between the two methods. If the incorporators adopt the bylaws, be sure to document this in a signed statement or certificate. If the directors adopt the bylaws (see below), reflect this action in your minutes of the first directors' meeting or, if you don't hold a meeting, in a written consent resolution of the directors.

Step 5. Hold a Directors' Meeting

The directors must do a number of things at the beginning to get the corporation on the right track. Historically, corporations have recorded these actions in a document called "minutes of first meeting of the board of directors." These minutes were written in language reflecting a formal parliamentary procedure that really doesn't match the less formal style of most small businesses.

Fortunately, in most states, there's a streamlined method for accomplishing this. You or your lawyer can prepare a consent form to be signed by the board of directors such as the one below.

SAMPLE CONSENT FORM FOR DIRECTORS

XYZ CORPORATION

CONSENT OF THE BOARD OF DIRECTORS

The directors of XYZ Corporation consent to the following:

1. BYLAWS: The attached bylaws shall be the bylaws of the corporation.

2. OFFICERS: The following people are elected to serve as officers of the corporation for the next year, or until their successors are elected:

    President:_____

    Secretary:_____

    Treasurer:_____

3. ISSUANCE OF STOCK CERTIFICATES. The President and Secretary are authorized and directed to issue stock certificates in the following amounts upon receipt of payment from the designated shareholders:

Name	Number of Shares	Amount to be Paid
1. _____	_____	_____
2. _____	_____	_____
3. _____	_____	_____

4. LEASE. The President is authorized and directed to enter into a three-year lease of space in The Village Green on the terms set out in the attached memorandum.

    Dated:_____,19____   _____
                                   Director #1

    Dated:_____,19____   _____
                                   Director #2

    Dated:_____,19____   _____
                                   Director #3

What actions should the board of directors take at its first meeting, either in formal minutes or through a consent resolution? The following are typical:

- adopt bylaws
- designate corporate officers
- approve the form of stock certificate
- approve bank account resolutions
- adopt the first fiscal year
- authorize issuance of stock
- approve lease
- approve employment contracts.

Step 6. Set Up a Corporate Bank Account

Remember, your corporation is a legal entity separate from its shareholders, directors and officers. For that reason, the corporation needs its own bank account so that its finances can clearly be kept separate.

If you're incorporating an existing business that already has a bank account, I recommend that you start fresh and set up a new bank account for the corporation. The bank will ask for a corporate board of directors' resolution authorizing the new account and an Employer's ID Number. (Employer's ID Numbers are discussed in Chapter 6, Section A.)

If you decide to simply continue the old account, do the following:

- Find out the bank's procedures for changing a sole proprietorship or partnership account into a corporate account. Most likely, the bank will want your directors to adopt a specific resolution, using language the bank will supply. The bank will want to see your articles of incorporation and a copy of the banking resolution. You'll also be asked to provide your Employer's Identification Number (issued by the IRS). You may not have this immediately, and the bank will probably let you start using the account for the corporation if you assure them that you've applied for the ID number.

- Keep detailed records showing exactly how much money was in the account when it was changed over to the corporation. Also keep track of any checks that were written by your existing business but haven't cleared yet. These checks should be treated as expenses of the unincorporated business and deducted from the amount considered transferred to the corporation. Preparing and retaining these records will save you headaches a year or two down the road when you try to figure out exactly what was transferred to the corporation.

Step 7. Issue Stock

The corporation should issue a stock certificate to each shareholder. The certificate is evidence of the shareholder's ownership interest in the corporation. Filling out the stock certificate is simple. Your main legal concern is whether you need to do anything to comply with federal or state securities laws.

Federal securities laws are administered by the Securities and Exchange Commission (SEC). In addition, each state has its own law regulating the sale of securities, intended to protect passive investors—people who put money into a corporation but are not active in the day-to-day operations of the business.

The bad news is that both the federal and state requirements are very complicated. The good news is that, as discussed earlier, the typical small company consisting solely of investors who are actively involved in the day-to-day operation of the company and often their close relatives is completely exempt from the complicated requirements. Nevertheless, some paperwork may be involved. For example, it's frequently advisable to give a "shareholder representation letter" to each prospective shareholder, even though it isn't strictly required under the state's securities laws. The letter gives you a way to confirm the purchaser's reasons for believing the transaction is exempt from the state's securities laws.

Example: Edgewater Inc. has been formed to build and operate a restaurant on the shore of a scenic lake. Chester, a wealthy investor who has been a partner in three major deals with Todd, the president of Edgewater Inc., is going to invest $75,000 in the new corporation and receive 75,000 shares of stock. To qualify a stock purchase as exempt under the state's "limited offering exemption," the purchaser must be an insider shareholder (a director, officer or promoter of the corporation), someone who's had a pre-existing business or personal relation with the corporation or one of its officers, or a "sophisticated investor." (Sophisticated investors are those who, because of their business or financial experience, are in a good position to protect their interests when buying stock in a new corporation.) Chester qualifies as both a sophisticated investor and one who's had a pre-existing business relationship with the corporate president. Todd prepares a shareholder representation letter reciting these facts for Chester to sign.

For sample shareholder representation letters and reliable information to prepare them for your corporation, see *How To Form Your Own Corporation* by Anthony Mancuso (Nolo Press) available in state-specific editions for California, Florida, New York and Texas.

Before you issue a stock certificate, make sure that the corporation has actually received payment for the shares. For example, if the shares are being purchased for cash, the corporation should receive the money before issuing the shares. If the corporation is issuing the stock in return for a promise of future payment by the shareholder (a practice allowed in some states but not others), the corporation should have in its possession a promissory note from the shareholder. If property is being transferred to the corporation in exchange for stock, the person transferring the property should sign a bill of sale at the same time the corporate shares are issued.

Step 8. Complete Any Initial Financial Transactions

Tie up any other loose ends relating to the financing of the corporation. As noted earlier, your corporation may borrow some of its start-up money from friends, relatives or other lenders. The corporation should issue written promissory notes as evidence that loans have been made. In addition, if you're leasing a building or equipment to the corporation, sign a lease.

Step 9. Set Up a Corporate Record Book

You can create a corporate record book in an ordinary loose-leaf binder. A more official looking way to do it is to buy a corporate record book from Nolo Press or a local stationer. Expect to pay about $75. These usually come with stock certificates and an embossed corporate seal.

The main items that you'll keep in the corporate record book are the articles of incorporation, the bylaws, the minutes of meetings (or consent resolutions) and the stock certificate stubs or ledger sheets showing who received the stock certificates and when. In many small corporations, shareholders prefer the convenience of simply leaving the completed stock certificates in the corporate record book even though each shareholder is, of course, entitled to possession of his or her certificate.

Step 10. Follow Through on State Government Requirements

Your state may require that you file documents in addition to the articles of incorporation. For example, in New York, you need to file a stock registration certificate certifying that you "keep a place for the sale, transfer or delivery of your corporate stock" at a certain address (normally your corporate offices). In California, you need to file a notice of stock transaction within 15 days after your first sale of stock and "an annual statement of domestic stock corporation" within 90 days after you file your articles of incorporation. To learn about requirements in your state, contact your corporate filing office.

Step 11. Comply With the Bulk Sales Act

If shareholders transfer assets of an existing business to the new corporation in return for stock, there are some special requirements. Called the bulk sales laws, they are designed to prevent business owners from secretly transferring their business assets to another company to avoid paying creditors. Basically, bulk sales laws require you to notify creditors that the assets of the business are being transferred.

Fortunately, state laws usually provide for some exemption or short cuts when the assets are being transferred to a new corporation that will be taking over and continuing an existing business. A key element generally is that your new corporation agrees to take over the business debts of the existing company. If you're forming a corporation to take over and continue a business formerly run as a sole proprietorship or partnership, compliance with the bulk sales law should be relatively easy.

Step 12.   File S Corporation Election

As discussed in some detail in Chapter 1, an S corporation is simply a corporation that decides to be taxed as a partnership. That is, it's not a separate tax entity like a regular corporation. Instead, the profits and losses of the corporation flow through to the individual shareholders who report them on their individual tax returns.

For purposes of incorporating under state law, the procedure is the same whether you're a regular corporation or an S corporation. But to become an S corporation, you need to file a form with the IRS. This is Form 2553, Election by a Small Business Corporation. All of the shareholders must sign this form. If you want to have S corporation status during the first tax year that your corporation exists, you need to file the election form before the 15th day of the third month of your tax year. In other words, you have a two-and-a-half month window during which you can file the election. When does your tax year start? For a new corporation, your tax year starts when your corporation (1) has shareholders, (2) acquires assets or (3) begins doing business, whichever happens first. If you miss the deadline, you have to wait until the next tax year to file the election form.

G. After You Incorporate

This chapter concentrates on steps you need to take to form your corporation. What must you do after incorporating? Obviously, you need to comply with federal and state tax filing rules. (See Chapter 6.) Your business may also need to get business licenses and permits. (See Chapter 5.) And it's smart to buy insurance before you begin doing business. (See Chapter 9.)

In addition, corporations must file annual reports with the secretary of state's office. Typically this is a form sent to you by the secretary of state's office which requires you to update information about corporate officers and location. Simply fill it out and return it with the necessary fee. If you forget to send the form back, your corporation may face fines and penalties and may even be automatically dissolved.

H. Business Practices for Your Corporation

Last week you were the sole proprietor of a catering business you called Feasts On The Go. Today you own all the stock of a new corporation, Feasts On The Go, Inc. In addition, you're the corporation's director, president, secretary and treasurer.

Or maybe last week you and Emily were partners in a used record shop called Around Again. Today you each own 50% of the stock in a new corporation called Second Time Around, Incorporated, which is running the old partnership business. Emily's the president, you're the secretary-treasurer.

What has changed? On a day-to-day level, not much. You still show up at the same place each day and do the same kind of work you did before you incorporated. In fact, your before- and after-incorporation lives will probably be so similar that it will be easy to forget the fact that you're now working for a corporation that is a separate legal entity.

But forgetting can be risky. If you're careless about maintaining the separation between the corporation and yourself, you can jeopardize your tax benefits or your freedom from personal liability—the main reasons to incorporate in the first place. While it's rare for a judge to disregard a corporation and impose personal liability on a shareholder, it does happen. When it does, it's almost always in a small corporation where the owners have allowed the line between the corporation and the shareholders to get very fuzzy or disappear. And the IRS also has the power to decide that a corporation is a sham if you fail to maintain it as a separate legal entity. Consider the following actual case:

> For 15 years, Walter Otto ran an export-import business in San Francisco. Then he incorporated his business. He filed articles of incorporation with the California secretary of state for "Otto Sales Company Inc." Next he invested $50 in the corporation. A few years later, the business became insolvent. A salesman sued for unpaid commissions, naming both the corporation and Walter as defendants. After a trial, the judge ordered Walter himself to pay the salesman over $18,000. Doing business through a corporation didn't protect Walter from personal liability.

What did Walter do wrong? Several things:

- He never issued any stock certificates to himself or anyone else.

- He contributed only $50 to the corporation as his "equity" in the business. (For more on equity and how to structure the financial side of a corporation, see Section B above.)

- He continued to use the same sales contracts that he used before he incorporated. These contracts said "Walter Otto" at the top. At the bottom, the contracts said: "Walter Otto, by_____, seller."

In the judge's view, Walter formed the corporation solely for his personal convenience and did not treat it as a real entity. So the judge "pierced the corporate veil" to make Walter personally liable for the debt. *Shafford v. Otto Sales Company*, 308 P.2d 428 (Cal. App. 1957).

Here are two more cases in which the owners of small corporations were found personally liable:

- J.C. Chou formed Oriental Fireworks Inc., a corporation that grossed from $230,000 to $400,000 annually. Its assets, however, never exceeded $13,000, and the company never bought liability insurance. Gregory Rice was seriously injured by fireworks distributed by the corporation. He sued and was awarded $432,000. Since the corporation lacked funds to pay the judgment—and didn't carry insurance—the court ruled that J.C. was personally liable.

  J.C.'s Main Mistake: Failing to provide even minimally adequate funds to the corporation (in legal lingo, failing to adequately capitalize the corporation) or to carry proper insurance. *Rice v. Oriental Fireworks Co.*, 707 P.2d 1250 (Or. App. 1985).

- Dusty Schmidt and Terry Ulven were partners in a business called Western Oregon Christmas Trees. At Christmas time, the partnership rented tents from the Salem Tent and Awning Company to display their trees. Later, Dusty and Terry formed a corporation—Western Oregon Christmas Trees Inc. They continued to rent tents from Salem but didn't sign rental agreements or checks as corporate officers. When several tents were destroyed by a storm, Salem sued the corporation and was awarded a judgment of $12,500. The court ruled that Dusty and Terry also were personally liable for the judgment.

  Dusty's and Terry's Main Foul-ups: Dusty and Terry made a $2,000 down payment on the tent using a check from their previous partnership— not from the corporation. Also, the pair commingled (mixed together) personal and corporate assets and failed to keep corporate records. *Salem Tent & Awning v. Schmidt*, 719 P.2d 899 (Or. App. 1986).

Even though these cases had unhappy endings for the owners of the small corporations, doing business as a corporation isn't all that dangerous. There are several simple steps you can take to preserve your corporate status so that you don't have to lie awake nights worrying about personal liability. These steps are not time-consuming—and they make good business sense.

1. Put Adequate Capital Into Your Corporation

Put in enough money and other assets to meet your foreseeable business requirements. The amount, of course, varies from business to business. What's reasonable to start a video store that requires a considerable inventory of films, a retail location and several employees may be vastly different than what's reasonable to start a typing service, which may need little more than a personal computer, printer, modem and copy and fax machines. See if you can get a recommendation from your accountant or someone in the same business.

2. Insure Against Obvious Risks

Try to determine if there's a substantial risk of customers or others being injured because of your business. If so, it's wise to obtain a reasonable amount of coverage. (See Chapter 9 for more on insurance.) There have been some cases—not many—in which a judge has felt that the failure of owners of a small corporation to buy insurance that was reasonably available was so reckless that it was a factor in disregarding the corporation and holding its owners personally liable.

Example: Eunice owns all the stock in a corporation called Roadside Enterprises Inc. The corporation sells and installs tires. It's obvious that an improperly installed tire can cause a serious accident. What if a Roadside employee forgets to tighten the lugs on a newly installed tire and the tire falls off, causing the driver to swerve into a tree? If the driver is killed, his or her family will probably sue Roadside. And if the corporation doesn't have reasonable insurance coverage (and hasn't set up a reasonable reserve fund), a judge could rule that Eunice has

some personal liability—even though she wasn't even at the tire store when the employee was inattentive.

Basically, it's a matter of exercising reasonable business judgment. If your business involves the risk of injury and you can buy liability insurance at a reasonable price, I recommend that you do so. On the other hand, if affordable insurance isn't available—an unfortunate reality in some industries today—it's highly unlikely that a judge would find fault with the owners of the corporation for not insuring against the risks.

3. Observe Corporate Formalities

Another way to protect yourself from the possibility that your corporation could be disregarded by a court is to always take it seriously yourself. Issue stock certificates to the shareholders before your corporation starts doing business. Keep a corporate record book containing your articles of incorporation, stock records, bylaws and minutes of shareholders' and directors' meetings. Comply with state law requirements that you hold annual meetings of shareholders or act by signed consent actions or resolutions. Either way you should document all actions taken such as election of officers for the next year.

Conference Calls: If it's not convenient for all the directors to meet at the same place, many states allow them to participate through a conference call. Follow up by documenting the telephone meeting in writing as soon as possible and sending a copy to each director.

Keep in mind that the annual meetings are minimum requirements. While it's not necessary or appropriate to preserve minutes or consent actions for every conference you have with your colleagues, if you take significant corporate actions during the year, it's wise to document them through minutes of a special meeting or a consent action form. Keep the minutes and consent actions in your corporate record book.

Here are some types of business activities that you should document with minutes of a directors' meeting or a signed consent action form signed by the directors:

- authorizing corporate bank accounts and designating who is eligible to sign checks and withdraw funds

- determining salaries and bonuses of officers

- contributing to pension and profit-sharing plans

- acquiring another business

- borrowing money

- entering into major contracts

- buying, selling or leasing real estate

- adopting or amending employee fringe benefits plans

- applying for trademark registration.

4. Separate Your Personal Finances From the Corporation's

The corporation needs its own bank account. (See Section F, Step 6.) Don't use the corporate bank account to pay your personal expenses. Get salary checks on a regular basis from the corporation (deducting employee withholding taxes); deposit the checks in your personal account; and then pay your own bills.

If you use personal funds to pay business expenses—for example, you pick up a ream of typing paper while you're out for lunch—you can have the corporation reimburse you, but be sure the corporation keeps the receipt for the paper to justify the payment as a proper business expense.

To further preserve the distinction between you and the corporation, document all transactions as if you were strangers. If the corporation leases property from you, sign a lease. If the corporation borrows money from you, get a promissory note. If you sell property to the corporation or use your property to buy stock, sign a bill of sale or other legal document formally transferring legal title to the corporation.

5. Use the Correct Corporate Name

Suppose the name of your corporation is The A.B. Smith Fitness Store Inc. Use that full business name in all your business dealings—on your stationery, business cards and phone book listings, on your signs, and in catalogues and computer database listings. Be careful not to use a different or abbreviated version (such as Smith Fitness Center) unless you file an assumed name certificate or fictitious name certificate as permitted by state law. For more on corporate names, see Section F and Chapter 4.

6. Sign as a Corporate Officer

In correspondence and on checks, sign your name as William Jones, President, rather than just William Jones. This makes it clear to those who deal with you that you're acting as an agent or employee of the corporation and not as an individual. Follow this practice on any other document you sign, such as contracts, order forms and promissory notes.

SAMPLE SIGNATURE OF CORPORATE OFFICER

> **JONES BAKERY INC.**
>
> **By:**_____
> William Jones, President

In some cases, you may have to sign the contract or promissory note as a guarantor. For example, banks usually won't lend money to a small corporation without the personal guarantees of the principals, and some extra-cautious landlords may insist on similar guarantees for leases. But even if you have to accept personal liability for some corporate obligations, it's better to do this as a guarantor than as the main signer. The reason: the guarantee provides further evidence that you and the corporation are separate legal entities.

7. Assign Existing Business Contracts to the Corporation

If you incorporate an existing business (such as a sole proprietorship or a partnership), the old business may have contracts still in effect, which the corporation will take over. For example, maybe the prior business leased space and the lease still has a year to go. Or maybe you're a computer consultant and, as a sole proprietor, you'd just gotten started on a contract to design customized billing software for a medical clinic.

It's usually a good idea to formally transfer these contracts to the corporation. Generally, unless the contract expressly prohibits an assignment, you're free to transfer it to your corporation without getting the consent of the other party. But bear this in mind:

Unless you get that consent and a release of personal liability, or unless your contract already specifically permits you to assign it to a new corporation and be free from personal liability, you're still going to be legally responsible for performance of the contract. This means that the landlord can turn to you if the corporation doesn't pay the rent, and the medical clinic can hold you personally responsible if you don't deliver the software you promised.

Important Tax Note: If your corporation will derive income from passive sources, such as rents, royalties or dividends, or from the performance of personal services, get professional tax advice before you transfer contracts to the corporation. A transfer could lead to a personal holding company penalty—which could be quite substantial.

To assign a contract, prepare a short document called "Assignment of Lease" or "Assignment of Computer Consultation Contract." A sample is shown below. Have the corporation agree to accept the assignment and to carry out the terms of the contract. From a business and legal standpoint, it makes sense to continue your business through a single entity—the corporation—rather than to do business simultaneously as a sole proprietor and as an employee of your corporation. Putting your eggs in one basket reduces the chances of blurring the distinction between the corporation and your personal business interests.

SAMPLE ASSIGNMENT OF CONTRACT

ASSIGNMENT OF RENOVATION CONTRACT

In consideration of the sum of $_____, receipt of which is acknowledged, Cecil Hardwick (d/b/a Hardwick Construction) assigns to Hardwick Building Company (a Nevada Corporation) all of his rights, duties and obligations under his contract with Plaza Building Associates dated _____, 19____ concerning the renovation of the Plaza Building.

Hardwick Building Company accepts this assignment and accepts all of Cecil Hardwick's duties under the assigned contract.

Dated:_____, 19___

ASSIGNOR: ASSIGNEE:

                                               Hardwick Building Company,

                                               A Nevada Corporation

_____   By: _____

Cecil Hardwick d/b/a   Cecil Hardwick

Hardwick Construction   President

 RECOMMENDED READING

Corporations in a Nutshell by Robert W. Hamilton (West Publishing Co.). A concise work written primarily for law students.

The Law of Corporations and Other Business Enterprises by Harry G. Henn and John R. Alexander (West Publishing Co.). A more detailed book used by lawyers.

Naming Your Business and Products

4

TRADEMARK TERMINOLOGY

Trademark: A word, phrase, design or symbol that identifies a product brand—such as Compaq computers, Nike shoes, Kodak cameras, Xerox photocopiers and Marathon gasoline.

Service mark: A word, phrase, design or symbol that identifies the provider of a service—such as Burger King (fast foods), Roto-Rooter (sewer-drain service), Kinko's (copy centers) and Blockbuster (video rentals).

Mark: Sometimes used to refer to both a *trademark* and a *service mark,* because the terms are nearly, but not completely, interchangeable.

Corporate Name: The name of a corporation as registered with one or more states. *Examples:* Time Inc.; Sony Corporation. The corporate name refers to the corporation only, and not to any product or services it offers.

Trade Name or Business Name: The name used to identify a business, as distinct from the product or service it offers. It may be the same as the product or service name; for example, Sony Corporation sells electronic equipment under the Sony trademark; McDonald's Corporation uses the service mark McDonald's on its fast food service. Or the trade name or business name may be different—for example, General Motors Corporation sells cars under the Buick trademark.

Assumed Name or Fictitious Name: A business name different from the owner's name. *Example:* Laura does business as Coffee Express. Partnerships and (in many states) corporations may also use assumed or fictitious names. In most places, you must register a fictitious name.(See Section B.2)

Federal Trademark Register: A list of all trademarks and service marks registered with the federal government. To be accepted, a trademark or service mark must be distinctive and not confusingly similar to an existing mark. All states maintain trademark registers too, and some maintain service mark registers; pre-existing federal trademark rights have priority.

Naming your business and products may not be as simple as it first appears. Some legal steps are mandatory; for example, if you incorporate, you must choose a corporate name acceptable to your state's secretary of state or corporations commissioner. And all businesses—corporations, partnerships and sole proprietorships—must comply with laws dealing with assumed names or fictitious names. (See Section B.)

Other legal steps are wise, but not mandatory. For example, before using a preferred name, it's smart to find out whether someone else already has rights to the name and can prevent you from using it or can limit how and where you use it. (See Section F.)

Some legal steps are of interest to only a limited number of small businesses—businesses that want to gain maximum protection for trademarks or service marks identifying their products or services.

If you're looking for the utmost protection for a trademark or service mark, you'll want to consider registering the mark under federal and state trademark laws. (See Sections C, D and E.)

Just how much effort and expense should you invest in protecting the name of your business, product or service? The answer depends on many factors, such as: the size of your business, the size of the market that you'll operate in, the type of product or service and your expectations for growth and expansion. For example, if you're starting a local computer repair service, you won't need as much business name protection as if you were planning to sell a new line of low-fat salad dressings in all 50 states.

To give you perspective on how to approach business names, we begin with some general guidelines. Like much of the other information in this chapter, these guidelines are drawn from *Trademark: How To Name Your Business & Product* by Kate McGrath and Stephen Elias (Nolo Press). That book discusses in great depth how to choose a legally protectable name and offers step-by-step instructions on how to file a federal trademark registration. Another useful book is *How To Protect Your Business, Professional, & Brand Names* by David A. Weinstein (John Wiley & Sons Inc.).

A. Business Names: An Overview

Once you get past the steps affecting business and product names required by law, you must make some judgment calls about how much protection to seek for your business name. You need to know both the legal guidelines and the practical, business realities. This section will help you sort out these issues.

1. Small Local Businesses

If yours is a small local business, such as a small retail store, a crafts shop, a typing service, a neighborhood restaurant or a repair facility, and you plan to stay small and local, you usually won't need to worry about registering a trademark or service mark. You will, however, want to avoid other businesses' claims of unfair competition. To that end, make sure that your name isn't confusingly similar to that of a local or regional competitor or a large national company in your field. You can feel relatively secure if you check state and local business directories and Yellow Pages for possible conflicts. (For more on how to conduct a name search, see Section F.)

If you incorporate, you'll also need to register your business name as part of the incorporation process—and perhaps locally as well. If you operate as a sole proprietor or partnership and use a business name other than your own name or names, you'll need to register that assumed name or fictitious name locally, as must a corporation that does business using a name other than its corporate name. (See Section B.)

> **Example:** Jeff wants to start a local typing service called "Speedy Typing for All." He'll be a sole proprietor. Since his is a small unincorporated local business, all he needs to do is to register the name as an assumed or fictitious name. In most states, registration is at the county level, but some states require it at the state level. (See Section B for more on assumed and fictitious names.) Jeff doesn't need to spend time and money to register the name as a state trademark or service. With a descriptive name and a small local business, there isn't much to protect.

However, Jeff should check to be sure there are no other typing services in his area using the same or a very similar name. If there are, Jeff should change his name or risk a claim of unfair competition.

2. Larger Local or Businesses

If you have a larger local business, such as a good-sized store, restaurant or service facility, or there's even a slight possibility that you'll eventually operate regionally, you'd be wise to go beyond the steps just suggested. For example, to avoid improperly using someone else's state or federally registered trade or service mark, consider conducting a wider name search—including the federal register of trademarks and service marks. If you conclude that your chosen name is free for use, you should look into registering your business name as a trademark or service mark. (See Section C.) On the other hand, if it's not likely that your business operations will go interstate for the first year or so, you can defer any action on federal registration.

3. Regional, Statewide or National Businesses

If your business is quite likely to operate on a regional or statewide basis or especially if you to plan conduct business in two or more states, you'll certainly want to make a wide search to avoid name conflicts with businesses using the same or a similar name. (See Section F.) And if you plan to do business across state lines, you should strongly consider gaining the protection offered by federal registration of your trademark or service mark. Especially if you're launching a new product, look into trademark registration as part of an effort to avoid conflicts with existing users and to acquire exclusive rights to the trademark. Although doing this can involve effort and cost, both will be far less than having to change a product name in midstream because you've infringed on someone else's trademark. For more on trademarks, see Sections C, D and E.

Example: Tony and Lars form a corporation that will design state-of-the-art sound systems for restaurants and jazz clubs. Their name—The Ears Have It Inc.—has been approved by the secretary of state for their state. Can they now safely use this name as a service mark to market their services? No. When the secretary of state accepted the corporate name, it simply meant that the name didn't duplicate the name of another corporation in that state.

Since Tony and Lars are hoping to market their services in several states, they (or a company they hire) should do a thorough name search, including checking federal and state trademark registers. If they don't, they may inadvertently find themselves in conflict with a company that's already using the name. If they find that their proposed name is clear, they should think about registering it as a federal trademark or service mark.

Again, if you decide that you want the protection of federal or state trademark registration, see *Trademark: How To Name Your Business & Product* by Kate McGrath and Stephen Elias (Nolo Press). You can probably handle the registration process yourself, but if you prefer to use a lawyer, the book will make you better able to take advantage of your lawyer's assistance.

B. Mandatory Name Procedures

As mentioned, there are name-related legal tasks that every business must pay attention to.

1. Corporations

As we saw in Chapter 3, as part of the process of creating a corporation, you need to choose a corporate name. Most states require certain words or abbreviations in your corporate name, so the public can recognize that your business is a corporation. This puts them on notice that, in general, you're not personally liable for debts of the corporation. (See Chapter 1 regarding limitations on the liability of corporate shareholders.)

Each state has its own laws dealing with what words you must include in your corporate name, so you should check your own state's statute. Most states will send you an information packet along with a sample printed form for the articles of incorporation. If so, the instructions will probably tell you the required words. Typically, the state will require one of the following in your official corporate name: *Incorporated, Corporation, Company* or *Limited,* or the abbreviations *Inc., Corp., Co.* or *Ltd.* If the name doesn't include one of the required terms, the state won't accept your corporate filing.

The law in your state will also likely list some words that can't be included in your corporate name or that can be used by only certain types of businesses.

Words That Are Typically Prohibited or Limited

Bank, banking, co-operative, engineering, trust, National, Federal, United States, insurance, acceptance, guaranty, pharmacy, credit union, medical, architect, indemnity, thrift, certified accountant, Olympic, surveyor.

This is by no means a complete list. For example, in New York you need the approval of a department of state government to use the words *Benefit, Council* or *Housing* in your corporate name.

To learn about the prohibited or limited words in your state, start by calling the office where you file the articles of incorporation. This is usually the secretary of state or the corporate commissioner's office. If they can't or won't tell you, go to a law library and look up the statute sections dealing with corporations.

Most states will reject a corporation name that's the same as one already on file or that's confusingly similar to the name of an existing corporation. If this happens to you and you've really got your heart set on the name you've picked out, there may be a way to get around the rejection. One approach is to change the name slightly or add something to it. Even a relatively small change may result in approval of the name. Or in some states, you can use a similar (but not identical) name if the prior holder of the name consents in writing. The document in which the other company gives its consent will have to be filed with the office that accepts corporate filings. Obviously, you're most likely to get cooperation from the other corporation if your business involves a completely different product or service.

> **Example:** Country Squire Inc. sells wood-burning stoves in the southern part of the state. It consents in writing to the use of the name "Country Squire Inn Inc." by a new corporation that will run a bed-and-breakfast in the northern part of the state. With the consent on file, the state corporations commissioner accepts the Country Squire Inn Inc. incorporation papers.

To avoid filing your corporate papers and then receiving word three weeks later that your name has been rejected, in many states you can call the government office that receives incorporation papers and ask if your proposed name is available. They may give you preliminary clearance by phone if the records show that no other corporation in your state is using the same or a similar name.

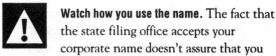 **Watch how you use the name.** The fact that the state filing office accepts your corporate name doesn't assure that you have the exclusive right to use the name in your state. An unincorporated business may already be using it as its trade name in your state. Or another business—whether incorporated in your state or elsewhere—may be using the name as a trademark or service mark. Depending on the situation, the prior use often gives the user the right to legally prevent your use of the name if your use of the name would be likely to confuse customers. It's always prudent to check further to avoid conflicts with other users. (See Section F for how to conduct a name search. For how to protect a name as a trademark or service mark, see Section C.)

If you expect some delay between the time you choose a name and the time you file your incorporation papers, find out if your state lets you reserve your preferred corporate name. Many states allow you to tie up a corporate name for two to four months by simply filing a form and paying a small fee.

2. Assumed and Fictitious Names

Sole proprietors sometimes choose to do business under names different than their own names, and partnerships usually select a partnership name other than the full names of all partners. Corporations may also decide to do business under names different than their official corporate names. Depending on state law, these adopted business names are will legally be called "assumed names" or "fictitious names." If your business uses such a name, you probably must register it.

a. UNINCORPORATED BUSINESSES

If you're a sole proprietor or partnership, in most states, you're required to file an assumed name or fictitious name certificate with the designated public office—usually at the county level—before you start doing business. Generally, there's a printed form for you to fill out, and you'll probably have to pay a small filing fee. In some states, the registration is good for a limited period, such as five years, and must be renewed. State law may also require that you publish notice of your business name in a local newspaper.

States require you to file the certificate for a simple reason: It lets members of the public know who is behind the name. If you don't register your assumed or fictitious name, you can have both legal and practical problems. For one thing, in many states, you may not be able to sue on a contract made or other transaction done under the business name. And in some states, you may be fined. In a number of states you can't open a bank account in the name of your business without filing.

TERMINOLOGY

Some people refer to an assumed name or a fictitious name as a "DBA." That's short for "doing business as"—for example, Albert White doing business as Al's Cabinet Shop. On legal documents such as contracts and lawsuits, this may appear as: Albert White d/b/a Al's Cabinet Shop.

---

b. CORPORATIONS

Most corporations operate under their corporate name which, of course, is on file with their state of incorporation. If, however, a corporation decides to do business under a different name, many states require it to file an assumed or fictitious name registration. All you have to do is complete a simple form and send it to the secretary of state or corporations commissioner with a modest filing fee.

Example: Miracle Widget Manufacturing Company wants to do parts of its business under the name "Widco" and other parts under the name "Industrial Innovators." In many states, it will have to register both of these names as assumed or fictitious names.

It's important to use your correct corporate name so that a creditor can't "pierce the corporate veil" and impose personal liability on you. (See Chapter 3.) If you're going to do business under a name that deviates from the official name on your articles of incorporation, it's essential that the name be properly registered. That way, you won't jeopardize the immunity from personal liability that's part of the reason for having a corporation.

If your state doesn't allow a corporation to do business under an assumed or fictitious name, there is sometimes an easy way to reach the same end while complying with the state rules.

Example: Contemporary Home Furnishings Inc. is incorporated in a state that doesn't allow registration of assumed or fictitious names. The company wishes to do operate a lamp store called "Bright Lights." It may be able to do this by calling the lamp store "Bright Lights, a division of Contemporary Home Furnishings Inc." or by saying "Bright Lights, owned and operated by Contemporary Furnishings Inc."

When it comes to products and service, a corporation is completely free to use names that are unrelated to its corporate name. In fact, this is common. Apple Computers, for example, sells products under the name Macintosh, and the Ford Motor Company sells Taurus automobiles.

C. Trademarks and Service Marks

A trademark or service mark consists of two parts. In reverse order, they are:

- The noun that specifies what kind of product or service you're talking about. *Examples:* automobile; health plan.

- The word or words that function as an adjective to identify a product or service as being different from all others. *Examples:* Buick automobile; Saab automobile; Blue Shield health plan; Kaiser health plan.

Think of these as the first and last names of products and services. The last name identifies the group; the first name uniquely specifies a member of that group. As such, the trademark is used as a proper adjective and is always capitalized.

Trademark law is the main tool that businesses use to protect the symbols and words that identify the origin of services and products. The basic premise is that the first user of a distinctive (that is, creative or unusual) name or symbol gets the exclusive right to use it. If you're the first user, you can make that right easier to enforce if you register the name or symbol with the federal trademark agency. The principal purpose of registration is to protect rights that already existed because you used the mark first. But registration can also confer other rights. For example, if you're using an unregistered mark without knowing that someone else used it first, federal registration can give you priority in areas outside the first user's market territory.

The twin goals of trademark law are:

- To prevent businesses from getting a free ride off the creativity of others in naming and distinguishing services and products, and

- To prevent customers from being confused by names that are misleadingly similar.

From a legal protection standpoint, the best trademarks are coined words, such as Kodak or Yuban, or arbitrary words such as Arrow for shirts or Camel for cigarettes, which have nothing to do with the product. Nearly as good are suggestive trademarks—ones that hint at some aspect of the product. For example, Talon suggests the gripping power of a zipper.

Trademarks that consist of creative, unusual or otherwise memorable terms are called "distinctive" and "strong." If you're the first to use such a name or symbol, you can legally stop others from using it in most situations.

Trademarks that consist of ordinary terms are called "weak," and competitors are free to use them. Merely descriptive words (such as Easy Clean for a cleanser) generally are not legally protectable. These weak marks can, however, become strong if they acquire a secondary meaning through prolonged usage. If that happens, they may be federally registered and may also be protected under the law of unfair competition if there's a local conflict with a similar mark. (See Section E.)

You can't acquire any rights in the name of the product itself; this is called a generic name. This means you can't adopt Bicycle or Refrigerator as your trademark for your version of those products. You can use the words as *part* of a distinctive name.

The law doesn't allow a business to claim the exclusive right to use descriptive words and generic names because competitors also need to describe their products. If you could tie up key words for your own exclusive use, your competitors would be unduly restricted in describing their goods. Also, descriptive terms aren't particularly memorable and don't further the purpose of trademarks and service marks.

D. Strong and Weak Trademarks

As noted earlier, with very few exceptions, only strong trademarks or service marks have the full protection of federal and state trademark laws. Remember, too, that trademark laws don't automatically protect a business name (the name of your company); to be considered a mark, a business name must be used to identify a product or service in the market place.

A trademark is considered weak when others can use it (or something similar) on products or services that don't compete directly with yours. Most ordinary trademarks are weak. *Examples:* Liquor Barn, Cuts Deluxe, Charlie's Auto Parts, 10-Minute Lube.

A trademark is considered legally strong when others can't use it or anything similar on related goods or services. There are two kinds of strong trademarks: ones that contain distinctive terms and ones that contain ordinary terms that have acquired distinctiveness through use.

1. Distinctive Terms

Distinctive trademarks are memorable, evocative, unique or somehow surprising—for example, 7-Up, Lycra or Cherokee apparel. The words themselves have little or no descriptive function; they serve to set the product or service off from others.

So if you're naming a service or product and want a strong mark, try for a name that is either unusual or used in an unusual way. A judge is likely to treat a distinctive name as a trademark or service mark and protect it from use by others—unless someone else has used a similar trademark on the same type of product or service first.

> **Example:** "Buick" distinguishes a line of cars from others, and the name means nothing apart from its trademark use. It's a distinctive name. Conversely, "Dependable Dry Cleaners" merely tells you something about the business; it doesn't help you distinguish it from rivals who might also advertise their services as reliable or efficient. So the name would probably not qualify for trademark or service mark protection unless it had been in use for a long time and developed a sizeable following—that is, a secondary meaning.

2. Ordinary Words

Generic terms can't be protected by trademark law; original and distinctive words can be protected. But what about other words used to identify products and services—ordinary words that are neither generic nor distinctive? This category covers place names (Downtown Barbers), surnames (Harris Sales), words that describe the product or service (Slim-Fast Diet Food) and words of praise (Tip-Top Pet Shop). Ordinary words receive limited legal protection as trademarks. It's more difficult to keep others from using them or something similar.

Even a weak trademark can acquire limited protection under unfair competition laws. For example, an ordinary name (a weak trademark) can be protected from someone else using the name in a confusing way. The law of unfair competition is generally based on state law (statutes and judge-made law) that supplements federal and state trademark laws. Owners of weak and unregistered names can get some relief from a rival's use of the identical name on the identical product or service in a competing market.

Weak trademarks can become strong ones through long use and extensive public familiarity with the mark. A trademark that starts out being ordinary or otherwise weak (like Dependable Cleaners) can sometimes, over time and through use, become identified in the public's mind with a specific product or service. When that happens, it can be transformed into a strong trademark.

> **Example:** Chap Stick brand of lip balm was originally a weak trademark. It simply described the condition the product was designed to cure: chapped lips. But it became strong as advertising and word of mouth helped the public develop a clear association between the name and a specific product. Over time, the name developed distinctiveness based on familiarity rather than any quality inherent in the name.

Lawyers describe a trademark that has become distinctive over time as one that has acquired a "secondary meaning." McDonald's is another good example of a weak mark that developed a secondary meaning over the years—and now qualifies for broad protection.

E. How To Protect Your Trademark

What do the words aspirin, escalator, cellophane and shredded wheat have in common? They are all former trademarks that have entered our language as product names. These words have lost their status as trademarks and are now generic terms. Other examples of former trademarks include harmonica, linoleum, raisin bran, thermos and milk of magnesia. In each of these cases, a business lost its exclusive right to use a valuable trademark.

Here are some steps that your business can take to prevent this from happening to your trademark.

- Use your trademark as a proper adjective that describes your product. You'll notice that ads refer to a Xerox copier, Jell-O gelatin and Band-Aid adhesive strips. If people continue to use the words Xerox, Jell-O and Band-Aid alone, these marks can easily go the way of other trademarks like nylon, mimeograph and yo-yo.

- Always capitalize the first letter of your trademark. And at some place on each ad or package, say specifically that the trademark is owned by your company.

- If your trademark has been placed on the federal trademark register, consistently give notice of that fact by using the ® symbol. If a trademark isn't federally registered or is registered only by a state, you may use the letters "TM" or "SM" to give notice of your claims. You may not use ® unless your mark is in fact on the federal register.

- Take prompt legal action if other businesses use your trademark without permission. A trademark may become weakened or even generic if others use it to describe their products and you do nothing about it. You or your lawyer should send a letter by certified mail (return receipt requested) demanding that the infringement cease. If your demand is ignored, be prepared to go to court to seek an injunction—but first do a careful cost/benefit analysis to satisfy yourself that it's worth the expense.

- If you discover that a newspaper or TV program has improperly used your trademark, send them a letter. Keep a copy in your records as proof that you have consistently enforced your trademark rights.

F. Name Searches

Most businesses should conduct some sort of name search to avoid possible conflicts with businesses already using the same name or a similar one. As noted in Section A, the extent of your name search will depend on a number of factors such, as the nature of your business and your plans for expansion. Typically, if you're naming a small local business, you can feel reasonably secure if you've searched for conflicts at the state and local level. A larger local business or one that has a chance of becoming regional needs to conduct a wider search.

- *Governmental Sources:* Check the records of the state office where corporations are registered—usually the Secretary of State or Corporations Commissioner—as well as the state office (if any) that maintains a list of assumed or fictitious names for corporations, partnerships and sole proprietorships. In addition, if assumed or fictitious names are filed at the county or local level, check the lists for the counties and localities in which you plan to do business now or in the foreseeable future. Finally, check your state's trademark registry, and (if it maintains one) your state's service mark registry.

- *Non-Governmental Sources:* Check telephone books and city directories for the cities in which you plan to do business, as well as for the surrounding areas and other major metropolitan areas. Many public libraries have excellent collections of phone books. While you're at the library, look at trade magazines for your industry and compilations of names of related businesses and products. The reference librarian should be able to help you.

ON-LINE RESOURCES

You can do all or part of your search by computer. On any of three subscriber databases—Compu-Mark, Dialog, and IntelliGate—you can find any identical federal or state trademarks within minutes for between $5 and $10 per mark searched. In addition, on Dialog you can do a partial common law search (a search for conflicting unregistered trademarks) for far less than what the search firms charge.

These services are bargains if you already have the equipment (computer, modem, printer), and you need to search for more than one name—for example, if you are naming new products regularly or if you want to check a number of possible choices.

You can also go to the nearest Patent Depository Library (there are 68 nationwide) and use Cassis, the government on-line system, for free.

If you plan to introduce products that will be marketed nationally or you plan to do business in several states, or if you merely want the extra peace of mind of knowing that your business or product name is safe and protected, you'll need to make a national search. This is especially true if you plan to register a trademark or service mark on the federal register or the state registers of several states. *Trademark: How To Name Your Business & Product,* by Kate McGrath and Stephen Elias (Nolo Press) explains in easy-to-understand detail how to make a national name search—and how to hire a company to conduct a search for you, which is the preferred route for most small businesses. Here are some companies that provide these services:

- Trademark Research Corporation, 300 Park Avenue South, New York, NY 10010, (212) 228-4084; outside New York, (800) TRC-MARK. This company is part of the Commerce Clearing House family.

- Thomson & Thomson, 500 Victory Road, North Quincy, MA 02171, (617) 479-1600.

- Compu-Mark, 500 Victory Road, North Quincy, MA 02171, (800) 421-7881. They're associated with Thomson & Thomson but use different data bases and their price is often lower.

- Prentice-Hall Legal and Financial Services, 1090 Vermont Avenue, NW, Washington, DC 20005, (800) 543-4502.

LICENSES AND PERMITS

5

You'll probably need a license or permit—maybe several—for your business. In some locations, every business needs a basic business license. But whether or not that is required, your business may need one or more specialized licenses. This is especially likely if you serve or sell food, liquor or firearms, work with hazardous materials or discharge any materials into the air or water.

There are licensing and permit requirements at all levels of government—federal, state, regional, county and city. It's not always easy to discover exactly what licenses and permits you'll need. But it's very important. You should thoroughly research this issue before you start a business, complete the purchase of a business, change locations or remodel or expand your operation. If you don't, you may face expenses and hassles you hadn't anticipated. In a worst case situation, you could be prevented from operating your planned business at a particular location but still be obligated to pay rent or a mortgage. For example, what if you sign a five-year lease for business space and then discover that the location isn't zoned properly for your business? What if you buy a restaurant and then find out that the liquor license isn't transferable? Or suppose you rent or buy business space thinking that you can afford to remodel or expand it, without realizing that remodeling means you must comply with all current ordinances? You might have to pay for $15,000 worth of improvements to comply with the local "access to the disabled" ordinance or $10,000 for a state-of-the-art waste disposal system.

Here are several examples that illustrate the types of licenses and permits many businesses need:

- Millie plans to open a new restaurant. Before doing so, she needs a permit from the department of building and safety for remodeling work and a license from the health department approving the kitchen equipment and ventilation system. She also needs a sign permit and approval of her customer and employee parking facilities from the city planning department. Finally, she has to get a sales tax license; even though in her state sit-down meals are not taxed, she must collect and report sales tax for take-out orders and miscellaneous items such as cookbooks.

- Leisure Time Enterprises, a partnership, buys a liquor store that also sells state lottery tickets. In addition to obtaining a basic business license issued by the city, the partners must have the state-issued alcoholic beverage license transferred to them. They also have to apply to the state lottery bureau for a transfer of the lottery license and to the state treasury department for a sales tax license.

- Electronic Assembly Inc., a corporation that assembles electronic components for manufacturers of stereo equipment, must obtain a conditional use permit from the planning and zoning board in order to conduct its "light manufacturing operation" in a commercial district. The company also needs clearance from a tri-county environmental agency concerned about possible air pollution and disposal of toxic chemicals. In addition, the new elevator must be inspected and approved by the state department of labor.

- Peaches and Cream, a new disco, has to get fire department clearance for its exit system and also must comply with the city's parking ordinance—which practically speaking means negotiating with the planning department for the number of off-street parking space the disco will provide for customers. The club also needs a liquor license from the state liquor control commission, a cabaret license from the city council and a sales tax license.

- Glenda needs an occupational license from the state department of cosmetology before she can open up her beauty shop. Because she carries a line of shampoos, conditioners and make-up, she needs a sales tax permit as well. In addition, because she's extending the front of her shop three feet into the front setback area, she needs a variance from the zoning board of appeals. Finally, because she's in an "historic preservation area," her sign must be approved by the local planning board.

In short, license and permit requirements can affect where you locate your business, how much you'll have to spend for remodeling and whether or not you'll have to provide off-street parking. If zoning requirements are too restrictive, you might even decide to avoid the hassle and move somewhere you don't have to fight City Hall for the right to do business. Similarly, if building codes require extensive—and expensive—remodeling to bring an older building up to current standards, you might want to look for newer space that already complies with building and safety laws.

Each state has its own system of licensing as does each unit of local government. Obviously, it's impossible to provide a comprehensive list of every permit and license in the United States. Fortunately, I can give you some general principles and a positive approach to help you learn about and comply with the licensing requirements that affect your business.

 Double check license and permit rules. When you investigate the type of licenses and permits you need for your business, check directly with the appropriate governmental agencies. Never rely on the fact that an existing business similar to yours didn't need a license or had to meet only minimal building code requirements. Laws and ordinance are amended frequently—generally to impose more stringent requirements. Often an existing business is allowed to continue under the old rules, but new businesses must meet the higher standards. Similarly, for obvious reasons, don't rely on the advice of real estate agents, business brokers, the seller of a business or anyone else with a financial interest in having a deal go through.

The Purpose of Licenses and Permits

Governments require licenses and permits for two basic reasons. One is to raise money; the whole point behind some licenses or permits is to levy a tax on doing business. In a way, these are the easiest to comply with—you pay your money and get your license.

The other basic purpose behind licenses and permits is to protect public health and safety and, increasingly, aesthetics. A sign ordinance that dictates the size and placement of a business sign or an environmental regulation that prohibits you from releasing sulphur dioxide into the atmosphere are two of many possible examples. Complying with regulatory ordinances can often be far more difficult than those designed simply to raise money.

A. Federal Registrations and Licenses

Small businesses don't have to worry about federal permits and licenses, but all businesses must know about federal tax registrations.

1. Tax Registrations

On the federal level, there are two tax registrations that you should know about. The first is the application for an employer identification number (Form SS-4), which should be filed by every business. If you're a sole proprietor, you may use your own social security number rather than a separate employer identification number, but I generally recommend that even sole proprietors obtain an employer identification number—especially if they plan to hire employees or retain independent contractors. It's one good way to keep your business and personal affairs separate. Employer identification numbers are covered in Chapter 6.

The second federal registration requirement applies if your business is a corporation and you want to elect status as an S corporation. In that case, you need to file Form 2553 (Election by a Small Business Corporation). S corporations are discussed in Chapter 1, Section D.2 and Chapter 3, Section A.2; the requirements for filing Form 2553 are discussed in Chapter 6, Section B.

2. Federal Licenses and Permits

The federal government doesn't require permits from most small businesses, but it does get into the act when certain business activities or products are involved. Below is a list of the business operations most likely to need a federal license or permit, along with the name of the federal agency to contact.

Business	Agency to Contact
Investment advisor	Securities and Exchange Commission
Ground transportation business such as a trucking company operating as a common carrier	Interstate Commerce Commission
Preparation of meat products	Food and Drug Administration
Production of drugs	Food and Drug Administration
Making tobacco products or alcohol, or making or dealing in firearms	Bureau of Alcohol, Tobacco and Firearms of the U.S. Treasury Department
Radio or TV station	Federal Communications Commission

B. State Requirements

It may take a little effort to discover which business permits and licenses your state requires. Fortunately, many states, eager to encourage the formation and growth of small businesses, are establishing small business assistance agencies to help cut through the thicket of state bureaucracy. These agencies often have free or inexpensive publications that list necessary licenses. For example, the Small Business Division of the Texas Department of Commerce offers a booklet called *Texas: A Guide to Licenses and Permits*. And the Office of Small Business of the California Department of Commerce offers *The California License Handbook* and *The California Permit Handbook*. In Appendix A to this book, you'll find a complete list of state agencies set up to help businesses in general and, often, small businesses in particular. An agency listed there is likely to be the best single source of information about state registrations, licenses and permits.

Beyond contacting these general purpose agencies, it's wise to call all state agencies that might regulate your business and ask what they require. In addition, you can often get valuable information from the state chamber of commerce and from trade associations or professional groups serving your business, profession or industry.

1. Licensing of Occupations and Professions

It should come as no surprise that states require licensing of people practicing the traditional professions, such as lawyers, physicians, dentists, accountants, psychologists, nurses, pharmacists, architects and professional engineers. Most states also require licenses for people engaged in a broad range of other occupations. The list varies from state to state but typically includes such people as barbers, auto mechanics, bill collectors, private investigators, building contractors, cosmetologists, funeral directors, pest control specialists, real estate agents, tax preparers and insurance agents. Since you can't always guess the occupations for which licenses are needed, you'll need to inquire.

Some licenses are taken out by the business entity (for example, your partnership or corporation), while others must be issued to the individuals who work in the business. For example, licensing laws for professionals—including lawyers, doctors, accountants and architects—tend to place requirements on individual professionals rather than on the partnership or professional corporation that is the business entity.

The procedures vary, but to get a license for a profession or occupation, you'll probably have to show evidence of training in the field, and you may have to pass a written examination. Sometimes you must practice your trade or profession under the supervision of a more experienced person before you can become fully licensed. For example, a real estate agent usually must work under the supervision of a licensed broker for several years before the agent is eligible to become a broker. Usually there's a formal application process, which may involve a background check. A license may be good only for a limited period, after which time there may be retesting before the license can be renewed. License laws for some occupations and professions require evidence of continuing education, usually in the form of short professional seminars.

2. Tax Registration

In all but the few states that still assess no taxes on income, chances are you'll have to register under your state's income tax laws in much the same way that you do under the federal laws. The state agency in charge (such as the treasury department or the department of revenue) can tell you what registrations are necessary. In addition, if you're engaging in retail sales, you may need to register for or obtain a sales tax license. There may also be registrations for other business taxes.

3. Employer-Employee Matters

As an employer, you may have to register with your state's department of labor or with agencies administering the laws on unemployment compensation and workers' compensation. As explained in more detail in Chapter 12, workers' compensation is a method of paying the medical bills and lost wages of employees injured in the course of their employment—regardless of who is at fault. Some state laws allow a business to be self-insured under some circumstances, but for most small businesses this isn't practical, so you'll have to carry workers' compensation insurance.

In addition, if your state has its own version of the federal Occupational Safety and Health Act (OSHA), your business may need to meet certain state-mandated requirements to protect your employees in the workplace.

Finally, a number of tax requirements relate to a business that has employees or works with independent contractors. For example, you'll need to get employer ID numbers from both the IRS and state tax authorities. And you'll have to withhold income taxes and Social Security taxes from the paychecks of employees, and report the figures to both the employee and the government. With independent contractors, you need to report income annually on a Form 1099 which goes to the independent contractor and the government. For more on taxation, see Chapter 6. For more on employees and independent contractors, see Chapter 12.

4. Licensing Based on Products Sold

Some licenses for businesses are based on the products sold. For example, there often are special licenses for businesses that sell liquor, food, lottery tickets, gasoline or firearms.

5. Environmental Regulations

Governmental regulation of environmental concerns continues to expand. As the owner of a small business, you may have to deal with regulators at the state or regional (multi-county) level. It's unlikely that you'll become involved with environmental regulations at the federal level.

Here are several activities that affect the environment and may require a special permit.

- Emissions into the air for an incinerator, boiler or other facility. For example, if you're going to be venting your dry cleaning equipment into the outside air, you may need a permit.

- Discharge of waste water to surface or ground water. For example, you may need a discharge permit if byproducts from manufacturing are being disposed of in a nearby pond. And you may need a storage permit if materials that you store on your site could contaminate ground or surface water.

- Handling of hazardous waste. If your business has any connection with hazardous waste, it's likely that the environmental agency will require you to at least maintain accurate records concerning the waste. You may need special disposal permits as well. Environmental regulations may also require you to register underground storage tanks holding gasoline, oil or other chemicals. And if there's a underground tank on your business site that's no longer being used, you may be required to remove it.

C. Regional Requirements

Increasingly, some environmental concerns are being addressed by regional (multi-county) agencies rather than by an arm of the state or local government. If so, you may need a permit or license from that regional body.

1. Environmental Regulations

In many areas, control of air pollution is now handled by a regional (multi-county or state) agency that issues permits and monitors compliance. For example, in northern California, the Bay Area Air Quality Control District covers at least seven counties. A regional body with environmental responsibilities may also have jurisdiction over waste water discharge or the storage or disposal of hazardous materials.

2. Water Usage

Questions affecting the use of water by a small business are usually dealt with at the local (city or county) level, but some issues may fall within the jurisdiction of a regional authority. For example, if your business is in a semi-rural area and plans to draw its water from a well rather than the public water supply, a regional health authority may test the purity of the water before you're allowed to use it. In scarce-water areas, a regional water management body may have authority to decide whether or not you may install a well or use an existing one.

Similarly, while regulation of septic systems typically is left to local health departments, in some areas permits may be under the control of a regional body.

D. Local Requirements

On the local level, begin by asking city and county officials about license and permit requirements for your business. A few larger cities that hope to attract economic growth may have a centralized office that provides this information. Otherwise, the city and county officials most likely to be of help are as follows:

- city or county clerk
- building and safety department
- health department

- planning (zoning) department
- tax offices (for example, tax assessor or treasurer)
- fire department
- police department
- public works department.

Non-official but often extremely helpful sources of information include local chambers of commerce, trade associations, contractors who have experience in building or remodeling commercial space, and people who have businesses like yours. You can also consult a lawyer who's familiar with small businesses similar to yours.

1. Local Property Taxes

Your city may impose a property tax on the furniture, fixtures and equipment that your business owns. If so, you may be required by law to file a list of that property with city tax officials, along with cost and depreciation information. You may have to update this information annually. Sometimes there's also a tax on inventory—which leads many retail businesses to run a stock reduction sale a few weeks before the inventory-taking date mandated by the tax law.

2. Other Local Taxes

Some cities, especially larger ones, tax gross receipts and income. Check with the city treasurer for registration and filing requirements.

3. Health and Environmental Permits

If your business involves food preparation or sales, you'll need a license or permit from the local health department. The health ordinances may require regular inspections as well. Whether you run a sit-down or a fast-food restaurant or a catering establishment, you can expect the health department to take a keen interest in the type of cooking equipment you use,

the adequacy of the refrigeration system and many other features of the business that can affect the health of your customers.

You may also run into health department regulations if you receive water from a well rather than a public water supply. In small towns or semi-rural areas, health departments routinely test well water for purity. Also, where septic systems are used for sanitary sewer disposal, the health department supervises the installation of new septic systems to make sure that there's no health hazard. (As noted in Section C, in some areas these matters are handled by regional rather than local authorities.)

Increasingly, local health departments are getting involved in environmental duties, including such things as radon tests and asbestos removal. Many other environmental problems, however, such as air and water quality, are still dealt with mainly at the state and regional level.

4. Crowd Control

If your business deals with large numbers of customers, you may need licenses or permits from the fire or police departments. These agencies are concerned about overcrowding and the ability of people to leave the premises in case there's an emergency. The role of the fire department may overlap with that of the building and safety department in prescribing the number of exit doors, the hardware on those doors, the lighting to be used and the maintenance of clear paths to the exits. The fire department will also be concerned about combustible materials used or stored on your business premises.

5. Building Codes

For anything but the most minor renovation (such as putting in track lighting or installing shelves), you're likely to need a permit—maybe several—from the building and safety department which enforces building ordinances and codes. Often, separate permits are issued for separate parts of a construction or remodeling project, including permits for electrical, plumbing and mechanical (heating and ventilating) work. If you don't have experience in these areas, you may need a licensed contractor to help you discover the requirements for your construction or remodeling project.

Building codes are amended frequently, and each revision seems to put new restrictions and requirements on the building owner. Municipalities often exempt existing businesses from laying out money to retrofit their premises—at least for major items such as elevators, heating and ventilating systems and overhead sprinkler systems. This is sometimes called "grandfathering"—slang for not imposing new rules retroactively. Grandfathering can create surprises. You may look at space in an older building and figure that you'll have no problems in doing business there because the current business owner or the one who just vacated the premises didn't. You could be in for a surprise. The prior occupant may have had the benefit of grandfathering language which didn't require him or her to bring the space up to the level of the current codes. A change in occupancy or ownership may end the benefits of grandfathering, and a new occupant or owner may be required to make extensive improvements. An experienced contractor can help you determine the building and safety requirements that apply to a particular space—for example, a code section mandating that railings on outside stairs be 36 inches high.

If You Build or Remodel

For any building or remodeling project, it's essential that you learn the applicable rules. If your city uses all or part of the Uniform Building Code, get a copy of it. Also look at the *Contractors' Guide to the Building Code* (Craftsman Book Company)—available through Nolo Press.

Other municipal ordinances may be administered by the building and safety department or by another unit of local government. There's no uniformity in how the responsibility for administering these other ordinances is assigned. A large municipality or county might have several separate departments to act as the enforcing agency. A smaller city or county would probably leave everything to the building and safety department.

6. Zoning Ordinances

Before you sign a lease, you absolutely need to know that the space is properly zoned for your usage. If it's not, it's best to make the lease contingent on your getting the property re-zoned or getting a variance or conditional use permit—whatever it takes under the ordinance to make it possible for you to do business there without being hassled by the city or county. In some communities, you must get a zoning compliance permit before you start your business at a given location. Other communities simply wait for someone to complain before zoning compliance gets looked at. Keep in mind that by applying for a construction permit for remodeling or by filing tax information with the municipality, you may trigger an investigation of zoning compliance.

Zoning laws may also regulate off-street parking, water and air quality and waste disposal, and the size, construction and placement of signs. In some communities, historic district restrictions may keep you from modifying the exterior of a building or even changing the paint color without permission from a board of administrators. Years ago, people tried to argue in court that such regulation of aesthetics wasn't a proper governmental function—that it wasn't related to the protection of the public health and safety. However, a carefully drawn ordinance seeking to preserve the special appeal of a historic district will very likely survive a legal challenge. So if you look at space in one of these protected neighborhoods, be prepared to suspend your freedom of choice and place the destiny of at least the exterior of the building in the hands of a panel of administrators.

In Chapter 11, dealing with home-based businesses, you'll find a discussion of zoning ordinances as they relate to businesses in the home. Take the time to review Chapter 11, Sections A and B, because zoning restrictions apply to all businesses.

E. How To Deal With Local Building and Zoning Officials

There's a certain amount of administrative discretion under building codes and zoning ordinances—enough, certainly that it can help greatly to have the administrators on your side. Here are some ideas for accomplishing this.

1. Seek Support From the Business Community

If you employ local people and will contribute positively to the economy, it may pay to make contact with city or county business development officials or even the chamber of commerce. If they see your business as an asset and don't want you to locate in the next city, they may be helpful in steering you through the building and safety department and may even advocate on your behalf before zoning and planning officials. Trade associations and merchants' associations may also come to your aid if you need building and safety officials to decide in your favor in areas in which they have some administrative discretion. Finally, contractors, lawyers and others who are familiar with the system and the personalities often know how to get things done and can be helpful to you.

2. Appealing an Adverse Ruling

The decision of a zoning or building official isn't necessarily final. If you get an adverse decision from the local Planning Commission, for example, you may be able to have a board of zoning adjustment or board of appeals interpret the zoning ordinance in a way that's favorable to you. Alternatively, you may be able to obtain a variance (a special exception to a zoning law) if a strict interpretation of the ordinance causes a hardship. In some cases, you can get a conditional use permit, which lets you use the property in question for your kind of business as long as you meet certain conditions set down by the administrative panel.

In dealing with administrators and especially with appeals boards, it's important to have the support of neighbors and others in your community. A favorable petition signed by most other businesses in your immediate area or oral expressions of support from half a dozen neighbors can make the difference between success and failure at an administrative hearing. Conversely, if objectors are numerous and adamant, you may not get what you're after. So if you sense opposition developing from those living or doing business nearby, try to resolve your differences before you get to a public hearing—even if it means you must make compromises on the details of your proposal.

LAW IN THE REAL WORLD

Strategic Planning Pays Off

Shelby, owner of Small World Books, is delighted to learn that the drug store next door is going out of business. He immediately seeks to buy or sign a long-term lease for the building so he can expand his profitable business. The future looks rosy.

Not so fast. Shelby learns that for his new business use of the building, he'll have to supply eight parking spaces to get a permit. Doing this in his desperately crowded neighborhood is totally impossible at anything approaching an affordable price.

Instead of giving up, Shelby asks the city planning commission for a variance to waive the parking spaces rule. A public hearing is scheduled. Shelby knows he has to put on a persuasive case, so he:

- Calls hundreds of local writers, publishers, critics, educators and book lovers to pack the hearing room and testify that an expanded book store will be a great community resource.

- Documents the prohibitive cost of buying or leasing the required parking spaces.

- Offers to validate parking at a lot four blocks away, just outside the worst of the congested area.

- Hires an architect who determines that a heavily used, nearby public garage can accommodate 20 more cars if the parking spaces are striped differently.

- Offers to pay for the re-striping.

Shelby gets the variance.

3. Going to Court

Every day, hundreds if not thousands of interpretations and applications of building and zoning laws are worked out through negotiation with administrators and through administrative appeals. But if these channels fail, it's possible in many instances to go to court. This can be very expensive and time-consuming. What good is it if you win your battle for a permit to remodel your premises but you waste two years getting to that point? Still, there are times when what you're seeking is so valuable and your chances of success are so great that you can afford both the time and money to get a definitive ruling from the courts. And in some instances, you can get a court to consider your dispute fairly quickly. If, for example, you submitted plans to the city that complied with all building and safety codes, and the building official refused to issue a building permit unless you agreed to put in some additional improvements you believe are not required by the ordinance, you could quickly go to court asking for an order of "mandamus" based on the fact that the administrator wasn't following the law.

Before you consider court action, however, get as much information as you can about the cost of litigation, how long it will take (you can win in the trial court, but the city might decide to appeal), and the likelihood of your ultimate success. This is a specialized corner of the law, so you're going to need someone who's had experience in the field—and there may not be that many to choose from in any given location. Look for a lawyer who's represented a similar business in a dispute with the city or someone who formerly worked as a city attorney and knows all the ins and outs of the local ordinances.

TAX BASICS FOR THE SMALL BUSINESS

6

No matter whether your business is organized as a sole proprietorship, partnership or corporation, you've automatically got a silent partner: Uncle Sam. The federal tax laws make this unavoidable. To guard against interest and penalties, you need to know what tax forms to file and when to file them. And to succeed in business, you need at least a basic, working knowledge of the tax system.

On a more positive note, by being aware of the fine points of the tax laws, you can often legally save a bundle of money—not to mention aggravation. For example, having a clear picture of what the IRS regards as a proper business expense will allow you to take deductions that otherwise might not occur to you.

 Get detailed information. The tax laws are vast and complicated, and you'll surely need much more information than you'll find in this chapter. Here I just hit the high points; it's up to you to deepen your knowledge.

In addition to what you learn from books and other publications, you may have to hire a bookkeeper and an accountant. If you're operating a one-person word processing business out of your home, you may be able to keep your books and do your taxes with no professional help at all—or perhaps get help just the first time you file your annual tax return, to make sure you've correctly completed Schedules C (Profit or Loss From Business) and SE (Social Security Self-Employment Tax). On the other hand, if you've formed a corporation that's operating a good sized dry-cleaning shop with eight employees, you may want an accountant to help set up your books and to prepare—or at least review—your business tax returns each year. And you may find that employing a part-time bookkeeper not only results in your records being well kept, but also frees you for more important tasks.

 RECOMMENDED READING

IRS publication 334, *Tax Guide for Small Business*. If you're just getting started, IRS publication 583, *Taxpayers Starting a Business* is also well worth reading. Both of these publications are free from your local IRS office or by calling (800) 829-3676.

Small-Time Operator by Bernard Kamoroff (Bell Springs Publishing). A modestly-priced and clearly-written book that covers not only taxes but also many other practical aspects of doing business, including bookkeeping.

Federal Taxes 2d (Prentice-Hall) and *CCH Federal Tax Guide* (Commerce Clearing House). These comprehensive tax guides are available in law libraries, business school libraries and the reference departments of major public libraries.

A word of caution about one other possible source of assistance: IRS employees. Most of them are hardworking and well-meaning, but their training and supervision are often inadequate. Unfortunately, it's common to receive poor oral advice in answer to questions. And if the advice proves to be so inaccurate that it results in your being assessed interest and penalties, the fact that you got it from an IRS employee won't get you off the hook. In short, it's often cheaper in the long run to rely on the advice of an experienced small business accountant than on a free oral opinion from the IRS.

State Taxes: In addition to federal taxes, you need to be aware of your state's taxes, which may include an income tax structured along the same lines as the federal version or one that has some major differences. Before you begin your business, contact your state's taxing authority to get detailed information.

A. Employer Identification Number

When you start your business, get an Employer Identification Number (EIN) from the IRS. Do this regardless of whether your business is a sole proprietorship, a partnership, an S corporation or a regular corporation. Technically, if you're a sole proprietor, you can use your Social Security number and don't need an EIN unless you have a Keogh plan or are required to file an employment, excise, fiduciary, or alcohol, tobacco and firearms return. Nevertheless, it's a good idea to get an EIN even though it's not required for your particular sole proprietorship. It helps you separate your business affairs from your personal affairs—something every small business person needs to do.

Electing S Corporation Status: If your regular corporation chooses to be taxed as an S corporation, it doesn't need a new EIN—the one you already have is still good. The same thing is true if you shift from an S corporation to a regular corporation.(See Section B to learn how to become an S corporation.)

To get an EIN, file form SS-4, Application for Employer Identification Number. The instructions tell you which IRS office to send the Form to. A Form SS-4 is shown below.

APPLICATION FOR EMPLOYER IDENTIFICATION NUMBER

Form **SS-4** (Rev. April 1991) Department of the Treasury Internal Revenue Service	**Application for Employer Identification Number** (For use by employers and others. Please read the attached instructions before completing this form.)	EIN OMB No. 1545-0003 Expires 4-30-94

Please type or print clearly.

1 Name of applicant (True legal name) (See instructions.)
Ted Anderson

2 Trade name of business, if different from name in line 1
The Poster Warehouse

3 Executor, trustee, "care of" name

4a Mailing address (street address) (room, apt., or suite no.)
555 Main Street

5a Address of business (See instructions.)

4b City, state, and ZIP code
Ann Arbor, MI   48104

5b City, state, and ZIP code

6 County and state where principal business is located
Washtenaw

7 Name of principal officer, grantor, or general partner (See instructions.) ▶

8a Type of entity (Check only one box.) (See instructions.)
☒ Individual SSN 555-55-5555
☐ REMIC
☐ State/local government
☐ Other nonprofit organization (specify) _____
☐ Other (specify) ▶ _____
☐ Estate
☐ Plan administrator SSN _____
☐ Personal service corp.
☐ National guard
☐ Other corporation (specify) _____
☐ Federal government/military
If nonprofit organization enter GEN (if applicable) _____
☐ Trust
☐ Partnership
☐ Farmers' cooperative
☐ Church or church controlled organization

8b If a corporation, give name of foreign country (if applicable) or state in the U.S. where incorporated ▶

Foreign country _____   State _____

9 Reason for applying (Check only one box.)
☒ Started new business
☐ Hired employees
☐ Created a pension plan (specify type) ▶ _____
☐ Banking purpose (specify) ▶ _____
☐ Changed type of organization (specify) ▶ _____
☐ Purchased going business
☐ Created a trust (specify) ▶ _____
☐ Other (specify) ▶ _____

10 Date business started or acquired (Mo., day, year) (See instructions.)
August 1, 1992

11 Enter closing month of accounting year. (See instructions.)
December

12 First date wages or annuities were paid or will be paid (Mo., day, year). **Note:** If applicant is a withholding agent, enter date income will first be paid to nonresident alien. (Mo., day, year) . . . . ▶ September 1, 1992

13 Enter highest number of employees expected in the next 12 months. **Note:** If the applicant does not expect to have any employees during the period, enter "0." . . . . ▶

Nonagricultural	Agricultural	Household
1	0	0

14 Principal activity (See instructions.) ▶ Sale of posters

15 Is the principal business activity manufacturing? . . . . ☐ Yes ☒ No
If "Yes," principal product and raw material used ▶

16 To whom are most of the products or services sold? Please check the appropriate box.   ☐ Business (wholesale)
☒ Public (retail)   ☐ Other (specify) ▶   ☐ N/A

17a Has the applicant ever applied for an identification number for this or any other business? . . . . ☐ Yes ☒ No
Note: If "Yes," please complete lines 17b and 17c.

17b If you checked the "Yes" box in line 17a, give applicant's true name and trade name, if different than name shown on prior application.

True name ▶   Trade name ▶

17c Enter approximate date, city, and state where the application was filed and the previous employer identification number if known.

Approximate date when filed (Mo., day, year)	City and state where filed	Previous EIN

Under penalties of perjury, I declare that I have examined this application, and to the best of my knowledge and belief, it is true, correct, and complete.   Telephone number (include area code)

Name and title (Please type or print clearly.) ▶ Ted Anderson, Owner   (313) 555-5555

Signature ▶ *Ted Anderson*   Date ▶ July 15, 1992

Note: Do not write below this line.   For official use only.

Please leave blank ▶	Geo.	Ind.	Class	Size	Reason for applying

For Paperwork Reduction Act Notice, see attached instructions.   Cat. No. 16055N   Form **SS-4** (Rev. 4-91)

The form isn't difficult to fill out following the IRS instructions. Here are a few pointers.

Space 1. Insert your official corporate name if you're a corporation. If you're a partnership, use the partnership name shown in your partnership agreement. If you're a sole proprietor, insert your full name.

Space 11. Here you're asked to state your fiscal year-end. Your answer, however, isn't binding. You make your binding election of a year-end on your first income tax return for the business.

Sole proprietors, partnerships, S corporations and "personal service corporations" are generally required to use the calendar year (ending December 31) for accounting purposes. (Personal service corporations are explained in Chapter 1, Section D.2.b.) A regular corporation can select a different fiscal year. Most small businesses find that the calendar year is the most convenient way to proceed but sometimes there are tax planning reasons to choose a different fiscal year.

Example 1: Radcraft Inc., a regular corporation, selects the calendar year for its fiscal year. In December 1992 it pays a $30,000 bonus to Jill, the president and sole shareholder. The bonus is included on Jill's 1992 income tax return, and tax on the bonus is due in April 1993.

Example 2: Jill selects a fiscal year of February 1 through January 31 for Radcraft Inc. (On Form SS-4, she lists January in space 11 for the closing month of the corporation's accounting year.) In January 1993, the corporation pays Jill a $30,000 bonus. The bonus is included in Jill's 1993 income tax return. The tax on the bonus isn't due until April 1994—although Jill must keep track of it when computing her quarterly estimates in 1993.

Your accountant can help you decide whether or not you and your corporation can realize a tax advantage by using a fiscal year-end other than December 31.

Space 12. The IRS will send you computer-generated tax forms based on your answer to this question.

Space 13. These numbers can be estimated. In case of doubt, make your estimate on the low side—it may stave off a premature avalanche of IRS forms.

Space 17a. This question refers to the entity, not the owner. Normally, a partnership or corporation has only one Employer ID Number. A sole proprietor may have several businesses, each with a separate number.

It takes about four weeks for the IRS to process a Form SS-4. Mail it in early so that you have your EIN before you need to file a tax return or make a tax deposit. Or complete Form SS-4, call the IRS and read the information to the IRS representative. You'll be assigned an EIN by phone. Then insert the assigned number in the SS-4 and mail it to the IRS.

Use your EIN on all your returns, checks and other documents you send to the IRS. If you're a sole proprietor who doesn't need and doesn't want an EIN, use your Social Security number instead.

You'll need a new EIN if any of these changes occur in your business:

- You incorporate your sole proprietorship or partnership.

- Your sole proprietorship takes in partners and begins operating as a partnership.

- Your partnership is taken over by one of the partners and begins operating as a sole proprietorship.

- Your corporation changes to a partnership or to a sole proprietorship.

- You purchase or inherit an existing business that you'll operate as a sole proprietorship. (You can't use the EIN of the former owner even if he or she is your spouse.)

- You represent an estate that operates a business after the owner's death.

- You terminate an old partnership and begin a new one.

B. Becoming an S Corporation

Many corporations derive tax benefits from electing S corporation status. The difference between a regular corporation, which is a separate tax entity from its shareholders, and an S corporation, whose income is reported on the owners' tax returns, is described in some detail in Chapter 1. If you're not thoroughly familiar with this material, please re-read it before going on.

To become an S corporation, all shareholders must sign and file IRS Form 2553 (Election by a Small Business Corporation) with the IRS by the 15th day of the third month of the tax year to which the election is to apply.

A number of technical rules govern which corporations can elect to become S corporations. Your corporation must meet these requirements:

- It must be a "domestic" corporation—one that's organized under federal or state law.

- It must have only one class of stock.

- It must have no more than 35 shareholders.

- It must have as shareholders only individuals, estates and certain trusts. Partnerships and corporations can't be shareholders in an S corporation.

- Its shareholders must be citizens of the United States. Nonresident aliens can't be shareholders.

There are other technical rules, but the vast majority of new, small corporations may become S corporations if they choose to do so.

To elect S corporation status, you need the consent of all shareholders. Unless yours is a one-person corporation, you should agree on this point before you form your corporation. An S corporation election doesn't have to be permanent. You can start out as an S corporation and then, after a few years, revoke your S corporation status and be taxed as a regular corporation. If you terminate your status as an S corporation, generally you'll have to wait five years until you can again become an S corporation— although you may be able to get permission from the IRS to shorten this waiting period.

Example: Nancy, Jerry and Agnes form a corporation, Phoenix Ventures Inc. They start to do business on September 1, 1992, and, like most businesses, use the calendar year for accounting and tax purposes. Their 1992 tax year will be a short one: September 1 through December 31. To obtain S corporation status for that first tax year, they need to file Form 2553 by November 15, 1992, which is the 15th day of the third month of that tax year. If they miss that deadline, their corporation won't qualify for S corporation status in 1992. But if they file Form 2553 by March 15, 1993, their corporation will get S corporation status for 1993.

Once the shareholders file a Form 2553, the corporation continues to be an S corporation each year until the shareholders revoke that status or it's terminated under IRS rules. What terminates S corporation status? For one thing, ceasing to qualify as an S corporation. For example, your corporation would no longer qualify if it had more than 35 shareholders or if you or another shareholder transferred some of your stock to a partnership.

C. Business Taxes in General

Three main categories of federal business taxes may apply to your business:

- income tax
- self-employment tax
- employment taxes.

This section looks briefly at each of these tax categories. Get IRS publication 509, *Tax Calendars*, to see when to file returns and make tax payments. It's updated annually.

Excise Taxes. In addition to the three main business taxes, the federal government imposes excise taxes on a few specialized transactions and products. These taxes almost never are of concern to small businesses. To see if your business if affected, see IRS publication 334, *Tax Guide for Small Business*.

1. Income Tax

You must file an annual federal tax return reporting your business income. Below is a list of the forms to use.

Business Income Tax Forms

Type of Legal Entity	Form
Sole Proprietorship	Schedule C (Form 1040)
Partnership	Form 1065
Regular Corporation	Form 1120 or 1120-A
S Corporation	Form 1120-S

a. SOLE PROPRIETORSHIP

If you're a sole proprietor, your business itself doesn't pay income tax. Your Schedule C income (or loss) is added to (or subtracted from) the other income you report on your personal Form 1040. If you have more than one business, file a separate Schedule C for each business.

Estimated Taxes

The money you earn as the owner of a sole proprietorship, a partner or a shareholder in an S corporation isn't subject to withholding—unless it is paid to you in the form of a salary. You may, however, need to send in payments of estimated taxes. First, figure out how much you'll earn from the business and how much from other sources. If withholding from other sources (such as a full- or part-time job) won't be enough to cover your tax bill for the year, make quarterly payments of estimated taxes during the year you earn the income. For more details, get IRS Publication 505, *Tax Withholding and Estimated Taxes.*

---

b. PARTNERSHIP

A partnership Form 1065 is an information tax return telling the IRS how much each partner earned. The partnership doesn't pay tax on this income. Each partner reports his or her share of income (or loss) on Schedule E, Supplemental

Income and Loss, and this amount is added to (or subtracted from) the other income the partner reports on Form 1040. In other words, a partner's income is treated like a sole proprietor's income on Form 1040: it's listed in a separate schedule and then blended with other income listed on the first page of the 1040.

 Passive losses. Losses from passive partnership activities—such as real estate investments or royalties in which the partnership plays the role of a passive investor—can usually only be taken as a credit against income from passive activities. This is explained in greater detail in IRS instructions.

c. S CORPORATION

The S corporation doesn't pay an income tax. Form 1120S filed by an S corporation is an information return telling the IRS how much each shareholder earned. As a shareholder, you report your portion of income or loss on Schedule E. Then you add that income to (or subtract a loss from) your other 1040 income.

d. REGULAR CORPORATION

A regular corporation reports its income or loss on Form 1120 or 1120-A and pays a tax if there is income. But in many small corporations, the shareholders are employees who receive all profits of the business in the form of salaries and bonuses, which are tax-deductible by the corporation as a business expense. In that situation, the corporation would have no taxable income. Not all small corporations, however, are able to pay out their income in the form of salaries and bonuses. If they don't, they must pay a corporate income tax.

> **Example:** Jenny and her twin sister Janet are the sole shareholders in Neptune Corporation which manufactures swimming pool supplies. In the second year of their corporate existence, to encourage growth, Jenny and Janet decide to pay themselves minimal salaries and to plow

most of the corporate income into inventory and the purchase of rehabilitated but serviceable equipment. The money that the corporation puts into inventory and equipment isn't available for distribution to Jenny and Janet; moreover, most of that money isn't a currently deductible business expense, so it is taxed at corporate income tax rates. (The equipment will be capitalized; depreciation deductions will be spread over several years.)

Corporate Income Tax Rates

First $50,000 of Taxable Corporate Income	15%
Next $25,000 of Taxable Corporate Income	25%
Remainder over $75,000	34%

Corporate taxable incomes between $100,000 and $335,000 are subject to an additional 5% tax.

If you have a regular corporation that expects to have taxable income, your corporation needs to make periodic deposits of its estimated income taxes. And if you're an employee of your regular corporation (as is almost always the case with an owner of a small business corporation), taxes and social security payments must be withheld from your paychecks.

2. Self-Employment Tax

If you're a sole proprietor or a partner, you must pay a federal self-employment tax in addition to income tax. You're undoubtedly aware that money is withheld from an employee's paycheck to cover the employee's income tax and the Social Security contribution. (The employer also pays toward Social Security.) Think of the self-employment tax as a similar Social Security tax for people who work for themselves. You compute this tax each year on Schedule SE which you then attach to your personal Form 1040. You add the self-employment tax to the income tax you owe. Here's a comparison of the social security tax for employees and the self-employment tax:

For 1993, the employer and the employee each pay 7.65% on the first $57,600 of the employee's wages, and 1.45% on wages from $57,600 to $135,000. (As Bernard Kamoroff points out in his excellent book, *Small-Time Operator*, Social Security tax is actually calculated and reported as two separate taxes: 6.2% on all wages up to $57,600 and an additional 1.45% on all wages up to $135,000.) These rates change annually.

Self-Employment Tax: In 1993, the base rate is 15.3% on earnings up to $57,600 and 2.9% on earnings over $57,600 up to $135,000. Adjustments on your income tax return, however, lessen the impact of this tax. First, in computing the self-employment tax, you reduce your earnings by half the tax rate—that is, you reduce your earnings by 7.65% on the first $57,600 and by 1.45% on earnings between $57,600 and $135,000. You then compute the self-employment tax based on the reduced amount. Second, you deduct half of your self-employment tax from your total taxable income before you figure your income tax. Confusing? Certainly, but the tax forms will walk you through these computations.

If you have income from another job that's subject to withholding—common for people just getting started in business—the income from your other job will reduce the tax base for your self-employment tax.

Example: Morton works 3/4 time as a chemistry instructor at a local college, where he receives an annual salary of $45,000. He also does consulting, as a sole proprietor, for several chemical companies and earns an additional $30,000 a year. The $45,000 salary at the college—which is subject to withholding by the employer—is used to reduce the $57,600 cap on income that's subject to the 15.3% self-employment tax. So Morton computes the tax at the rate of 15.3% on $12,600 of his consulting business income. On the remaining portion—$17,400—he computes the tax at the rate of 2.9%.

Be sure that your quarterly payments of estimated income tax are large enough to include the self-employment tax. If you forget about the self-employment tax, you may underestimate your total tax liability and wind up paying a penalty.

Tax Tip: If you're a sole proprietor and want to reduce the size of your self-employment taxes, consider incorporating your business and electing S corporation status. This won't significantly affect your income taxes, but it can reduce your self-employment taxes if you receive some corporate earnings in the form of dividends rather than salary. Be aware, however, that this is a somewhat aggressive strategy and is in an area that's ripe for more stringent regulation by the IRS. Check with your tax advisor if this is your main reason for incorporating.

3. Employment Taxes

If you have employees, be aware of these taxes:

- federal income tax withholding
- Social Security tax
- federal unemployment tax (FUTA).

These taxes are all explained in great detail in an IRS publication, *Circular E, Employer's Tax Guide*. In summary, here's how they work.

You withhold income taxes from your employees' paychecks based on the number of dependents (withholding allowances) declared by the employee and on the size of the employee's salary. Each employee gives you a signed Form W-4 stating the withholding allowance. Use the tables in *Circular E* to figure out how much income tax to withhold.

In addition, as noted in the previous section, you must withhold the employee's share of the social security tax, and you must also pay the employer's share. You can learn the current amounts by consulting the latest edition of *Circular E*.

Finally, there's the federal unemployment tax (FUTA) that you must report and pay. You pay this with your business's funds—it's not withheld from the employee's pay. The FUTA rate for 1993 is 6.2% of the first $7,000 of the employee's wages for the year. Employers who pay promptly are given a credit

for participating in state unemployment programs. Use Form 940 or 940EZ to report federal unemployment tax.

Payroll Taxes Made Easy

If you're overwhelmed by the requirements for calculating payroll taxes and the fine points of when and where to pay them, you can pay a bank or payroll service to do it for you. A reputable payroll tax service that offers a "tax notification service" will calculate the amount due, produce the checks to pay the employees and the taxes and tell you when the taxes are due.

You don't send the money you withhold directly to the government; instead, you deposit it in a bank that's qualified as a federal tax depository. That's where an advantage of a payroll service comes in. If a bank did the payroll, it would withhold the amount of the tax from your account when the payroll is done, even though the tax isn't due yet. That means the bank, not you, gets the use of the money for awhile. If your payroll service offers tax notification, it will prepare the checks and tell you when they must be deposited. Depending on how often you must make payments, that can give you the use of the money for an extra month or more.

At the end of each quarter, the payroll service will produce your quarterly payroll tax returns and give you instructions for filing them. At the end of the year, the service will prepare W-2 forms and federal and state transmittal forms.

Payroll services can be cost-effective for even very small businesses, but when you look for one, it pays to shop around. Avoid services that charge set-up fees (basically, a fee for putting your information into its computer) or extra fees for W-2's or quarterly and annual tax returns.

You must periodically deposit the withheld income tax and the employer's and employee's shares of social security taxes at an authorized financial institution, usually a bank. The IRS sends you coupons to use in making these deposits. How often you're required to deposit these funds depends on the size of your payroll and amounts due; a typical small business makes monthly deposits

 Deposit taxes on time. Be sure to withhold taxes as required by the tax laws—and to pay (deposit) those taxes on time. There are substantial penalties if you don't. Moreover, if you're an owner of a small business and personally involved in its management, you can be held personally liable for these taxes and penalties if the business lacks the funds to pay.

D. Business Deductions

Of all the federal taxes that may affect a small business, income tax is the one that business owners are most concerned about. The general formula is that you first figure out your gross profit—your gross receipts or sales less returns and allowances and the cost of goods sold. Then you subtract your other business expenses to find the net income or loss of your business. For an in-depth analysis of what business expenses can be deducted, see IRS Publication 535, *Business Expenses*.

In this section, we'll look at common categories of deductible business expenses.

Home-based businesses: If you have a home-based business, you'll find special tax pointers in Chapter 11.

1. Depreciation

If you buy equipment or machinery that has a useful life longer than one year, the IRS generally won't let you deduct the full cost in the year you buy it. Instead, you deduct a portion each year over the term of the item's useful life. Exceptions are made for inexpensive items for which the cost of detailed record keeping would be prohibitive. For example, your $75 desktop calculator may last for five years but you'd undoubtedly be allowed to deduct its entire cost in the year you buy it. You'd probably treat it as part of your office supplies.

IRS tables list the useful life of various types of equipment and machinery. You may choose one of two methods—straight-line or accelerated—for figuring depreciation.

a. STRAIGHT-LINE DEPRECIATION

The straight-line method means that you deduct an equal amount each year over the projected life of the asset. Actually, that's a bit of an over-simplification; something called the "half-year convention" makes things slightly more complicated. That rule allows only a half-year's worth of depreciation to be deducted in the first year.

> **Example:** Norbert buys a $1,000 fax machine in 1992 which can be depreciated over five years according to the IRS table. Under a strict application of the straight-line depreciation method, he'd deduct $200 each year for five years. But the half-year convention allows him to deduct only a half year's worth of depreciation—$100—the first year. So Norbert would deduct $100 the first year; $200 a year for the next four years; and the final $100 in the sixth year.

(Exceptions to the half-year rule are explained in IRS publications.)

b. ACCELERATED DEPRECIATION

Most small businesses will want to use the accelerated depreciation tables instead of the straight-line method. It allows them to write off a large amount of the purchase price in the years immediately following purchase of the machinery or equipment. That, of course, makes the tax savings available sooner.

Another tax rule—one especially helpful to small businesses—lets you get around the depreciation rules to some extent. You can, if you choose, write off up to $10,000 ($5,000 for a married person filing a separate return) of depreciable assets in the year of purchase.

Example: Bertha buys an $8,000 computer in 1992. Ordinarily, she'd have to use IRS depreciation tables and spread the cost over several years. But she has the option to deduct the cost all at once for 1992. This is known as a Section 179 capital-expense deduction.

There are a few important limitations to this deduction. The first, which doesn't affect many businesses that are just starting out, applies if you purchase more than $200,000 in depreciable assets in one year. If you do, the $10,000 is reduced, dollar for dollar, by the amount you exceed $200,000. For example, if you spend $205,000 on depreciable assets, you can write off—as an expense deduction—only $5,000 worth.

Furthermore, the amount you write off can't exceed the total taxable income that your business received in that year. You may, however, carry forward any disallowed part of this write-off so that you get some tax benefit in future years.

2. IRS Guidelines for Business Deductions

The IRS has broad, general guidelines for what constitutes deductible expenses. For example, to be deductible, a business expense must be ordinary and necessary—something that's common in your type of business, trade or profession. If you have an expense that's partly for business and partly personal, you must separate the personal from the business part. Only the business part is deductible.

So much for generalities. Here's a partial list of the kinds of expenses that your business can normally deduct:

- advertising
- bad debts
- car and truck expenses
- commissions and fees
- conventions and trade shows
- depreciation on property owned by the business
- employee benefit programs
- insurance
- interest
- legal, accounting and other professional services
- office expenses
- pension and profit-sharing plans
- rent
- repairs to and maintenance of business premises and equipment
- supplies
- taxes and licenses
- trade publications
- travel, meals and entertainment
- utilities
- wages.

This list isn't all-inclusive. You can also deduct any other expenses that you believe—and can convince the IRS—are ordinary and necessary business expenses. For example, if you're a free-lance movie critic, you could claim the cost of movie tickets.

Now let's look at the rules affecting a number of specific expenses (deductions) in more depth.

3. Employees' Pay

You can deduct salaries, wages and other forms of pay that you give to employees as long as you meet certain IRS tests listed below. If you're both an employee and a shareholder of your business, your own salary must meet the same tests for deductibility as salaries paid to any other executive or employee.

For a salary to be deductible, you must show that:

- The payments are ordinary and necessary expenses directly connected with your business.

- The payments are reasonable. Fortunately, you have broad discretion to decide what's reasonable. Short of a scam—such as paying a huge salary to a spouse or relative who does little or no work—the IRS will almost always accept your notion of what's reasonable pay.

- The payments are for services actually performed.

- The payment was actually made during the tax year.

If you use the cash method of accounting (very common among small businesses), you can deduct salaries and wages only for the year in which they were paid. However, you can deduct employee taxes your business withheld in the year your business withheld them; you can't deduct (until paid to the government) the employer's matching portion of these taxes. Businesses using the accrual method have more latitude in when they can deduct salaries and payroll taxes.

You can also deduct bonuses you pay to employees if they're intended as additional payment for services and not as gifts; most bonuses qualify for deduction. If your business distributes cash, gift certificates or similar items of easily convertible cash value, the value of such items is considered additional wages or salary regardless of the amount. If a gift is considered as part of an employee's wages or salary, it's subject to employment taxes and withholding rules.

Certain non-cash gifts are deductible if they are less than $25 per person per year.

Example: To promote employee goodwill, Pebblestone Partnership distributes turkeys, hams and other items of nominal value at holidays. The value of these items isn't salaries or wages, but the partnership can deduct their cost as a business expense.

4. Employee Benefits

A number of employee benefits can be deducted, including:

- health and dental insurance
- group term life insurance
- educational assistance programs
- moving expenses
- qualified employee benefit plans, including profit-sharing plans, stock bonus plans and money purchase pension plans
- employee benefit plans that allow employees to choose among two or more benefits consisting of cash and qualified benefits.

If your business can afford these benefits, not only are they tax deductible by your business— they are not taxed to the employee.

While these benefits sound attractive, there are two serious drawbacks. First, many small businesses—particularly those just starting out—can't afford them. Second, plans that mainly benefit the owners of the business are not tax-deductible. (See Chapter 1, Section D.2.b, for a more thorough discussion.)

5. Meals, Entertainment and Travel

If you're a sole proprietor, deduct the allowable portion of your own business travel, meals and entertainment expenses on Schedule C of your Form 1040. Use Schedule C to report the amounts that you reimburse or allow your employees for these expenses. (Consult IRS Publication 463, *Travel, Entertainment, and Gift Expenses* for an in-depth treatment of this subject.)

If you're a partner or a shareholder of a corporation in which you play an active management role, it's usually best to have your partnership or corporation reimburse you for your business-related travel and entertainment expenses. The business can then deduct these amounts to the extent allowed by law.

To be treated as a business deduction, travel expenses need to be ordinary and necessary in your type of business. Basically, these are any reasonable expenses you incur while traveling. You (or your business) can't deduct expenses for personal or vacation purposes, or any part of business expenses that is lavish or extravagant. But if you're on the kind of tight travel and entertainment budget common to most small business people, you won't have to worry about this last restriction. Here are examples of deductible travel expenses:

- air, rail and bus transportation while traveling on business

- operating and maintaining your own car. (See Section 6 for more on car expenses.)

- taxi fares or other costs of transportation between the airport or station and your hotel, from one customer to another, or from one place of business to another

- baggage charges and transportation costs for sample and display material

- meals and lodging while traveling on business

- cleaning and laundry expenses

- telephone and fax expenses

- public stenographers' fees

- tips incidental to any of these expenses.

Travel expenses don't include expenses for entertainment such as sports events and concerts, and they don't include expenses for transportation while you're not traveling. The IRS says that you're traveling away from home if (1) your duties require you to be away from the general area of your tax home substantially longer than an ordinary day's work, and (2) you need to get sleep or rest to meet the demands of your work. (Napping in your car doesn't count.) Generally, your "tax home" is your main place of business regardless of where your family home is.

If a trip is entirely for business, you can deduct your ordinary and necessary travel expenses. If your trip was primarily personal, you can't deduct any travel expenses—even if you did some business at your destination. What if your trip was primarily for business but you took a vacation-like side trip? Then you need to allocate your expenses; see IRS

publication 463 for instructions. The IRS does give you one break; if you legitimately need to fly somewhere for business, you can write off the entire plane fare, even though you stay over for pleasure after your business is completed.

Meal and entertainment expenses have special rules and restrictions. You can generally deduct only 80% of your business-related meal and entertainment expenses. In addition, the IRS may disallow extravagant and excessive expenses. But short of fraud or obvious gross excess, the IRS doesn't monitor where you go for your business meals. So in practice, for most small business people, 80% of all business-related meal expenses are deductible.

As an employer, this 80% limit applies to your business even if you reimburse your employees for 100% of their expenses.

 Excessive expenses may trigger an audit. Your overall travel and entertainment budget may result in a tax audit if these expenses are out of proportion to what the IRS thinks is reasonable, given your type of business and income. For most honest small business people, this isn't usually a problem unless they have some extraordinary need to travel.

Example: Ben starts a marble importing business and spends his first year visiting 200 prominent architects and interior designers from coast to coast to introduce his business. His high travel expense triggers an audit, but Ben is able to show that these trips were necessary to get his business off the ground.

If you are audited, you'll need to show the IRS complete and accurate records of your travel and entertainment expenses, including actual receipts. Also, since you need to tie each trip and meal to a specific business purpose, it makes good sense to keep a log stating the purpose. Otherwise, if challenged, you may have trouble recalling the details.

6. Automobile Expenses

If you use your car for business, you may be able to deduct some or all of your car expenses. Deductible items include:

- gas
- oil
- tolls
- tires
- garage rent
- lease fees
- rental fees
- parking fees
- repairs
- licenses
- depreciation.

The following discussion assumes you use your car more than 50% for business. Special rules apply if you use your car 50% or less for business. For complete information about deductions for your car, see IRS publication 917, *Business Use of a Car*.

If you use your car for both business and personal purposes, you must divide your expenses between business and personal use. (This rule applies to all items you use for both business and personal use.) The miles you put on your car driving from your home to your main place of business are considered to be commuting miles—a personal use, not deductible. The same thing applies to fees you pay to park your car at your place of business.

Example: Tricia has a catering business that requires her to call on customers. She drives 20,000 miles during the year: 12,000 for business and 8,000 for personal use (including her daily trips from home to her shop). She can claim only 60% of the cost of operating her car as a business expense. The coins she fed the parking meter in front of her shop each day would be a personal (commuting) expense and not deductible; fees paid for parking while calling on customers would, however, be deductible.

What about depreciation? As with other business assets, you can deduct the cost of a car (but only the portion used for business), but you must spread the deductions over several years. IRS depreciation tables have special schedules for cars. Cars are depreciated over five years, and you can't depreciate a total of more than $16,000. The maximum annual deductions for car depreciation are as follows:

First Year	$2,660
Second Year	$4,200
Third Year	$2,550
Fourth Year	$1,475
Fifth Year	$1,475

Depreciation for Employees' Cars: If your employees use their cars in their work, they can't take a depreciation deduction unless this use is for your convenience as their employer and you require it as a condition of employment.

If you don't want to keep track of your car expenses and you want to avoid the complexity of the depreciation rules, the IRS offers a second method for deducting car expenses. You can use the standard mileage rate for your business mileage. In 1992 the rate was 28¢ per mile. The rate changes periodically, so check IRS publications for the latest figure. If you're going to use the standard mileage rate, you must start by using it in the year you begin using your car for business. If you don't use the standard mileage rate that first year, you can't use it for that car later on. If you use the standard mileage rate, you can also deduct tolls and parking fees that you paid while on business.

If you take a deduction for car expenses, you must file Form 4562 with your tax return. If you give an employee a car for business and personal use, the employee must report as income the value of the personal usage. For example, an employee who keeps a company car at home and drives to and from work must report that commuting usage—and any other personal usage—as income.

If you lease rather than own your car, you can deduct the part of each lease payment that's for your use of the car in business. If you use your leased car 60% for business, you can deduct 60% of each lease payment. You can't deduct any payments you make to buy the car even if the payments are called lease payments. A lease with an option to buy may be a lease or a purchase contract, depending on its wording.

Keep accurate records of your car usage so that if you're challenged by the IRS, you can demonstrate the extent of your business use. The best procedure is keep a daily log in your glove compartment to record the following about each business trip:

- date
- destination
- mileage
- business purpose.

BUYING A BUSINESS

7

For those who have some money put aside, buying an existing business may be a better approach than starting from scratch. After all, there's something attractive about letting someone else find a location and sign a lease; test the market and develop a customer base; buy furniture, fixtures, equipment and inventory; hire employees; and perform the countless other chores that go with starting a business. In short, there's something very attractive about letting someone else prove that the business works.

If you find yourself looking for an existing business to buy, keep an open mind. It's not always possible to buy a business you'll be happy with at a price you can afford. Many people who buy existing businesses do very well, but others, having explored the opportunities and finding nothing to their liking, return to the idea of starting their own business. And some people pay too much money for a poor business or one they may never really enjoy operating.

This chapter first looks at how to find a business to buy. Then it turns to the nuts and bolts of actually buying a business, including how to structure the purchase, what to investigate before closing the deal and the legal documents needed for a business to change hands.

Selling a business: This chapter focuses on buying a business, but a seller's concerns are also discussed briefly in Section I.

A. Finding a Business To Buy

Before you look for a business to buy, narrow your field of possible choices. First, decide whether you want to be in a service, manufacturing, wholesale, retail or food service business. Once you make this choice, consider the specific type of business you're interested in—perhaps a desktop publishing center, a management consulting business, a direct mail processing business, a dance studio, a flower shop or a used book store.

Your choice of business should be motivated by the type of work you've done in the past, courses you've taken, special skills you've developed through a hobby, or perhaps just a strong yearning to work in a particular field. It's almost always a mistake to consider buying a business you know little about, no matter how good it looks. For example, if you hate mechanical and electronic equipment, buying an auto tune-up shop or a business that installs security systems makes little sense even if the business looks irresistible from a financial point of view.

If you're currently employed by a small business you like, what are the chances of that business becoming available to you? Maybe the current owner wants to retire, is in bad health, is moving out of the city or is just getting bored. If you know the inner workings of the business and are sure that it's doing well—or at least that it has the potential to flower under your able leadership—that would be an ideal place to start. Failing that, perhaps business associates or friends can provide you with leads to similar businesses that may be available.

Here are some other time-tested ways to search for an available business:

- *Newspaper Ads:* This is a traditional starting point and can quickly put you in touch with people who are actively seeking a buyer for their business.

Unfortunately, ads are only the tip of the iceberg. Many of the best business opportunities never get into the papers but surface primarily by word of mouth.

- *Professionals Who Advise Small Businesses:* Bankers, lawyers, accountants, insurance agents and real estate brokers who regularly work with small businesses often know about available businesses before they go on the market. Think about who you know who is plugged into this network and get on the phone. A few well-placed phone calls may be enough to identify likely candidates in your area.

- *Business Suppliers:* Another great way to tap into the grapevine is to contact the network of suppliers for that business. For example, if you're thinking of opening a flower shop, a floral wholesaler in your area will probably know who is thinking of retiring or selling out for other reasons.

- *Trade Associations:* Almost every business has a local or regional trade association—for example, the Northern California Booksellers Association or the Michigan Pest Control Association. The secretary or a long-time employee of such a group may have heard about a business owner who's thinking of retiring.

- *The Direct Approach:* If there's a business that you've admired from afar, simply drop in and politely ask if the owner has ever thought about selling. Who knows? Maybe he or she has been thinking about moving to another part of the country or changing to a different type of business. Once in a while, you'll be in the right place at the right time. A long shot? Probably—but you have nothing to lose by trying it.

- *Business Brokers:* Finally, there are business brokers—people who earn commissions from business owners who need help finding buyers. As is true in all endeavors, not all business brokers are created equal. A few are honest, ingenious and hardworking. Many more are adequate but nothing special when it comes to competence, energy and integrity. More than a few are sleazy, incompetent and interested almost exclusively in earning a commission. In short, before working with a broker, it pays to carefully check out his or her reputation. Several glowing recommendations from a banker, accountant or fellow small business person should raise your confidence level. On the other hand, if the feedback you get is lukewarm, look for someone else.

It's foolish to rely on a broker—who gets paid only if the deal goes through—for advice about the quality of the business or the fairness of its price. If you do, he or she is almost sure to paint an unrealistically rosy picture. Also, because the seller typically pays the broker, the broker's loyalty will be to the seller—not to you. Use a broker only to find a business, not to negotiate the purchase price and other terms. Have your own lawyer advise you on drafting the documents involved, particularly the purchase agreement. (See Section G.)

B. What's the Structure of the Business You Want To Buy?

If you find a business you're interested in, one important question is: What kind of legal entity owns the business—a sole proprietorship, partnership or corporation?

1. Buying From a Sole Proprietor or Partnership

Legally, it's simplest to buy a business from a sole proprietor, because one person owns the business and the assets are in his or her name. Buying from a partnership is almost as simple, although partnership agreements typically require the consent of all partners before the business can be sold. If you're dealing with only one partner, to avoid disappointment, promptly ask to see the partnership agreement and make sure that the person negotiating the deal has received proper authority from the other partners. Beyond that, get a clear understanding early on about whether you'll only be buying just the assets of the business, or whether the seller is also trying to get you to assume responsibility for all liabilities.

Changing a Business's Structure. A new owner is free to change the legal form of a business. For example, you can buy a business from a sole proprietor and then operate it through a partnership or corporation.

2. Buying From a Corporation

When you buy a business owned by a corporation, you run into a special problem: figuring out the best way to structure your purchase. You can buy the corporate entity itself (the stock) or you can buy only its assets, leaving the seller still owning the corporation minus the assets you purchased.

In almost any purchase of a business, you'll be much better off buying the assets rather than the corporate stock (but see Section c, below). Most sales of small businesses—a whopping 94%—involve the sale of assets rather than corporate stock. Buying assets has four distinct advantages:

- It helps you avoid the liabilities of the existing business.

- It gives you significant tax advantages..

- You can avoid acquiring unwanted assets from the corporation.

- You generally can get a higher tax basis for depreciable assets, which means there's less taxable gain to report if you later sell the assets.

Example of Stock Purchase: Brown Manufacturing Inc. is a small corporation owned by Joseph Brown and his two sons. The company, which makes specialized computer circuit boards, owns a small factory, several machines, raw materials, an inventory of completed items, office furniture and equipment and two delivery trucks. The corporation owns all of the assets of the business. In a stock purchase, you'd buy 100% of the stock of the corporation from Joseph Brown and his sons. As the new owner, you'd elect yourself (and anyone else you choose) to the board of directors; the board would then typically appoint you to the office of president.

Example of Asset Purchase: You want to buy the business operated by Brown Manufacturing Inc., but instead of buying the corporate stock, you have the corporation sell you all or most of its assets, such as the factory, the machines, the trucks and several patents and trade secrets associated with circuit board assembly. The seller would continue to own Brown Manufacturing Inc. minus its assets. You would use these assets to run the manufacturing business as a sole proprietorship or partnership (if you have one or more business associates), or perhaps you would choose to place the assets in a new corporation of your own.

a. LIABILITIES OF THE CORPORATION

If you buy the stock of a corporation, you're buying not only the assets but any liabilities as well. This is fine if there aren't any, but this can be difficult to determine. Maybe the corporation owes federal income taxes that you don't know about. Or maybe a customer slipped in the entryway of the business three months ago, broke his leg and is right now visiting a lawyer to prepare a million dollar lawsuit. Hidden liabilities can surface for injuries caused by defective products, discrimination against employees, or environmental or safety violations to name but a few.

In addition, the business may have contracts that you don't want to assume. For example, the corporation may have a five-year maintenance contract for service on the computers it owns—and there may be four more years to go at a rate you consider exorbitant.

You can protect yourself against some unknown liabilities. A good investigation will uncover many (though not all) potential liabilities. And personal warranties from the seller guaranteeing payment of any liabilities not disclosed can give you someone to turn to if unknown or undisclosed liabilities suddenly surface. Insurance may cover some of these risks, such as claims for injuries caused by defective products. But the point remains—if you buy a corporation, it's almost impossible to get 100% protection from its obligations.

In contrast, by buying the assets of the corporation rather than the corporate stock, you can avoid virtually all of these liability problems as long as you notify creditors of your purchase under the terms of your state's bulk sales statute (see Section G.10) and you don't lead creditors to believe that you're picking up the liabilities of the corporation.

It's important to realize, however, that under some circumstances, if you continue the business of the prior corporation, you or your new corporation may still be subject to some liabilities incurred by the old corporation even if you only purchase assets. Known in legal lingo as "successor liability," the most common area of concern is products liability—liability to a person injured by a defective product. This is particularly likely to arise if you buy the assets of a corporation that manufactured a potentially hazardous consumer product and you directly continue the business. Each state has its own legal rules governing what constitutes a sufficient link (often called continuity) between the first manufacturer and the second to hold the second liable. One court ruled that there may be such a link if:

- there is a continuation of the management, personnel, physical location, assets and general business operations of the selling corporation.

- the selling corporation quickly ceased its ordinary business operations and then liquidated and dissolved.

- the purchasing company assumed the liabilities and obligations of the seller ordinarily necessary for continuing the business operations of the selling corporation.

In addition, depending on state law, a company that's just a continuation of an earlier corporation may be liable for other legal problems of the earlier corporation—for example, a wrongful discharge case brought by an ex-employee—or even for contractual obligations such as a union contract. The good news is that if you're fully informed about the law in your state, you can usually anticipate any successor liabil-

ity problems and structure your purchase to avoid them. Or you may be able to buy insurance—often called "tail coverage"—to protect you from the long tail of the old corporation's liabilities.

b. TAX ADVANTAGES

You may be able to get several kinds of tax advantages in an asset purchase because you can allocate the purchase price among various assets you buy. As long as this allocation is based on an arm's length negotiation between you and the seller, it's likely to be upheld by the IRS.

You want to allocate the greater portion of the purchase price to assets you can write off against earnings immediately or through depreciation. These include things like the inventory of the business, supplies, machinery, equipment and vehicles, furniture and fixtures. Normally, you'll also want to assign some value to the seller's non-competition agreement. The value of the promise not to compete is spread over its duration (often three to five years), and an equal amount is deducted each year. On the other hand, you'll want to assign minimally reasonable values to assets that can't be deducted as current expenses, depreciated or amortized. This includes such assets as good will, trademarks, customer lists and trade names. (How to allocate purchase price to different assets you're buying is discussed in Section G.)

In addition, by buying assets rather than corporate stock, you can depreciate assets that the seller has already fully depreciated.

Example: Arthur is buying a dry cleaning business. The business has dry cleaning equipment that's ten years old but in excellent condition. The owner has fully depreciated it. Arthur and the seller allocate $30,000 of the purchase price to the equipment. That way, Arthur can start to depreciate it a second time. If Arthur bought the corporate stock, he wouldn't be able to take any depreciation for this equipment.

c. EXCEPTIONS: WHEN PURCHASING STOCK IS BETTER

In some limited circumstances where the corporation has a uniquely valuable asset that can't be transferred, it may be better to buy the stock of the corporation rather than its assets. For example, the corporation may have tax benefits such as a net operating loss carryover (NOL) that you want to take advantage of. The NOL carryover would be lost if you purchased the assets rather than the corporate stock. Also, if a store had a favorable five-year lease with a five-year option to renew that wasn't freely assignable, that could provide an incentive to you to buy the corporate stock. Or suppose a computer retail business had a hard-to-get distributorship for a particular brand of popular computers. If the distributorship contract couldn't be assigned to you and you weren't sure you could qualify for a similar contract yourself, you might consider buying the corporate stock because the corporation would likely continue to have the rights to be a distributor.

 Investigating distributorships. Even in a stock purchase, you'd want to read the distributorship documents carefully and check with the manufacturer to confirm that the manufacturer didn't reserve the right to cancel the distributorship if the corporate stock changed hands.

d. HOW TO PROTECT YOURSELF IF YOU BUY CORPORATE STOCK

If you do decide to purchase a corporation's stock instead of its assets, protect yourself to the maximum extent possible. One way is to get a warranty from the seller that he or she will pay for certain types of problems such as tax liabilities, obligations to former employees or damage claims by the landlord. Then arrange to pay for the business in installments spread over a number of years. Most liabilities will come to light in the first few years after you purchase the business. If the seller fails to make good on his or her warranty, you can pay for these liabilities and then withhold the amounts from the balance you owe the seller. Also, as mentioned earlier, insurance may be in place or obtainable to protect against products liability and other personal injury claims.

C. Gathering Information About a Business

Buying a business takes weeks or months. During that time you'll need to diligently gather information—lots of information—about the business so that you don't get stung on the purchase price or have surprises later about income, expenses or undisclosed liabilities. Eventually, this information will help you structure a sound sales agreement.

In most small business purchases, the buyer learns everything possible about the business before signing the sales agreement. By contrast, business brokers sometimes advise making a quick formal offer to purchase with a number of contingencies that allow you to terminate the deal if all the facts don't turn out as represented by the seller. I recommend against this approach. Why invest your time, effort and money in a complete investigation of the business if the preliminary review of records convinces you that this isn't the business for you or that the price is too high? Better to request early access to financial records that will help you decide if you're really interested in the business. Then if you're satisfied with the finances you can sign a sales agreement with appropriate contingency clauses or wait until closing (legal lingo for the transfer of the business) to sign.

If you and the seller are strangers to one another, however, the seller may be reluctant to turn over sensitive business information until he or she is confident that you're a serious buyer. The seller may suspect you have some secret plan in mind, like using the information in a competitive business or some other improper purpose. To allay these fears, consider giving the seller a confidentiality letter like the one below.

SAMPLE CONFIDENTIALITY LETTER

Carlos Mendez, President
Mendez Furniture Company Inc.

Dear Mr. Mendez:

As you know, I am looking into the purchase of your furniture business. Our conversations have been helpful but I'm now at the stage where I would like to see your company's financial records, including your tax returns, for the past five years.

I know that the information that I'm requesting is confidential and that improper use of the information could damage your business. Consequently, I will use this confidential information only to help me decide whether I want to purchase your business and the terms of that purchase. I will disclose this confidential information only to my co-investors, my lawyer and my accountant. I'll make sure that each of these people knows that this information is confidential, and I'll ask them to sign confidentiality agreements before I release the information to them.

If I don't buy your business, I will return all of the confidential information, including any copies, to you and will continue to treat in confidence the information you have disclosed to me.

I look forward to receiving this information.

Sincerely yours,

Suzanne Gerstein

That kind of letter will satisfy many sellers. But a few sellers may prefer a longer, more formal confidentiality agreement drafted by a lawyer. That's okay, but you (and perhaps your lawyer as well) should make sure that the proposed document contains no binding commitment to buy the business. It should be limited to your agreement to treat the information as strictly confidential and use it only to investigate the purchase of the business and to the other terms set out in the letter. If the proposed agreement goes further than that, find out why and get legal advice.

Don't be surprised if the seller wants to learn about your own financial status, job or business history. Remember that most purchases of a small business are usually done on an installment basis, where the seller receives a down payment and periodic payments over a period of time. The seller is interested in your financial stability, your reputation for integrity and your general business savvy because the seller, in effect, will be extending credit to you.

D. Valuing the Business

Does it sound impossibly demanding to determine a fair purchase price for a business? It's really not—especially if you take the sales price with a grain of salt. Most sellers ask for way too much, and far too many inexperienced buyers don't bargain aggressively enough. Lots of little businesses are worth no more than the fair current value of inventory and equipment. Good will, over and above the value of the continuing hard work of the owner, is commonly a myth.

1. What Are You Buying?

Generally, the assets of a business consist of inventory, fixed assets (furniture, fixtures, equipment) and intangible assets (such as a lease, trade name, customer list and good will). The most important factor in establishing the fair market value of these assets is this: Given the realities of the business and the industry in which it operates, what kind of return would a buyer reasonably expect on his or her investment? To arrive at this number, an appraiser will look both at the business's earnings and what similar businesses typically earn.

2. Good Will Can Be a Myth

Be very careful about what you pay for good will—the portion of the purchase price attributed to such intangible factors as the reputation of the business, its location and the loyalty of its customers. Despite what sellers will almost surely tell you, many small businesses have little or no value beyond the value of the hard assets such as furniture, fixtures and equipment. How can this be, if a business earns a good yearly profit? Easy. Most of the profit is commonly attributable to the hard work, clear vision and good judgment of the owner, not to the inherent value of the business. Think of it this way: most rug cleaning businesses, hardware stores, print shops and restaurants don't make a substantial profit. Those that do are usually run by uniquely talented people. When these people move on, many of those businesses quickly lose their luster.

Example: Joe and Monte own Caretti Brothers, a highly successful produce store that they've operated for 20 years. They sell the business to Anna Marie, who pays $200,000, including $100,000 for good will. Anna Marie continues to run the business as Caretti Brothers and does her best to preserve the store's distinctive atmosphere. Nevertheless, in her first year she earns only one-third the profits generated by the former owners.

Unhappily, she realizes that Joe and Monte succeeded because customers valued their extroverted personalities and their rare ability to select only the freshest and tastiest tomatoes and grapefruit. Too late, she understands that she should have paid little or nothing for good will, which was largely personal to the Carettis and couldn't be transferred to her.

Good will isn't always a myth. Some profitable businesses—usually those that have been established for years and have strong name recognition—are worth significantly more than the value of their tangible assets, because they have a good reputation. Even if the owner retires or sells out, this reputation will continue to bring in business. Unfortunately, deciding that a business has good will is easier than deciding how much. One approach is for buyer and seller to try and agree on a multiplier—the number by which earnings (or sometimes sales) must be multiplied to determine the value of the business.

Where does the multiplier come from? In some industries, there are rough norms. For example, certain types of businesses typically sell for five times earnings, while other often sell for ten or more. Construction companies, retail stores and restaurants are examples of businesses where you can often obtain standard multipliers from business evaluators or appraisers who specialize in that industry.

 Be critical of all multipliers. Never accept a multiplier without loads of caution. The facts of a particular business, the state of the local economy and industry trends change so quickly that last year's sensible multiplier can be completely off base this year.

3. Evaluating the Business's Financial Health

To properly evaluate the business, ask for access to the following documents:

- Tax returns, profit and loss statements and balance sheets for five years.

- Loan documents, if you're going to assume any obligations of the old business.

- Papers relating to specific assets; for example, the lease if you're taking over seller's space or title documents if you're purchasing the seller's building.

- Patents, trademarks, copyrights and licenses.

- Documents that relate to lawsuits, administrative proceedings and claims against the corporation.

- All accountants reports including compilation reports, reviews and audit reports. (See "Types of Accountants' Reports," below.) A full-fledged audit report is the best, but not all small businesses have one available. Whatever type report the business has, specifically ask for a list of all assets and the depreciation schedules.

In addition, if you're purchasing corporate stock, ask for:

- Corporate contracts with major suppliers, as well as contracts obligating the corporation to deliver goods or services.

- Employment agreements, union contracts and any other documents concerning wage levels and fringe benefit obligations.

Types of Accountants' Reports

Reports from Certified Public Accountants come in three basic varieties:

Compiled: The CPA compiles the balance sheet of the company and the related statements of income and retained earnings and cash flows for a specified year. The compilation simply presents, in the form of a financial statement, the information gathered by the owners of the company. The accountant doesn't audit or review the information or offer an opinion about it.

Reviewed: The CPA goes a step further by asking questions of company personnel and analyzing the financial data presented by the owners. Short of a full-scale audit, the CPA certifies only that he or she isn't aware of any material modifications that should be made to the financial statements to conform to generally accepted accounting principles.

Audited: Here, the CPA examines, on a test basis, evidence supporting the amounts and disclosures in the financial statements. For example, the CPA may visit the warehouse to see if it really contains the inventory that's claimed. Also, the accountant assesses the accounting principles used by the owners and evaluates the overall financial statement. If everything is in order, the CPA signs an opinion that the financial statements are accurate and maintained in conformity with generally accepted accounting principles.

Once the books are in your hands, have an experienced small business accountant study them. You and your accountant should look especially hard at the years before the last one. It's relatively easy for a business owner to pump up earnings and depress expenses for a year or two, so assume that the results for the last year at least have been manipulated. One way to see if earnings have been exaggerated is to see if there are fewer employees now than previously— almost any business can operate shorthanded for a limited time. Also, check to see if equipment maintenance or replacement has been deferred by comparing maintenance and replacement costs for the last year with those of the years before.

4. Expert Help

Consider hiring an experienced appraiser to appraise the business as a whole as well as the individual assets. Check references and be sure the person you pick understands the type of business you are entering. For example, if you're thinking of buying a traditional typesetting business, work with someone who thoroughly understands the mostly negative implications that the rapid improvement of desktop publishing techniques holds for this business. Appraisals do cost money, but it's money well spent if it saves you from overpaying for the business.

Where can you turn for an accurate assessment of the value of a business? Here are three suggestions:

- Consult a member of the American Society of Appraisers who specializes in business valuations. For a list of such appraisers, write to ASA National Headquarters, P.O. Box 17265, Washington, DC 20041.

- Check with a respected firm of certified public accountants. Many CPA firms offer business valuation services.

- Seek guidance from an experienced business broker. But use caution. Brokers are best at making deals. They often lack the technical training needed for placing a value on a business.

E. Other Items To Investigate

Now let's look at some other items that are worthwhile investigating before you close on the purchase of a business.

1. Title to Assets

If real estate is included in the sale, ask to see the deed and the title insurance policy. The title should be re-checked to make sure no new encumbrances appear, and the title insurance policy will need to be updated. Also ask to see ownership documents for any cars and trucks.

It's a good idea to check with the appropriate county or state offices to see if there are liens on any of the vehicles or other equipment or merchandise. Lenders who have taken a security interest in the business or suppliers who have extended credit may have filed a UCC (Uniform Commercial Code) financing statement with the appropriate state agency to record the fact that they have a security interest in some assets of the business. Any bank lending officer, small business lawyer or accountant should be able to tell you where and how to check in your state.

2. Litigation

Ask to see copies of any lawsuit papers and letters from any people threatening lawsuits. Also check with the court clerk in the main counties in which business is conducted. What you're looking for are actual or threatened lawsuits involving injuries or claimed breaches of contract. This type of investigation is particularly important where you're buying the stock of a corporation, but you may also turn up information that will be valuable to an asset purchase. For example, if the business manufactures or distributes aluminum stepladders, finding product liability lawsuits pending will help you determine whether the ladders are safe or need to be redesigned. Also, remember in a few circumstances even those

who purchase assets of a corporation may be held liable for the existing business's liabilities. (See Section B.2.)

3. Warranties and Guarantees

If you buy the stock of a corporation, you want to know what types of warranties the corporation has extended to its customers so you can anticipate claims. For example, if you buy a business that writes customized computer software, you'll want to know what promises have been made should bugs be discovered in already installed programs.

4. Workers' Compensation Claims and Unemployment Claims

Check with the workers' compensation insurance carrier to learn the claims history of the business and current insurance rates. Also check with the state office handling unemployment affairs to learn what rate is currently applied to the payroll of the business. These facts will be primarily of concern if you're planning to purchase the stock of a corporation, because they'll indicate how much you'll probably have to pay for workers' compensation insurance or unemployment coverage. But in some states, even purchasers of corporate assets may have their future workers' compensation insurance rates affected if it looks like the new business is simply a continuation of the old one.

5. Employee Contracts and Benefits

This is a concern primarily if you're buying the stock of a corporation and will be subject to its contracts. However, if you intend to keep the same employees, you need this information for other purchases as well so that you'll know the employees' expectations when they come to work for your new business entity. They won't be happy campers if you offer them less pay or benefits than they're currently getting. If it's a concern, ask the seller for permission to talk to key employees to see if they'll stick with you after you buy the business. (Strictly speaking, permission isn't required, but being polite helps bring about a smooth transition.)

6. Maintenance of Trade Secrets

Not every business has trade secrets, but if the one you're purchasing does—and those secrets are a valuable asset for which you're paying—you want to be sure they've been properly safeguarded. Ask what the business has done to protect its trade secrets and other proprietary information such as customer lists. Has this information been disclosed only to key employees? Have those employees signed confidentiality agreements and covenants not to compete? If not, and key employees leave and set up a competing business, you may be buying a lot less than you bargained for.

7. Taxes

Again, this applies primarily to a purchase of corporate stock because you want to know what tax liabilities are hanging over the head of the corporation. But whatever kind of purchase you're making, you can gain valuable information about the income and expenses of the business, including the kinds of items that have been tax-deductible in the past. Check on state and local property taxes and sales taxes, federal and state income taxes, and any special taxes levied by federal and state governments.

8. Leases

Look carefully at all space and equipment leases. How long does the lease have to run? Is it renewable? And, most important, if you're purchasing the assets, is it transferable? If the lease isn't clearly assignable, check with the landlord or equipment lessor about taking over the lease. If they respond favorably, get a commitment in writing. (For more on real estate leases, see Chapter 10.)

9. Other Contracts

If the business has contracts with suppliers or customers, become familiar with their terms. In the case of an asset sale, the important question is whether or not the contracts are assignable by the seller. Often, you need the consent of the supplier or customer. For example, if you're buying a gas station, does the oil company have to approve your taking over the contract for that brand of gasoline? Where a contract is freely transferable if all the conditions have been met, make sure the seller isn't in default or otherwise in noncompliance. If so, you may not be able to enforce the contract.

10. Patents and Copyrights

Many small businesses don't own patents or copyrights, but as information becomes a more and more valuable part of many businesses, they do crop up fairly often. Of course, if you're interested in buying a book, software or music publishing company, you can be pretty sure that the business's most valuable assets will be its intellectual property.

If patents or copyrights are involved, get hold of the basic registration documents and any contracts that give the business the right to exploit these rights. If you're not fully familiar with these matters, have the documents and contracts reviewed by a lawyer who specializes in this area of law. These lawyers are usually listed in a separate category in the Yellow Pages under "Patent and Trademark."

11. Trademarks and Product Names

Trademarks, service marks, business names and product names may be important business assets. If so, make sure that you'll have the continuing right to use them. Ask about the extent of any searches for conflicting marks and names, and what has been done to register or otherwise protect the marks and names you'll be taking over. (See Chapter 4 for more on business and product names.)

12. Licenses and Transferability

Check into any special licenses that you'll need to continue the business. For example, if you're buying a restaurant with a liquor license, is the license transferable? Has the existing business obtained an environmental permit for disposal of its wastes? If so, what about transferability? The same goes for other special permits the existing business has, such as a health department license, or a federal license for trucking or broadcasting. (For more on licenses and permits, see Chapter 5.)

13. Zoning

The existing business may be operating under a temporary zoning variance or a conditional use permit that has important limitations. Learn exactly what the requirements and conditions are and whether you can continue operating under the variance or conditional use permit. Also, if you buy the business assets rather than corporate stock, you may find that you're no longer covered by prior zoning or building preferences; you may, for example, need more parking, better access and different signs. (See Chapter 5, Section D, and Chapter 11, Section A, for more on zoning and related requirements.)

14. Toxic Waste

If the business must dispose of toxic waste, or if its activities have any possible adverse impact on the purity of water and air, look into what licenses or permits are needed. Also, especially if your purchase involves real property, check carefully to see how toxic waste has been handled in the past. You could find yourself stuck with liability for past improprieties.

15. Franchisor Approval

If you're looking at a business that's operating under a franchise, the seller undoubtedly will need the approval of the franchisor before assigning the franchise to you. Look at the franchise agreement to see exactly what's involved in obtaining the franchisor's approval and then speak directly to the franchisor to see how the approval process can be expedited. (For more on franchises, see Chapter 8.)

16. Availability of Credit

Find out whether banks and major suppliers will be willing to extend credit to you. Credit may mean the difference between success and failure in your business.

17. Scuttlebutt

Never rely entirely on documents and public records. You can learn a lot simply by talking to people who have had contact with the existing business—bankers, key customers, suppliers, neighboring businesses and former employees. When talking to key people, take your time and pay attention to subtleties. Many people may be reluctant to talk frankly until they've sized you up, and others will have ties of friendship to the seller or be worried about their own possible legal liability if they divulge unfavorable information about the business.

F. Letter of Intent To Purchase

If all goes well, you and the seller may eventually agree on most major aspects of the purchase. But you still may not be quite ready to put together a formal sales agreement. Perhaps you need time for additional investigation, or maybe your lawyer, business advisor or key lender is out of town for a week or two. One device that can be helpful to keep momentum is a non-binding letter of intent to purchase. The same objective can be accomplished through a more formal "memorandum of intent to purchase"—but a memorandum usually turns out to be more legalistic and, therefore, more threatening to a seller.

Giving the seller a modest, earnest money deposit along with the letter of intent is also helpful, because it shows you're sincerely interested in pursuing the purchase and are not wasting the seller's time. But because details of the purchase have not solidified at this point, be sure to provide that the deposit is to be refunded if the purchase falls through.

A sample non-binding letter of intent is shown below.

LETTER OF INTENT TO PURCHASE

Robert Tower, President
The Tower Mart Inc.
25 Glen Blvd.
Arlington Heights, IL

Dear Bob:

Thanks for meeting with me again last week. I continue to be interested in purchasing the assets of the Tower Mart Inc. If we reach an agreement regarding my purchase, I plan to transfer these assets to a new corporation that I'm forming. My new company would then run a convenience store similar to what you're currently operating.

I'm interested in purchasing the following assets: the inventory, fixtures, equipment, leasehold improvements and business name. In addition, I will need all necessary licenses and permits transferred to me. I will expect you to give me a covenant not to compete stating that for three years, you won't open a similar store in our city. The purchase price for all of the assets as well as the good will and your covenant not to compete would be $150,000, as we have already discussed.

> [Before referring to a covenant not to compete, see the discussion of such covenants in Section G.5, below]

As an indication of my good faith in pursuing this matter, I am enclosing a check for $1,000 as earnest money. I would pay an additional $49,000 in cash at closing. The balance of $100,000 would be amortized in equal monthly installments over a period of 10 years with interest at the rate of 10% per annum.

Regarding the inventory, we will check this at the time of closing. If the inventory is valued at less than $45,000, the purchase price would be reduced accordingly. Also, as you and I discussed, your corporation would remain responsible for all liabilities of the present business and these would not be assumed by my new corporation.

Before I have my lawyer draft a sales agreement, there are some things I need to investigate:

1. I want to meet with your landlord to make sure that I can take over the existing lease and that I can get an option to extend it for another five years.

(continued)

2. I need to have my accountant review all of your tax returns and business records for the past five years so that I can satisfy myself regarding the financial condition of your business.

3. I want to make sure that the state liquor board will approve a transfer of the beer and wine retail license to my new corporation.

Assuming that I'm satisfied with these items and all other aspects of the proposed purchase, I will have my lawyer draft a sales agreement and then we can close approximately 45 days from now.

This letter states my intent but it is not a legally binding contract or commitment on either my part or yours. Upon further investigation I may change my mind. If the deal doesn't go through for any reason, I'd be entitled to my earnest money back.

If my letter has captured the essence of what we talked about and you're still interested in pursuing the sale, please let me know. I believe that we are moving toward a transaction that can be advantageous to both of us.

Sincerely,

Mary Beyer

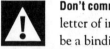 **Don't commit yourself.** Make it clear in a letter of intent that it is not intended to be a binding contract. You may or may not need your lawyer's assistance in writing a letter of intent, but I do recommend that you call your lawyer to at least check on the adequacy of the language you use to describe the non-binding nature of the letter.

G. The Sales Agreement

The sales agreement is the key legal document in buying business assets or an entire corporation. I recommend that you consult a lawyer experienced in small business concerns, but the first job is yours. You should create a written outline of the terms that you and the seller have agreed on. Next, have your lawyer review it and help draft the next version of the agreement. Once you and your lawyer are satisfied, present the agreement to the seller.

Why take on the document drafting yourself, rather than letting the seller do it? Because even though it's more time consuming, this approach will almost surely give you more control over the overall shape of the transaction. By seizing the initiative, you may well wind up with 95% or more of what you want.

This section briefly reviews the principal types of clauses in a business sales agreement. Remember, as discussed earlier (Section B.2), it's almost always better to buy the assets from the corporation than to buy its stock. Accordingly, these clauses are geared primarily to an asset purchase. If for some reason you decide to buy corporate stock, make corresponding changes in your sales agreement.

1. Names of Seller, Buyer and Business

Your sales agreement will start with the name and address of the seller and the buyer. It will also identify the business by its current name.

- *Purchase From or By a Sole Proprietor.* Name the sole proprietor, adding the business name if it's different from the individual's. *Example:* Mary Perfect doing business as Perfect Word Processing Service.

- *Purchase From or By a Partnership.* Use the partnership's legal name and the names of all partners. *Example:* Ortega Associates, a Colorado partnership of William Ortega and Henry Cruz.

- *Purchase From or By a Corporation.* Simply use the corporate name and identify it by the state where it's registered. *Example:* XYZ Enterprises Inc., a Massachusetts corporation.

If you're going to operate the business you're purchasing as a corporation, I recommend either of two procedures: Set up the new corporation before signing the sales agreement and name the new corporation as the purchaser. Or list the purchaser as yourself as the agent of a corporation to be formed. Using either of these methods, the assets can go directly into your corporation rather than having a two-stage process in which you receive the assets and then transfer them to the corporation. If you're going to be putting the assets into a corporation, the seller undoubtedly will want you (and probably your spouse as well) to personally guarantee the payment of any part of the purchase price that's being paid on an installment basis.

2. Background Information

Often, before a sales agreement gets into the terms of the transaction, it outlines some background facts. For example, the sales agreement might state that "Mildred Johnson currently owns a business in Cincinnati which produces ice cream, sorbet and other dessert products" and that the sales agreement "applies only to the portion of the business operated at seller's west side location at 123 Maple Street."

You can also include some statements about the buyer; for example, "the buyer is a building contractor licensed under the laws of the state of Maine." These statements aren't usually a key section of a purchase agreement, but if they are included, it's important to be accurate.

3. Assets Being Sold

This is where you list what you're purchasing. You can put the details, such as lists of equipment, on a separate page which is sometimes referred to in the body of the agreement as a schedule or exhibit and specifically made part of the contract. Here's an example of how a sales agreement might list assets being sold:

a. All furniture, trade fixtures, equipment and miscellaneous items of tangible personal property owned by seller and used in the business, listed and described in Exhibit A which is hereby made a part of this agreement.

b. Customer lists and all other files and records of the business.

c. Assignment of the seller's interest (as tenant) in the lease dated March 1, 1991 for the building located at 123 Main Street owned by Central Property Associates (landlord).

d. Assignment of the seller's interest (as lessee) in the computer equipment lease with CompuLease dated March 1, 1991.

e. All telephone numbers of the business and the right to use the business name, "The Tower Mart." Seller will cease using that name on the day of closing.

If you have so agreed, also include a statement that you're not acquiring any of the liabilities of the business or that you're acquiring only those that are specified.

Except as otherwise specified in this agreement, buyer is not assuming responsibility for any liabilities of the business. Seller will remain responsible for all liabilities of the business not specified in this agreement, and will indemnify buyer and save buyer harmless from and against such liabilities.

4. Purchase Price and Allocation of Assets

After stating the purchase price, allocate the price among the different categories of assets. Some typical allocations are shown below.

Allocation for a Retail Business

Merchandise on Hand	$75,000
Tangible Personal Property	$30,000
Assignment of Lease Agreement	$ 4,000
Trade Name and Good Will	$ 8,000

Allocation for a Small Computer Company

Inventory (Computers and Software)	$100,000
Covenant Not To Compete for Five Years	$ 30,000
Patents and Copyrights	$ 40,000
Building Owned by Seller	$100,000
Trade Name and Good Will	$ 5,000

For tax reasons, as a buyer, you want most of the price assigned to the assets that give you the fastest recovery of your investment: inventory and depreciable assets. You want the least allocated to items like good will, which can't be depreciated and give you no tax benefits until you sell the business. The seller should be willing to accommodate you; there's little

if any tax advantage to the seller in allocating the price differently.

In each example, above, since the price you pay for a trade name and good will can't be depreciated, it's assigned a relatively low value. In the second example, the seller's building, which is included in the sale, could reasonably be valued at anywhere from $100,000 to $130,000 depending on whose appraisal is used. I've assigned the lowest reasonable value to the building because, under IRS guidelines, it must be depreciated over a period of 31-1/2 years. The covenant not to compete, on the other hand, is assigned a relatively high value because it can be depreciated over a five-year period.

If the seller is going to provide consulting services to you for a year or so, consider assigning a portion of the purchase price to those services so that you can write off that amount quickly as a business expense. Better yet, remove an appropriate amount from the purchase price and put it in a separate agreement for consulting services.

5. Covenant Not To Compete

Especially if the seller is well known and would be a threat to your business if he or she opened a rival outfit, you want a covenant (promise) not to compete. In such a covenant, the seller agrees not to compete directly or indirectly with you in the operation of the type of business that you've purchased. If the seller violates the covenant, judges or arbitrators will usually enforce it unless it unreasonably limits the seller's ability to earn a living.

To increase chances that your agreement will be enforced, it's wise to place a reasonable geographic limitation on the seller's right to run a similar business (for example, within 25 miles of your business) and also a reasonable time limit (for example, three years). If you're purchasing a business from a corporation, have the individual operators of the business sign their own personal promises not to compete.

Obviously, whatever geographic limitations you and the seller agree on should fit the area. In New

York City, a 25-mile zone would take in a huge chunk of New Jersey and some 15 to 20 million people—probably an unreasonable restraint on the seller's future ability to earn a living. In drafting a covenant not to compete, get help from a savvy lawyer who knows what the state courts enforce.

An example of a covenant not to compete is shown below.

Covenant Not To Compete

Seller shall not establish, engage in, or become interested in, directly or indirectly, as an employee, owner, partner, agent, shareholder or otherwise, within a radius of 10 miles from the city of _____, any business, trade or occupation similar to the business covered by this sales agreement for a period of three years. At the closing, the seller agrees to sign an agreement on this subject in the form set forth in Exhibit B.

LAW IN THE REAL WORLD

Why You Need a Covenant Not To Compete

Sid is buying a travel agency from Mary Jones, who has been in the travel business for 25 years and is well known in the community. Part of the reason Sid is buying her business is the excellent reputation and following her business has earned.

Two months after Sid takes over the business, Mary—who quickly tired of retirement—opens a new travel agency four blocks away. Inevitably some, perhaps many, of her old customers will abandon Sid and patronize Mary's business. Sid should have included a covenant not to compete in the sales agreement to protect himself against this possibility.

---

6. Adjustments

You'll probably need to adjust the sales price slightly at closing. For example, you should reimburse the seller for payments the seller has made for such items

as rent, utilities or insurance for periods after you take over. On the other hand, if salaries and wages are paid every two weeks and you take over the business halfway through that period, the purchase price should be reduced at closing to reflect the fact that you'll be paying salaries for a period when the seller still owned the business. Adjustments may also be made for license fees, maintenance contracts, equipment leases and property taxes.

7. Terms of Payment

Nearly 80% of small business purchases are handled on an installment basis, with the seller extending all or most of the credit. Typically, a buyer puts down about one-third of the purchase price and pays the balance over four or five years. For example, in the purchase of a $250,000 business, you may negotiate a contract that requires you to make a $50,000 down payment at closing with the balance paid in five annual installments of $40,000 each plus interest at 10% per year.

At the closing, you'll sign a promissory note for the unpaid portion of the purchase price. The seller generally will want to retain an ownership (security) interest in the equipment and other assets of the business until the purchase price has been paid. Sometimes called a "lien," this is akin to a mortgage on your home. Just as the bank could sell your home to pay off your loan if you fell behind in your payments, the seller of a business who retains a lien on or security interest in your business assets could, if you were delinquent in making payments, take possession of those assets and sell them to cover the balance owing.

Here's a sample terms of payment clause:

Purchaser will pay seller $_____ at closing and will pay the balance of $_____ according to the terms of a promissory note purchaser will sign at the closing, in the form set forth in Exhibit __. The promissory note will provide for monthly payments of $_____ each. The payments will include interest on the unpaid balance at the rate of ____%

---

per annum from and after the date of closing. The first installment will be due on the first day of the month following the closing and the remaining installments will be due on the first of each month after that until the principal and interest is fully paid. Payments will be applied first on interest and then on principal. The unpaid principal and interest shall be fully paid no later than ____ years from the date of the note. There will be no penalty for prepayment.

Until purchaser has paid the full balance of principal and interest on the debt, seller will retain a security interest in the business assets being purchased. As evidence of such security interest, purchaser, at closing, will sign a security agreement in the form set forth in attached Exhibit __ and will also a sign a Uniform Commercial Code Financing Statement, to be recorded at the appropriate county and state office.

It's a good idea to attach the proposed promissory note as well as the proposed security agreement as exhibits to the sales agreement.

Tax and Usury: Charge Reasonable Interest

The IRS will accept the interest rate agreed to by the seller and buyer if it is reasonable in terms of the current financing market and the risk involved in extending credit. If the interest rate is outside the reasonable range, the buyer may not be able to deduct the excess interest paid. To avoid this, stick close to prevailing interest rates.

Also be aware that state usury laws limit the rate of interest that can be charged. Here, it's the seller rather than the buyer who runs the risk of running afoul of the law. Not only may the seller not be able to collect excessive interest, but he or she may also face criminal penalties.

---

8. Inventory

Because the inventory of saleable merchandise is likely to fluctuate between the time you sign the sales

agreement and the closing, consider putting a provision in the sales agreement that allows for adjustment. For example, you might say that you'll pay up to $75,000 for merchandise on hand at the closing based on the seller's invoice cost. You might also provide that if there's more than $75,000 worth of merchandise on hand when you close, you have the right to purchase the excess at the seller's cost, or to choose $75,000 worth and leave the rest in the hands of the seller.

Here's another way to handle this problem. Simply provide that a physical count of all merchandise will be made on the day of sale or another mutually-agreeable date. You might define the word merchandise to include only unopened and undamaged merchandise. In a retail business, you can agree to value the merchandise at its current wholesale cost, or at the seller's current retail price less a certain percentage. If you don't have experience doing an inventory, you might also put in the sales agreement that you and the seller will split the cost of hiring an inventory service company to determine the amount of the purchase price of the merchandise.

In a manufacturing or service business, you may have the analogous problem of placing a value on work in progress.

9. Accounts Receivable

Usually the accounts receivable of an existing business remain the property of that business and aren't transferred to the buyer. But a seller who prefers to be free of collection problems may want to include them. Be very careful. When a business changes hands, accounts can be hard to collect. A considerable percentage will probably never be collected, so you should get a substantial discount. How much depends on how collectable these accounts are. By now you should know this through your close examination of the seller's books and, if most of the money is owed by only a few accounts, by checking with them personally.

10. Bulk Sales Compliance

If the business you're buying involves the sale of merchandise from a stock that you'll keep on hand, you must comply with the "bulk sales" law of your state. These laws apply to transfers of a major part of the seller's materials, supplies, merchandise or other inventory. Generally, they don't apply to transfers where the seller's business consists primarily of selling personal services rather than merchandise. But some states have broadened the definition of businesses covered by the bulk sales provisions. For example, in Michigan, enterprises covered by the law include restaurants, cafes, taverns, hotels, clubs and any other establishment that dispenses food, or any enterprise that manufactures what it sells.

A seller covered under the bulk sales law must give you a list (sworn to under penalty of perjury) of all business creditors and tell you the amounts due each one. Also, the seller must tell you about any claims made by potential creditors, even if the claims are disputed. Then you send notice to the creditors so that they'll know that the business is changing hands. If these things are not done, the creditors of the old business will continue to have a claim against the merchandise that you're buying. Sending proper notices protects you from such claims.

Sometimes, to avoid the need to comply with the bulk sales law, a contract will say that the seller will pay all outstanding debts of the business before the closing or out of the proceeds of the sale at the time of closing, and will furnish an affidavit to that effect at closing.

11. Seller's Representations and Warranties

In the sales agreement, the seller should guarantee the basic facts of your transaction. Here's an example of the guarantees when the seller is a corporation:

Seller and seller's shareholders represent and warrant that:

1. Andover Corporation is in good standing under the laws of Wisconsin.

2. Andover Corporation's board of directors has authorized (through board resolutions to be delivered to buyer at closing) the signing of this sales contract and all of the transactions called for in the contract.

3. Andover Corporation has good and marketable title to the assets that are being sold and will convey them to buyer free and clear of all encumbrances, except for the assets listed in Exhibit A which will remain subject to the encumbrances listed there.

4. The balance sheet that Andover Corporation gave buyer correctly reflects the assets, liabilities and net worth of the business as of October 31, 199_, and there will be no material changes between the balance sheet date and the closing.

5. The income statement that Andover Corporation gave buyer accurately reflects the income and expenses of the company during the period covered, and no significant changes in the level of income or expense will occur between the contract date and the closing.

6. The lease under which Andover Corporation occupies space at 789 Oak Avenue is in full effect and is assignable to buyer. Andover Corporation will take all necessary steps to assign the lease to buyer.

7. Between the contract date and the closing, Andover Corporation will operate the business as usual and will take no action out of the ordinary.

8. Andover Corporation has complied with all applicable laws and regulations of the federal, state and local governments.

9. There are no lawsuits or claims pending or threatened against Andover Corporation other than those listed in Exhibit __, and Andover

Corporation does not know of any basis for any
other lawsuit or claim against the business.

10. Andover Corporation has disclosed to buyer all
material facts that would reasonably affect a
prudent investor's decision to purchase the
assets covered by this agreement.

In addition, if the seller made specific statements
to you about the business and these influenced your
decision to buy it, have the seller reiterate these
statements in writing in this section of the
agreement.

 Don't rely on the seller's promises. Never
use the seller's warranties and representations as an excuse for not thoroughly
checking all important facts yourself, as discussed in
Section C above. Enforcing a warranty against the
seller or suing for a misrepresentation can involve a
long and expensive lawsuit.

If you're buying a business or the assets from a
corporation, have the principal owners sign the
warranties as individuals in addition to signing them
as officers of the corporation. That way, you'll be able
to go after their personal assets if they've misrepresented facts or if their warranties are violated.

The contract should also say that the warranties
survive the closing. This gives you the right to sue if
you discover some unpleasant facts about the business several years after you purchase it. Here's some
wording to consider:

> The representations and warranties of the parties to
> this agreement and those of the seller's sharehold-
> ers shall survive the closing. The act of closing
> shall not bar either party from bringing an action
> based on a representation or warranty of the other
> party.

12. Buyer's Warranties and Representations

The seller may expect the buyer to sign representations and warranties as well. For example:

Buyer represents and warrants that:

1. Buyer is a corporation in good standing under
the laws of Wisconsin.

2. Buyer has the authority to enter into and
perform the buyer's obligations under the sales
agreement.

3. Buyer has had an opportunity to inspect the
assets of the business and agrees to accept
the assets as is, except for the items referred to
in Exhibit C.

The first representation in this example assumes
you've established a corporation. You wouldn't
include this statement if you were buying as a sole
proprietor or signing on behalf of a partnership.

In the second representation, a corporate buyer
would agree to furnish the seller with a board of
directors resolution approving the terms of the sales
agreement and authorizing the signing of the
purchase documents.

13. Access to Information

By the time you sign the sales agreement, you should
have seen a lot of financial information involving
the business, but you may still want to see more to
verify that everything is as promised. So it's a good
idea to include a paragraph or two in the sales
agreement covering your right to get full information. In exchange, the seller will probably want to
include language assuring that you'll deal with the
information in a responsible manner—that is, that
you won't make unnecessary disclosures. (For a
discussion of sellers' concerns about confidentiality,
see Section C, above..)

Here's some language you might place in the
sales agreement:

> Before the closing, seller will provide to buyer and
> buyer's agents, during normal business hours,
> access to all of the company's properties, books,
> contracts and records, and will furnish to buyer all

the information concerning the company's affairs that buyer reasonably requests.

Buyer acknowledges that the company's books, records and other documents contain confidential information, and that communication of such confidential information to third parties could injure the company's business if this transaction is not completed. Buyer agrees to take reasonable steps to assure that such information about the company remains confidential and is not revealed to outside sources. Buyer further agrees not to solicit any customers of the company disclosed from such confidential information.

The confidential information that may become known to buyer includes customer lists, trade secrets, channels of distribution, pricing policy and records, inventory records, and other information normally understood to be confidential or designated as such by seller.

14. Conduct of Business Pending Closing

Unless the sales agreement is signed at the closing, be sure that the seller doesn't make any detrimental changes in the business between the time you sign the sales agreement and the time you close. We considered some commitments along this line in Section G.11 dealing with the seller's warranties and representations. In addition, if you're purchasing the stock of a corporation, get a commitment that no change will be made in the articles of incorporation or in the authorized or issued shares of the corporation. Also, if you're dealing with a corporation, get a commitment that no contract will be entered into by or on behalf of the corporation extending beyond the closing date, except those made in the ordinary course of business.

Finally, have the corporation agree that it won't increase the compensation paid to any officer or employee and won't make any new arrangements for bonuses.

15. Contingencies

A contingency clause is a safety valve that lets you walk away from the transaction if certain things don't pan out. For example, if the location of the business is a crucial part of your decision to buy, you'll want to reserve the right to cancel the deal if you find out that the lease can't be assigned to you. The same thing might be true of a required license; if you're buying a bar, you would make the deal contingent on the state transferring the liquor license to you. If you plan to expand the business or move to a new location, make the deal contingent on your being able to get approval from the local zoning and building officials. Here's a sample contingency clause:

This agreement is contingent upon buyer receiving approval, by _____ 19___ from the landlord and the city's building and safety department for a remodeling of the premises leased by the business as shown in the plans and specifications attached as Exhibit __.

16. Seller To Be a Consultant

Sometimes it pays to have the seller stay on for a few months as a consultant or employee to help ease your transition into the business and reassure long-time customers and suppliers that the business is in good hands. If you make these kinds of arrangements with the seller, be sure to capture them in the sales agreement, using language such as the following:

_____, as an independent contractor engaged by buyer, will provide consultation, customer relations, general assistance and information to buyer pertaining to the company for up to 20 hours per week as requested by buyer for a period of 8 weeks following closing. For such services, buyer will pay _____ $_____ per week.

The consulting fees are tax-deductible as current business expenses.

17. Broker Fees

If a business broker is involved, specify who is responsible for paying the fee, unless you independently hired the broker to help you locate the business. Normally, the seller is responsible.

18. Notices

It's customary to state addresses for both the seller and the purchaser where any notices and demands can be sent—for example, if a payment were late or other contract term not met. Typically, sales agreements provide that notices can be given by first-class mail, but it is appropriate to require notice by registered mail with a return receipt requested.

19. Closing Date

Include a date for the closing. That's when you'll make your down payment, and both parties will sign any documents that are necessary to transfer the business to you.

H. The Closing

Finally, the big day has arrived—you're about to become the owner of a business. In an ideal world, you'd simply give the seller a check and the seller would give you the keys. Unfortunately, there's lots of additional paperwork involved.

There's also a certain amount of stress and pressure at a closing (after all, it's not every day that you buy a business). Working with your lawyer or other advisor, make a checklist in advance listing all documents to be signed at the closing. Review this carefully a couple of days before the closing and be sure you have all your paperwork ready to go. If anything is unclear or doesn't make sense to you, ask your lawyer to redraft the language in plain English so that you and everyone else can understand it.

Checklist for a Typical Closing

- *Adjust purchase price* for prorated items such as rent payments or utilities, or changes in the value of inventory.

- *Review documents promised by seller*—for example, a corporate board resolution authorizing the sale or an opinion of the seller's lawyer stating that the corporation is in good legal standing and that the sale has been properly approved by the shareholders and/or directors.

- *Sign promissory note* if you're not paying all cash for the business. The seller may require your spouse's signature as well so that your joint bank account will be a source of repayment if the business doesn't produce enough income.

- *Sign security agreement* giving the seller a lien on the business assets if you don't pay the full price in cash at closing. (If you fail to keep up your payments as promised, the seller can take back the assets subject to the security agreement.) You may also be asked to sign a UCC Financing Statement to be filed with the county clerk or secretary of state, giving public notice of the seller's lien.

- *Sign assignment of lease* if you're taking over an existing lease. If the landlord's approval is required, be sure it has been obtained before the closing.

- *Transfer vehicle titles* if cars or trucks are among the business assets.

- *Sign bill of sale* transferring ownership of other tangible business assets.

- *Sign transfer of patents, trademarks and copyrights* if included in the sale.

- *Sign franchise transfer documents* if you're buying a business from a franchisee. This should include the signed approval of the franchisor.

- *Sign closing or settlement statement* listing all financial aspects of the transaction. Ideally, everything in the closing or settlement statement should be based on clear language in the sales agreement so that nothing need be negotiated at the closing table.

- *Sign covenant not to compete* if seller agreed to one.

- *Sign consultation or employment agreement* if the seller has agreed to stay on as a consultant or employee.

I. Selling a Business

Obviously, when you're just starting out in business, selling it isn't at the forefront of your mind. But there's a good chance that, sooner or later, you'll need to or want to sell. The reasons can vary widely—from not liking working for yourself, to a need to relocate, to one spouse selling to the other as part of a divorce, to retirement.

Let's look at some things you can do get a good price for your business and protect your legal position.

1. Valuing Your Business

When you contemplate selling all of a business or only part (which might occur if you take in a partner or sell out to your co-owner spouse as part of a divorce), your first task is to determine the value of your business.

> **Example:** Pauline has built a thriving retail business with three locations and 24 employees. Now she's getting divorced. She and her husband have agreed that she'll keep the business rather than liquidate it. Pauline must put a value on the business so that she and her husband can arrive at a reasonable property settlement.

You can get help from an appraiser (see Section D above) or a business broker. If you do use a broker to sell your business, carefully read the listing agreement. Consider these issues:

- Does the broker have the exclusive right to sell your business or can you sell it directly without paying a commission?

- Do you have the right to reject a proposed purchaser because of the purchaser's credit history or for other reasons without having to pay the broker's commission?

- If there's an installment sale, will the broker receive his or her total commission out of the down payment or in installments as you're paid?

If you do business through a corporation, you'll probably be selling only the assets the corporation owns—not the corporation itself—although, from a tax and liability standpoint it's more advantageous for you to sell the corporate stock.

Timing of a sale can be critical to getting the best price. Suppose your company has had earnings of $400,000 per year for the past three years. And suppose, too, that you have good reason to believe you'll jump to $600,000 next year. You can, of course, tell a prospective buyer why you expect an increase in profits. But there's often a better tactic: hang on to the business for another year so that you have actual numbers to point to—not just a theory.

Would-be buyers will have much more confidence in your figures if you can show them several years worth of financial statements audited or reviewed by a CPA. (The distinctions between the types of CPA reports are discussed in Section D above.) Also, keep detailed schedules of expenses so that buyers can compare your business with others in your industry.

Getting a Good Price for Your Business

- Show steadily increasing profits at or above the industry average. Plan ahead. To show strong profits, you may need to give up some hidden perks. Don't fret; you'll be handsomely rewarded at sale time.

- Put your business in good general condition. Everything should be neat, tidy and in good working order. Machinery should be in good repair; your inventory should be well balanced and current.

- Maintain adequate personnel. A buyer will be put off—and discount the price—if the first chore in running the business is to recruit and train new employees.

- Get a written appraisal supporting your sales price. This can help persuade the buyer that the price is right.

These suggestions are from *Valuing Small Businesses and Professional Practices* by Shannon Pratt (Dow Jones-Irwin).

---

2. Read Your Lease

Your lease may say that a new business owner can't take over your space without the landlord's consent. If so, such consent will be needed if you signed the lease as a sole proprietor or partner. It will also be needed if the purchaser is buying the assets of your corporation rather than its stock. Find out early whether your landlord will be an obstacle to selling the business and, if so, how you can get his or her support.

3. Protect Your Privacy

A prospective purchaser will want to investigate your business thoroughly before signing a purchase agreement. To protect your privacy, use a confidentiality or nondisclosure agreement in which the potential purchaser promises not to use or disclose confidential information about your business—unless, of course, he or she decides to buy it. (A sample agreement is shown in Section C above.) A prospective purchaser who violates this agreement can be sued for damages and injunctive relief.

4. Sign a Letter of Intent

In Section F, we looked at the non-binding letter of intent from the standpoint of a buyer. There's no reason why such a letter can't be drafted by a seller who wants to summarize the terms of the proposed transaction as part of testing whether a potential buyer is serious.

5. Draft a Sales Agreement

To understand the elements of a sales agreement, read the previous sections of this chapter, particularly Section G. Here are some points to consider from the seller's viewpoint:

a. STRUCTURE OF THE SALE

The sales agreement structures the sale. As noted in Section B.1, if you're doing business as a sole proprietor or partnership, the structure of the sale is a foregone conclusion: you'll sell the assets of the business to the buyer. But if you're doing business as a corporation, the matter is more complicated. It's almost always better for you to sell your corporate stock than to have the corporation sell its assets. But for tax and liability reasons, buyers prefer to buy corporate assets rather than corporate stock—and, in practice, the vast majority of small corporate businesses are sold on an asset sale basis. (See Section B above.)

b. EXCLUDED ASSETS

If you're selling the assets of the business or the business itself—whether it be a sole proprietorship, a partnership or a corporation—the purchase agreement lists the assets being transferred. Typically, this includes furniture, fixtures, equipment, inventory and vehicles and the business name. Equally important, specify any items excluded from the sale, for example: cash, accounts receivable, life insurance policies or your personal desk or computer.

c. ALLOCATION OF PURCHASE PRICE

In Section G, we focused on the allocation of the purchase price from the buyer's standpoint. The buyer wants to assign relatively high value to items that can be written off immediately or depreciated quickly. It rarely makes any difference, tax-wise, to the seller. A tax pro can quickly size up your particular sale. Allocation of purchase price is usually a win-win situation in which you can accommodate the buyer's reasonable tax needs without penalty.

d. ADEQUATE SECURITY FOR INSTALLMENT SALES

In most purchases of small businesses, the buyer puts down 20% to 40% of the purchase price and pays the balance in installments over three to five years. Plan ahead in case the buyer doesn't keep up the payments as promised. Insist that the buyer's spouse sign all closing documents jointly with the buyer. That way, if you need to sue the buyer because of nonpayment, you have a chance of collecting the judgment out of a house owned jointly by the buyer and spouse, or from bank accounts in their joint names. If the couple's credit is weak, insist that the documents be signed by an outside guarantor.

The purchase agreement should require the buyer to give you a security interest (also called a lien) in the business assets. A financing statement that's filed with county or state officials will give public notice that you have a claim on the business assets.

If you're doing business as a corporation and are selling your stock, consider placing the stock certificates in escrow. That way, the buyer won't receive the certificates until the purchase price has been paid in full.

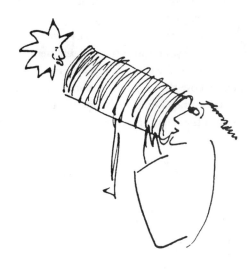

e. LOOKING TO THE FUTURE

The buyer may want to hire you for several months or years as a consultant or employee. If so, spell this out in the sales agreement or in a separate document signed at the same time. Be specific about the types of services you'll be expected to render, the amount of time you're committing and the amount you'll be paid. Sometimes, compensation for a seller's post-sale services is simply folded into the purchase price so the seller receives no additional payment.

If you've agreed not to compete with the buyer, the terms should be specified in a covenant not to compete. Cover such matters as precisely what business or activities you won't engage in, being careful not to burn all of your bridges. Think carefully about how long you're willing to refrain from working in a competing enterprise and how large a geographical area should be barred during the non-competition period. (See Section G.5.)

f. WARRANTIES

Sales agreements typically contain numerous warranties and representations by the seller and a few by the buyer. (See Sections G.11 and G.12 for examples.) Read your warranties and representations carefully to make sure they don't go too far. For example, suppose the proposed warranty language says: "Seller warrants that the business name does not conflict with the name of any other business." What happens if the day after the sale a business that you didn't know about surfaces and complains that it had the name first? With the warranty wording given here, you could be liable for damages whether or not you know about the other company.

If you see a warranty that's too far-reaching, have it rewritten. In our example, you might say something like "Seller warrants that, to the best of seller's knowledge, . . ." Or perhaps you could say: "Seller warrants that it has received no notice that its business name conflicts with that of any other business."

FRANCHISES: HOW NOT TO GET BURNED

8

"The incidence of fraud and misrepresentation in franchise sales is no longer confined to a small number of underfinanced operators, but increasingly involves established national franchise companies."

—Rep. John J. LaFalce, Chair, Small Business Committee, U.S. House of Representatives[1]

In other words, be careful.

Many people have done extremely well after buying a franchise. Many more have lost their shirts. To avoid falling into the second category, you need to thoroughly investigate a franchise proposal and get sound legal and financial advice before you pay a cent or sign a contract locking you into a deal.

In this chapter, you'll learn more about what a franchise is, legally speaking, and how you can increase the chances of success if you decide to buy one. You'll also be introduced to two important legal documents: the offering circular and the franchise agreement.

A. An Overview of Franchises

Buying a franchise falls somewhere between working for somebody else as an employee and starting a business of your own as an independent entrepreneur. The main appeal is that you're not in business all by yourself but can sell a recognized product or service. In addition to name recognition, good franchises offer two other benefits:

1. **A Proven Plan for Running the Business.** The franchisor (the company that sells a franchise) will have an operations manual that can serve as a roadmap to get you started. This is particularly helpful if you don't have business experience.

2. **Help From the Franchisor If You Run Into Problems.** The better franchisors have people available who are experienced in real estate (including locating a site for your franchise business), marketing, personnel policies, accounting and day-to-day operations. With a well-run franchise organization, being able to call on these resources can be a real plus.

Now for some negatives. If you have a strong independent streak, a franchise may not be the answer. Innovation by individual franchisees is often discouraged. It's a little like the Army: you must follow the system as dictated from above. Another built-in down side of franchises is that the franchisor gets a piece of your financial action. Franchisors have figured out many ways to make money on your business including:

- *Franchise fees*—You must always pay up-front for the right to be a franchisee. These can get very pricey, especially for a successful, nationally established franchise.

- *Royalties*—Commonly, the franchisor gets a percentage of the income your franchise earns. Income usually means gross sales, not profits. If your franchise takes in $200,000 from gross sales and your contract calls for a 10% royalty, the franchisor will be entitled to receive $20,000 whether or not your business earns a profit. Other operating expenses may eat up the remaining $180,000 of gross income, leaving nothing—or even less.

- *Markups on equipment, goods and supplies*—The franchisor may add dollars to the cost of equipment, goods and supplies that the franchisor furnishes. Many franchise agreements require you to buy certain items from the franchisor rather than from outside suppliers; others let you buy through outside sources if the items meet the franchisor's specifications. If, for example, you're required to purchase cooking equipment from the franchisor, you may pay lots more than you'd pay a restaurant supply store.

- *Training fees*—Often you must pay the franchisor to train you and your employees whether or not you need the training.

---

[1]Quoted in the *Wall Street Journal*, July 11, 1991.

- *Co-op ad fees*—These fees cover advertising for the entire group of franchises or a regional group. For example, you may have to contribute to a fund for national advertising or for advertising for all the franchisees in your metropolitan area.

- *Interest on financing*—You may have to pay for deferring payment of a portion of the franchise fee, the cost of improving your business premises or buying equipment.

- *Leases*—Your franchisor may charge you rent on real estate or equipment. Typically, the franchisor does not lease real estate or equipment to you at the franchisor's cost but adds on a profit factor. But because relatively few franchisors own the premises where their franchisees do business, real estate lease charges are relatively uncommon.

Another problem in buying a franchise is that you may not get everything that's promised to you in the sales presentations. Some franchisors are notorious for misrepresenting the facts about their organization or what you can reasonably expect to earn. Others are fly-by-night outfits operating entirely with smoke and mirrors.

LAW IN THE REAL WORLD
Going It Alone

Phil, a real estate broker, wanted to open his own shop. He first considered going it alone, but then decided he might do better by purchasing a franchise from one of the national organizations. He contacted several and was amazed to find that he couldn't buy a one-office franchise directly from them. Instead he was told that in his region a "master" franchise had already been sold and that he would have to contact this company to purchase a sub-franchise.

When he did, he learned that his region had been divided into hundreds of sub-regions or territories, each of which was for sale through a local real estate office. All training, quality control and recruiting was done by the master franchise holder, not the national organization.

Eventually, Phil decided not to purchase any of the local franchises he was offered, concluding that the territories had been divided too narrowly. In the meantime, he has opened his own office and is doing fairly well. He might still affiliate with a franchise organization, but only if he can find one that sells good-sized territories at a reasonable price.

In sum, buying a franchise, like starting your own business, doesn't guarantee success. If success does come, it's likely to be at least as much the result of your hard work as any inherent value in the franchise.

In considering a franchise, don't assume there's a governmental safety net. Neither the state nor the federal government is going to thoroughly investigate the accuracy of information in the offering circular or bail you out if things go wrong. True, you may get limited help from a government agency to close down or even prosecute a fraudulent operator. But even in the case of blatant dishonesty by the franchisor, you'll be pretty much on your own in trying to get back your money. Keep this in mind when you listen to sales puffing from the people trying to sell you a franchise. You're almost surely not receiving a balanced, objective point of view. No matter what they say about peace, brotherhood and all prospering together, most franchisors look at their job as simply to sell as many franchises as possible, as fast as possible, at the highest price possible.

B. What Is a Franchise?

There are many definitions of what constitutes a franchise, including definitions found in state statutes. The most convenient analysis and definition comes from the Federal Trade Commission (FTC)—the one government agency that has nationwide regulatory power in this field. The FTC recognizes two types of business relationships that qualify for regulation as franchises:

The Package Franchise. The franchisor licenses you to do business under a business format it has established. The business is closely identified with the franchisor's trademark or trade name. Examples include fast food outlets, motels, car washes, transmission centers, tax preparation services and quick copy shops.

The Product Franchise. You distribute goods produced by the franchisor or under the franchisor's control or direction. The business or goods bear the franchisor's trademark or trade name. Examples include gasoline stations and car dealerships.

This chapter deals primarily with package franchises, which are more common.

The FTC definition is broad. It covers all of the businesses that you and I would ordinarily think of as franchises. Generally, the FTC (and many state agencies that regulate franchises) will classify your business relationship as a franchise if three conditions exist:

- You have the right to distribute goods or services that bear the franchisor's trademark, service mark, trade name or logo. You have the right to operate under these names or symbols.

- The franchisor significantly assists you in operating your business or significantly controls what you do. For example, a franchisor might assist in site selection, training you and your employees, or furnishing a detailed instructional manual. A franchisor might exercise control by telling you where your business must be located and how your shop must be designed, or by dictating your hours, accounting and personnel practices and advertising program.

- You pay a fee to the franchisor of more than $500 for the first six months of operations. (In the real world, you're going to be paying a franchisor much more—probably anywhere from $10,000 or $20,000 up to $1 million, although not all of it will necessarily be due in the first six months.)

C. Investigating a Franchise

The franchise concept works best when a franchisor's standardized operations, high name recognition and efficiencies of scale all contribute to success. Fast food is an obvious example. In many other businesses, however, the benefits of being a franchisee are less clear. For example, while the franchise route is one way to get started in the copy shop or quick stop market business, you may enjoy equal or greater success by setting up your business without a franchise. You could better tailor your operations to the local market and perhaps run more profitably than you could as a franchisee—especially when you subtract the costs you must pay the franchisor.

After you've identified a few businesses in which you believe being a franchisee could be beneficial, investigate the franchisors in those fields. A good track record counts. Find out how many franchises the franchisor has in actual operation—information that's readily available in the offering circular. (See Section D.20.)

Next, carefully evaluate whether the specific franchise operation you're thinking about makes economic sense. Is there really a demand out there for the product or service that you'll be selling? Can you make a decent profit given how much you can charge and your cost of doing business? Don't forget to count all those franchise fees. The franchisor may give you actual or hypothetical projections of how much money a typical franchisee can earn. Distrust these. Chances are they're full of hype. Ask for financial details about individual franchise operations that are geographically and demographically similar to the one that you're considering.

Most important, speak to a number of other franchisees. The names and addresses of those in your state will be listed in the offering circular. (See Section D.20.)

The more you know about the franchisor, the better. Visit the home office, even if it's in another city or state. Get to know the people you'll be dealing with if you buy. What's the background of the owners, officers and management staff of the franchisor? Do they have the experience and competence to give you promised technical support?

Be especially suspicious of franchises that promise big profits for little work and offer a money-back guarantee. Rarely do you get something for nothing in this world and almost never do you get your money back when business deals go awry.

Learn how much help you can expect from the franchisor in:

• selecting a site

• negotiating a lease

• writing and placing help wanted ads for employees

• interviewing prospective employees

• getting the necessary business licenses

• ordering equipment.

Make sure all key promises are in writing; oral statements don't count. Often they're not legally enforceable, but even where they are, proving in court what someone said years before may be impossible. One good way to get things in writing is to take notes when you talk to the franchisor. Then write up your notes, review them with the franchisor and ask for the signature of someone in authority.

With a larger franchisor, many of your contacts will be with a district or regional manager. Meet these people and find out what they're like.

Ask about whether any franchise operations have closed. Obviously, this a sensitive topic for a franchisor. Ideally, the franchisor will be honest in discussing failures with you, but you can't count on this. If the franchisor seems to be stonewalling, try to get the names of franchisees whose operations failed from existing franchisees and talk to them directly.

Investigate the area where your franchise will be located. Talk to people who work or live nearby to learn more about the behavior and tastes of potential customers. What do other business owners have to say about your customer base? How do they think your franchise will fit into the community?

RECOMMENDED READING

Owning Your Own Franchise by Herbert B. Rust (Prentice-Hall). This book offers practical advice from one who's spent years working in the franchise industry.

Other sources of information include *Franchise Opportunities Handbook* (U.S. Department of Commerce), *Evaluating Franchise Opportunities* (U.S. Small Business Administration), and various publications of the International Franchise Association (IFA). The IFA publishes a membership directory that will give you valuable information on franchisors who are members of the association. You can write to the IFA at 1350 New York Avenue, N.W., Suite 900, Washington, DC 20005 or call (202) 628-8000.

D. The Uniform Franchise Offering Circular

The Federal Trade Commission requires franchisors to give prospective franchisees an offering circular containing details about the franchise. In addition, the franchisor must give you a copy of the proposed franchise agreement and related documents. But FTC rules don't dictate the terms of the deal you and the franchisor agree to. As long as there's full disclosure, the deal can be very one-sided in favor of the franchisor and still be legal.

The FTC does list the items that a franchisor must include in an offering circular and provides a format for the franchisor to follow. Most states that regulate franchise sales prefer a slightly different format called the "Uniform Franchise Offering Circular." Since the FTC says it's okay for a franchisor to use that format, practically every national franchisor does.

Although the FTC requires the disclosure, it doesn't verify or vouch for the information the franchisor discloses. It's up to you to check out anything you don't understand or that sounds too good to be true.

Under FTC rules, if you're a prospective franchisee, the franchisor must give you the offering circular at the earliest of either:

- Your first in-person (face-to-face) meeting with the franchisor, or

- Ten working days (not counting Saturdays and Sundays) before you sign a contract or pay money to the franchisor.

If a franchisor violates these or other FTC rules, there are heavy civil penalties. Also, the FTC may sue the franchisor, on your behalf, for damages or other relief, including cancellation of a franchise contract and refunds.

State laws often provide other avenues of relief for violation of disclosure and other requirements. For example, in some states, you may have the right to sue the franchisor who fails to make disclosures properly. In other words, you won't have to rely on the state to make your case for you.

Knowing that these legal avenues are open to you may give you some peace of mind—but don't relax your guard too much. If the franchisor becomes insolvent or goes into bankruptcy, chances are you'll recover only a minuscule part of your loss, or maybe nothing at all.

Here are the 23 items included in the Uniform Franchise Offering Circular and brief comments about how to think about each:

1. The Franchisor and Any Predecessors

Here you'll learn the name of the franchisor and its predecessors and the name under which the franchisor does business. You'll also find out if the franchisor is a corporation, a partnership or some other type of business.

The franchisor then describes its businesses and the franchises being offered, and lists the business experience of the franchisor and its predecessors. You can find out how long the franchisor has operated the type of business you'd be franchising. You can also learn whether the franchisor has offered franchises in other lines of business and the number of franchises sold.

2. Identity and Business Experience of Persons Affiliated With the Franchisor

The franchisor must list its directors, trustees or general partners, as well as principal officers and other executives. For each, his or her principal occupation and employers must be stated for the past five years.

3. Litigation

This is where you learn the legal history of the franchisor and its people. If the franchisor or its people associated have a history of legal problems, watch out. If the franchisor follows the FTC rule, you'll discover, for example, whether or not there are administrative, criminal or civil cases alleging:

- violation of any franchise law
- fraud
- embezzlement
- restraint of trade
- unfair or deceptive practices or
- misappropriation of property.

If such an action is pending, the offering circular must provide full information.

Furthermore, the franchisor must disclose whether, in the past ten years, the franchisor or its people have been convicted of a felony, pleaded no contest to a felony charge or have been held liable in a civil action involving any of the offenses listed above. And there's more. If the franchisor or associated person is subject to an injunction (court order) relating to a franchise or involving any laws on securities, antitrust, trade regulation or trade practice, the franchisor must disclose this information. This can provide an early warning of potential problems.

Don't rely on the franchisor's explanations of lawsuits involving the company. You can look at the court files, which are open to the public and identify all litigants. Call the people on the other side and get their version of events.

4. Bankruptcy

The franchisor must state whether the franchisor or its officers have gone through bankruptcy or been reorganized due to insolvency during the past 15 years. The information required is far-reaching. The franchisor must disclose if any officer or general partner was a principal officer of any company or a general partner of any partnership that went bankrupt or was reorganized due to insolvency within one year after the officer or general partner was associated with the company or partnership.

5. Franchisee's Initial Fee or Other Initial Payment

Read this section carefully to learn how much you'll be charged when you sign the franchise agreement and whether you'll be paying a lump sum or installments. The franchisor must tell how it will use or apply your franchise fee or initial payment and under what circumstances your money is refundable.

If the franchisor doesn't charge an identical initial franchise fee or other initial payment to each franchisee, the franchisor must tell what method or formula is used to determine the fee or payment.

6. Other Fees

Here's where you get details about required fees. (See the list in Section A.) The franchisor must set out the formula used to compute fees and the conditions for refunds.

7. Franchisee's Initial Investment

These are estimates (or a high-low range) of expenses you'll be responsible for. You'll be told who the payments are made to, when the payments are determined and the conditions for refunds. If part of your initial investment may be financed, you'll learn the details, including interest rates.

Listed expenses include those for:

- real estate, regardless of how it's financed and whether it's bought or leased
- equipment, fixtures, other fixed assets, construction, remodeling, leasehold improvements and decorating costs
- inventory required to begin operation
- security deposits, other prepaid expenses and working capital required to commence operation
- any other payments you must make to start operations.

Don't invest everything in a franchise. These fees can add up to far more than you first expected and dangerously stretch your budget. Never put every last cent into a franchise. Even with an honest franchisor, there's a good chance you won't make any money the first year. Keep enough money in reserve to live on during the start-up phase. And always be wary about pledging your house for a loan needed to buy a franchise. It's one thing to risk your savings; it's quite another to risk the roof over your family's head.

8. Obligations of Franchisee To Purchase or Lease From Designated Sources

Here, the franchisor states whether you are obligated to purchase or lease from the franchisor—or companies designated by the franchisor—any of the following: goods, services, supplies, fixtures, equipment, inventory or real estate.

The franchisor also must say if and how the franchisor may derive income from these required purchases or leases. As mentioned in Section A, many franchisors mark up the products they require their franchisees to buy from them.

9. Obligations of Franchisee To Purchase or Lease in Accordance With Specifications orFrom Approved Suppliers

Will the franchisor require you to purchase goods, services, supplies, equipment or anything else according to the franchisor's specifications? Or lease those goods or services from suppliers approved by the franchisor? If so, the franchisor must give details including how specifications are issued and changed and how approval is granted or revoked to suppliers. Check with existing franchisees. Do they say the quality of the franchisor's goods and services is good? Or do they sing the blues?

10. Financing Arrangements

Look for the terms and conditions of any financing arrangements offered to help franchisees afford the purchase. It's important to know if the franchisor sells or assigns notes and contracts to a third party. If you're dealing directly with the franchisor in financing arrangements, you can often withhold payment if the franchisor isn't meeting its obligations to you. But if the note or financing contract has been transferred to somebody else, you may be obligated to pay regardless of how poorly the franchisor is performing.

 Beware of finance changes. Paying finance charges and interest on notes held by the franchisor is a real financial burden. If you can't afford to pay all of the franchise fees up front, maybe you shouldn't buy the franchise. Think long and hard before you pledge your house as security for these obligations—and before you ask your spouse or a relative to be a co-signer or guarantor of the debt.

11. Obligations of the Franchisor

What are the franchisor's obligations to you before you open your franchise business? How will the franchisor select a location for your business? What's the typical length of time between the signing of the franchise agreement and the first payment of any money for the franchise and the opening of your business? What kind of assistance must the franchisor give you once your business is operating?

Look for detailed answers to these questions as well as a description of the training program the franchisor will provide, including: the location, length and content of the training program; when the training program will be conducted; experience that instructors have had with the franchisor; any charges for the training; the extent that you'll be responsible for travel and living expenses of people enrolled in the training program; and whether any additional training programs or refresher courses are available or required.

12. Exclusive Area or Territory

Here the franchisor describes whether or not you have any territorial protection. Check to see if the franchisor has established another franchisee or company-owned outlet in your territory, or has that right in the future. Obviously, your business will be in trouble if the franchisor defines your exclusive territory very narrowly and then floods the market with outlets offering similar products or services.

If you have exclusive rights in a territory, you may have to achieve a certain sales volume or market penetration to keep your exclusive rights. Make sure you understand under what conditions your area or territory can be altered.

13. Trademarks, Service Marks, Trade Names, Logotypes and Commercial Symbols

Most likely your franchise will require you to use the franchisor's trademarks, service marks, trade names, logotypes or other commercial symbols. Fine. In many ways, these represent much of the value of a franchise. The franchisor must tell you in the offering circular whether or not the franchisor's trademarks and symbols are registered with the U.S. Patent Office and with appropriate state agencies. If they're not, don't buy a franchise.

The franchisor must also describe any agreements, administrative proceedings or court cases that may affect your right to use these trademarks and symbols.

Franchisors should stand behind their trade names and trademarks. Even if a trademark is properly registered, it can still be challenged in court by a company that used it before the franchisor used it or registered it. Make sure that your franchisor is obligated in writing to defend any challenges against its names and trademarks and to indemnify you against any damage awards for using them. The franchisor should also agree to reimburse you for out-of-pocket expenses if you have to replace signs and print new

supplies because of an adverse court ruling regarding names or trademarks.

14. Patents and Copyrights

The franchisor must give full details about any patents or copyrights that relate to the franchise and the terms and conditions under which you can use them.

15. Obligation of the Franchisee To Participate Personally in the Actual Operation of the Franchise Business

Some franchisors permit someone to own a franchise without actively participating in the operation of the business. Other franchisors want the owner fully involved. The franchisor must state whether or not you must participate personally in operating the franchise business, and also whether or not the franchisor recommends that you participate.

Often a franchisor allows a franchisee to send a manager to be trained.

16. Restrictions on Goods and Services Offered by Franchisee

If you're going to be restricted in the goods or services you can offer or the customers you can sell to, this must be spelled out in the offering circular. Find out if you'll be required to carry the full range of the franchisor's products. For example, with a food franchise, do you have to offer the full menu? Can you add items to the menu?

17. Renewal, Termination, Repurchase, Modification and Assignment of the Franchise Agreement and Related Information

You're entitled to know the conditions under which you may renew, extend or terminate your franchise and also the conditions under which the franchisor may refuse to deal with you. (See Section E.8 for more on termination.)

18. Arrangements With Public Figures

Some franchisors use celebrities to promote franchise operations. The franchisor must disclose any compensation or other benefit given or promised to any public figures for using their names or endorsements. You also need to be told the extent to which celebrities are involved in the actual management or control of the franchisor and how much—if anything—they have invested in the franchise operation.

19. Representations Regarding Earnings Capability

The franchisor has a choice. It can disclose actual or potential sales, profits or earnings of franchisees. Or it can say nothing on the subject—which is what most franchisors choose to do. If the franchisor does make any earnings claims, the offering circular must describe the factual basis and material assumptions that underlie the claims.

For earnings claims to make sense, you need to know the franchise locations that the numbers are based on and the number of years that they have been in operation. Actual figures are, of course, more helpful than hypothetical projections. Before you buy a franchise, have your accountant go over the numbers with a fine tooth comb and check with a number of existing franchisees to see how they're doing.

20. Information Regarding Franchisees

The information in this part of the circular can be a gold mine if you take advantage of it. The franchisor must list the total number of franchise locations and state how many of them were in operation when the offering circular was prepared and how many are covered by franchise agreements but are not yet in operation. The franchisor also must list the names, addresses and telephone numbers of all franchises in your state.

A company with a hundred franchises up and running has had a chance to test its business formula and has experience in helping franchisees get started. A company with only eight or ten units in operation is relatively young and still has a lot to learn. But be leery of a franchise that's merely on the drawing board and isn't yet in actual operation. It may never open and, even if it does, may not prosper. Obviously, a franchise that's not yet open can't give you hard information about sales or profitability.

In addition, the franchisor must tell you how many franchises the franchisor has canceled or terminated in the last three years; how many have not been renewed by the franchisor; and how many have been reacquired by the franchisor.

Contact franchisees in your state or in nearby states. Ask questions: "How's it working out? Was it a good deal? Would you do it again? Are you making a profit? How much?" Franchisees sometimes feel locked in and are reluctant to admit that they used bad judgment in buying a franchise, but they might level with you if you ask, "Would you feel comfortable recommending that I put my life savings into this deal?"

Ask franchisees if they get help and support from the home office and how often they see someone from headquarters. Spend a day or two at a few franchises. Picture yourself in that setting. How does the system seem to be working? If there's a franchisee organization, see if you can attend meetings and get old newsletters. Don't rely on what one or two franchisees tell you—they could have unrevealed ties to the franchisor or be unrealistically positive because they're trying to unload their own franchise or will be paid a commission if they help reel you in.

21. Financial Statements

The franchisor must file audited financial statements showing the condition of the company. Unless you have experience in interpreting financial statements, get an accountant with experience with franchises to interpret the figures and help you develop tough questions. You want a franchisor to be financially strong enough to follow through on training commitments, trademark protection and support services. If a franchisor is financially weak—many are—and folds overnight, your franchise may not be worth much.

To find an accountant with the right experience, seek recommendations from owners of successful local franchises who have been in business for a while.

22. Contracts

The franchisor must attach to the offering circular a copy of all agreements that you'll sign if you purchase the franchise. This includes lease agreements, option agreements and purchase agreements. Read them carefully, and don't sign until you understand everything.

23. Acknowledgment of Receipt by Prospective Franchisee

The last page of the offering circular is a detachable receipt, which you sign as evidence that you received the offering circular.

E. The Franchise Agreement

If you buy a franchise, you and the franchisor will sign a long document called a franchise agreement. There probably will be other documents to sign at the same time, but the franchise agreement is far and away the most important. Whether or not any terms of the agreement are negotiable depends on whether the franchisor is new or long established and on prevailing market conditions. A new franchisor eager to penetrate the market may be more flexible and willing to make concessions than an established franchisor whose franchises are in hot demand.

Again, if the franchisor has made any promises to you, make sure that they're in the franchise agreement. Otherwise, chances are you won't be able to enforce them.

Let's look at a few sensitive areas of a franchise deal that you must be aware of before you plunk down your money and sign an agreement.

1. Franchise Fee

Your personal liability for the franchise fee and other franchise obligations is a crucial part of the deal.

Does the franchise agreement allow you to avoid personal liability for franchise-related debts by forming a corporation to serve as the franchisee? Or does the franchisor require you (and perhaps your spouse as well) to be personally responsible for all franchise obligations? At the risk of being repetitive, I strongly recommend against pledging your house or other assets as security for payment of the franchise fee. (See Section D.5 for how the franchise fee is dealt with in the offering circular.)

2. Advertising Fees

If the franchise agreement requires you to pay an advertising fee to the franchisor, make sure that part of that fee is earmarked for local advertising that you'll have some control over. Perhaps the franchisor will agree to match any money you spend on local advertising. This is especially important if your franchise will be in an area where there are only a few other franchise locations. Otherwise the franchisor may spend all the advertising money 1,000 miles away where there are more franchisees.

3. Royalty Fees

Typically, the royalty fees you pay the franchisor are a percentage of your gross sales. (See Section A.) They may, however, be a flat weekly or monthly charge. Be cautious about a franchisor who charges a small initial franchise fee but then charges you a high percentage of monthly sales.

Example: Compare two fast food operations. Franchisor A charges an initial fee of $5,000 and monthly royalties of 8% (in addition to advertising fees). Franchisor B charges a franchise fee of $20,000 and monthly royalties of 5% (not including advertising). Let's say that each franchise has annual sales of $500,000. In the first year, each franchisee will pay $45,000 to the franchisor. But look at succeeding years. Franchisee A will pay $40,000 each year to its franchisor, while Franchisee B pays only $25,000.

Franchise royalties are costly. Remember that many franchises simply are bad business deals. In a world where it's very hard for any small business to make a 10% profit, giving a huge chunk of money to the franchisor as a royalty often doesn't make sense.

4. Hidden Costs

Read the franchise agreement carefully to uncover any hidden costs—many of which are mentioned earlier in this chapter. (See Section A.) It's to your advantage if the income received by the franchisor is primarily based on royalties. That way, the franchisor has a direct interest in making your business profitable. The franchisor's incentive to promote your profitability is somewhat reduced if the franchisor begins to see itself as primarily your landlord or supplier rather than as a business partner.

If you must buy equipment, supplies or inventory from the franchisor, make sure that the prices you'll pay are competitive with those charged by outside sources. You don't want to sign up with a franchisor who plans to gouge you on these items—especially if they're of iffy quality. Yes, the franchisor has a legitimate interest in seeing that all franchisees run standardized operations, and this can require that certain items such as food supplies be exactly the same. But this need for specialization should be balanced against your need to make a decent profit. Franchisors often allow you to buy equipment and goods through an approved supplier, as long as the franchisor's specifications are met.

5. Quotas

Some franchise agreements require you to meet sales quotas. For example, your agreement might state that if you don't maintain a certain volume of business, you'll no longer have the right to an exclusive territory. In some cases, the franchisor may also reserve the right to terminate your franchise if quotas aren't met. Watch out for this one. If the quotas aren't realistic or it takes you longer than you expected to master the business, you face the horrible prospect of losing some or all of your investment.

6. The Franchise Term

Typically, a franchise agreement provides for a term of five to 15 years. Beware of an agreement that states that the franchise can be terminated "at will" by the franchisor upon written notice. See Section E.8 for a further discussion of termination provisions.

Also carefully study your renewal rights. Is renewal entirely in the hands of the franchisor? If you do renew, will a renewal fee be charged? Will you have to sign a new franchise agreement containing whatever terms are in effect when you renew? This could change the whole ball game, because ten years from now, when you go to renew, a new franchise agreement could have higher royalties or advertising fees.

Under some franchise agreements, the franchisor can require a franchisee to install expensive improvements in the business premises—even beyond the start-up installations. If the franchise agreement doesn't grant you the automatic right to renew your franchise on the same terms, seek language limiting the franchisor's right to force you to put expensive improvements into the business beyond the initial alterations. You want to be sure that if you're forced to put more money into the premises, you have enough time to recover that investment.

7. Assignment

Usually, a franchise agreement says that you first need the written approval of the franchisor to transfer or assign your franchise agreement to someone else? But what happens if you have a serious health problem that prevents you from running the franchise? Could you transfer the franchise to a family member? If you die, would your spouse automatically be able to continue the business for you?

And if you die, is there a deadline (such as 90 days or six months) during which the franchise must be transferred to a new owner to avoid termination of the franchise by the franchisor? Find out how long it takes, if someone wants to buy your franchise, to learn whether the franchisor approves or disapproves of the sale.

One way of dealing with the possible death of the owner of a franchise is a clause allowing your survivors a period of time to elect to keep and operate the business, as long as they meet the franchisor's training requirements.

Some franchisors may be willing to give you the right to sell, subject to a right of first refusal in the franchisor to meet any bona fide offer. For example, if someone comes to you with an offer to buy your franchise, you would have to give the franchisor 30 or 60 days to meet the terms of the purchase.

8. Termination

Study carefully what the franchise agreement says about the franchisor's right to terminate the franchise. If the franchisor can terminate your franchise because of defaults or breaches of the agreement, you want to be notified in writing of the franchisor's intent and given at least 30 days in which to clear the defaults or correct the breaches. On the other side of the coin, you may want to have the right to terminate the agreement yourself if the franchisor is in default.

Commonly, the franchisor has the right to terminate the franchise if you fail to operate the business, understate your gross revenues, don't pay royalties when due or participate in a competing business.

 Termination without good cause. Watch out for franchise agreements that give the franchisor the right to terminate a franchise whether there is good reason or not. It's harsh and unfair—so much so that 16 states limit the right of a franchisor to unilaterally terminate a franchisee. Typically, under such statutes, the franchisor would have to show "good cause" before terminating you.

9. Competition

It's critical to know where you stand in terms of competition with other franchisees. Typically, the franchisor grants you a protected territory for your franchise operations. Within your territory, your franchisor agrees not to grant another franchise or operate a business itself. If you don't have a protected territory, will the franchisor at least give you first crack at buying any proposed new location near yours?

A franchise agreement also usually restricts you from competing in a similar business during the term of the franchise and for several years after a termination. Generally, courts enforce these restrictive covenants if they're reasonable as to time and geographic scope. Franchisors want to make sure their trade secrets aren't misused. You, on the other hand, don't want to give up your right to earn a living in a field that you know best. So take a close look at the non-competition language and make sure that it doesn't restrict you too severely. Maybe you can live with a provision that says that you won't go into a competing business in the same county as your franchise for two years after a termination; maybe you can't.

F. Solving Problems With a Franchisor

If you do opt for a franchise, try to keep open the lines of communication with your franchisor. Talk about problems as soon as they begin to emerge. It's expensive, time consuming and quite often frustrating or even hopeless to litigate with a franchisor. Often, several franchisees can gain negotiating power by banding together or even forming a franchisee's organization to try to work out their mutual grievances with a franchisor. If that doesn't work, look into whether the FTC— or perhaps the attorney general who enforces the franchise laws in your state—will take up the cudgels for you.

As a final resort, hire a lawyer familiar with franchisee rights to evaluate your prospects of winning a lawsuit. Be aware that franchise law is a relatively specialized area; not all business lawyers are experienced in this field.

Insuring Your Business

9

A well-designed insurance program can protect your business from many types of perils. Consider the following:

- A fire destroys all the furniture, fixtures and equipment in your restaurant.

- Burglars steal $75,000 worth of computer equipment you use in your book publishing business.

- A customer visiting your yogurt store slips on the just-washed floor and shatters her elbow.

- On the way to an office supply store to pick up some fax paper, one of your employees runs a stop sign and injures a child.

- A house painter has a severe allergic reaction to a solvent that your company manufactures and distributes.

- One of your employees is hospitalized for four weeks with a severe back injury she received while trying to lift a heavy package.

- The building where you're located is severely damaged by a wind storm. You're forced to close your doors for two months while repairs are made. In addition to having to pay $35,000 for continuing business expenses, you lose the $25,000 of profits you expected for that period—a total loss of $60,000.

- A client installs a lawn sprinkling system based on specifications you recommended as a landscape architect. Because you hadn't checked soil conditions carefully, the system malfunctions, flooding your client's basement and ruining the antique furniture stored there. Your client sues you for professional negligence.

Maybe none of these will happen to your business—but unless you consider yourself permanently exempt from Murphy's Law ("What Can Go Wrong Will Go Wrong"), don't bet on it. Fortunately, insurance is available to cover each of these events and for many, if not most of them, is reasonably cost-effective.

Not every small business needs every type of coverage. In fact, a business that tried to buy insurance to cover all insurable risks probably wouldn't have money left over to do anything else. Deciding on insurance coverage usually involves some difficult choices. Here are some general rules to start with:

- Get enough property and liability coverage to protect yourself from common claims. These are the most important kinds of insurance for a small business.

- Buy insurance against serious risks where the insurance is reasonably priced.

- Keep costs down by selecting high deductibles.

- Self-insure if insurance is prohibitively expensive or the particular risk is highly unlikely.

- Adopt aggressive policies to reduce the likelihood of insurance claims, particularly in areas where you're self-insured.

Sections C, D and E look at the standard types of insurance available to small businesses and how you can put together a reasonable insurance program.

A. Working With an Insurance Agent

Find and work with a knowledgeable insurance agent—one who takes the time to analyze your business operations and to come up with a sensible program for your company. Generally, it's best to work with a single insurance agent for all your business needs so that coverages can be coordinated. But be sure to find out whether any agent you're speaking to is locked into one insurance company. If so, it may be wise to look elsewhere. The agent you choose should be willing to obtain quotes from several companies so that you don't pay more than is necessary.

To find a competent insurance agent or broker, talk to local business people, particularly those in your line of work. Other people in the same field should be able to give you good leads on insurance agents. Working with an agent who knows your business is advantageous because that person is already a fair way along the learning curve when it comes to helping you select an affordable and appropriate package.

Example: Louisa, who owns a plant nursery, wants insurance coverage for risks associated with bugs and toxic substances. She finds an insurance agent who already works with similar businesses. The agent knows what insurance is available for a plant nursery and how to tailor the coverage to Louisa's business so that it will be affordable.

INSURANCE TERMINOLOGY

In some parts of the country, the term "insurance agent" refers to a person who represents a specific company, and "insurance broker" refers to a person who is free to sell insurance offered by various companies. Elsewhere, the term "insurance agent" is used more broadly to cover both types of representatives—and that's how it's used in this chapter.

Steer clear of an agent who, without learning the specifics of your business, whips out a package policy and claims it will solve all your problems. Yes, the insurance industry has developed some excellent packages that cover the basic needs of various businesses. For example, there are packages offered for offices, retail sales operations, service businesses, hotels, industrial and processing companies and contractors. One of these may meet your needs, but neither you nor your insurance agent will know for sure until the agent asks you a lot of questions and thoroughly understands your business. If the agent is unable or unwilling to tailor your coverage to your particular business, find someone else.

Be frank with your agent when discussing your business. Reveal all areas of unusual risk. If you fail to disclose all the facts, you may not get the coverage you need or, in some circumstances, the insurance company may later take the position that you misrepresented the nature of your operation and, for that reason, deny you coverage for exceptional risks. Make sure you have a clear understanding of what your insurance policy covers and what's excluded. Does the policy exclude damage from a leaking sprinkler system? From a boiler explosion? From an earthquake? If so, and these are risks you face, find out if they can be covered by paying a small extra premium.

Also ask how much the agent will help in processing claims if you do have a loss. Ideally, the insurance company should have a local or regional office that's readily accessible to you. That's normally a better arrangement and more personal than dealing with an insurance company that hires an independent claim service to investigate and deal with claims. It's a good idea to talk to several agents before making a final selection. Ask for written recommendations on comparable coverage and what the cost will be. There should be no charge for providing this information, because the agents will be eager to get your business.

Is the Insurance Company Solvent?

In recent years, many insurance companies have become insolvent. If you wind up with a company that goes broke and you have a loss covered by a policy, you may receive only a paltry portion of the coverage that you paid for or none at all. The best way to minimize this risk is to work with a company that appears in good financial shape.

You can check out insurers in these standard reference works, which rate insurance companies for financial solvency:

- *Best's Insurance Reports* (Property-Casualty Insurance Section)

- *Moody's Bank and Financial Manual* (Volume 2)

- *Duff & Phelps* (Insurance Company Claims-Paying Ability Rating Guide)

- *Standard & Poor's*

Each publication has strengths and weaknesses. In my opinion, the best overall sources on the list are *Moody's* and *Duff & Phelps*. Some commentators think that *Best's* is too lenient in its ratings. And *Standard & Poor's* is sometimes incomplete because some companies prefer not to pay the huge fee it takes for a listing. Your insurance agent should be able to give you the latest ratings from these publications. You can also check the reference department at a public library.

Also consider the services offered by Weiss Inc., which is reputed to be tougher (more conservative) in its ratings. Weiss offers the following reports on the solvency of an insurance company:

- $15 over-the-phone rating

- $25 short-form written report

- $45 long-form written report.

You can call Weiss toll-free at (800) 289-9222 and charge the report to your credit card.

B. Property Coverage

In considering property coverage, there are four main issues to think about:

- What business property should you insure?

- What perils will the property be insured against? In other words, under what conditions will you be entitled to receive payment from the insurance company?

- What dollar amount of insurance should you carry? (Obviously, the higher the amount, the higher the premiums. You don't want to waste money on insurance but you do want to carry enough so that a loss wouldn't jeopardize your business.)

- Should you buy coverage for replacement cost or for the present value of the property?

 Section B.6 outlines property insurance from a renter's point of view. Renters may want to skip ahead, then return here and read the general information on how property insurance works.

1. Property Covered

Your insurance policy will contain a section called Building and Personal Property Coverage Form, which lists exactly what property is covered. If you own the building you're occupying, be sure the building is covered, including:

- completed additions

- permanently installed fixtures, machinery and equipment

- outdoor fixtures (such as pole lights)

- property used to maintain or service the building (such as fire extinguishing equipment).

The policy may also cover additions under construction as well as materials, equipment, supplies and temporary structures on or within 100 feet of the main building.

Be sure that your business personal property is also covered. A typical policy covers the following items located on the business premises:

- furniture and fixtures
- machinery and equipment
- inventory
- all other personal property used in the business (such as technical books and cassette tapes)
- leased personal property, if you're contractually obligated to insure it
- personal property of others that's in your custody.

 Be sure that everything is covered. Check carefully to be sure the policy covers all the types of personal property that you own or expect to own: furniture, equipment, goods that you sell, products that you manufacture, and raw materials used in the manufacturing process.

Typically, various items are excluded, such as accounting records, currency, deeds and vehicles held for sale. If you need coverage on excluded items, you can usually arrange it, for an additional premium.

2. Perils Covered

More than 90% of the time, property insurance for small businesses are written in one of three forms: Basic Form, Broad Form and Special Form. Special Form coverage is the most common and affords the best protection.

Whichever policy you decide on, read it carefully before you pay for it—not just when you've suffered a loss. You may discover that some coverage is narrower than it first seemed. For example, smoke loss may refer only to loss caused by a faulty heating or cooking unit; it may not cover smoke damage from industrial equipment. Similarly, an explosion may not include a burst steam boiler. Fortunately, most insurance policies today are written in plain English so you should have little problem in understanding what's covered and what isn't. If you need coverage

not provided in the policy, talk to your agent about how to add it on.

Basic Form coverage includes losses caused by fire, lightning, explosion, windstorm or hail, smoke, aircraft or vehicles (but not loss or damage caused by vehicles you own or operate in the course of your business), riot, vandalism, sprinkler leaks, sinkholes and volcanoes. The policy defines these perils—and also lists some exclusions, such as nuclear hazards, power failures or mud slides.

Broad Form coverage contains everything that's in the Basic Form and adds protection from a few more perils, including breakage of glass (that is part of a building or structure), falling objects, weight of snow or ice and water damage. Again, these terms are defined in the policy and, again, exclusions are listed.

Special Form policies are constructed differently than Basic and Broad Form policies and offer wider and slightly more expensive coverage. Instead of listing specific perils such as fire and lightning, Special Form policies simply say that your business property is covered against all risks of physical loss unless the policy specifically excludes or limits the loss. This type of policy offers the most protection. For example, it's a convenient way to insure against loss by theft, which isn't covered by Basic and Broad Form policies (Section D.2 discusses theft insurance).

 If you need additional coverage. If you're concerned about property loss caused by perils not covered or, in the case of a Special Form policy, excluded from an insurance policy, you can often get the additional coverage through an endorsement (add-on page) to the policy by paying an additional premium. For example, such coverage is usually available for losses due to earthquakes and floods.

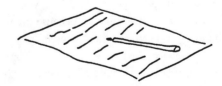

Earthquake and Flood Insurance

Earthquake insurance can be handled through a separate policy or an endorsement to Basic, Broad or Special Form coverage. Deductibles in an earthquake endorsement are typically stated as a percentage—such as 10%—rather than as a dollar amount. This means that the higher your policy limit, the bigger the deductible. As a result, some business people choose a $200,000 policy with a $20,000 deductible rather than a $400,000 policy with a $40,000 deductible. They reason that the deductible on the latter policy is so high they're unlikely to ever collect anything.

Flood insurance, by contrast, is usually handled through a separate policy called "Difference in Conditions."

Combining Property and Liability Insurance in One Policy. You can purchase property insurance as a stand-alone and buy a separate stand-alone policy for liability coverage (discussed in Section C), or you can buy a policy that combines both coverages. It's often—but not always—cheaper to buy a combination policy. Here's where comparison shopping definitely pays off.

3. Amount of Coverage

Be sure to carry enough insurance on the building to rebuild it. But there's no need to insure the total value of your real property (the legal term that includes land and buildings), because land doesn't burn. Especially if you're in an area where land is very valuable, this is a big consideration.

If you're in doubt as to how much it would cost you to rebuild, have an appraisal made so you know that your idea of value is realistic. Because the value of the building and other property may increase, it's wise to get a new appraisal every few years. Your insurance agent should be able to help you do this.

Usually it's best to insure your property for 100% of its value. If doing this is prohibitively expensive, consider a policy with a higher deductible rather than underinsuring.

Underinsuring to get a reduced premium is a false economy for several reasons. Not only are you not covered if you suffer a total loss, but it may also reduce your ability to recover for a smaller loss. This is because most insurance policies carry a co-insurance clause which states that to recover the full policy amount, you have to carry insurance to cover at least 80% (this percentage may vary) of the property's replacement cost or actual cash value. If you don't, you become a co-insurer if there's a loss, even if it's less than the policy maximum; the policy will only pay off a percentage of its face value.

Example 1: Fluoro Corporation owns a $100,000 building. If Fluoro carries $80,000 worth of insurance or more, the insurance company will pay Fluoro for the full amount of any loss up to the policy limit. For example, if the loss is $50,000 Fluoro will get the full $50,000. If the loss is $90,000, Fluoro will receive only $80,000, the policy limit.

Example 2: Pluto Associates owns a similar $100,000 building. To get a reduced premium, the partners decide to carry only $40,000 worth of insurance. If there's a fire and Pluto has a loss of $20,000, its insurance company will pay only $10,000. Because Pluto carried only half of the 80% figure mentioned in the policy, it's entitled to only a proportional payment.

4. Replacement Cost vs. Current Value

Historically, in case of a loss, a basic fire insurance contract covered the actual current value of the property, not its full replacement value. Today, policies are routinely available with replacement cost coverage. This is the coverage you want.

Example: Sure-Lock Corporation owns a 20-year-old building. The current cash value of the building (the amount someone would pay to buy it) is $150,000. But if the building burned down, Sure-Lock would have to pay $200,000 to replace it. If Sure-Lock buys insurance based on the building's cash value and the policy has an 80%

co-insurance clause, the company will need to insure the building for $120,000. If Sure-Lock buys insurance based on replacement cost, it will need to insure for $160,000, which is 80% of $200,000.

The real cost of insurance is reduced when you consider that insurance premiums for a business are a recognized business expense—which means they are tax-deductible.

5. Ordinance or Law Coverage

If you're purchasing insurance for an older building—either because you own it or your lease requires it—understand that a normal Basic Form, Broad Form or Special Form policy designed to replace your existing building should it be destroyed probably won't be adequate. The problem is that legal requirements adopted since the building was constructed will normally require that a stronger, safer, more fire resistant building be constructed. Doing this can cost far more than simply replacing the old building. To cope with this possibility, you want a policy that will not only replace the building but pay for all legally required upgrades. This coverage is called "Ordinance or Law Coverage."

Example: Time Warp Inc., sells antique furniture and building materials removed from old homes. In keeping with its image of days gone by, Time Warp does business in a 100-year-old building in a historic part of town. Time Warp carries insurance for the full replacement cost, $100,000. One day a fire destroys 50% of the building. The insurance pays $50,000 toward reconstruction, but the Time Warp owners learn to their dismay that re-building will cost much more and that the additional costs are not covered by their insurance policy. The items excluded by their typical property insurance policy include the following:

- *The cost of meeting current health and safety codes.* The old building was of wood frame construction and lacked an elevator and sprinkler system. That was OK before the fire. The building pre-dated the health and safety ordinances and was "grandfathered"—specifically exempted from the new construction

requirements. After the fire, it's a whole new ball game. In re-building, Time Warp must spend an additional $100,000 for masonry construction, an elevator and a sprinkler system required by current health and safety codes.

- *The cost of rebuilding the undamaged portion of the building.* The local ordinance requires that if a building built before current codes is destroyed by fire to the extent of 50% or more, the entire building must be replaced. The cost of replacing the undamaged 50% of the building is another $200,000.

- *The cost of demolition.* The local ordinance requires that, because of the extent of damage, the entire building—both the damaged and undamaged portions—must be torn down before reconstruction begins. That will cost another $25,000.

"Ordinance or Law Coverage" would pay for all of these items.

6. Tenant's Insurance

If you're a tenant, read the insurance portion of your lease. You may have agreed to insure the building and protect the landlord against any liability suits based on your activities, in which case you'll need the type of coverage an owner would carry. This is available through a renters commercial package policy, which also provides routine product liability coverage for businesses not involved in hazardous activities and allows you to name your landlord as an additional insured.

Even if you haven't agreed to provide insurance coverage in your lease, a renter's commercial policy can make excellent sense. Not only will it cover any of your "leasehold improvements," such as paneling and partitions, but it will also cover damage to the premises caused by your negligence. For example, if the building you rent suffers fire or water damage as a result of an employee's negligence (a fire in an area where food is prepared spreads and damages the walls and ceiling), you may be liable. This is true even if the building owner is insured and recovers from his or her insurance company, because the owner's insurer has the right to try and recover.

What the insurer will pay you for loss to lease-hold improvements is based not on replacement value but on what's called the "use interest" in the improvements. Basically, the insurance company looks at how long you would have had the use of the improvements and reimburses you for the use you lose.

Example: Court Reporting Associates (CRA) installs $20,000 worth of paneling in their rented offices. They have a five-year lease with an option to renew for five more years—which, for insurance purposes, is treated as a ten-year lease. Two years into the lease, a fire destroys the paneling. Because CRA used up 20% of the lease before the fire, it will receive payment for only 80% of value of the paneling.

Insurance clauses in leases vary widely. (See Chapter 10, Section D.13, for more on such clauses.)

C. Liability Insurance

The second major category of insurance coverage for a small business is liability insurance. Your business can be legally liable to people injured and for property damaged because you or your employees didn't use reasonable care. For example, if a customer falls on a slippery floor and then sues you, you may be liable because you negligently failed to provide safe premises.

As you probably know, when it comes to personal injuries, judges are broadening the scope of what people can sue for—and juries are increasingly generous in awarding damages. Because an injured person can collect not only for lost wages and medical bills but also for such intangibles as pain, suffering and mental anguish, a single personal injury verdict against your business has the potential to wipe it out. For that reason, unless you have a very unusual business that has no personal contact with customers, suppliers or anyone else, your insurance program should include liability coverage.

Some intentional acts not involving bodily injuries are also usually covered under the liability portions of an insurance policy. Examples are libel, slander, defamation, false imprisonment and false arrest.

Toxic Waste Clean-up

Suppose the government orders your company to clean up a toxic waste problem on your property. This can and does regularly occur even if the pollution occurred years before you bought the property. Will your liability insurance policy cover the clean-up costs (called the "response costs")? Most courts that have considered this question ruled that response costs are covered by a liability insurance policy, but a significant minority have ruled otherwise. If you have a business or own property that by any stretch of the imagination could become involved in a toxic waste or pollution problem, try to find out exactly how far your liability coverage extends in environmental situations. You may need to buy supplementary coverage (if available and affordable) to cover this risk.

Keep yourself informed on this subject. It's likely that faced with court decisions saying that general liability coverage requires insurance companies to pay for response costs under clean-up orders, insurance companies will tighten up their policy language to exclude these expenses. You may need to buy special coverage if your business faces the possibility of a clean-up order.

---

1. General Liability Policies

Liability policies are designed to protect you against lawsuit judgments up to the amount of the policy limit plus the cost of defending the lawsuit. They provide coverage for a host of common perils, including customers and guests falling and getting mangled by your front door or otherwise being injured. Liability policies usually state a dollar limit per occurrence and an aggregate dollar limit for the policy year. For example, your policy may say that it will pay $500,000 per occurrence for personal injury or a total of $1 million in any one policy year.

 Excluded claims. Punitive damages—damages intended to punish your business for willful or malicious behavior rather than compensate the injured person—are not covered by the typical general liability policy. And liability coverage won't protect your business if an employee intentionally assaults a customer. In addition, a general liability policy doesn't cover injuries caused by defective products or motor vehicles, or by an employer's liability for injuries received by workers on the job. Special coverage for these types of liability is discussed in the next three sub-sections.

As noted, both building owners and tenants may purchase liability coverage separately or as part of a package policy that also provides a number of other types of insurance, including fire insurance for the building itself.

2. Products Liability Insurance

Products liability insurance covers liability for injuries caused by products you design, manufacture or sell. You may be liable to a person injured by a defective product or one that came without adequate instructions or warnings. Product liability insurance can be very expensive, but if your business manufactures, distributes or sells a product that may injure people, you should seriously consider it. For example, if you manufacture medical instruments or chemicals, you'll definitely want to consider this type coverage. If you're a retailer and sell products in their original packages and provide no product assembly or service or advice, your exposure is drastically reduced; the manufacturer is primarily liable and the products liability coverage provided by standard renters commercial policies should be adequate.

The amount of products liability insurance that you need depends on the nature of your product and not on your gross sales. Obviously, a company that

sells $2 million of paper clips a year will need less coverage than a firm that manufactures gauges critical to the safe operation of heaters and also has $2 million worth of sales annually.

3. Vehicle Insurance

Make sure your business carries liability insurance not only on its own cars and trucks but also on employees' cars and trucks when those vehicles are used for business purposes. This coverage is known as Employer's Non-Owned Automobile Liability and is relatively inexpensive—a premium of $65 to $100 may buy you coverage of $1 million for one year. Vehicle insurance isn't provided under general liability policies.

It wouldn't hurt to check your employees' driving records before you entrust company vehicles to them or send them on business errands using their own cars, but failure to check won't be a problem under most vehicle policies unless the insurance company has listed that employee as an excluded driver. To do this, insurance companies periodically ask businesses for the names of employees who are driving on company business. They then check the names against state driving records. If this results in the discovery of a poor driving record for a particular employee, the insurer will likely exclude that driver from coverage and notify you.

Coverage for injury or property damage while using leased vehicles can be added to either your motor vehicle policy or your general liability policy—which is what a company would do if it owned no vehicles. This is known as Hired Vehicle coverage.

Most vehicle policies also cover physical damage to the car or truck caused by collision, fire or theft.

4. Workers' Compensation Insurance

As the name implies, workers' compensation insurance covers your liability for injuries received by employees on the job. All businesses with employees are required to provide for some kind of workers' compensation coverage.

Usually, an injured worker can't sue your business for negligence. But as a trade-off, he or she can collect specified benefits from your business for work-related injuries whether or not the business was negligent. All the worker must prove is that the injury came about in the course of employment—a concept that has a very broad definition in many states. For example, an employee injured at a company picnic may have a valid workers' compensation claim.

The amount of money that the employee can recover is limited. The worker can recover for medical treatment and lost wages and, in serious cases, for impaired future earning capacity. But there are no awards for pain and suffering or mental anguish. A growing portion of workers' compensation claims, however, result from mental or emotional stress. In California, an employee who proves that as little as 10% of his or her disability was caused by job-related stress can qualify for worker's compensations benefits.

As a sole proprietor, you usually can't be personally covered by workers' compensation insurance for any work-related injuries you sustain; only your employees can be covered. Workers' comp coverage of a partner or of an officer of a small corporation usually isn't required but can be obtained if you choose.

Each state has a law setting out what an employer must do to provide for workers' compensation benefits. Sometimes an employer can self-insure. Usually, that isn't practical for small businesses because they can't afford the type of cash reserve required by state law. Most small businesses buy insurance through a state fund or from a private insurance carrier. Insurance rates are based on the industry and occupation, as well as the size of the payroll. Your business's safety record can also influ-

ence the rate; if you have more accidents than is usually anticipated, your rate is likely to be increased.

Although workers' compensation laws cover virtually all injury claims by an employee against an employer, in a few instances employees can still sue an employer for pain and suffering resulting from a work-related injury. For example, in some states, an employer whose gross negligence or intentional conduct caused an injury can be sued. A second part of a workers' compensation policy (sometimes called Coverage B or employer's liability) insures the employer against liability for these types of claims. I recommend policy limits of $500,000 for most businesses for this coverage.

Workers' compensation insurance is required only for employees—not for independent contractors. (Independent contractors are covered in greater detail in Chapter 12, Section I.) Small businesses sometimes buy services from independent contractors to save money on workers' compensation insurance, as well as taxes and other expenses normally associated with employees. That's fine as long as you correctly label people as independent contractors rather than employees. But if you make a mistake, and a person improperly labeled as an independent contractor is injured while doing work for your business, you may have to pay large sums to cover medical bills and lost wages which should have been covered by workers' compensation insurance.

In addition, you can sometimes have a problem with a properly classified independent contractor who hires employees to perform some work for you. If you hire an independent contractor who has employees, insist on seeing a certificate of insurance establishing that the employees are covered by workers' compensation insurance.

Example: You hire Sharon, who is doing business as Superior Painters, to paint your store. Sharon will be doing the work along with two of her employees. If Sharon doesn't carry workers' compensation insurance for her employees, and any of them are injured on the job, they may be treated as your employees, which would increase your own workers' compensation premiums. Also, have Sharon show you that she has general liability coverage;

if she or one of her employees injures one of your customers while painting your store, such injuries may not be covered by your own insurance.

The Expanding Boundaries of Workers' Comp

Premiums for workers' compensation insurance are on the rise—partly because judges are extending the types of claims for which workers can receive payment. A key factor in many cases is stressful working conditions. Money has been awarded to:

- A worker who suffered a heart attack after an argument with his boss.

- A truck driver who blacked out while driving and was then unable to drive because of anxiety that he might black out again.

- A worker who fainted, fell and suffered a head injury after his supervisor told him he would be transferred to a new department and had to take a pay cut.

Judges have also expanded the right to receive workers' comp in other situations. For example, benefits were awarded to the family of a convenience store clerk who died after getting into a fist fight with a disorderly customer. And a woman who bought a cold tablet from her employer received payments when the tablet caused her to have tremors due to a congenital condition.

In another case, a cocktail waitress at a resort was on her way home when she stopped to help a resort guest who was having car trouble. The guest sexually assaulted her. The waitress was awarded workers' comp for injuries she received in the assault. The court's reasoning: the waitress had been told to be "very cordial and nice to guests." Therefore, her offer of assistance on the road was related to her employment.

D. Other Insurance To Consider

There are many forms of business insurance on the market today. You won't need them all, but some specialized coverage may make sense for your business.

1. Bonds Covering Employee Theft

If you're seriously concerned that employees might embezzle money from the business, look into bonds that cover all workers, including those hired after the bond goes into effect. Then, if an employee steals from you, the bonding company reimburses you for the loss.

2. Crime Coverage

Crime insurance covers losses when the criminal isn't connected with your business. Your policy should cover not only burglary and robbery but also other thefts and loss or disappearance of property. Depending on the kind of business and the part of the country you're in, you may be more concerned about losses by theft than from fire. Computers and other high-tech equipment are relatively lightweight and easy to carry away. A mid-sized publisher or word processing company, for example, could easily suffer a $100,000 loss in a night if its computers were stolen.

Usually, your company's business insurance covers only property owned by the company, not your personal property.

Example: Management Concepts Inc., a small consulting firm, is using an expensive computer that's the personal property of Patricia, the corporation's president. If the computer is stolen from the corporate offices, the corporation's insurance policy normally won't cover it. To protect against this kind of problem, Patricia should sign a Bill of Sale formally transferring legal title to the computer to the corporation. Or she should make sure that the corporation has an insurance policy that specifically protects property of officers or employees that's used in the business.

Probably the most convenient way to insure your business against loss by theft is to purchase the Special Form of property insurance, which includes such coverage (see Section C.1).

If property is stolen from your business, you will, of course, have to document the loss. I recommend that you keep a computerized list of your business property, updated periodically. And keep a copy at home or in a fire-proof box in case the computer and your records get stolen or destroyed.

3. Business Interruption Insurance

If your business property is damaged or destroyed and you can't use it, your business losses will far exceed the cost of repairing or replacing the damaged property. Your business may be unable to function until you can find a new location and purchase more goods. For example, if you're in California and an earthquake levels your retail warehouse, or if your business is in Indiana and a tornado rips the roof off your store, or a fire burns you out, you may be out of business for weeks or months while your inventory is replaced and new buildings are located.

Business interruption insurance—a valuable but often overlooked kind of insurance—is intended to cover your lost income while your business is closed, as well as the expenses you incur in keeping your business going while the lost property is repaired or replaced. This insurance coverage also pays the cost of renting temporary quarters. It's also possible to guard against losses if your business is interrupted because disaster strikes someone else.

Example: Tom operates a small bakery. Half of his income comes from supplying bread, rolls and pastry to a large restaurant. If the restaurant burns down, Tom's income will be drastically reduced. He might sensibly look into business interruption insurance that covers not only losses that would occur should his property be damaged but also those that would result if a major supplier or customer were suddenly forced to stop or curtail operation.

Before you buy business interruption insurance, run through a contingency plan of what you'd do in case of a disaster. Let's say that your warehouse were destroyed by fire. Assuming the contents of the warehouse were covered by your fire or multi-peril insurance, you need worry only about how much it will cost you to be out of business until you can set up a temporary warehouse and get more merchandise. Could you replace key merchandise quickly and take other steps to minimize the harm? If it's reasonable to believe that you'll be partially back in business in a couple of weeks and be in fairly good shape within 30 days, business interruption insurance might not really be worth the cost.

Will Your Customers Pull You Through?

Ben runs a successful book store. His inventory is covered, by a multi-peril contract, from loss from most hazards. But he worries that if he is burned out of his historic building, it might take a year or more to get repairs approved and made. Ben asks his insurance broker whether or not business interruption insurance makes sense.

After establishing that Ben could get new merchandise within a couple of weeks because book wholesalers and publishers would be anxious to help (Ben's credit is good), the broker recommends against it, pointing out that within a mile of Ben's building there are a dozen empty stores that Ben could rent very reasonably and be back in business almost immediately. The fact that Ben's loyal customers would likely support him after a disaster might even mean that sales would go up.

---

4. Industry-Specific Insurance

Supplementary insurance policy packages are often available for retail or manufacturing businesses, or even for specific types of businesses—a bookstore, barber shop or restaurant—and can be well worth looking into. For example, a manufacturing policy may have broader coverage for losses caused by malfunctioning equipment and machinery than a standard Special Form policy.

RECOMMENDED READING

- *Insurance and Risk Management for Small Business* by Mark R. Greene (U.S. Small Business Administration). The book is now out of print but may be available at your local public library. It's a well-written and comprehensive resource, and provided the basis for some of the information in this chapter.

- *Insurance Law in a Nutshell* by John F. Dobbyn (West Publishing Co.) is a concise statement of the basic legal principles. It's written primarily for law students, but useful to business people as well.

E. Saving Money on Insurance

This chapter is based on the sensible premise that few businesses can really afford to adequately insure themselves against every possible risk. You need to decide what types of insurance are really essential and how much coverage to buy. While this is no easy task, here are some guidelines that should help.

1. Set Priorities

Start by looking at what coverage is required by state law. For example, there may be minimum requirements for coverage on business-related vehicles, and you will almost surely be required to carry workers' compensation insurance if you have employees.

Next, if you rent, you'll need to purchase any insurance required by your lease. See Section B.6 and Chapter 10, Section D.13 for a discussion of insurance language in a lease.

Beyond the required coverages for your business, ask these questions: What types of property losses would threaten the viability of my business? What kinds of liability lawsuits might wipe me out? Use your answers to tailor your coverage to protect against these potentially disastrous losses.

Be less concerned about insuring against smaller losses. For example, if you're in the self-help publishing business, consider a package especially tailored to printers and publishers that includes liability coverage for errors and omissions (such as leaving some vital information out of an instruction booklet you publish), but be less concerned about protecting yourself against claims of libel—after all, your material never comments on personalities.

2. Increase the Amount of Your Deductibles

Deductibles are used primarily for real and personal property insurance, including motor vehicle collision coverage. The difference between the cost of a policy with a $250 deductible and one with a $500 or $1,000 or even higher deductible is significant—particularly if you add up the premium savings for five or ten years. For example, the difference between a $250 and a $500 deductible may be 10% in premium costs, and the difference between a $500 and $1,000 deductible may save you an additional 3% to 5%. Most businesses can afford to be out of pocket $500 or even $1,000—especially if taking this risk means you pay significantly lower premiums. Consider using money saved with a higher deductible to buy other types of insurance where it's really needed. For example, the amount you save by having a higher deductible might pay for business interruption coverage.

3. Initiate Loss Prevention and Risk Reduction Measures

Good safety and security measures may eliminate the need for some types of insurance or lead to lower insurance rates. Ask your insurance agent what you can do to get a better rate. Sometimes something simple like installing deadbolt locks or buying two more fire extinguishers will qualify you for a lower premium. Here are some other ideas to cut losses and premiums.

- Install a fire alarm system, if one can be found at a reasonable cost.

- Install fire-proofing materials to minimize fire damage in susceptible areas of the premises.

- Isolate and safely store flammable chemicals and other products.

- Provide adequate smoke detectors.

- Install a sprinkler system.

    Ideas for preventing theft include:

- Install tamper-proof locks.

- Purchase a secure safe.

- Install an alarm system.

- Install better lighting.

- Hire a security service to patrol your property at night.

    Also consider placing bars on doors or windows. This may create a negative impression; an innovative architect or contractor may be able to help you design and install these security devices in ways that are not unsightly.

    To prevent injuries to customers, employees or members of the public, you might:

- Check each applicant's driving record and not hire people to drive who have poor records.

- Give additional training to drivers you do hire.

- Set up a system for safer operation of machinery.

- Conduct fire drills.

- Give your employees protective clothing and goggles if necessary.

Although how to protect against some types of risks may be obvious to you, how to protect against many others won't be. Get help from people who are experienced in identifying and dealing with risks. One excellent resource is your insurance company's safety inspector; your insurance agent can tell you whom to contact.

Another good approach is to ask your employees to identify all safety risks, no matter how small. Also ask them to propose cost-effective ways to eliminate or minimize them—they may have cheaper and more practical ideas than you do.

Example: Adventure Apparel Corporation sells recreational and travel clothing by mail order from its well-stocked warehouse. The 25 employees of the corporation all take turns serving on the safety committee, which meets regularly to discuss safety issues ranging from the best way to operate computer terminals to reduce the possibility of repetitive motion injuries to making sure that the electric pallet lifters are run only by trained people. The system works because the employees are in a unique position to monitor safety hazards and to suggest practical solutions.

In the long run, a safety program will reduce your losses and, in turn, lower your insurance rates. In the short term, simply putting these practices into effect and letting insurance companies know about them may put you in a lower rate category. And of course, your employees will appreciate the care you show for their well-being—a significant plus in a world where keeping good employees is a real business asset.

4. Comparison Shop

No two companies charge exactly the same rates; you may be able to save a significant amount by shopping around. But be wary of unusually low prices—it may be a sign of a shaky company (see Section A for information on how to check out an insurance company). Or it may be that you're unfairly comparing policies that provide very different types of coverage. Make sure you know what you're buying.

Review your coverage and rates periodically. The insurance industry is cyclical, with alternating phases of low prices and high prices. When competition for insurance customers increases in a particular field, you really can achieve savings. But don't dump a loyal agent for a few cents. Ask your agent to look around and meet or come close to meeting the competition.

You can make the cyclical nature of the insurance industry work for you. If you're shopping for insurance during a time when prices are low, try locking in a low rate by signing up for a contract for three or more years.

5. Transfer Some Risks to Someone Else

Here are some possibilities:

- *Indemnification by Manufacturer*. Suppose you run a store that sells exercise equipment, and primarily from one manufacturer. If you're buying a significant amount of equipment, the manufacturer may be willing to provide insurance that indemnifies your business from any claim by a customer injured by the equipment.

- *Leasing Employees*. Some businesses lease employees at least in part because the leasing company takes care of carrying workers' compensation and liability insurance on the employees (among other things); but be cautious—the overall cost of leasing employees may be greater than if you hire directly. You may also to be able to transfer some risks by simply engaging independent contractors to handle the more hazardous aspects of your business operations. (See Chapter 12.)

6. Find a Comprehensive Package

Look for a small business package that includes a full range of coverage. This is often much cheaper than buying coverage piecemeal from several different companies. Group plans often offer these packages.

7. Seek Out Group Plans

Is there a trade association in your industry? If so, it may be a source of good insurance coverage. Trade associations often get good affordable insurance rates for the members because they have superior bargaining power.

8. Self Insure

Using this technique, you simply don't buy insurance and hope to maintain your own reserve fund to cover likely losses or liabilities. There are two drawbacks. First, despite good intentions, most small business don't have enough funds to set aside for this purpose. Second, unlike insurance premiums, money put into a reserve fund isn't tax-deductible until or unless you spend it.

F. Making a Claim

As soon as a loss occurs, gather and preserve evidence to help prove your claim if it becomes necessary. (If you followed my suggestion and have a comprehensive list of your property, get it out now.) Take pictures of any damaged property. Collect documents such as receipts showing what you paid for the lost property. If you can, secure the damaged property in a safe place so that it will be available for inspection later and for possible use in a lawsuit. Gather names of any witnesses who can help substantiate how the loss occurred and the extent of the damage.

Your next step is to request a claim form from your insurance agent. For small, routine losses you or someone else in your company can probably complete the form, with a little help from your agent. If more money is at stake, a lawyer can help you structure and justify your claim. (See Chapter 20 for information on how to find and hire a good lawyer.)

Damage to Rented Space: If you're renting the space your business occupies, start by figuring out whose insurance policy covers the loss—yours or the building owner's. For example, if a pipe breaks, you'll have to look at both insurance policies to see which one covers this risk. Ideally, your insurance company will pay you for damage to your inventory and equipment, and the owner's insurance company will pay for damage to the building. To make this happen and avoid squabbles, it helps to have a "mutual waiver of subrogation" in your lease. Without it, you can get caught in the cross-fire between two insurance companies. (See Chapter 10, Section D.13.)

Often there's a time limit on filing your claim, but you may need more time to analyze all of your damages. Don't feel rushed. Take the time you need. Simply file the claim form within the required time limit, listing the losses you're sure of at that time. Indicate that the list of losses is partial and that you're still gathering information.

If you're served with a lawsuit or are informed that an injured person is going to make a claim against your business, get the lawsuit papers and related information to your insurance company as soon as possible. Contact your agent promptly.

Negotiating a Favorable Lease

10

Almost all small businesses start out in leased premises; many businesses prefer to use leased space throughout their business lives. By leasing rather than owning, you avoid tying up valuable working capital. Also, it's easier to move to new quarters if your space needs change. This chapter looks at how to find the right place for your business and how to negotiate your lease.

A. Finding a Place

Your first step is to find the right space. Begin by analyzing the specific needs of your business. Real estate professionals are fond of saying that the three most important factors in choosing a business space are location, location and location. For certain types of retail stores and restaurants, this may be true. For example, a sandwich shop requires a location with a high volume of foot traffic. Or maybe you'll benefit if you're near other businesses that are similar to yours; restaurants often like to locate in a restaurant district.

But for many other businesses, where you're located doesn't matter much. For example, if you repair bathroom tile, run a computer-based information search business, import jewelry from Bali, or do any one of ten thousand other things, it won't help you to be in a high-visibility, high-rent district. Chances are your businesses can efficiently operate in a less pricey area, where you can negotiate a lower rent and the landlord is likely to be far more flexible on other lease terms as well.

After you've analyzed what you need, it's time to begin searching for the right spot. Go to the neighborhoods where you might like to locate; spend a day or two driving or walking the streets to see what may be available. Don't just look for vacant space. A store, office, studio or workshop that's good for your business may be occupied by a tenant who is going out of business—or moving to larger quarters in a few months. If you find a desirable location, call the landlord to see if the space will be coming on the market soon. There's a lot of turnover among small businesses, and you may get lucky.

Because some of the best opportunities come to light through word of mouth, ask friends, associates and other business people if they know of available space. Business owners—particularly those in the part of town that you're interested in—may know of businesses that are moving or going out of business long before these vacancies are announced in newspaper ads. And if you get there early, the landlord, relieved that he or she can avoid a period of vacancy and uncertainty, may offer you a favorable lease.

For-rent ads in newspapers are an obvious place to look. If the selection there is limited, call a real estate office that deals primarily with business space. The agent's fee—usually, a percentage of the rent that you'll be paying—is generally paid by the landlord. If your space needs are special, consider hiring an agent to search the market for you. But if you follow this somewhat unusual approach, you'll probably have to pay the agent's commission.

B. Leases and Rental Agreements: An Overview

A lease is a contract between you and the landlord. A lease can be for a short term (as little as one month) or long term, and it can be written or oral—although a lease for more than a year must be in writing to be legally enforceable. Some people use the phrase "rental agreement" to describe a short or oral lease for which rent is typically paid once a month and the tenancy can be terminated on a 30-day written notice. (See Section C below for more on short-term leases.) To avoid confusion, I'll stick to the word "lease."

TERMINOLOGY

Sometimes a written lease talks about the "Lessor" and the "Lessee." The lessor is the landlord; the lessee is the tenant.

In theory, all terms of a lease are negotiable. Just how far you can negotiate, however, depends on economic conditions. If desirable properties are close to full occupancy in your city, landlords may not be willing to negotiate with you over price or other major lease terms. On the other hand, in many parts of the country where commercial space has been over-built, landlords are eager to bargain with small businesses to fill empty units. Even in a tight market you may come across some acceptable space that, for one reason or another, the landlord is anxious to fill, giving you greater bargaining power. This is often true where there's a new building or one under construction and the landlord needs cash. Also, if you're one of the first tenants in the building, you may get an especially attractive deal, because your presence may help the landlord attract other tenants.

If you find a landlord willing to negotiate, what should you ask for? After you read Section D, you'll have a good understanding of the kinds of terms that usually go into a lease. Since you're not likely to get everything you want, it's important get your priorities straight in your own mind and concentrate on achieving what's most important. What do you really care about? What would be nice to have but not essential? What benefits can you offer the landlord for things you really need?

A lower rent is likely to be high on everybody's bargaining list. But how about physical changes in the building? Would you want the landlord to redesign the entryway? Add some office space at the back of the warehouse? Customize the interior for your needs? More or better parking for your customers might be worth more than slightly lowered rent. Your priorities may be unique to your business, so think them through carefully before making proposals and counter-proposals to the landlord.

Let's look at how you might approach the matter of rent. A landlord who is reluctant to lower the basic rent may be willing make other adjustments—which may be even more valuable. The landlord might do this so he or she can truthfully tell other prospective tenants that you're paying a high dollar amount per square foot. (It may sound silly, but some landlords do play this game.) For example, in a slack market, the landlord may be willing to give you a move-in allowance. Also, check out what the landlord is willing to do in paying for improvements (often called build-outs) to the space. (See Section D.9.)

C. Short Term Leases (Month-to-Month Rentals)

Once you've found the space you want, the next step, usually, is to sign a lease. (See Section D.) Occasionally, a small business that's just starting out prefers an oral lease permitting the tenant to occupy the space from month to month. This might seem attractive if you just want to test the waters, have great uncertainty about the prospects for your business and wouldn't mind leaving on short notice if the landlord terminated the lease. But even if you only want to make a very short-term commitment, it almost always makes far more sense to negotiate a written month-to-month lease or rental agreement. A written lease clarifies what's been agreed to and helps avoid disputes.

Whether oral or written, the key feature of a month-to-month lease is that you can move—or the landlord can require you to move—on short notice. You can negotiate how notice is required, but if you don't, the law in your state will dictate the amount of time. In many states, this is 30 days, although states don't always compute the time period in the same way. Some, such as California, allow either the landlord or tenant to give notice at any date during a month; the 30 days runs from the notice date. Other states require that the notice be given at least 30 days before the first day of the next monthly rental period;

furthermore, the termination date must coincide with the beginning of a new period.

Example: Albert is a tenant under an oral month-to-month lease in Michigan. He and the landlord haven't agreed on a specific notice period, relying instead on the law in their state, which requires a 30-day notice. Albert pays his rent on the first of each month. On July 15, Albert's landlord notifies him that he's terminating the lease as of August 15. Does Albert have to move by August 15? No. He can stay until September 1. That's because under the court interpretations in his state, he's entitled to notice 30 days in advance of a full rental period. Because Albert's rental period begins on the first day of each month, he can't be kicked out in the middle of a month. He's entitled to stay for at least one full rental period. If the landlord wanted Albert out by mid-August, he should have given Albert his notice before July 1.

 Notice requirements vary from state to state. For information about what's required in your state, you'll need to check the statutes or case law. (Chapter 20 suggests ways to do basic legal research.)

The clauses in a month-to-month lease, other than those dealing with the length of the tenancy, are much the same as those in any other written lease, so be sure to consult the following sections of this chapter.

D. Written Long-Term Leases

Many small businesses and landlords prefer the protection of a written lease that lasts a year or more. But when you talk to the landlord, you'll probably be presented with a typed or printed lease prepared by the landlord or the landlord's lawyer. Because the terms typically favor the landlord, consider it as no more than the starting point. Chances are excellent that you'll be able to negotiate at least some significant improvements. But keep in mind that you have two sometimes conflicting goals: to get a favorable lease and to have a good long-term relationship with your landlord. In the interest of long-term harmony,

there are times when it makes sense not to fight for the last scrap of a concession as if you were a starving pit bull.

To eliminate a proposed lease's one-sidedness, ask for equal treatment for you and the landlord for all clauses where this is relevant. For example, if the lease requires you to cure your lease defaults within ten days after you receive notice from the landlord, it should also require the landlord to cure his or her defaults within ten days after you give notice. Similarly, if you're required to pay for your landlord's attorney fees in enforcing the lease, the landlord should be required to pay for your attorney fees if you have to enforce the lease.

Now let's look at some common lease terms and how you might approach them.

1. Who Should Sign the Lease?

Leases begin by naming the landlord and the tenant. Make sure that the person, partnership or corporation named as landlord is the owner of the property. Although this may seem to go without saying, believe me, it often doesn't. A husband may not have legal authority to sign leases for space in a building owned solely by his wife. A management company or on-site manager may have only day-to-day management powers that fall short of the right to approve new leases. Or if they can sign a lease, they may be able to offer only certain terms and concessions. If you have any doubts about whom you're dealing with and what authority they have, ask to see a deed or title insurance policy to verify that the named landlord really owns the building. Here are the rules about who's authorized to sign a binding lease on behalf of the landlord:

- If a building owned is by an individual, that person (or an authorized agent) should sign the lease.

- If a building is owned by a general partnership, insist on the signature of one of the partners.

- If a building is owned by a limited partnership (not uncommon for rental properties), require the signature of a general (managing) partner; a limited partner usually lacks the power to bind the partnership.

- If a building is owned by a corporation, get the signature of a corporate officer or an executive with authority to sign leases.

- If you're dealing with a rental agent who will be negotiating the lease and signing it on behalf of the owner, ask for written confirmation from the owner that the agent has that authority. Obviously, you need to worry less about this step if the rental agent is part of an established and respected real estate management company, but it never hurts to request documentation.

Who should be named as the tenant? Before you sign a lease as an individual or a partner, be aware that you'll be personally liable for the rent if your business run into financial problems. If your business fails, the landlord can (and probably will) go after your personal assets such as your car, home and bank account. To avoid this exposure, consider incorporating. Then you can sign the lease as President of XYZ Inc.—and you're personally off the hook. (Personal liability for business debts is discussed in Chapter 1.)

 Beware of personal guarantees. In addition to signing in your corporate capacity, you may be asked to personally guarantee the lease. Doing this makes you personally responsible for the rent and means that the corporation doesn't shield your personal assets. One approach is to offer to guarantee the lease only up to a maximum amount—say, three months worth of rent. For even greater protection, see if the landlord is willing to release you from your personal guarantee if all rent is paid on time during the first year.

2. Defining the Space You're Leasing

The lease should identify the space that you'll be occupying. If you're leasing the whole building, that's easy: simply give the street address. If you're leasing less than the whole building, specify your space more precisely. One way is to refer to building or floor plan drawings. For example, you might say "Suite 2 of the Commerce Building as shown on the attached drawing" or "The south half of the first floor of the Entrepreneur Plaza."

In describing the space you'll be occupying, don't overlook the common areas—space you'll be sharing with other tenants. This often includes hallways, rest rooms, elevators, storage space and parking. Spell out in your lease that your business (and your customers) have the right to use these additional spaces and facilities. If your business keeps unusual hours, remember to define when you have access to your space and the common spaces. You don't want to find yourself locked out some evening or weekend.

Because commercial space is often priced by the square foot, find out what method is used to compute square footage. Sometimes it's measured from the exterior of the walls or from the middle of walls' thickness. If this is the case, you'll be paying for some space that's not really usable. This isn't necessarily bad. But you need to find out about it in advance, because it affects rent negotiations.

The square footage rate is usually stated in annual terms—$20 a square foot means $20 per square foot per year. However, it's sometimes stated by the month—$.60 a square foot means 60 cents per square foot per month. Obviously you need to know exactly what any numbers you're quoted mean. Also find out if the quoted figure applies only to the space occupied by your business or whether you're expected to pay for a proportionate share of the common areas. If your rent is computed on the basis of dollars per square foot, and if you're asked to pay for a share of the common areas, it's reasonable to seek a lower square footage rate for common areas.

If your landlord has agreed to set aside some parking spaces for your business or to let you use a storage building or other outbuilding, get it in writing in the lease. Also specify if indoor storage space will be shared or is reserved exclusively for your use.

3. Starting Date of the Lease

Your lease should clearly state its starting date. This can sometimes be a problem, especially if you're renting space in a building that's still under construction or space currently occupied. If you sign a lease before ground has been broken or if the building is only partially complete, what happens if your space isn't ready by the time you need it? This too should be addressed in your lease. Otherwise there may be little pressure on the landlord to meet deadlines. One possibility is to negotiate a cut-off date by which you have the right to cancel the lease if the building (or your unit) isn't ready for occupancy. You may also be able to collect damages from the landlord if you suffer losses because your space isn't ready on time. But in negotiating such a clause, remember it's always hard to prove lost profits—particularly if you're just starting out in business—so it's better to negotiate a pre-set amount for your damages.

Also, with a building to be constructed or under construction, state in your lease that until local building officials have issued a certificate of occupancy for the building, no rent will be due. You may think that this is so obvious it doesn't need to be spelled out in your lease, but some landlords have actually tried to collect rent even before building officials have approved the building for occupancy.

In a slight variation on this problem, some leases call for the landlord to erect a shell building. Then you, the tenant, finish off your own space. Obviously, you want to avoid having to install improvements in a partially-constructed building, which may not be completed for many months. One good solution: a lease clause saying you don't have to start work on your space until the building is enclosed and the common areas—such as hallways and rest rooms—

are done. The lease could also require the landlord to have the building and safety department make a preliminary inspection of your space before you start making improvements. The inspection would make sure the landlord has correctly installed the electrical and plumbing lines, and heating, ventilating and air-conditioning facilities within your leased space. You don't want to risk the possibility that you'll have to rip out and re-do your interior work because the landlord's contractor made a mistake.

With space that's currently vacant, ask the landlord to agree to let you have immediate access to decorate and install equipment. That way, you'll be ready to do business when you start paying rent. Spell this out in the lease.

4. Ending Date of the Lease

The lease should state its termination date, although you may have an option to renew. (See Section 5.) Some leases state that if the tenant remains in possession after the termination without exercising an option to renew, the tenancy is from month to month during the holdover period. (See Section C for information on month-to-month tenancies.)

5. An Option To Renew a Lease

When you first negotiate a lease, you can often bargain for a clause that gives you the right to renew or extend your lease when its term ends. Let's say you're negotiating a new two-year lease. You like the location, the rent is favorable and you'd like the right to stay for an extended period if your business is doing well. But at the same time, you're nervous about signing a four-year lease in case your business doesn't prosper. A two-year lease that includes a option to renew for two more years may be ideal. Typically, you exercise an option to stay by notifying your landlord in writing a set number of days or months before the lease expires. The amount of notice required is negotiable.

Getting the landlord to include an option in your lease may not be easy. Put yourself in the landlord's shoes. You might well go for a firm commitment from the tenant for eight years with adequate rent increases built in. You'd find it less attractive to grant a series of successive two-year options, which introduce an element of uncertainty—they allow the tenant the right to stay if the location turns out to be profitable but to leave if it's a dud. Not surprisingly, as a landlord, you'd look for some economic incentive to make the deal more attractive.

Now that you understand the landlord's point of view, you won't be too surprised if you find that the rent rate for a short lease with an option to renew is more than the rate you can lock in with a long-term lease. Also, the landlord will likely want a higher rent for the renewal period, either in a fixed amount or an increase tied to a cost-of-living index.

 Drawbacks of options to renew. An option to renew isn't always a good idea. If your business isn't particularly sensitive as to its location (maybe you publish a newsletter on how to raise fish or sell advertising for trade shows), think twice before you waste bargaining clout or pay extra for an option to renew. Sure, you may have to move, but in a high-vacancy climate, you might even find space with a lower rent.

6. The Right To Expand

If future expansion is a good possibility, you may want the lease to give you the right to add adjacent space or to move to larger quarters in the building. Sometimes this is done through a right of first refusal—the landlord promises in the lease that before any other vacant space is rented to someone else, the landlord must offer it to you on the same terms and conditions.

7. Rent

Leases usually state the rent on a monthly basis, for example, $1,000 per month, and indicate when payment is due—typically the first of the month in advance. The lease may also say that the rent for your two-year lease is $24,000 payable in monthly installments of $1,000 per month on the first of the month. Sometimes there's a late charge if you're more than a few days late.

This isn't the only way to compute rent. Depending on the type of building and local custom, here are the main ways that the rental amount is set:

- *Gross leases:* These require the tenant to pay a flat monthly amount. The landlord pays for all operating costs for the building—taxes, insurance, repairs and utilities. Under one common variation, the tenant pays for its own electricity, heat and air conditioning; if your lease uses this method and you are in a building with other tenants, see if there are separate meters available so that you can control these costs. If not, ask to see copies of the bills—you don't want to agree to pay for utilities if someone else in the building runs up huge bills.

- *Net leases:* The tenant must pay a monthly base rent plus some or all of the real estate taxes. If you sign this kind of lease and you're leasing just a portion of the building, make sure that the portion of the real estate taxes allocated to your space is fair.

- *Net-net leases:* This type goes further and requires the tenant to pay the base rental amount plus real estate taxes and the landlord's insurance on the space you occupy (which is different than your own liability insurance, discussed in Chapter 9). In a standard lease, the landlord insures the entire building against property damage caused by fire, flooding and the weather, as well as negligence and vandalism. The landlord's insurance also cov-

ers claims against the landlord brought by people injured on the property. In a net-net lease, the cost of this insurance is allocated among the tenants, usually on the basis of the proportion of space each one occupies.

- *Net-net-net ("triple net") leases:* The tenant pays the base rental amount plus the landlord's operating costs, including taxes, insurance, repairs and maintenance. Such leases are not often used for space rented by a small business but there are exceptions, such as store fronts in popular areas of large cities.

- *Percentage leases:* These leases are used most commonly for retailers in a shopping mall. The tenant pays base rent plus a percentage of gross income. (See Section F for a discussion of shopping center leases.)

If the lease is for more than one year, the landlord may want to build in a rent increase for future years. For example, a three-year lease may provide for rent of $1,000 per month in year one, $1,100 in year two and $1,200 per month in year three. Sometimes the increase is tied to some external measure, such as the Consumer Price Index. If the CPI increases 5% during the base year, so does your rent in year two.

Some landlords want the rent to be increased if their taxes or maintenance costs go up. If you're moving into a new building and the landlord proposes this last kind of formula, be particularly careful. No one really knows what operating costs will be in this situation—they may jump 50%. You'll at least want to negotiate a cap on how much the rent can go up because of increased operating costs.

As emphasized throughout this chapter, leases are normally negotiable. For example, depending on market conditions, you may be able to convince the landlord to turn a triple net lease into a gross lease. Or the landlord may be willing to put a cap on the amount of taxes, insurance and maintenance costs you'll have to pay. If vacancies rates are high, the landlord may be willing to give you a few months of free rent in return for your agreeing to take the space on a triple net basis.

8. Security Deposit

Landlords commonly request a security deposit in the amount of the last month's rent plus an additional amount equal to a half month's or full month's rent. So if your rent is $1,000 per month, you may have to cough up $2,500 to $3,000 before you take possession—$1,000 for the first month and $1,500 to $2,000 for the security deposit. This is all negotiable.

Ask the landlord to hold the security deposit in an interest-bearing bank account for your benefit. If you're concerned about the landlord's solvency, you might go further and suggest that the security deposit be held in escrow by a third party—but don't be surprised if the landlord balks at either suggestion.

The security deposit is intended to cover unpaid rent if you move out early and any damage you cause during your occupancy over and above normal wear and tear. Usually, your right to be free from liability for normal wear and tear is recognized under state law; you don't have to worry about this unless the lease the landlord proposes tries to make you responsible for it. So if your lease obligates you to return your space "in tip-top condition," you'll want to ask for a change. Similarly, it's normally considered unreasonable for the landlord to require you to pay to re-paint the space before you move out or install new carpeting—unless, of course, you caused an unusual amount of damage.

9. Improvements by the Landlord

Unless you rent a raw or recently remodeled space designed for a business such as yours, the space will often need to be fixed up or modified before it's suitable for your use. At the inexpensive end of the spectrum, you may need only a few coats of paint on the walls, or perhaps to have the carpet cleaned. At the big bucks end of the spectrum, you might need hundreds of thousands of dollars' worth of improvements before you could open a elegant new restaurant (for up-to-date kitchen equipment and an appealing decor) or a small manufacturing facility (pollution control equipment and a loading dock). In between

these two extremes, your business might need more lighting and electrical outlets, air conditioning or perhaps a partitioned office or work area. Who's going to pay for these things—you or the landlord? It's all negotiable.

Your lease should specify the improvements the landlord is to make. Ideally, the landlord should agree to have improvements in place before your move-in date. The next best thing is a stated deadline within the first months of your lease.

Try to get the landlord to agree to pay for all or most of these improvements. But be forewarned that the landlord's willingness to pick up the tab will depend on a number of factors including the condition of the building, your type of business, the extent and cost of the improvements, whether the improvements would be useful to a future tenant, the length of your lease, and—very important—how much rent you'll pay. For example, if you're starting a fancy restaurant, the landlord isn't likely to make $200,000 of improvements—but this might change if you're a famous chef who the landlord is counting on as an anchor tenant. But if you're opening a bookstore, the landlord may agree to install shelving for you. If the building is in bad repair, you can probably convince the landlord to put it in decent shape for you and maybe to make needed modifications in the process. If you're paying a hefty rent for five years, you can expect more than if you're signing up for one year at a low rent.

Improvements to leased space usually become the property of the landlord. (See the discussion of fixtures in Section 10.) This means that after you move out, future tenants will continue to use the space in its improved condition, and the landlord will continue to collect rent for the improved space. In other words, if your improvements are sensible, the economic benefits to the landlord will outlast your lease. This is a good negotiating point; you shouldn't be expected to bear the major financial burden for improvements that have a long useful life. On the other hand, if you have specialized needs—for example, you're running a photo lab or a dance studio—and your dark room or hardwood floor would be of limited value to most future tenants, don't expect the landlord to willingly pick up the costs of the improvements. The landlord may even want to charge you something to cover the cost of remodeling the space after you leave.

After you agree with the landlord on improvements, make sure the lease is clear on what's being done. Attach drawings and specifications so later there can be no doubt about what was promised. If extensive improvements are to be made, insist on drawings and specs prepared by an architect or construction specialist. Think about all your needs: partitions, special lighting, soundproofing, special floor coverings, painting, wall coverings, woodwork, cabinetry and so on. Many landlords can be very flexible and open to making improvements if you approach them before the lease is signed.

Here is some language you might include in the lease:

> Before the beginning of the lease term, Landlord, at its expense, will make improvements to the premises as set forth in Exhibit A (Plans and Specifications for Improvements). These improvements will be completed in a workmanlike manner and comply with all applicable laws, ordinances, rules and regulations of governmental authorities.

Improvements to raw space—particularly in a new building—are often called the "build-out." Sometimes the landlord offers a standard build-out to every tenant. For example, the build-out might include a certain grade of carpeting or vinyl floor covering; a particular type of drop-ceiling; a certain number of fluorescent lighting panels per square feet of floor space; and a specified number of feet of drywall partitions, with two coats of paint. Once you understand the landlord's standard build-out, see if you can get some upgrades or extras thrown in. You may wind up with better carpeting, more lighting or fancier woodwork.

If the landlord offers a build-out allowance based on the cost of the improvements (for example, up to $30 per square foot of rented space), see if you can negotiate a higher figure. Generally, the longer the lease, the better the deal you can negotiate on the build-out. This makes sense. With a lease of three or five years, the landlord has an incentive to do far more for you than if you sign up for only 12 months.

10. Making Improvements Yourself

You may want to make improvements or alterations that go beyond what the landlord is willing to provide. The lease proposed by the landlord may require the landlord's permission before you can make improvements or alterations to the premises. Meet this clause head on by submitting your plans to the landlord before you sign the lease—and don't sign unless you get approval.

Also, provide that the landlord won't unreasonably withhold consent to future improvements you may wish to make.

11. Removing Improvements When You Leave

At the end of the lease, you may want to remove some of the items you've installed and take them to a new location. Leases sometimes prohibit the removal of improvements. The landlord has a legitimate concern in preventing you from removing items in a way that damages the space or impedes renting to a new tenant. If your lease doesn't spell out your rights, the state law on "fixtures" will normally say that anything you've attached has become part of the real estate and is therefore the landlord's property. This can lead to arguments. For example, who owns the window air-conditioner that you attached with metal brackets?

The best way to avoid argument is to specify what you can remove and what belongs to the landlord. List all items you'll want to remove—either in the lease itself (if there's room) or on an extra sheet attached to the lease. (See Section G for how to do this.) Even if you have permission to remove certain items, make sure that you install them so they can be removed later without damage to the building. It may cost a little more to install easy-to-remove shelves, cabinets, light fixtures and air conditioning units. In the long run, however, it will be well worth it, because you can keep these items without having to make extensive repairs to the landlord's property.

12. Zoning Laws, Permits and Restrictions on Use of the Space

If the lease says nothing about the use of the space, you can use it for any lawful purpose. However, leases are often quite specific about what you can and can't do. For example, if your business sells and repairs bicycles, the landlord may insist that the lease limit you to these activities. This may seem okay now, but what if you want to do other things in the future? Define the permitted uses broadly enough to encompass any needs you anticipate. A poster business, for example, might want to provide that the space can also be used for classes on making and framing posters. A private post office might want to be free to do photocopying, fax transmissions and the retail sale of greeting cards.

No lease or landlord can give you the right to do something that's prohibited under the zoning laws. So it's an excellent idea to check with your local building or zoning department to be sure your anticipated uses are permitted under the local zoning ordinance. A bicycle shop may not be permitted in an office zone, for example. In addition to zoning ordinances, other planning, building, safety and health ordinances can affect your intended use. An ordinance may require a certain number of off-street parking spaces for some types of businesses, an entrance accessible to handicapped people or a restroom for customers—a common requirement for a restaurant. (For more on this subject, see Chapter 5, Section D.6.)

13. Required Insurance

Most landlords want their tenants to carry insurance to cover damage the tenant does to the building and injuries suffered by customers and other visitors on the premises. This is something that any business would be wise to do even if it weren't required by a lease. (Chapter 9 covers the types of insurance you should consider.) But when you get down to specifics, it can be one of the most complicated parts of the lease.

Look carefully at the policy limits the landlord wants you to carry. Is a $2 million liability policy reasonable for your business? Some landlords want you to buy a policy to cover the landlord's liability for injuries as well as your own. This is often considered unreasonable; bargain to eliminate such a requirement, if you can.

At the very least, your landlord should agree to pay for casualty insurance on the building so that funds are available to repair it if it's destroyed or damaged by a fire or windstorm. And if you're in an area where floods or earthquakes are common, insist that the landlord also include these non-standard coverages.

With both you and your landlord buying insurance, there's always the possibility of unnecessary duplication of coverage. Ask for a copy of your landlord's policy and review it with your agent.

When a landlord and tenant each carry property insurance, you can run into complications because of the legal concept of "subrogation." Ordinarily, if an insurance company pays an insured business for damaged property, the company has the right to turn around and sue any third party that caused the damage. The insurance is said to be subrogated to the rights of the insured business to collect damages—in other words, the insurance company steps into the shoes of the insured business.

Example: Pericles Corporation is a tenant in a building owned by Town Development Associates. Pericles carries insurance on its property and Town Development carries insurance on the building. One evening, employees of Pericles forget to turn off the coffee maker before leaving.

The coffee boils away, the machine overheats and a fire breaks out, seriously damaging the building, furniture and equipment of Pericles. Pericles' insurance company pays for replacement of the damaged furniture and equipment, and Town Development's insurance company pays for repair of the building. However, since the fire was caused by the negligence of a Pericles employee, Town Development's insurance company steps into the shoes of Town Development and sues Pericles to collect the money paid out to repair the building. In doing so, the insurance company is exercising its right of subrogation.

You can head off this kind of headache by including a clause such as the following in your lease:

Mutual Waiver of Subrogation

Landlord and Tenant release each other from any and all liability to each other for any loss or damage to property, including loss of income and demolition or construction expenses due to the enforcement of ordinance or law, caused by fire or any of the Extended Coverage or Special Coverage perils, even if such fire or other peril has been caused by the fault or negligence of the other party or anyone for whom such party may be reponsible.

If you don't have such a clause in your lease and try to waive subrogation rights after a loss occurs, you may be out of luck. Most insurance policies provide that a waiver of rights is effective only if it is made in writing before a loss.

14. Subletting Your Space or Assigning the Lease

Someday you may want to share your space with another business. For example, if you run a toy store, you might want to rent a portion of your floor space to someone who sells children's books. You'd do this by subletting the space. When you sublet, you're still responsible to the landlord for paying the entire rent and honoring all other provisions of the lease. Obviously, subletting is of more concern with a long lease than with a short one.

Another possibility is that you'll want to move out of the space during the term of the lease, because you've found better space or you've decided to go out of business. If you found another tenant to take over your space, you could sublease the whole space to the new tenant; in that case, you'd still responsible to the landlord under the lease. But ideally, you'd want to assign your lease to the new tenant. Assigning your lease takes you out of the picture entirely. The new tenant pays the landlord directly and you have no further liability under the lease.

Landlords often are reluctant to give tenants an unlimited right to assign their lease or sublet their space. They're afraid of winding up with an occupant who is a deadbeat or who may damage the property or who runs a business that will adversely affect the image of the building, making it harder to attract good tenants. A typical provision drafted by a landlord looks like this:

Tenant agrees not to assign or transfer this lease or sublet the premises or any part of the premises without the written consent of Landlord.

In my opinion, such a clause is unfair from a tenant's point of view. To make it fairer, ask to add the following wording:

Consent of Landlord will not be unreasonably withheld.

With this additional wording in your lease, if you find a reasonable occupant to sublet to, and the landlord refuses to let you sublet, courts will generally rule that you're off the hook for rent after you move out.

 Uncooperative landlords. If you find yourself with a landlord who objects to a subtenant you've found, check with your lawyer or do some research to learn your legal rights in your state.

LAW IN THE REAL WORLD

When Corporate Status Comes in Handy

Elena formed a corporation called Elena's Mediterranean Deli Inc. As president of her new corporation, she signed a five-year lease for space in a popular food court. Buried in the lease's small print was a sentence that said the lease couldn't be assigned and the space couldn't be sublet without the landlord's permission.

A few years later, Elena wanted to sell her business to Arnold for a handsome profit. Arnold planned to continue running the business at the same location. Elena told the landlord about her plans to sell and sublet. The landlord, who wanted to install his nephew in Elena's space, objected, saying he wouldn't let Elena assign the lease or sublet the space. The landlord was willing to excuse Elena from the rest of the lease—but this wouldn't allow her to reap the profit from a sale of her business.

What to do? Fortunately, because the corporation rather than Elena was the tenant, the lease was legally a corporate asset. Elena realized that she didn't need to sublet or assign her lease. She sold the corporation to Arnold, which meant that the corporation—although owned by a new shareholder—was still the tenant. Elena used the profits to go to grad school.

---

15. The Landlord's Right To Enter Your Space

Some leases give the landlord a broad right to enter your premises at all times to make inspections or repairs. This is an unnecessary invasion of your privacy, and most landlords will settle for a more limited right of entry. It's reasonable to provide that the landlord can only enter your leased space during normal business hours, unless there's a genuine emergency, such as a burst pipe or electrical hazard.

Because repairs can be disruptive, you might also require the landlord to consult you before making repairs and schedule them for a mutually convenient time. For many businesses, this won't be a problem. But if repairs could be disastrous—for example, you're a doctor renting space for your allergy practice or the owner of a shop that assembles delicate electronic components—you'll want to tightly control when the landlord can repaint or install new carpeting.

A related issue comes up near the end of a lease. Does the landlord have an unlimited right to enter your place to show it to prospective tenants? Depending on the type of business you have, this can be disruptive and annoying. It's a good idea for your lease to limit this type of intrusion to a slow period (say, 9 a.m. to 11 a.m., Monday through Friday) and to require 24 hours' notice.

16. Signs

Many types of businesses need one or more external signs. Check the lease to see if it gives your landlord the right to disapprove signs before they go up. One way to be sure the landlord won't be unreasonable is to have your signs approved when you sign the lease. If you do, attach a drawing or photo of the signs to the lease so that there can't be any argument later about what you agreed on.

 Don't forget municipal sign ordinances. In some communities, signs are heavily regulated by ordinances which restrict their size, number, color and location. In a few communities, there are even limitations on the content of signs—for example, in a few places in Southern California, there are limits on the number of non-English words you can use. So besides providing for your signs in your lease, check with local building and planning officials to see what ordinances and regulations may affect you.

17. Cancelling Your Lease

In general, you can't cancel your lease before it runs out without pointing to a specific reason stated in the document itself—unless, of course, your landlord agrees to end the lease early. The right to end your lease early is definitely something you should think about during your negotiations. The future of your business may look rosy, but especially with a new business, no one knows for sure.

One approach for a new business is to propose a provision that allows you to cancel your lease if your gross income projections haven't reached a stated level by a certain time—say, six months after you take occupancy. Although this would be a somewhat unusual clause, a landlord with vacant space and no other tenants in prospect might accept it.

An even more compelling reason for ending your lease early would be that the building has been damaged by a fire or flooding and you can't conduct your business there. In most states, if you rent space in just a portion of a building, the law provides that you can terminate your lease if the building is destroyed. But what if it's only heavily damaged? If the landlord doesn't make repairs promptly, state law may allow you to terminate based on "constructive eviction"; the landlord's inaction, you would argue, constitutes an eviction. But if the landlord disputes this, you'll be stuck with what a judge rules. A better approach is to provide in your lease that if you can't run your business in your space for 30 days because of damage that you didn't cause, you can cancel the lease. Also, if relevant, make sure your 30-day provision covers the possibility that you and your customers can't get access to your space because of damage to another part of the building.

For more information on getting out of a lease, see Section I.

18. Mediation or Arbitration

I recommend that all small business leases have a clause requiring mediation or arbitration of landlord-tenant disputes. With mediation, an outside party helps the disputants arrive at their own settlement, which can then be recorded as a legally binding agreement. Arbitration is more like a private court action with the arbitrator in the role of a judge listening to the dispute and rendering a decision. But because no court is involved, it tends to be far faster and cheaper than a full-blown lawsuit. (Mediation and arbitration are covered in Chapter 18.)

19. The Fine Print

Study the lease thoroughly so that you're sure your responsibilities and those of the landlord are clear and reasonable. In addition to the major items already discussed, make sure the lease deals with all possible costs, including any of the following that concern you:

- *Real estate taxes.* If nothing is mentioned in the lease, this is normally the landlord's responsibility.

- *Utilities*—water, electricity, natural gas, heating oil, etc. These are usually the tenant's responsibility if not specifically mentioned in the lease.

- *Maintenance of the building and of your premises.* Without a lease provision to the contrary, the landlord must pay for maintaining the building; you pay for maintaining your own space. If you're leasing an entire building, you are normally responsible for all maintenance unless the lease specifies otherwise.

- *Repair and maintenance of the interior walls, ceiling and floors in your space.* This is normally the tenant's problem in the absense of a lease provision.

- *Repair of malfunctioning plumbing, electrical and mechanical systems (heating, ventilation, and air conditioning—commonly called* HVAC). Without a lease provision, payment responsibilities are debatable. Generally, the landlord is responsible for systems that affect the entire building— although the opposite is usually true if you lease the entire building. When you rent less than an entire building, the responsibility for mechanical or electrical facilities within the four walls of your space isn't always clear; you could find yourself arguing over who must pay for replacing a defective light fixture or a thermostat that goes haywire if the lease doesn't cover it.

- *Janitorial services.* These are normally the tenant's responsibility unless the lease says otherwise. Landlords usually provide janitorial services for bathrooms and other areas used in common by several tenants.

- *Window washing.* Without specific lease language, the landlord normally doesn't have to wash windows. In smaller buildings, leases usually leave window-washing to the tenant, with the possible exception of windows serving common areas such as hallways, entryways and storage areas. In larger, multi-storied buildings, the landlord usually accepts responsibility—at least for the exterior of the windows.

- *Trash removal.* Without lease language to the contrary, this is the tenant's chore.

- *Landscape care and snow removal.* This is generally the landlord's duty unless you lease the entire building, in which case the burden shifts to you. It's always wise to address this issue in the lease— particularly if you're a tenant in a professional or other building where projecting the right image is important.

- *Parking lot maintenance.* This is something the landlord usually must pay for unless the whole parking lot is under your control, in which case it's usually your job unless the lease provides otherwise. In addition to maintenance, be sure the lease is clear regarding the landlord's duty to make a certain number of spaces available, keep the lot or garage open during normal business hours and provide security.

On service items such as janitorial services and window washing, specify how often this will be done. If the landlord is responsible for heating and air conditioning, will these services be available weekends and at night? If you business keeps long hours, you want your space to be comfortable at all times.

Regarding repairs, you and your landlord may find it convenient to allow you to make certain minor repairs not exceeding a fixed sum (say $300) and to deduct those outlays from your next month's rent.

E. Additional Clauses To Consider

Most of the above lease clauses are relatively common. Here are a few more, which are seen less often but which can be valuable to you as a tenant.

1. Option To Purchase the Building

If the situation warrants, consider a clause giving you an option to buy the building someday. It could give you the right to buy at a specified future time at a specified price, or a right of first refusal, in which if your landlord receives an offer from someone else to purchase the building, you'll be given a chance to match that offer. Many landlords will give you this right because it doesn't cost them anything. If you decide not to exercise your right of first refusal, the landlord simply sells the property to the person who made the offer.

2. The Right To Withhold Rent

Suppose your landlord violates the lease by not furnishing air conditioning for a sweltering July—or heat for a frigid January. Can you withhold rent? The traditional legal view is that your obligation to pay rent is independent of the landlord's obligation to perform under the lease. In other words, tenants are expected to quietly pay their rent except in the most extreme circumstances. But in the last 25 years, a tenants' rights revolution has taken place—mainly in the area of residential leases. For example, in the case of housing, many states recognize an "implied warranty of habitability." This means that regardless of what the lease obligates the landlord to do, the landlord must put dwelling units in a habitable condition—and keep them that way throughout the lease. If the landlord fails to do so, the tenant can withhold all or part of the rent without fearing eviction. Unless the parties come to an accommodation, a judge will ultimately decide how much of a rent reduction (the technical term is "abatement") the tenant is entitled to.

Commercial tenants, however, have not fared as well. The courts in most states still say that a commercial tenant must continue to pay rent despite the landlord's failure to meet implied or expressed duties. But this may be changing. Courts in several states have shown concern for the rights of commercial tenants. For example, a Texas court ruled that there is an implied warranty by a commercial landlord that leased premises are suitable for their intended purpose. The ruling came in a case where the landlord didn't provide adequate air conditioning, electricity, hot water, janitorial services or security to a business tenant. The tenant stopped paying rent and moved out. The court upheld the action of the business tenant.[1]

How far the courts will go to protect your rights as a commercial tenant is still uncertain. Certainly a one-day failure to provide air conditioning wouldn't be enough to let you withhold rent or move out. But

what if you and your customers have to sweat it out for two weeks? Or six weeks? That may be enough in some states, assuming you've given the landlord prompt notice of the problem and a chance to make repairs.

I recommend that you deal with all this legal uncertainty by requesting a lease clause giving you the right to withhold rent if, after reasonable notice, the landlord violates the lease in a way that seriously interferes with your ability to do business. Here's a sample clause:

> If, within ten days after notice from Tenant, Landlord fails to cure a default by Landlord that materially affects Tenant's ability to conduct its business, Tenant shall be entitled to a reasonable abatement of rent for the period of default and may withhold all rent until Landlord has cured the default.

F. Shopping Center Leases

Leases for space in a shopping center are a special breed of animal. They often charge a percentage of sales as part of the rent and restrict competing businesses, to mention just two major differences.

It can be hard to read a shopping center lease and decide whether it offers a square deal or not. So, in addition to reading the lease language carefully, one of your first steps should be to check if the shopping center has a tenants' association; many shopping centers have them, and it can a source of invaluable information. If there's no formal association, drop in on some current tenants. Either way, learn as much as you can about the center's management and how tenants are really treated. Also, try to find out which lease clauses the owner considers negotiable. This sort of information as to problems and opportunities will give you a definite advantage in your lease negotiations.

Now let's look at a typical shopping center lease. Many of the lease clauses discussed earlier in this chapter also appear in a shopping lease, but there are

---

[1]*Davidow v. Inwood North Professional Group - Phase I*, 747 S.W.2d 373 (Tex. 1988).

likely to be a number of different wrinkles you should know about.

1. Percentage Rent

Retail businesses moving into a shopping center often find that the landlord expects to receive a percentage of gross sales in addition to a fixed "base rent." For example, the lease might provide:

a. The landlord will receive $2,000 a month as base rent.

b. In addition, if your gross sales exceed $200,000 a year, the landlord will receive 5% of the amount of your gross sales over the $200,000 figure.

c. The amount received by the landlord under the percentage rent clause won't exceed $25,000 a year.

In addition to trying to negotiate more favorable terms, be specific in how you define gross sales. Depending on your type of business, certain items should be deducted from gross sales before the percentage rent is determined. Here are some possibilities:

- returned merchandise
- charges you make for delivery and installation
- sales from vending machines
- refundable deposits
- catalog or mail-order sales
- sales tax.

In short, make sure your lease excludes all items that overstate your sales from the location you're renting.

2. Anchor Tenants

You may be attracted to a certain shopping center because one of the tenants is a major department store or supermarket. These superstars, known as anchor tenants, attract customers to the shopping center. Insist on a provision letting you out of the lease if an anchor tenant closes or, with a new shopping center, if the center never opens. Also seek the right to cancel your lease if center occupancy falls below a certain percentage. There's nothing worse than having a store in a half-empty mall.

3. Competing Businesses

How many record or running shoe stores can a mall support? You may want to negotiate a limit on the number of competing businesses allowed in the mall. Similarly, the landlord may want you to agree not to open a second store within a two-mile radius of the mall; the fear is that a second store too close might decrease gross sales from your mall location—thereby reducing the money the landlord gets under the percentage rent clause. At any rate, remember that these issues are usually negotiable. Many shopping centers (especially older ones) can no longer afford to dictate coercive terms to small businesses, and you may find much more landlord flexibility than you expect.

4. Duty To Remain Open

Your lease may compel you to remain open for business during all mall hours—typically 10 a.m. to 9 p.m. Monday through Saturday, and noon to 5 p.m. on Sunday. With a small business, think about whether you can afford to run your business during all of those hours or if it's appropriate to do so. For example, not many people buy children's shoes at 8:45 on Tuesday evening, but there is often a line on Saturday morning that justifies opening at 8:30 or 9 a.m. instead of 10, when the rest of the mall opens. If you need reasonable changes, ask for them.

G. How To Modify a Lease

As discussed in this chapter, there are a number of constructive ways to modify the lease presented by the landlord. The most important thing is to put the changes in writing. Never rely on oral understandings. In this day of computers and word processing software, the simplest method for making changes may be to have the landlord or landlord's lawyer print out a revised version of the lease—or you can make small changes on the lease itself by crossing out unacceptable wording and adding new language. You and the landlord should initial each of these changes.

If changes are extensive and it's not practical for the landlord to include them in a fresh draft, it's best to prepare an addition to the lease—in legal parlance, an "addendum." The addendum should refer to the main lease and state that in case of any conflict, the terms of the addendum supersede the original lease. A sample addendum is shown below.

Addendum

This is an Addendum to the Lease dated
_____, 19__, between
_____ (Landlord) and _____
_____ (Tenant) for commercial space at
_____.

The parties agree to the following changes and additions to the Lease:

[Insert changes and additions]

In all other respects, the terms of the original Lease remain in full effect. However, if there is a conflict between this Addendum and the original Lease, the terms of this Addendum will prevail.

Keep in mind that a lease can be modified even after it's been signed. For example, if six months into your lease your landlord agrees to install some partitions for $2,000, you can sign an addendum then.

H. Landlord-Tenant Disputes

There's almost no limit to the kinds of disputes that landlords and tenants can have. Your landlord may claim that you're damaging the building, or that you're consistently late paying rent, or that you or your customers or visitors park in other tenants' spaces. You may feel that your landlord hasn't been furnishing services that were promised, such as security, janitorial or landscaping, or that your landlord is failing to attend to the leaky roof or having the windows washed frequently enough.

No matter what the cause, it's usually best to compromise a landlord-tenant dispute through negotiation. Sometimes a frank discussion and a little give and take by each side can resolve what seems like an impossible problem. If the dispute is serious and not amenable to face-to-face negotiations, have your lawyer help you analyze your legal rights. They may be stronger than you think. Legal trends in many parts of the country have improved the tenant's position.

If your lease has a mediation or arbitration clause, this is the obvious next step. But even if it doesn't, you may wish to suggest one or both of these approaches. Going to court can be expensive and time-consuming—something the landlord probably wants to avoid. In short, a sensible landlord has good reason to listen to your complaints and to mediate or arbitrate disputes. (See Chapter 18 for more on mediation and arbitration.)

1. Put Your Complaints in Writing

If you think your landlord has violated the lease, put your concern in writing in a straightforward, non-hostile way. State specifically what the violation is and what part of the lease it involves. Deliver your notice or letter to the landlord either in person or by certified mail (return receipt requested). Putting a landlord on early notice can help bolster your legal position if the dispute ever goes to court. If rent withholding is allowed in your state or by a specific clause in your lease (see Section E), you may want to write a letter or two to the landlord before you hold back on the rent. An example of such a letter is shown below.

SAMPLE LETTER TO LANDLORD

August 5, 1992

Arnold Ace
Ace Real Estate Associates
1234 Main Street
Anytown, U.S.A. 12345

Dear Mr. Ace:

I am writing to you about some problems we are having with our store space at 567 Enterprise Drive.

As you know, paragraph 12 of our lease specifically says that Ace Real Estate Associates will maintain the heating and air conditioning system and keep it in good repair. I have called your office twice this week and left word that the air conditioning is not working. No one has come to fix it or given us a date by which the work will be done. Our customers have complained, and on Tuesday we had to close early.

Also, under paragraph 14 of our lease, the Landlord agreed to replace the broken floor tiles in the entry area within two weeks after we took possession. We have been here for six weeks now and nothing has been done about the tiles. The broken tiles are hazardous.

These are serious violations of our lease. I am requesting that you immediately repair the air conditioning and promptly replace the broken floor tiles. We cannot operate without the air conditioning during this hot weather. Its lack has already caused us to lose substantial revenues and has damaged customer relationships.

If you do not take care of these matters within five days, I plan to have the work done myself and to deduct the cost from next month's rent.

If the cost of fixing the air conditioning is excessive, I may choose to terminate the lease and to sue your company for damages caused by your breaching the lease, including moving expenses and lost profits.

I hope that this will not be necessary. Please proceed at once to make the repairs as required by the lease.

Very truly yours,

Peter Olsen

2. Coping With the Threat of Eviction

Many leases contain stern language that appears to give the landlord the right to enter your space and regain possession if you don't pay your rent on time or fail to live up to some other lease obligation. Don't be intimidated. No matter what the lease says, in most states a landlord can't evict you without going to court and getting a court order first. This process requires that you be given notice and an opportunity to present your side of the dispute.

A hearing by a judge—or, if your lease so provides, by a mediator or arbitrator—gives you a chance to explain any legal defenses you have. For example, perhaps the reason you didn't pay your rent by the first of the month was that the landlord failed to repair the air conditioning as required by the lease. The right to a court hearing also gives you valuable time to develop your case and perhaps resolve the dispute. Court hearings don't take place instantly. You usually have some breathing space in which to build your legal response.

I. Getting Out of a Lease

Suppose that your business doesn't work out or—more optimistically—that you outgrow the space that you've leased. How free are you to simply vacate the space and walk away from the lease? Unless your landlord has done something to make your space unusable, you're legally responsible for the entire rent for the remaining portion of the lease if the landlord can't find another suitable tenant.

But especially if you have desirable space and a favorable lease, getting out of it—or most of it anyway—may be less difficult than you think. If you find that you need to move out, you have two options:

- *Buy your way out.* Try working out a deal in which the landlord keeps all or a part of your security deposit (including, perhaps, the last month's rent) in return for releasing you from the lease. If the lease still has a fairly long time to run or it will be hard to find a new tenant, you might

need to sweeten the deal by offering an additional month or two of rent.

- *Find a new tenant.* Find a new tenant to take over the space. Present the new tenant to the landlord along with information about the person's credit and business history. Especially if your lease says that your landlord can't unreasonably refuse to consent to a sublease, you're in a strong legal position if the new tenant has good financial credentials and runs a business of a type permitted by your lease. But again, even without this provision (or if your lease flat out prohibits subletting or assignment), the law in your state may recognize the landlord's duty to mitigate damages—that is, try to find a replacement tenant and minimize his or her loss. If so, you're in a pretty good legal position. If the landlord accepts a new tenant who agrees to pay as much or more than you do, you're free of the lease at no further cost. If the landlord turns down the new tenant and then sues you for lost rent, you can argue that the landlord acted unreasonably and that the landlord—not you—should absorb any losses.

In addition, in states that recognize the landlord's duty to mitigate damages, usually the landlord must make a good faith effort to fill the space. Some landlords claim to meet this duty by placing a few ads in the newspaper and listing the property with a real estate agent (why should they do more since you're still obligated?). You're better off to use your own efforts to find a new tenant if possible.

J. When You Need Professional Help

A basic lease that sticks to routine clauses like those listed earlier in this chapter and is written in clear English should be no problem to negotiate yourself. However, it still may be prudent to have a lawyer with small business experience look over the final draft of the lease before you sign it. A visit of one-half hour or less should be sufficient. A real estate or small business expert may also be able to assist you. But make sure the person you check with doesn't stand to profit from putting the deal together—a circumstance that all but guarantees you won't get objective advice.

For non-routine leases, seek assistance earlier in the game. You may need considerable help in negotiating and drafting some critical clauses. This may cost a few dollars, but compared to a confusing or landlord-slanted lease, a fair, well-drafted lease that contains the provisions you need is almost always a bargain.

 For more on leases, see *Landlord and Tenant Law in a Nutshell* by David S. Hill (West Publishing Co.).

HOME-BASED BUSINESSES 11

RECOMMENDED READING

- *Working from Home* by Paul and Sarah Edwards (Jeremy P. Thatcher Inc.). This encyclopedic volume by the reigning gurus of home-based businesses covers everything from how to live with computers, faxes and voice mail to juggling family, friends, children and work.

- *Your Home Office* by Norman Schreiber (Harper & Row). In addition to providing many practical suggestions, this book offers an extensive catalog of helpful high-tech office items, publications, audiotapes and videotapes.

Ah, Home Sweet Home. Or is it Home Sweet Workplace? One of the major business trends is the dramatic increase in the number of consultants, artists, craftspeople, therapists, mail order specialists, professionals and others who use their homes as a business base.

One reason for this trend is the amazing array of electronic equipment that makes it possible to be productive and in touch with the rest of the world without leaving the comforts of home. By investing in a computer, a copier, a fax and an extra phone line or two, you can now duplicate conditions that until recently were practical only in leased commercial space.

But the upsurge in home-based businesses also reflects a new emphasis on the quality of life. Working at home gives you the chance to spend more time with your family, to be more flexible in the hours that you work and to avoid the gridlock of the highway.

From a legal standpoint, a home-based business isn't much different than any other business. You still need to pick a business name; decide whether to be a sole proprietor or to form a partnership or corporation; purchase insurance; pay taxes; sign contracts; and collect from customers. But a few special legal issues are peculiar to the at-home business, including land use restrictions, insurance and special tax provisions.

A. Zoning Laws

Planned communities and condominiums often have their own detailed rules affecting home-based businesses. Typically, these rules are stricter than local zoning ordinances. Skip ahead to Section B if your home is subject to these rules.

Is it legal to run a a business in your home? The answer depends on where you live and what you do. To understand how this works, let's start with the case of Bob Mullin, whose plight made its way into the lawbooks.[1] Bob ran his insurance business from his two-bedroom home in Indianapolis. He thought he was on safe legal ground. After all, unlike some cities, the local zoning ordinance allowed people to use their homes for "home occupations." As long as a home was used primarily as a residence, it could also be used for "professions and domestic occupations, crafts or services." The ordinance specifically allowed homes to be used for such occupations as law, medicine, dentistry, architecture, engineering, writing, painting, music lessons and photography. Also, people could use their homes for such businesses as dressmaking, tailoring, hair grooming, washing, ironing and cabinet making. So why not an insurance business?

Bob Mullin used his living room as a reception room and office, complete with a secretary's desk and filing cabinet. He put his own desk in the dining room in place of a dining room table. The photocopier stood in the kitchen next to the stove and refrigerator, and he converted one of the bedrooms into an office.

The zoning board took Bob to court, claiming he'd gone too far. The Indiana Court of Appeals

---

[1]*Metropolitan Development Commission v. Mullin*, 339 N.E.2d 751 (Ind. App. 1979).

agreed. The court ruled that it was okay for Bob to conduct an insurance business at home, but that Bob's usage was excessive. The business had taken over the house to the point that the primary use was no longer residential. The court told Bob to cut back or close down.

This case demonstrates but one of the many ways that local zoning ordinances can have a devastating effect on a home-based business. The good news is that by learning the law and using discretion, you may find that zoning isn't a real problem for your business.

1. How Zoning Ordinances Are Organized and Applied

Most cities have zoning ordinances. Areas outside of cities are usually covered by zoning ordinances adopted by county, village or township governments. Zoning ordinances come in many shapes and sizes, but they all do basically the same thing: they divide the area into districts in which various types of activities are allowed or prohibited. For example, there are usually residential districts for single-family and two-family homes and other districts for apartments. Other areas or zones are earmarked for commercial usage. Ordinances often break down the types of commercial usage; in some zoning districts, only offices or retail and service businesses are allowed. Usually some part of town is reserved for manufacturing operations, which are typically broken down into light and heavy industrial.

In some areas, more than one use is allowed in a district; for example, commercial and light industrial, or residential and commercial. Outside of cities, zones allow various types of agricultural activities.

Some zoning ordinances, especially in affluent areas, exclude home-based businesses. More commonly, zoning ordinances restrict—but don't prohibit—using a home for a business. An ordinance might say, for example, that in general you can't run a business from your home, but then go on to list several types of business that are permitted. The

Indianapolis ordinance mentioned earlier specifically allowed professions such as law, medicine and architecture, as well as painting, music lessons and photography. Some ordinances are vague, simply allowing "customary home occupations"—a term that must be interpreted by a judge if a given use is challenged.

Zoning ordinances that regulate home businesses frequently also limit:

- the amount of car and truck traffic
- outside signs
- on-street parking
- the number of employees
- the percentage of floor space devoted to the business.

It's not always easy to tell whether or not a particular business is allowed in a home under the zoning ordinance you're looking at. Some zoning ordinances were written years ago and don't adequately deal with many contemporary businesses that people wish to operate from home—especially sophisticated businesses that depend on high-tech communications equipment.

The level of enforcement varies widely. In more enlightened communities, zoning officials recognize that residential zoning is intended primarily to preserve the residential character of a neighborhood—not to prohibit low-profile businesses. Officials don't go out looking for violations but take their cues from the neighbors: If people living near a home-based business don't complain, why search for a possible technical violation? Even where it's clear that there's a violation, these officials work with the business owner to see if changes can be made to make the business conform to the ordinance before ordering the owner to end the business or taking administrative or court action.

On the other hand, you may have the misfortune of living in a community that believes in strict enforcement of all ordinances. In such a community, your home-based business may be at the mercy of fairly rigid bureaucrats—although, as we'll see, you may fight arbitrary or unreasonable action.

If municipal officials are determined to close down your home-based business, their first step is to write you a cease and desist letter. If you ignore this, you'll probably get another letter or two followed eventually by a misdemeanor prosecution (seeking a fine or, in an extreme case, a jail term) or a civil lawsuit requesting an injunction—a court order prohibiting future violations of the ordinance. If you violate such an injunction, the judge can fine you for contempt of court or even put you in jail.

2. Investigating Zoning Laws

Before setting up a home-based business, it's a good idea to learn not only what your local zoning ordinance provides but also to find out about enforcement attitudes. If you're in a strict enforcement community and you file for a local business license or tax permit, this may trigger an inquiry about whether you comply with the zoning ordinance. Talk to people who run other home-based businesses, local contractors, your city's business development office, small business advisors and lawyers about how to make the fewest legal waves.

You may find yourself in a gray area. Your planned home-based business may or may not violate a vaguely worded local ordinance—for example, a computerized information searching business in an area that allows traditional home-based businesses. It's hard to predict whether the local zoning officials will take action against you or not. One approach is to just go ahead and chance it. If you're simply planning to set up your desk and computer in an unused room in a home you already own, you have little to lose. This approach is far less sensible if you plan to buy or renovate a house to accommodate your business. Before you spend a significant sum to house your business, you want assurance that you won't be closed down. It's best to approach the city, explain your plans and ask for an official green light. If a purchase is involved, put a clause in your offer making

the deal contingent on getting approval from the zoning authorities. Then, if your use isn't approved, you're free to cancel your purchase.

If you plan to operate out of your existing residence and decide that your business is doubtful legally, or that you could be closed down if the ordinance were strictly enforced, you can minimize the risks. Start by being a good neighbor. Make sure that your business has little if any impact on the people who live around you. For example, if all you do is convert one room to an office equipped for a consulting business, it's unlikely that anyone will complain—as long as you have no employees and see only an occasional client or customer at your home. This is true even if you generate $1 million a year in gross income. You'll also be in a better position if you cleared your plans with your neighbors or if several of them also have home-based businesses.

What kinds of things are most likely to get you trouble? Anything that a neighbor can see, hear or smell outside of your home that causes inconvenience or smacks of a commercial venture. Increased traffic, parking problems, signs, outside storage of supplies, noises or unpleasant odors emanating from your home—any of these can lead to neighborhood complaints. Pollution is another red flag.

Example: A craftsman who worked at home with stained glass and even taught classes there was doing quite well until he started dumping lead-laced fluids down a storm drain. The neighbors properly insisted that the city attorney put him out of business.

LAW IN THE REAL WORLD

Get the Neighbors on Your Side

Ted operates a business in his home helping non-lawyers prepare their own divorce and bankruptcy forms. Several customers come and go each day, often in the early evening and on Saturdays. One of Ted's neighbors, who has no idea of what Ted is doing, jumps to the conclusion that he's dealing drugs.

She calls a meeting of other neighbors and convinces the others that there can be no other explanation for all the coming and going. They complain to the police and zoning board. When the truth comes out, the police laugh and leave.

The zoning officials are another matter. They cite a local ordinance prohibiting businesses that generate traffic and tell Ted to close down. Eventually, when Ted gets all his chagrined neighbors to sign a statement saying a few cars a day aren't a problem, the zoning officials reverse their position.

Ted could have avoided this time-consuming, anxiety-producing process if he'd simply told folks what was going on when he began his business.

3. Dealing With Zoning Officials

Suppose you receive a complaint from the city. What steps can you take? Start by going to City Hall and talking to the person who administers the zoning law—someone in the Zoning or Planning Department. There are both practical and legal reasons for attempting to resolve zoning matters without filing a lawsuit. On the practical level, administrative (agency) relief is quicker, less expensive and often more flexible than a judicial solution. And the law usually requires you to pursue your available administrative solutions before you go to court; this is known in legal lingo as "exhausting your administrative remedies."

The kind of response you can hope for at City Hall depends greatly on community attitudes. If some home-based businesses are allowed, you clearly want to show that yours meets the spirit of the criteria for allowing businesses. Emphasize how small and unobtrusive your business is. When faced with the facts, the city may become more reasonable. Or you may be able to negotiate a settlement under which you scale down your operations. For example, you might agree to limit your business to weekdays from 8 a.m. to 5 p.m. and to provide off-street parking for your one employee.

If you can't negotiate with the city staff, there are more formal approaches. Most places have a planning or zoning board with power to grant exceptions (variances or conditional use permits) if compliance with an ordinance would cause unreasonable hardship. For example, a zoning board might allow a physically handicapped person to operate a therapy practice at home even though some traffic is generated. The board may also have power to overturn a zoning official's interpretation of an ordinance. If you appeal to a local zoning or planning board, try to get neighbors to attend the hearing to speak on your behalf. If that is too inconvenient, ask as many neighbors as possible to write letters or sign a petition stating that they support your business use. Neighborhood support or opposition is likely to be crucial to the success or failure of your appeal. Also, come to the hearing with any photographs or documents that accurately show the nature and extent of your business.

In many cities, if you're turned down by a zoning or planning board or commission, you can appeal to a second board—often the city council itself. While it's less likely that you'll prevail at this level, it does happen.

Going beyond administrative channels, you may be able to get the zoning ordinance amended by the city council or county legislative body. For example, in some communities moves are afoot to change ordinances that allow "traditional home-based businesses" to include those based on the use of computer and other high-tech equipment—businesses that are unobtrusive, but hardly traditional.

To push through an ordinance change, you'll probably have to lobby some city council members or planning commissioners. You may also need to enlist the local Chamber of Commerce and other groups representing business people. With increased use of homes for businesses, the time may be ripe in your community for ordinance revisions of this sort. It's politically attractive to revamp an archaic ordinance to allow more home-base businesses, especially if the city is struggling with traffic and parking problems.

Also consider trying to get your property rezoned. This works best if your home is on the edge of a commercial district. Ask the city to move the boundary line separating the two zoning districts so that your home falls within the commercial district—which, of course, would give you much greater latitude to run your business out of your home.

4. Going to Court

If you decide municipal officials are being unreasonable in attempting to close down your home-based business and you can't get administrative relief or an ordinance amendment, you may want to take the matter to court yourself before the city starts a prosecution or requests an injunction. By acting first, you have a chance to frame the factual and legal issues more favorably, putting the municipality on the defensive. At this stage, you'll probably need a lawyer's help; zoning cases are relatively complicated and specialized. Consulting and perhaps hiring a lawyer who works in this area regularly will be well worth the fee. Make sure you find a lawyer who's familiar with zoning practices (see Chapter 20 for more on finding and working with lawyers). You needn't turn the whole case over to a lawyer—there's plenty you can do to organize support from neighbors and other home-based businesses as well as researching how courts have decided other similar cases.

You can assert several legal theories in a zoning lawsuit, including the following:

• The city's legal interpretation of its zoning ordinance was incorrect. For example, you might

claim that your word processing business is a "home occupation" even though the zoning officials decided that it isn't. You'd ask the judge to issue a judgment declaring that your business does qualify as a home occupation.

Example: Dr. William Brady lived in Beverly Hills, California. He wrote a syndicated column and, with the help of secretaries, mailed out 150,000 pamphlets a year from his home office. The city tried to close his business because the local zoning ordinance prohibited home businesses that involved the purchase or sale of materials for profit. But the court ruled that the doctor wasn't violating the zoning ordinance; sending out the pamphlets was basically the same as a person answering his or her mail.[2]

• The ordinance is invalid because it violates the state statute (called an "enabling law") that gives cities authority to enact zoning ordinances. For example, you might claim that the zoning ordinance is invalid because it doesn't permit home owners to have "reasonable accessory uses" or "home occupations" as required by the state enabling law.

• The ordinance is invalid because the city didn't use proper procedures in adopting or enforcing it. For example, the city may not have held the necessary public hearings before it amended the zoning ordinance to prohibit certain types of home-based businesses.

• The authorities have acted in a discriminatory manner by enforcing the ordinance against you. For example, they've allowed similar home-based businesses for years but now have singled you out for special treatment.

You aren't limited to just one legal theory. Your lawsuit can allege as many theories as apply.

Lawsuits are expensive, but yours may be settled before there's a full-scale hearing or trial. The city may agree on an acceptable compromise to avoid the expense or inconvenience of fighting your lawsuit, or may not want to put its zoning ordinance in jeopardy

---

[2]*City of Beverly Hills v. Brady*, 215 P.2d 460 (Cal. 1950).

just for the sake of closing down one in-home business.

B. Private Land Use Restrictions

Zoning ordinances are not the only source of potential problems for a home-based business. You must also check out private restrictions on your use of your home, condo or co-op unit. Depending on the part of the country and the type of ownership arrangement, use restrictions commonly are found in the following documents:

- property deed (the restrictions are called "restrictive covenants")
- a subdivision's Declaration of Building and Use Restrictions or Covenants, Conditions and Restrictions (CC&Rs)
- planned Unit Development (PUD) rules
- condominium regulations
- co-op regulations
- leases.

Language in these and similar documents is likely to restrict or even prohibit business uses. If your residence is covered by a title insurance policy (virtually every piece of real estate is), use restrictions may be identified there. If you've lost your deed or your subdivision, condo or co-op restrictions, get a copy from your association or go to the county office where title papers are recorded (usually the county recorder or register of deeds) and purchase a copy.

If your neighbors believe you're violating these restrictions, they may take action to stop you. Often—especially for condo, co-op or PUD units—they can take you before an owners' association board empowered to enforce regulations. If you don't come into compliance, you may lose privileges and face other penalties. Beyond these private sanctions, your neighbors can take you to court and try to stop your business. Judges can be very strict in enforcing these private restrictions. Here are three real-life instances where a judge sided with the neighbors.

Example 1: Salvador, a field manager for a brush manufacturer, supervised a staff of door-to-door salespeople and supplied them from his residence in Metairie, Louisiana. He interviewed prospective salespeople at his home and received stored merchandise in his garage. The court ruled that merely receiving samples wouldn't violate the restrictive covenants in the deed to Salvador's property. But Salvador had a problem because he used his home to hire and outfit new employees with samples stored at home. He wasn't using his home "for residential purposes only" as required by the restrictive covenants. *Woolley v. Cinquigranna*, 188 So.2d 701 (La. App. 1966).

Example 2: Sheldon and Raye practiced psychotherapy in their home in Illinois. The subdivision restrictions covering their home said that "No lot shall be used except for single residential purposes." Their neighbors took them to court, claiming a violation of that restrictive rule. The judge ordered Sheldon and Raye to discontinue their professional use of their home even though the exterior appearance of the home as a single-family home hadn't been altered. *Wier v. Isenberg*, 420 N.E.2d 790 (Ill. App. 1981).

Example 3: Myrtle operated a part-time beauty parlor in her Sunnyvale, California home, receiving six customers per day. Myrtle didn't advertise her services, there was no external evidence of her business, and neighbors weren't inconvenienced. Still, the judge ruled that Myrtle violated the subdivision restriction that said "No lot shall be used except for residential purposes." *Biagini v. Hyde*, 3 Cal. App. 3d 877, 83 Cal. Rptr. 875 (Cal. App. 1970).

If you're taken to court, you have two main lines of defense. The first is that your neighbors or the condo association are misinterpreting the restrictions and that your business use is allowable. Second, if the neighbors did not object to prior business uses, they have, in legal effect, waived the right to do so now. In other words, their inaction in the past has nullified the restrictions.

Judges are often sympathetic to homeowners seeking to enjoy the use of their property. If neighbors have been lax or the restriction is vague, you have a good chance of getting a favorable ruling if your business use doesn't really hurt your neighbors or change the residential character of your neighborhood. On the other hand, if the legal restrictions are tightly drafted and your neighbors acted swiftly to enforce them whenever a violation came to their attention, even a sympathetic judge won't be able to help you.

But slugging it out in court should be a last resort. If you're both dogged and diplomatic, you may be able to find a way to operate your home-based business. Look first at the rule to see how restrictive it is. Some specifically allow certain types of home-based businesses while others simply adopt the standard in your municipality's zoning ordinance (see Section A, above), which in turn may be fairly permissive. If you don't qualify under the rules, consider trying to change them. Other people in your subdivision may also feel they are too restrictive. Often the document creating restrictive covenants says that restrictions can be changed if a certain number—say 70%—of the homeowners in the subdivision agree. Similarly, condo regulations can often by changed by agreement of a specified number of owners.

Leases. If you live in a rented house or apartment, read your lease carefully. Your landlord may have the right to evict you if you use the premises for business. It's best to get clearance in advance, written into the lease. Most landlords won't care if you use the property partly for business as long as you don't cause any damage or create any problems with your neighbors.

C. Insurance

Chapter 9 discusses insurance coverage for small businesses. The same general principles apply to home-based businesses, but there are also some special considerations you should be aware of.

Never rely exclusively on your normal homeowner's policy. If you do, bad things can happen:

- After your computer is stolen, you may find out that it's not covered by your homeowner's policy because business property is excluded.

- After your house burns down, you may find that the fire coverage is void because you didn't disclose your business use to the insurance company.

- After the UPS delivery person slips on your front porch and breaks his back, you may find you're not covered for injuries associated with business deliveries.

It's easy to avoid these nasty surprises. Sit down with your insurance agent and fully disclose your planned business operations. It's relatively inexpensive to add riders to your homeowner's policy to cover normal business risks. You may need separate policies for other business-related coverage.

When it comes to business equipment and furnishings, figure out how much it would cost for replacements after a fire, theft or other disaster. Don't overlook things such as the specialized business software you run on your computer. Depending on the nature of your business, replacing equipment and furniture could run into many thousands of dollars. Ask your insurance agent what it takes to insure this valuable property, allowing for a good-sized deductible to keep costs down. (See Chapter 9, Section E, on how to buy affordable insurance.) Make sure that the coverage on equipment and furnishings is for the full replacement cost—not just the depreciated value, as can be the case in some homeowner's policies.

Your homeowner's policy may also not adequately protect you from liability to business visitors. Accidents—such as people getting hurt when they trip and fall—are more likely to happen at home than in a well-planned office building. Your homeowner's policy probably protects you if you're sued by a social guest or someone at your home for a non-business purpose—a florist's truck driver delivering flowers or the meter reader who's checking on gas usage. But it may not cover a business associate, employee, customer or delivery person who is injured on your property.

Some home-based businesses need special kinds of insurance. If you render professional services, look into professional liability insurance. If you manufacture, distribute or sell products that may hurt someone, think about products liability insurance. Also, if you have employees, you'll need to provide worker's compensation coverage. (All this is covered in Chapter 9.)

If you do some business away from your home, be sure that your car insurance covers injuries that occur while you're on business errands. And see about the extent of your general liability coverage if you should accidentally injure someone or damage their property while away from home on business. You may need a rider or special policy to cover this risk.

D. Taxes

Chapter 6 discusses the main tax basics that apply to all small businesses. This section looks at some special concerns of the home-based business.

1. Deducting the Cost of Your Home Office

The IRS has rules for determining if you can take a deduction for business use of your home. These rules apply to sole proprietors, partners and corporations that have elected S corporation status (to be taxed as a sole proprietorship or partnership would be). They don't apply to regular for-profit corporations. Whether or not you qualify for these deductions that relate to your home, your business is still entitled to take deductions for regular business expenses as outlined in Chapter 6. For more details, see IRS publication 587, *Business Use of Your Home*.

According to the IRS, your "home" can be a house, condo or apartment unit—or even be a mobile home or boat. But wherever you live, to deduct for the use of part of your home as a business, you must use that part exclusively and regularly:

- as your principal place of business, or
- as a place to meet or deal with patients, clients or customers in the normal course of your business, or

- in connection with your business if you're using a separate structure (such as a garage) that's not attached to your house.

As you might expect, these terms have acquired definite meanings as the IRS has interpreted them over the years.

a. EXCLUSIVE AND REGULAR USE

"Exclusive use" means only for business. If you use part of your home for your business and also use it for personal purposes, you don't meet the exclusive use test.

> **Example:** You use a den in your home to write legal briefs and prepare tax returns. You also use the den for poker games, watching TV and hosting your book club. Result: you can't claim business deductions for using the den.

There are two exceptions to the exclusive use rule: using part of your home to store inventory and using part of your home as a day-care facility. Where these exceptions apply, you can claim some business deductions even though that part of your home is used for both personal and business purposes. Check IRS publications for more information.

"Regular use" means you're using the part of your home business on a continuing basis—not just for occasional or incidental business.

b. PRINCIPAL PLACE OF BUSINESS

As noted above, to take deductions relating to your home, your home must be your "principal place of business." This is simple if you have only one type of business and conduct it only at home. It gets more complicated if you have several businesses or conduct a business from more than one location.

The IRS says that you can have a principal place of business for each trade or business in which you engage. So if you use your home for a part-time business, it may qualify as a "principal place of business" for that business.

Example: A teacher's principal place of business is the school where he or she teaches. If the teacher also has a public relations business and uses a part of his or her home as the principal place for that business, expenses for this business use of the home may be deductible.

Here are some factors the IRS looks at to determine whether or not your home is your principal place of business for a particular trade or business:

- The total time you regularly spend doing your work at home.

- The facilities you have to work there.

- The relative amount of income you get from doing business at home.

 Home-connected expenses. As noted earlier, the IRS rules discussed above apply to home-connected expenses, not to other business expenses. If you have a bona fide business and don't qualify for home-connected expenses, you can still deduct other business expenses—for example, the cost of supplies, postage, advertising and long-distance phone calls.

2. Allocating Home-Connected Expenses

If your business use of your home meets all of the above tests, your next step is to determine how much of your home is used for business purposes. That's because expenses related to the business use of your home are tax-deductible business expenses, but only in the same proportion as your business use of your home. Expenses are divided on an area basis.

Example: You pay a painter $1,000 to repaint the interior of your entire house. You use 20% of the house for business purposes only. You can deduct, as a business expense, 20% of the $1,000 expense.

Here are two common methods for figuring your business percentage.

Square Footage Method: Divide the number of square feet of space used for business by the total number of square feet of space in your home. For example, if your home measures 1,200 square feet

and you use one 240-square foot room for your business, one-fifth (20%) of the total area is used for business.

Number of Rooms Method. If the rooms in your home are about the same size, figure the business portion by dividing the number of rooms used for business by the number of rooms in the home. If you use one room in a five-room home for business, one-fifth (20%) of the total area is used for business.

You must also figure out which expenses are tax-deductible because they relate to your home-based business. The IRS has three categories of home-connected expenses: direct expenses, indirect expenses and unrelated expenses. (Again, these categories do not affect deductions for normal business expenses unconnected with your home expenses —supplies, business equipment and so on).

In the IRS scheme of things, home-connected expenses are "unrelated" to your business—and, therefore, never deductible as a business expense—if they benefit only the personal parts of your home that you don't use for business. Examples: repairs to personal areas of your home, lawn care and landscaping.

Direct and indirect home-connected expenses are both deductible as business expenses. "Direct expenses" are those home-connected expenses that benefit only the part of your home used for business. Examples are painting or repairs made to the specific area or room used for business. You can deduct all of these expenses.

Indirect expenses are for keeping up and running your entire home. They benefit both the business and personal parts of your home. Examples include:

- real estate taxes

- deductible mortgage interest

- casualty losses

- rent

- utilities and services

- insurance

- repairs

- security system

- depreciation.

You can deduct the business portion of your indirect business expenses if they relate to the part of your home used for business. Generally, you use the percentage you figured based on square footage or number of rooms, but see IRS publications for exceptions and more details.

Example: Your $400 electric bill includes electricity for lighting, cooking, laundry and TV. Only the lighting is used for business. If $250 of the bill is for lighting, and you use 10% of your home for business, then $25 is deductible as a business expense.

 Depreciation deductions. Before you decide to take a depreciation deduction for part of your home, consult a tax advisor. This is a complicated area of the tax law, and it's easy to make costly mistakes. Taking a deduction for depreciation on your current tax return isn't the problem. The problem comes later when you sell your home and have to figure out your cost basis so that you can determine the gain—which may be taxed at the time of sale or rolled over into your next home. Usually, if you're using 10% or 20% of your home for your business, it's best to forget about taking a tax deduction for depreciation on your home (business equipment is another matter). But get specific advice from a tax expert before you make this decision.

3. Deducting for Home Computers

The IRS has special rules for taking a deduction for a home computer. Different rules apply depending on when you placed your home computer in service (before 1990 or afterwards) and whether or not you use the computer more than 50% of the time for business. For more information, get IRS publication 534, *Partial Business Use of Listed Property*.

EMPLOYEES AND INDEPENDENT CONTRACTORS

12

This chapter deals with how to hire and fire employees and how to comply with laws that affect them. We'll also look at hiring independent contractors, instead of employees, for certain tasks (Section I).

(Chapter 6 covers the employer's responsibility to withhold and report taxes.)

A. Hiring Employees

As we go through the technical legal rules for hiring and firing employees, don't lose sight of three even more important concepts:

- Hire excellent people
- Treat them well
- Do whatever you can to create a workplace where employer and employees cheerfully combine their energies for the common good.

The first step in the hiring process is to write a job description. This will help both you and applicants by defining what exactly the job consists of and what skills are necessary. Then you can begin soliciting applications and interviewing applicants.

Here are some suggestions to help you in the hiring process. Your hiring procedures must also comply with federal and state laws that prohibit discrimination. (See Section B.)

1. Don't Promise Too Much

Painting a positive picture of the job is okay—just don't go overboard and make promises you can't keep. If you make exaggerated statements about job benefits or job security, you may wind up with a disgruntled employee who quits or even takes you to court. Some courts have ruled that an employee may acquire some job rights under an implied contract based on statements and promises that the employer made at the time of hiring. (See "Employment at Will," below.)

Employment At Will

Normally, employment is "at will"—meaning that you can fire an employee for any reason or no reason at all. Likewise, an employee can quit at any time. However, you and the employee can change the at-will relationship by entering into an employment contract. To prove the existence of a contract that guarantees job security, an employee traditionally has had to point to specific wording in a document—a luxury reserved mostly for professional athletes and upper-echelon officers of major corporations. But in recent years, judges have sometimes found a guarantee of job security in oral contracts based on enthusiastic statements made by the employer.

The at will employment doctrine is showing additional signs of gradual erosion. It's possible that during the 1990s, many workers will acquire limited rights to job security regardless of whether they have any contract, oral or written.

2. Give Written Policy Guidelines to New Employees

Often, applicants and new employees hear only what they want to hear about the job. To avoid disputes about what was said, hand the applicant or new employee a written list of job duties. If your business has more than a handful of employees, develop a set of basic employee guidelines for new employees. The guidelines may cover such things as how work assignments are made, policies for dealing with the public, standards for attire, overtime obligations, vacations and sick leave.

A new small company doesn't need a full-fledged employee handbook or personnel manual when it hires its first few employees, but you should consider having one by the time you have 15 or so employees. The personnel handbook should explain not only job benefits but also an employee's duties. In the handbook, avoid describing any employees as having "permanent status." The word "permanent" may suggest that your business fires employees only for good cause. It's better to talk about "regular" or "full-time" employees. Also, state that your business reserves the right to change its policies and benefits from time to time.

Your personnel guidelines should make it absolutely clear that no employee is under contract unless he or she has a separate written agreement signed by both the employer and the employee. They should state that there will never be oral or implied contracts. Have prospective employees state in writing that they've received a copy of your personnel handbook.

Employee handbooks can be a two-edged sword. They help your business by clarifying the ground rules for employment. But because your employees have a right to rely on any promises or benefits in the handbook, be very careful not to make statements that you don't plan to live by.

For an excellent model of an employee handbook, see *How To Comply With Federal Employee Laws* by Sheldon I.

London (London Publishing Company Inc.). Using this model or others like it, you should be able to prepare a draft of an employee handbook that fits your needs. Then have a small committee of employees review and comment on your draft—a cost-effective way to ensure the handbook and the workplace are as good a match as as possible. You may also want to have a lawyer with experience in employment law look it over before it's final.

LAW IN THE REAL WORLD
Watch Your Enthusiasm

Joy, the owner of a successful vegetarian restaurant called Joy's Garden, hires Allison to keep the books. "If you do a good job," Joy tells Allison, "you'll have a great future here." Unfortunately, Joy becomes increasingly unhappy with Allison's work and, after four months, fires her.

Allison sues Joy's Garden. Based on Joy's statement, she claims that she had an implied contract that she couldn't be fired without good cause. In court, Joy has a few anxious moments when the judge rules that Joy's enthusiastic reassurance at the time of hiring gave Allison a right to keep her job unless there was good reason to discharge her.

When it's time for Joy to tell her side of the story, she produces a copy of the written job description she gave Allison before she hired her. It clearly says that the bookkeeper is to compute and deposit payroll taxes and maintain the restaurant's checking accounts. Joy also has copies of penalties asessed by the IRS because Allison had twice deposited the taxes late. She also produces Allison's personnel file, which contains three warnings about Allison's substandard performance.

Joy breathes a sigh of relief when the judge rules that Joy had good cause to fire Allison. Case dismissed.

3. Respect the Applicant's Privacy

Increasingly, courts and legislatures are protecting the privacy of employees and job candidates. Your company's application form should stick to basic questions, such as: Where do you live? Have you ever been employed under another name? Who are your previous employers? Who are your character references?

Use your form to tell the applicant the records you want to see, such as college transcripts and personnel records from prior employers, and include a specific statement authorizing you to get access to them. Also state on your form that if the applicant gives inaccurate information or omits significant information, he or she won't be hired.

If any of the items listed below are particularly important to your business, check the law in your state. Your state's civil rights commission and the human resource committee of your state chamber of commerce are good places to start.

- *Skills:* A short skills-based test is often appropriate. Most new businesses operate on a slim profit margin and need to know that employees will be up to speed from day one. As long as the skills you're testing for are genuinely related to the job duties, a skills test is generally legal.

- *Criminal Records:* If you plan to ask about an employee's criminal record, be sure you know what your state allows. In many states, you can't ask an applicant about juvenile crime records or about adult arrests that didn't result in a conviction. In some states, you can't ask about convictions for misdemeanors (minor offenses) that go back more than five years if the applicant has had a clean slate since that time.

- *Credit History:* Credit information isn't always relevant to employability, but it does come into play when you hire someone who will handle money. If you want to order a credit report on a job applicant, some states require you to get the applicant's consent first. Also, the federal Fair Credit Reporting Act requires you to let appli-

cants know if they've been denied employment partly because of something in a credit report.

- *Smoking:* Some employers don't want to hire people who smoke—in part because it can result in greater absenteeism and higher health insurance premiums. But you're on shaky ground if you fire or refuse to hire someone because he or she smokes during non-working hours. Laws in at least 15 states say that this is illegal discrimination. You can, however, regulate smoking on the job. At least 15 states and many municipalities have laws restricting smoking in privately owned workplaces. For example, the law might require that if any smoking is allowed, it be restricted to a certain room or floor within a building. Even in places without such laws, judges likely will uphold your right to prohibit smoking on the job.

- *School and College Transcripts:* If you want to see these records, have the applicant sign a written release acknowledging your right to obtain them. Many schools, however, only release transcripts directly to the former students.

- *Personnel Records:* Many employers wisely get permission from applicants to speak to their former employers; usually this is part of the application form. But this generalized permission doesn't automatically mean you have authority to obtain personnel records. If this is a concern, get specific written permission from the applicant to obtain the records you want.

- *Drug Testing:* Laws on drug testing vary widely from state to state. Some states allow testing employees only in a narrow range of jobs, such as those concerned with safety. But, in Iowa, for example, you can test any job applicant as part of a pre-employment physical, as long as you use the services of a state-approved lab and obtain a confirming test for any positive result. Before testing an applicant for drug use, learn the law in your state. If your state permits testing of applicants or employees and you plan to do such testing, use the application form to inform applicants of this policy.

- *Honesty Tests:* Lie detector tests—rarely used by small businesses anyhow—are now virtually outlawed by the federal Employee Polygraph Protection Act. About the only time they can be used is in connection with a criminal investigation. Some employers use paper-and-pencil honesty tests as a way of screening job applicants, but the legality of such tests is doubtful in many states. In any case, many of these tests are sophomoric. It's hard to see why a business would insult the intelligence of prospective employees by using one.

- *Marital Status or Sexual Orientation:* Some cities and a few states prohibit discrimination against applicants based on marital status or sexual orientation. If you're going to inquire about this delicate area (but why would you?), make sure you're up-to-date on the law in your area.

- *HIV Status:* In recent years, courts have generally—but not always—ruled that being infected with HIV (Human Immunodeficiency Virus) or having AIDS is a physical handicap, and that the Federal Rehabilitation Act and many state and local anti-discrimination laws make it illegal to discriminate in employment-related matters on the basis of HIV infection or AIDS. Some states and cities have also passed laws limiting HIV

testing of employees and job applicant to positions such as those in hospital, where the virus could conceivably be passed from employee to patient. The Americans With Disabilities Act clearly prohibits any company with 15 or more employees from discriminating against workers infected with HIV.

4. Watch Your Words in Offering a Job

Earlier, I pointed out that it's dangerous to promise too much in describing a job to an applicant. The same rule applies when you reach a formal employment agreement. One good approach when offering someone a job, whether in a letter or a proposed contract, is to refer to your company's employment guidelines and handbook, if you have them. (See Section A.2.) Make it clear that these personnel policies are part of the employment agreement and that you're not making any additional oral promises now or in the future.

SAMPLE EMPLOYMENT LETTER

DATE:_____

Dear _____:

I am pleased to offer you a full-time position with our company as
__(Insert Job Title)__ beginning __(Insert Date)__ . Your starting salary will be
$_____ per week.

When you applied, I gave you a written list of your job duties which are as
follows:

(Insert List of Job Duties)

Also, when you applied, I gave you a copy of our employee handbook. The handbook
sets out our current employment policies and describes your job benefits including
medical coverage, paid vacation and sick leave. It also describes your responsibilities to the company. Each time the handbook is updated, you'll receive a revised
copy.

The company's commitments to you and its other employees are stated in the handbook. The company has made no oral commitments to you. No one at the company is
authorized to make oral commitments regarding employment—either now or in the
future.

While I hope that everything works out here, this is an at-will employment. You
have the right to terminate the employment at any time and so does the company.

If this offer of employment is acceptable to you, please sign a copy of this
letter and return it to me within 10 days. I look forward to having you join our
staff.

Sincerely,

_____
(Your Name and Signature)

ACCEPTANCE _____ _____
                          Signature   Date

Here's other language to consider putting in your application forms, offers of employment or employment contracts:

> I understand that I have the right to terminate my employment at any time and that XYZ Company has the same right. I acknowledge that I will have no contractual rights of employment, either now or the future, unless such rights are expressly stated in a written agreement.

5. Comply With the Immigration Reform and Control Act

Federal immigration law is intended to crack down on the hiring of illegal aliens; hiring such aliens is now a crime. You must follow the statutory hiring procedures for all new employees, even new employees who were born and raised in the town where your business is located. You should become thoroughly familiar with Form I-9 (Employment Eligibility Verification) published by the Immigration and Naturalization Service (INS). This is a one-page form that you and the employee must complete to ensure that the employee can legally work in the United States and as proof of identity.

The law requires you to review certain documents—such as drivers licenses, birth certificates, passports and naturalization certificates—for each new employee. You must determine from the documents whether or not it's legal for that person to work in the United States. Besides U.S. citizens, permanent resident aliens can work here legally. And if someone has applied to become a permanent resident alien, he or she may be able to work here for a limited time. The same is true of students on working visas. If in doubt, check with the INS.

It's your responsibility to see if the employee's documents appear genuine. No specifics for doing this are set out on the employer's portion of Form I-9. It's a good idea to keep photocopies of the employee's documents to prove that you reviewed these papers if the INS questions your hiring practices in the future. In addition, in the employee's portion of Form I-9,

the employee must verify that he or she is a U.S. citizen or an alien entitled to work here.

Hang on to the I-9 for at least three years. If the employee stays with your company longer than that, keep the form for at least one year after he or she leaves. The INS has the right to see your I-9s. You can be fined up to $1,000 per employee if you can't produce them.

6. Check References Carefully

Some job applicants exaggerate or even lie about their qualifications and experience. So be sure to contact as many former employers as possible to try to get the inside story. Unfortunately, in today's legal climate, former employers are often reluctant to say anything negative for fear that if they speak frankly, they may be hit by a lawsuit for defamation. You need to learn to read between the lines. If a former employer is neutral, offers only faint praise or over-praises a person for one aspect of a job only ("great with numbers" or "invariably on time"), there's a good chance some negative information is hiding in the wings. If the reference isn't glowing and doesn't take in all aspects of the job, check several other references—and perhaps call back the applicant for a more directed interview.

Negligent hiring suits. Be particularly diligent in checking the background of employees such as drivers and security guards whose work may affect the public safety. Businesses have been successfully sued for negligence when obviously unfit employees have caused serious harm. Some of these cases arose where an employee with a history of criminal convictions or violent conduct was hired for sensitive work. In one case, a Texas company advertised for truck drivers and then hired a man without asking to see his driver's license or checking his driving record. A week later, the driver was in a serious accident. An injured person sued the employer for negligent hiring. It turned out that the employee had received at least five speeding tickets in the 18 months before he was hired, and he had hardly any experience in driving a truck. This led to a $500,000 damage award against the employer.

If you're running a bar, think twice before hiring a bouncer who was fired from a previous job for using excessive force. Or if your business gives financial advice or handles a customer's money, don't hire anyone who has a history of fraud or negligent financial dealings.

To protect yourself against claims of negligent or discriminatory hiring, keep a written record of your pre-employment checking. Write down the names of the people you spoke to, when you spoke to them and what they said. Also keep a copy of any records or tests that you looked at in making your hiring decision.

7. Insist on Adequate Experience

Once you have a pool of applicants, it's usually best to hire the person who has the strongest combination of experience and inherent ability. Most small businesses don't have the time or resources for extensive training. If you hire a bookkeeper, publicist or warehouse manager, that person needs to be able to perform the job from the very beginning. In short, it's usually a mistake to pick someone with loads of

charm or an old friend or relative over someone who knows the job.

8. Establish a Probationary Period

Consider hiring employees with the understanding that there's an initial probationary period, such as 90 days. Put the details in writing. During this period, the employees typically get a salary, but no benefits, and should receive periodic performance evaluations. The probationary period gives both you and the employee a fair chance to judge whether things will work out. After the probationary period, the employee becomes a "regular employee" qualifying for fringe benefits. But, as noted above, never talk or write about permanent employment, as that kind of language can imply a long-term contract and cause trouble if you have to fire the worker.

RECOMMENDED READING

- *Your Rights in the Workplace* by Dan Lacey (Nolo Press). An up-to-date treatment of such issues as illegal job discrimination, wage and hour laws and workplace safety. Although written from the perspective of the employee, this book is quite useful to employers as well.

- *Every Manager's Legal Guide to Hiring* by August Bequai (Dow Jones-Irwin). Clear, practical advice. The chapters on interviews and reference checks are particularly useful for a small business.

- *Negligent Hiring, Fraud, Defamation and Other Emerging Areas of Employer Liability* by Ronald M. Green and Richard J. Reibstein (The Bureau of National Affairs Inc.). A round-up of recent court cases dealing with an employer's liability to employees and to people injured by employees. Good if you're curious about the cutting edge of the law in this area.

B. Complying With Non-Discrimination Laws

Numerous federal and state laws are intended to promote equal opportunity and to prevent bias in hiring. Generally, these laws prohibit discrimination based on a individual's race, color, religion, sex or national origin. In addition, the Pregnancy Discrimination Act of 1978 prohibits discrimination on the basis of pregnancy, childbirth or related medical conditions. And the Age Discrimination in Employment Act prohibits discrimination against people aged 40 to 70. Some states also prohibit discrimination based on a person's height, weight or marital status.

The Americans With Disabilities Act (ADA) currently applies to employers with 25 or more employees. Beginning in July 1994, it will apply to employers with 15 or more employees. If you're

covered by the ADA (or a similar state law), you can't discriminate against employees or job applicants with disabilities. Furthermore, you may have to reasonably accommodate disabled people who are otherwise qualified for a position.

Exemptions from anti-discrimination laws may be available for a bona fide occupational qualification. For example, a manufacturer may need a person who fits a certain height-weight profile to safely operate a particular type of equipment, or a store specializing in the books of one religion may need clerks of that persuasion to effectively serve customers.

The pre-employment chart below outlines the type of information that you can ask for in applications and during job interviews. This chart was developed by the Michigan Department of Civil Rights. Follow the chart to comply with federal laws and those of practically every state.

PRE-EMPLOYMENT INQUIRY GUIDE

Subject	Lawful Pre-employment Inquiries	Unlawful Pre-employment Inquiries
Name	Applicant's full name Have you ever worked for this company under a different name? Is any additional information relative to a different name necessary to check work record? If yes, explain.	Original name of an applicant whose name has been changed by court order or otherwise. Applicant's maiden name.
Address or Duration of Residence	How long a resident of this state or city?	
Birthplace		Birthplace of applicant. Birthplace of applicant's parents, spouse or other close relatives. Requirements that applicant submit birth certificate, naturalization or baptismal record.
Age	Are you 18 years old or older?	How old are you? What is your date of birth?
Religion or Creed		Inquiry into an applicant's religious denomination, religious affiliations, church, parish, pastor, or religious holidays observed
Race or Color		Complexion or color of skin.
Photograph		Any requirement for a photograph prior to hire
Height		Inquiry regarding applicant's height.
Weight		Inquiry regarding applicant's weight
Marital Status	Is your spouse employed by this employer?	Requirement that an applicant provide any information regarding marital status or children. Are you single or married? Do you have any children? Is your spouse employed? What is your spouse's name?
Sex		Mr., Miss or Mrs. or an inquiry regarding sex. Inquiry as to the ability to reproduce or advocacy of any form of birth control. Requirement that women be given pelvic examinations.
Handicap/Disability		Inquiries regarding an individual's physical or mental condition which are not directly related to the requirements of a specific job and which are used as a factor in making employment decisions in a way which is contrary to the provisions or purposes for the Michigan Handicappers' Civil Rights Act.

Citizenship	Are you a citizen of the United States? If not a citizen of the United States, does applicant intend to become a citizen of the United States? If you are not a United States citizen, have you the legal right to remain permanently in the United Sates? Do you intend to remain permanently in the United States? (To avoid discrimination based on national origin, the questions above should be asked after the individual has been hired even if it is related to the Federal I-9 process.)	(Questions below are unlawful unless asked as part of the Federal I-9 process.) Of what country are you a citizen? Whether an applicant is naturalized or a native-born citizen; the date when the applicant acquired citizenship. Requirement that an applicant produce naturalization papers or first papers. Whether applicant's parents or spouse are naturalized or native born citizens of the United States: the date when such parent or spouse acquired citizenship.
National Origin	Inquiry into language applicant speaks and writes fluently.	Inquiry into applicant's (a) lineage; (b) ancestry; (c) national origin; (d) descent; (e) parentage, or nationality, unless pursuant to the Federal I-9 process. Nationality of applicant's parents or spouse. Inquiry into how applicant acquired ability to read, write or speak a foreign language.
Education	Inquiry into the academic vocational or professional education of an applicant and public and private schools attended.	
Experience	Inquiry into work experience. Inquiry into countries applicant has visited.	
Arrests	Have you ever been convicted of a crime? Are there any felony charges pending against you?	Inquiry regarding arrests which did not result in conviction. (Except for law enforcement agencies.)
Relatives	Names of applicant's relatives already employed by this company.	Address of any relative of applicant, other than address (within the United States) of applicant's father and mother, husband or wife and minor dependent children.
Notice in Case of Emergency	Name and address of person to be notified in case of accident or emergency.	Name and address of nearest relative to be notified in case of accident or emergency.
Organizations	Inquiry into the organizations of which an applicant is a member, excluding organizations the name or character of which indicates the race, color, religion, national origin or ancestry of its members.	List all clubs, societies and lodges to which you belong.

*This question may be asked only for the purpose of determining whether applicants are of legal age for employment.

(Issued by Michigan Department of Civil Rights)

In addition to observing the anti-discrimination guidelines when preparing application forms and interviewing job candidates, be careful when you advertise for employees. Obviously, it's illegal to run an ad specifying that applicants be of a certain race, sex or religion. But to further guard against claims of discrimination, it's important to describe jobs in neutral, non-sexist terms such as "salesperson," "manager" or "server"—not salesman, foreman or waitress. Or a job can specifically be designated "male/female" to make clear that applicants of both sexes are welcome.

Sexual Harassment

Legally, sexual harassment on the job is a form of sex discrimination prohibited by federal law—and many state laws. Sexual harassment comes in two basic varieties:

- **Quid Pro Quo**—a Latin phrase meaning something for something. This type of harassment occurs when, for example, employer Joe tells employee Ann that he'll fire her unless she sleeps with him. (The vast majority of sexual harassment claims involve a male supervisor and a female subordinate.) Quid quo pro harassment is also present if an employee's pay or assignment are dependent on submission to sexual requests.

- **Hostile Work Environment**—more subtle, perhaps, but equally illegal. It occurs when unwelcome sexual conduct interferes unreasonably with an employee's work performance or creates an intimidating or offensive environment. The work environment can be poisoned by such things as off-color jokes, pornographic pictures, unwanted touching and sexually charged horseplay. Courts have ruled that when a woman claims sexual harassment based on a hostile work environment, the test is whether or not a "reasonable woman" would see the remarks or behavior as offensive.

As an employer, you should take steps to prevent sexual harassment. The Equal Employment Opportunity Commission suggests that you affirmatively raise the subject, express strong disapproval, develop appropriate sanctions and inform employees of their right to raise harassment issues.

For an excellent treatment of this subject, see *Sexual Harassment on the Job* by William Petrocelli and Barbara Kate Repa (Nolo Press).

If you're a federal contractor or subcontractor, your ads must state that all qualified applicants will be considered without regard to race, color, religion, sex or national origin. The phrase "an equal oppor-

tunity employer" may also be required. In any case, it's wise to use it. And even though most small businesses are exempt from state and federal affirmative action laws, many progressive companies actively try to attract a racially diverse workforce.

C. Protecting Trade Secrets

In hiring and working with employees, some business owners need to protect their unique assets from misuse. For example:

- a restaurant's recipes for a special salad dressing and a muffin that draw people from miles around.

- a heating and cooling company's list of 500 customers for whom it regularly provides maintenance.

- a computer company's unique process for speedily assembling circuit boards.

If they are treated as such, the recipes, the customer list and the assembly process are all trade secrets. Other examples are an unpatented invention, engineering techniques, cost data, a formula or a machine. Trade secrets are your property and are entitled to legal protection if you take sensible steps to keep employees, competitors and others from making unauthorized use of them.

To qualify for legal protection as a trade secret, two preliminary criteria must be met.

First, you must show that you've taken steps to keep the information secret. If you disclose the trade secret in a trade journal, a speech or even in conversation with someone outside your company without getting a specific commitment from that person to keep it secret, you'll lose the right to legal protection.

Most lawsuits involving trade secrets are against former employees who learn the trade secret on the job, but later leave and try to profit from it.

Example: Sue works at the Speedy Copy Shop. She has daily access to the list of larger accounts that are regularly billed more than $2,000 per month. Sue quits to open her own competing shop. Before she does, she copies the list of major accounts. One of her first steps in getting her new business going is to contact these people to try and get their business away from her former employer. Speedy takes Sue to court.

Has Sue stolen trade secrets? The answer depends in large part on whether or not Speedy took steps to treat its list of larger accounts as a trade secret in the first place. If Speedy kept the list in a secure place, permitted access to employees on a need-to-know basis only and had them sign non-disclosure agreements, a judge likely will rule that trade secrets were stolen. But if Speedy's owners took no precautions at all, there's a good chance the judge won't recognize the list as as trade secret.

Second, the information must not be freely available from other sources. If the recipe for a restaurant's "special" salad dressing can be found in a standard American cookbook or re-created by any competent chef, it simply isn't a trade secret. On the other hand, if the restaurant's chef found the recipe in a medieval French cookbook in a provincial museum, translated it and figured out how to adapt it to currently available ingredients, it probably would be considered obscure enough to receive trade secret protection. That's because the recipe isn't readily available to other American restaurants.

In addition to these two primary legal tests, judges look at several other factors in deciding whether you have a trade secret:

- how valuable the information is to you and your competitors

- how much money and effort you spent in developing the trade secret

- how easily the information could have been acquired from other sources.

Here are some steps you can take to protect your legal position so that an employee doesn't make improper use of trade secrets.

- Before you hire someone who will have access to secrets, find out if the job candidate was trusted with trade secrets in the past. If so, did the prospective employee honor his or her obligations regarding the secrets?

- Have the employee sign a written agreement which specifies the things that you want to be treated as trade secrets and states that the employee will keep them secret.

- Keep confidential documents under lock and key and give access to the fewest possible employees. With computerized information, limit access by creating passwords that you divulge only to select employees who state in writing that they'll keep the password and protected information confidential.

- When an employee is fired or talks about quitting, quickly restrict the person's access to trade secrets and remind such an individual in writing that he or she mustn't use or reveal any of your trade secrets. Also, require the departing employee to turn in any written materials, equipment, samples or other items that may contain secret information.

- Require employees with access to trade secrets or other valuable proprietary information to sign a promise not to compete. It's best to do this when the employee first comes on board.

Even if you haven't obtained a confidentiality agreement or agreement not to compete from an employee, you may still be able to obtain a court order forbidding an employee or former employee from improperly using trade secrets and other confidential information that you disclosed.

D. Wage and Hour Requirements

The Federal Fair Labor Standards Act (FLSA) deals with both minimum wages and overtime pay. Legislation in your own state may deal with this subject as well. In Alaska, for example, the minimum hourly wage in 1992 is $4.75, more than the federal minimum of $4.25. Your state department of labor can tell you about the laws in your state.

Generally it's wise to pay more than the legal minimum even for positions that usually command only the minimum wage. Paying a little more than the going rate lets you recruit above-average people, which more than compensates for the extra cost. Workers work better and feel happier, and turnover is reduced.

1. Coverage of the Federal Fair Labor Standards Act

The FLSA sets the minimum wage; it doesn't require vacation, holiday and sick pay, premium pay for weekend or holiday work (unless it's for overtime), fringe benefits or formal notices for job terminations. Also, it doesn't place any limit on the number of hours that people 16 years of age or over can work— but it does give them rights to overtime pay for extra (more than 40 hours per week) work.

Almost every worker is covered by the FLSA, but the law doesn't apply to unincorporated family businesses that employ only family members.

Employees Who Receive Tips

A "tipped employee" is one who customarily and regularly receives more than $30 a month in tips. In 1992, the minimum wage is $4.25 an hour. For employees who earn tips, you can deduct up to $2.13 an hour—as long as the amount deducted doesn't exceed the value of the tips actually received.

If you're going to deduct something from the minimum hourly wage for a tipped employee, you must tell the employee about the tip credit allowance and allow the employee to keep all tips (either individually or through a pooling arrangement). Finally, you must show that the employee receives at least the minimum wage when you add together the direct wages and the tip credit.

The Wage and Hour Administration lets you employ learners, apprentices and handicapped workers at hourly wages lower than the minimum wage. The rate can be as low as 85% of the minimum wage for apprentices or as low as 50% of the mini-

mum wage for handicapped workers. As of April 1, 1991, you could pay "trainees" a minimum wage of $3.62 an hour; the training must be genuine and other rules apply.

Also under the federal law, you can pay a minimum wage of 85% of the prevailing minimum for full-time students who work at a retail service establishment. If you have a small retail or service business and want to hire up to six full-time students at the reduced rate, you must get a certificate for this preferential treatment. Send an application to the regional office of the Wage Hour Division of the Department of Labor. If you want to hire more than six full-time students at the preferential rate, the paperwork is more extensive, which may put a damper on your enthusiasm.

Many states, such as California, have labor departments that aggressively investigate employee complaints about wage and hour violations.

2. Overtime Pay

Be warned: This is a complicated subject. The overtime premium required by the federal Fair Labor Standards Act is one-and-a-half times the regular rate. It applies to all hours worked beyond a 40-hour work week. However, under a special provision of the law, an employee of a retail or service establishment who gets commissions is exempt from overtime if two conditions are met:

- The regular rate of the employee is more than one and a half times the prevailing minimum wage; and

- More than half of the compensation for a "representative period" (not less than one month) is commissions on goods or services.

In computing overtime pay, treat each work week as a separate unit. You can't average hours over two or more weeks. Many small businesses try to get around overtime pay by offering compensatory time off—usually if the employee receives a fixed salary. Legally, that's permitted as long as the comp time is awarded at the rate of one and one-half times the overtime hours worked and made available during the same pay period that the overtime hours were worked.

Example: Solstice Products pays John a fixed salary every two weeks. John's standard work week is made up of five shifts, each eight hours long. During the first week of a pay period, he works 44 hours, earning four hours of overtime pay. During the second week of the pay period, Solstice allows John to take six hours off (4 hours x 1.5) so that he works only 34 hours that week. Solstice pays him his regular salary as though he'd worked 40 hours each of these two weeks.

 Watch Out for Comp Time Violations. Often employers and employees agree that comp time will be taken long after the extra work was done. If the employee doesn't complain, that's fine, but you should know that if the employee objects, this is a violation of federal law.

 RECOMMENDED READING

- *Your Rights in the Workplace* by Dan Lacey (Nolo Press)—useful for employers even though written from an employee's perspective.

- *How To Comply With Federal Employee Laws* by Sheldon I. London (London Publishing Company Inc.).

E. Occupational Safety and Health

The Occupational Safety and Health Administration (OSHA) is part of the U.S. Department of Labor. Many states also have agencies dealing with safety and health issues on the job. To keep the workplace free from recognized hazards, the federal agency publishes minimum standards for each industry and conducts inspections. Most small businesses,

however, never see an OSHA inspector, because there are not enough of them to go around. And workplaces with ten or fewer employees are exempt from safety inspections unless they're in a high-risk industry.

OSHA publishes a self-inspection checklist that you may find helpful in spotting hazards. On your own, you should be alert for hazards such as eye irritants, strong odors, fumes, excessive noise or leaking chemicals.

Some workplace health and safety issues affect virtually every small business. For example, OSHA requires employers to warn workers of potentially hazardous chemicals. This can include photocopier supplies or solvents commonly used in offices and retail stores.

Today, many workers are requesting a smoke-free environment. Some employers accommodate both smokers and non-smokers by setting aside a special area where smokers can light up during a coffee break. Legally, the picture is unsettled. As noted in Section A.3, at least 15 states and many municipalities have laws restricting smoking in privately owned workplaces. Several states protect smokers by making it illegal to discriminate against employees who smoke during non-working hours.

With the increasing presence of computers in the workplace, there's considerable interest in the safety of video display terminals. While there's not yet widespread regulation in this field, it's very likely that we will be seeing pressure on employers to provide computer workers with frequent breaks and with furniture that reduces physical wear and tear on the workers, such as eye strain and wrist and back problems. With or without legislation, it makes sense for employers to encourage employees to take measures to avoid injury.

F. Workers' Compensation

Chapter 9 covers workers' compensation generally. One key to avoiding workers' compensation claims is to watch out for employees with pre-existing injuries—a task made difficult by the American With Disabilities Act (ADA). To comply with the law, follow these guidelines:

- Make sure your job descriptions emphasize the essential duties of the job.

- In job interviews, don't ask about general health or physical conditions. Inquire only about conditions that apply to essential job duties. It's OK to ask, "Can you perform these tasks?" Or, "Do you have any disability that would prevent you from performing the essential functions of the job?"

- Don't require medical exams before making a job offer. After you make a job offer, it's all right to require a job-related medical exam—if you require such an exam for all candidates for the same type of work.

G. Unemployment Claims

Employees who are terminated because of cut-backs or because you decide they are not a good fit for the job are generally entitled to unemployment benefits. Employees who are fired for serious misconduct (stealing, repeated absenteeism) or who voluntarily leave a job are not entitled to unemployment payments. In between these clear categories are many gray areas. For example, say you and an employee get into an argument that results in her leaving your employment. Did she quit? Was she fired? It's sometimes difficult to say.

1. An Overview of the System

Although the details vary in each state, some general principles apply in most cases. As a private employer, you contribute to an unemployment insurance fund in your state. Think of your contributions as a payroll tax you're responsible for. The rate is based on two factors: the size of your payroll and the amount of unemployment benefits paid from your account. Employers with smaller payrolls and low levels of unemployment claims will, over time, pay lower taxes, which means you'll save money if you recognize and successfully oppose questionable claims. If an ineligible claimant receives benefits, sooner or later you'll pay a higher tax than you should.

Typically, this is how a claim is processed:

Step 1: The former employee files a claim with the state agency that runs the unemployment program.

Step 2: You receive written notice of the claim and can file a written objection—usually within seven to 10 days. Don't miss this deadline. If you do, you may be cut off from raising your objection.

Step 3: The state agency makes an initial determination of eligibility. Usually there's no hearing at this stage.

Step 4: You or the former employee can appeal the eligibility decision and have a hearing before a referee. This is the most important step in this process. First of all, at the hearing, people testify and a record is made. Usually, any further appeal is based solely on what takes place at that hearing. You won't get a chance to add testimony later. Second, the referee's decision sometimes controls what happens in a related civil lawsuit. For example, if the referee rules that the employee quit because of sexual harassment, that may be decisive in a later case that the employee brings against your business for wrongful discharge.

Fortunately, unemployment hearings are usually quite informal—with no difficult procedures or rules of evidence. Employers with a minimum of savvy can represent themselves quite competently.

Step 5: Either side can appeal the referee's decision to an administrative agency—based solely on the testimony and documents used at the referee's hearing.

Step 6: Ultimately, either side can appeal to the state court system. This is rarely done because it's expensive.

The two most common defenses that an employer can raise are that the employee quit voluntarily without good cause, or that the employee was fired for willful misconduct.

2. Keeping Unemployment Benefit Costs Down

As with workers' compensation, there are ways you can defeat questionable claims and save thousands of dollars in unemployment taxes. Here are some tips for reducing the costs of unemployment benefits:

- Double check the information your state unemployment agency uses to compute your tax rates and to compute benefits paid to former employees. Clerical errors are frequent and can be costly.

- A former employee may be eligible for benefits at first but may later become ineligible. For example, three weeks after being fired, a claimant may decide to return to school full time, making him or her unavailable to take a new job. Or a former employee may receive retirement or vacation pay that affects the level of unemployment benefits. If you have information about such events, notify the state agency promptly.

- Before the referee's hearing, ask to see the agency's complete file on the claim. This will give you a chance to refute inaccurate statements.

- Bring all pertinent employment records to the referee's hearing. Also line up witnesses who can give first-hand testimony about why the former employee was guilty of misconduct, quit voluntarily or is otherwise ineligible for benefits.

- Consider having a lawyer or other specialist represent you or help you prepare key segments of your case—although the simple, informal procedures are not difficult to master. In some states, you can hire experienced non-lawyer specialists to oppose claims at a fraction of what lawyers charge.

A clerk in the referee's office may know who performs these services in your area.

H. Firing Employees

There's been a huge increase in recent years in the number of fired employees who sue their former employers for wrongful discharge—and win. True, the larger verdicts are usually against big companies, but even a small business is exposed to the risk of a costly judgment in favor of an ex-employee.

The basic rule of law in this field is the "at will" employment doctrine described in Section A. This doctrine states that unless a specific employment agreement fixes the length of employment, you're free to fire the employee for any reason or no reason at all, and the employee is free to resign at any time, either with or without a reason. But over the years, statutes and case law have somewhat eroded the employment at will doctrine. Today, there are a number of legal grounds on which a fired employee can base a wrongful discharge lawsuit against you.

But remember this: poor performance or a legitimate need to reduce your staff are both still valid reasons for firing an employee. In court where there's a welter of claims and counter-claims about why you terminated an employee, establishing that poor performance was the real reason can be a challenge. To ease the burden, always let your employees know what's expected of them and warn them if their performance declines. One good way to do this is to give them written evaluations and warnings and keep copies in your personnel files.

Now let's look at the legal grounds an employee can assert in fighting a firing. The details vary from state to state, but the basic rules are universal.

1. Illegal Discrimination

You can't fire employees because of their race, skin color, religious beliefs, national origin, gender or (in a few places) sexual orientation. In addition, age discrimination protections apply to employees over the age of 40, and the federal Pregnancy Discrimination Act protects female employees from being fired because of pregnancy, childbirth or related medical conditions. The Americans With Disabilities Act (ADA) makes it illegal to discriminate against people because of their physical condition. If a worker becomes disabled, either on the job or elsewhere, you may have to make a reasonable accommodation such as providing mechanical aids or adjusting the job duties.

2.   Public Policy

There are "public policy" limitations on firing employees. You can't fire an employee for refusing to perform an illegal act, such as fudging a report to an environmental protection agency, or for insisting on performing a legally permissible act such as reporting a health or safety problem to an appropriate public agency. Some states have laws that specifically protect whistle-blowers—employees who report violations or suspected violations of laws and regulations.

Example: Geri is an accountant at an EquipCo, an equipment rental company. She develops health problems which she believes are caused by fumes from a defective furnace. EquipCo refuses to repair the furnace. Geri reports the problem to the local building and safety department. Three days later, EquipCo fires her. Geri can

sue EquipCo under her state's whistle-blower protection law.

On the basis of public policy, judges have ruled that you can't fire an employee for filing a workers' compensation claim, or displaying an offensive bumper sticker.

3.   Employment Contracts

You can't fire an employee without a good reason if the employee has a written or oral contract assuring that a firing will only be for just cause. Sometimes the assurance of continuing employment isn't expressed in so many words but is implied from statements that employers make at the time of employment or in employee handbooks.

Example: Charles applies for a job at BlueCo, which decides to hire him. On the day the company hires Charles, the president tells him: "As long as you do your job, you'll be with this company until the mandatory retirement age of 65. You'll never have to look for another job." Charles is also given an employee handbook which says that employees will be discharged "for just cause only." A year later, the company fires Charles, and he sues for wrongful discharge. The judge rules that Charles has an implied contract that he can be terminated only for just cause. The implied contract results from Charles' "legitimate expectations" based on the president's statements and the employee handbook.

For more information about employee handbooks, see Section A.2.

I.   Independent Contractors

Independent contractors differ from employees in two primary ways:

- They control both the outcome of a project as well as the means of accomplishing it.
- They offer their services to the public at large—not to just one company.

Typically, a small business hires many independent contractors. Common examples are a lawyer or accountant, a painter who spruces up your office, or a computer consultant who installs specialized software at your store and teaches your employees how to use it.

Generally, independent contractors have special skills that you need to call upon only sporadically. But sometimes your company may have needs that can be filled equally well by an employee or an independent contractor. If you weigh both possibilities and conclude that you can save money and reduce paperwork by using an independent contractor rather than employee, fine. But be sure he or she really qualifies for independent contractor status under the IRS rules. If you classify a worker as an independent contractor when the worker should have been treated as an employee, and the IRS or a state unemployment or labor commissioner's office investigates and rules against you, you can face fairly severe penalties. Section 2, below, discusses the IRS rules for determining who is an independent contractor and who is an employee.

1. Advantages and Disadvantages of Independent Contractor Status

By hiring a person as an employee, you assume some financial burdens that you don't have if you hire the same person as an independent contractor. The cost of carrying an employee goes far beyond the amount on the employee's paycheck. You must make an employer's contribution for the worker's Social Security. You're also responsible for withholding federal and state income taxes and the worker's share of Social Security taxes, and for keeping records and reporting these items to the federal and state governments. Each year, you must send the employee a Form W-2 showing how much he or she earned and how much was withheld. (See Chapter 6, Section C.3, for details on an employer's tax responsibilities.)

That's not all. As an employer, you must carry workers' compensation insurance for the employee

and may have to make payments into an unemployment protection fund. Health insurance, retirement plans and other fringe benefits may add to the cost. Finally, most employers provide paid vacations and sick leave for employees.

Now, contrast this situation with hiring an independent contractor. When you use an independent contractor, you're not required to withhold taxes from the amount you pay the worker, and you don't have to pay any portion of the worker's Social Security. Your only responsibility is to complete a Form 1099-MISC at the end of the year if you paid the independent contractor $600 or more during the year. The form is sent to the IRS and the employee.

By hiring an independent contractor rather than an employee, you also save the expense of providing an office or other work space for the worker and the ongoing expenses of fringe benefits and insurance. Furthermore, if you become unhappy with the person's work, you can turn to another independent contractor without going through the trauma often associated with firing an employee who works each day on your premises. Another benefit of hiring someone as an independent contractor is that your company generally won't be liable for the negligence of the person that you hire. If you hire employees, however, you would be liable if, for example, the employee carelessly injured someone while at work.

Of course, there are tradeoffs. A business doesn't enjoy day-to-day control over the work of an independent contractor. Not having the person always available may be inconvenient. Furthermore, because an independent contractor must charge enough to cover the costs of doing business and still make a profit, he or she may charge a higher price for services than the hourly rate paid to an employee. And if an independent contractor is injured because of some dangerous situation at your business premises or in a place that you have control over, the independent contractor can sue your business for injuries. An employee in the same situation would be limited to workers' compensation benefits. But if you carry adequate liability insurance to protect you from claims by any injured person who is not an employee, this isn't a significant drawback.

Given a choice, many workers prefer to be treated as independent contractors rather than employees. Some like the fact that there's no withholding of taxes; they feel that they have a better cash flow, even though they're ultimately responsible for paying their taxes, and the employer isn't picking up any part of the Social Security tax. Workers may also see benefits in being treated as independent contractors because they're more easily able to deduct business expenses, including money spent on cars, home offices, and travel and entertainment. On the other hand, some workers prefer employment status that gives them paid vacations, medical care and other fringe benefits at the employer's expense—and freedom from worry about the paperwork required of people who are in business for themselves.

2. Employee or Independent Contractor: The IRS Rules

To determine whether someone is an employee or an independent contractor, the IRS looks at the degree of control you have over the worker. Basically, if you control—or can control—not only what is to be done but also how it's done, the worker is an employee. The IRS acknowledges that people in an independent trade, business or profession who offer their services to the public generally are not employees even though they occasionally work for you.

The IRS doesn't care what you call the relationship. You can designate someone as a partner, co-adventurer, agent or independent contractor. But if the person really is an employee, that's how the IRS says you must treat the person. The IRS's list of factors is shown below.

Factors Tending To Show the Worker Is an Employee

- You require—or can require—the worker to comply with your instructions about when, where and how to work.

- You train the worker to perform services in a particular manner.

- You integrate the workers' services into your business operations.

- You require the worker to render services personally; the worker can't hire others to do some of the work.
- You hire, supervise and pay assistants for the worker.
- Your business has a continuing relationship with the worker, or work is performed at frequently recurring intervals.
- You establish set hours of work.
- You require the worker to devote substantially full time to your business.
- You have the worker do the work on your premises.
- You require the worker to do the work in a sequence that you set.
- You require the worker to submit regular oral or written reports.
- You pay the worker by the hour, week or month, unless these are installment payments of a lump sum agreed to for a job.
- You pay the worker's business or traveling expenses.
- You furnish significant tools, equipment and materials.
- You have the right to discharge the worker at will, and the worker has the right to quit at will.

Factors Tending To Show the Worker Is an Independent Contractor

- The worker hires, supervises and pays his or her assistants.
- The worker is free to work when and for whom he or she chooses.
- The worker does the work at his or her own office or shop.
- The worker is paid by the job or receives a straight commission.
- The worker invests in facilities used in performing services, such as renting an office.

- The worker can realize a profit or suffer a loss from his or her services, such as a worker who's responsible for paying salaries to his or her own employees.
- The worker performs services for several businesses at one time—although sometimes a worker can be an employee of several businesses.
- The worker makes his or her services available to the general public.
- The worker can't be fired so long as he or she meets the contract specifications.

In most situations, the status of a worker is determined by these factors (called "common law factors"). Certain workers, however, fall into special categories, and the usual IRS criteria don't apply to them. For example, the federal tax law says that certain workers are automatically employees, including:

- officers of corporations who provide service to the corporation
- food and laundry delivery drivers
- full-time salespeople who sell goods for resale
- full-time life insurance agents working mainly for one company
- at-home workers who are supplied with material and given specifications for work to be performed.

Federal law also provides that licensed real estate agents and door-to-door salespeople are generally treated as "non-employees" or "exempt employees," but may be treated as employees for the purpose of liability and workers' compensation.

As a sole proprietor or partner in your own business, you're neither an employee nor an independent contractor. You're responsible for paying your own income tax and Social Security self-employment tax. If you're a shareholder in a corporation but provide services to the corporation, you're generally an employee.

3. Additional State Rules

The IRS list of common law factors is similar to the standards followed in most states for state taxes and unemployment rules, but there can be some differences. For example, in California, a person working for a licensed contractor who performs services requiring certain state licenses is an employee unless the worker has a valid contractor's license. If you plan to hire independent contractors, check with the employment office in your state to see if special rules are in effect.

4. How the Independent Contractor Rules Are Applied

To better understand how the IRS common law tests are applied, let's look at two workers who provide the same type of services but fall into different legal categories.

Example 1: The Employee. Wendy teaches advertising part-time at a community college. In addition, she does work for ABC Enterprises writing the company's newspaper ads, as well as its catalogs and consumer information leaflets. Wendy works at the company's offices every Wednesday and Friday. She receives a fixed salary each week for her two days of work. Wendy reports to the owner of the company and receives direct supervision and instructions from the owner. The company furnishes a desk and the supplies that she needs to do her job. Wendy writes advertising exclusively for ABC Enterprises; she's not allowed to do this kind of writing for anyone else. Wendy is an employee of the company.

Example 2: The Independent Contractor. XYZ Distributors has similar needs for advertising copy on an occasional basis. But when XYZ needs a newspaper ad or catalog, it calls upon Frank to do the work. Frank works out of his home and occasionally farms out some of his overflow work to other writers, whom he pays directly. Frank owns his own computer and word processing software and pays for his own expenses of doing business. Each time he completes a job for XYZ Distributors, he sends the company an invoice. Frank writes ads for half a dozen different companies and is constantly seeking new customers. He clearly is an independent contractor and not an employee.

If you can't decide whether a person is an employee or an independent contractor under the IRS tests, the IRS will give you a written report of its determination. You'll have to file Form SS-8 with the IRS. Your local IRS office will tell you where you can mail the form.

5. The Risks of Misclassification

There are at least three ways for the IRS to learn about your hiring and classification practices. First, the IRS may look into the affairs of an independent contractor who hasn't been paying his or her income taxes. Second, disgruntled employees may complain to the IRS if they think independent contractors are getting favored treatment. Third, during tax audits, the IRS routinely checks to see if workers have been misclassified as independent contractors.

The presumption is that the worker is an employee unless proven otherwise. If the status of a worker is questioned, it's up to you to prove that the worker is an independent contractor rather than an employee.

If it turns out that an employee was in fact misclassified, the cost to your business will be heavy. You'll be responsible for paying the employee's Social Security tax, federal income tax and federal unemployment insurance for up to three years. In addition, the IRS can add penalties and interest.

State government officials are also interested in businesses that misclassify employees as independent contractors. A state employment office may audit your business to see if there's been any misclassification. The audit can be the result of a spot check by the state employment office or a request by an independent contractor for unemployment or workers' compensation benefits. You may wind up owing money to a state unemployment insurance fund.

A Worker's Status May Change

John operates a small desktop publishing shop spe-cializing in writing and designing brochures, flyers and other promotional materials for small businesses. At first, John does most of the work himself, turning any overload over to others with similar skills. John collects from the customer and pays these people as independent contractors. So far, so good.

As John's business grows, he arranges for part-time help on a fairly regular basis. Sue, Ted and Ellen regularly handle the overflow, working in John's offices under his broad supervision an average of about two days per week each. The rest of the time they work for themselves. John continues to treat them as independent contractors. By law, he shouldn't. He's tempting fate—and the IRS. John is exercising significant control over these workers and using their services in-house on a regular basis. Under the IRS guidelines—the common law factors— summarized in Section 2, they are part-time employ-ees. John should withhold income taxes and pay the employer's share of Social Security taxes as well as carry workers' comp insurance and pay into the state's unemployment fund.

6. Avoiding Problems With Independent Contractor Classification

Here are some suggestions that will help you to have a worker classified as an independent contractor:

- Sign a contract with the independent contractor spelling out the responsibilities of each party and how payment is to be determined for each job. The contract should allow the independent con-tractor to hire his or her own assistants. A sample contract is shown below.

- Require the independent contractor to furnish all or most of the tools, equipment and material needed to complete the job.

- Have the independent contractor do all or most or the work at his or her own place, not at your business premises.

- Make it clear that the independent contractor is free to offer services to other businesses.

- Pay for work by the job rather than by the hour, week or month. Have the independent contractor submit invoices for each job before you make payment.

- Specifically state in your contract that the con-tractor will carry his or her own insurance, including workers' compensation coverage.

A lawyer or accountant can help you analyze specific situations and avoid problems with the IRS or state taxing and employment offices. For more information on independent contractors, I recom-mend *Guide To Hiring Independent Contractors* by Carolyn Usinger (American Chamber of Commerce Publishers).

SAMPLE CONTRACT WITH INDEPENDENT CONTRACTOR

AGREEMENT

This AGREEMENT made on _____, 19___ between _____
                                                                                    Client

of _____and _____
            Business Address   Contractor

of _____
            Business Address

1. **Services To Be Performed.** Contractor agrees to perform the following services for Client:

[Description of services]

2. **Time For Performance.** Contractor to complete the performance of these services on or before _____, 19____.

3. **Payment.** In consideration of Contractor's performance of these services, Client agrees to pay Contractor as follows:

[Description of how payment will be computed]

4. **Invoices.** Client will submit invoices for all services performed.

5. **Independent Contractor.** The parties intend Contractor to be an independent contractor in the performance of these services. Contractor shall have the right to control and determine the method and means of performing the above services; Client shall not have the right to control or determine such method or means.

6. **Other Clients.** Contractor retains the right to perform services for other clients.

7. **Assistants.** Contractor, at Contractor's expense, may employ such assistants as Contractor deems appropriate to carry out this agreement. Contractor will be responsible for paying such assistants, as well as any expense attributable to such assistants, including income taxes, unemployment insurance and social security taxes, and will maintain workers' compensation insurance for such employees.

8. **Equipment and Supplies.** Contractor, at Contractor's own expense, will provide all equipment, tools and supplies necessary to perform the above services, and will be responsible for all other expenses required for the performance of those services.

CONTRACTOR   CLIENT

_____   _____

 Trade secrets. In some situations, you may disclose trade secrets of your business to an independent contractor. If so, include a clause in the agreement prohibiting the independent contractor from disclosing or making any other unauthorized use of the trade secrets.

THE IMPORTANCE OF EXCELLENT CUSTOMER RELATIONS

13

Customers (you may call them clients or patients) are the lifeblood of any small business or professional practice. To thrive, you not only need a steady stream of people who keep coming back for more goods or services; you also need them to enthusiastically recommend your business to their friends. To build a loyal following, you must do more than just give people what the law requires. Yes, knowledge of your legal rights and those of your customers is important, but it's even more important not to let legal technicalities take priority over a key objective of your business: to keep happy customers coming back and sending other people your way.

Example: When Sandra brought her white wool blazer home from the dry cleaner's, she was dismayed to see that it had a very slight pink tint. Sandra reported the problem to Milt, the owner of the cleaning shop. Milt could have legally responded in a number of ways, including the following:

- "The problem is scarcely noticeable. You're being fussy."

- "How do I know the blazer wasn't like this when you brought it in?"

- "Didn't you see our sign? We're not responsible for any problems once you take the cleaned garment from the shop."

- "That's a two-year old blazer. Used clothing isn't worth much. I'll pay you $20 for the damage—not a penny more."

- "I've never had this type of complaint before. I want to send the blazer to an independent testing lab to see if the fabric is sub-standard. If it is, it's your problem—not mine."

But Milt was a wise business person. He didn't stand on his legal rights. Instead he told Sandra: "I'm sorry this happened. We use state-of-the-art cleaning processes, but apparently something went wrong. In any case, we guarantee your complete satisfaction. Since we can't fix this type of damage, let me know the purchase price of an equivalent new blazer." Sandra did, and Milt reimbursed her the full amount.

As a result of his enlightened attitude, Milt had a happy customer. In the two years since the blazer problem, Sandra and her husband have taken more than $500 worth of cleaning business to Milt's shop. They not only continue to be loyal customers, but—even more important—every time Sandra wears her new blazer, she tells the story of how Milt bought it for her and she recommends his business. Because Milt treated Sandra well, the blazer now ranks as one of Milt's all-time best investments.

Now consider what would have happened if Milt had responded with a strictly legalistic approach, offering Sandra the value of a two-year old blazer. Sandra might have grumbled and accepted the $20 payment, or she might have taken Milt to small claims court and perhaps have won a few dollars more. But this much is certain: Sandra and her husband would never have taken any more cleaning to Milt's place. Even worse, they'd likely have told others about Milt's inadequate service for years to come and might have complained to local better business and state regulatory agencies. So while Milt was thinking of himself as a tough business person who knows his legal rights and never lets customers rip him off, he actually would have foolishly lost many thousands of dollars of business.

Whether you run a restaurant, a hardware store or a sand and gravel business, if a customer complains about your product or service, don't quibble. It's much smarter to point to your customer satisfaction policy as you eliminate or reduce the charges—and maybe even give the customer something extra as a reward for putting up with the problem. Maybe you won't make any money on that transaction; you'll probably even take a small loss. And yes, once in a blue moon someone will take unfair advantage of your policy. So what? When you consider the good feelings that customers will have about your business—and the fact that you'll receive positive rather than negative word-of-mouth from everyone you treat generously—it's a bargain. Consider, too, that a customer whose problem you resolve is unlikely to complain to any agency or board with power to license or otherwise oversee your business. Anyone who has had to cope with an investigation knows that even if the complaint that triggered the inquiry has no merit, the process can be worrisome and, if lawyers are involved, expensive.

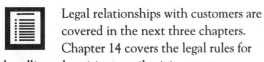 Legal relationships with customers are covered in the next three chapters. Chapter 14 covers the legal rules for handling advertising, retail pricing, returns, warranties and other customer transactions. In Chapter 15, you'll find information about checks and credit cards. Chapter 16 explains how to extend credit and get prompt payment.

A. Developing Your Customer Satisfaction Policy

Whether you're selling products or services, go further than is legally required in anticipating and responding to the problems of your customers. How you do this depends in part on the nature of the products or services you offer. But for starters, consider the policy of Eddie Bauer—a highly successful national company that sells outdoor goods through its catalog and retail outlets:

OUR GUARANTEE

Every item we sell will give you complete satisfaction or you may return it for a full refund.

OUR CREED

To give you such outstanding quality, value, service and guarantee that we may be worthy of your high esteem.

Over the years, my family and I have bought many items from Eddie Bauer. We've never had to return anything for a refund. But just knowing that the company stands behind what it sells has given us confidence in Eddie Bauer products. And that, of course, is the point: by reassuring customers in advance that they control the resolution of any problems, Eddie Bauer's good customer service is a marketing advantage.

Some department store chains such as Nordstrom's have also built solid businesses based in large part on their guarantee of customer satisfaction.

But it's not just the big-time operators who successfully use a customer recourse policy as a business-building technique. Nolo Press—the small California company that published this book—has more than held its own in the highly competitive book business in part because of consumer-oriented policies such as this one:

OUR NO-HASSLE GUARANTEE

If for any reason, anything you buy direct from Nolo Press does not meet your needs, we'll cheerfully refund your purchase price and we'll pay for your cost to return it to us via U.S. Mail (Priority). No ifs, ands or buts.[1]

Short and simple. No legal technicalities. No complicated rules. As additional evidence of its desire to serve its customers, Nolo offers another customer satisfaction policy almost unheard of in the industry: Nolo gives people 25% off on any current title if they return the cover of a prior, out-of-date edition. Why? Because out-of-date law books can be dangerous, and a customer who uses them is poorly served.

Businesses that treat customers generously can reap an unexpected dividend: higher morale among workers. Employees are not robots. They hate defending miserly policies that result in stressful confrontations with customers. They make great ambassadors for businesses they truly feel good about.

---

[1]Incidentally, Nolo's guarantee applies to this book.

LAW IN THE REAL WORLD

Listening to Your Employees

Rose, the owner of a retail store, overhears clerk Ned tell an unhappy customer that there is nothing he can do—the time to return a particular item ran out yesterday. Rose intervenes to solve the customer's problem by graciously taking the merchandise back. Now, Ned is unhappy. "I was just following your policy," he tells Rose. "You undercut me and made me feel really stupid." Rose realizes it is unwise to adopt a strict policy and then throw it out on a whim. After all, if she hadn't overheard the conversation, she would have lost a customer and made an employee feel bad about being a tough guy. Rose meets with her employees, and together they come up with a much more customer-friendly policy. They post it conspicuously in the store so that everyone knows what the new, fairer rules are.

Businesses that offer services have different problems than restaurants and retail outlets. But they still have many opportunities to enhance customer satisfaction and favorable word-of-mouth. On longer-term jobs, you can set time-performance standards in advance so that both you and the customer can judge if everyone's expectations are being met. Often this consists of little more than committing yourself to meeting interim deadlines. For example, a toxic materials contractor removing asbestos from heating ducts in a three-story building might agree to get the entire job done in 30 days with the first floor clean and ready to re-occupy in 10 days and the second floor in 20 days. A home remodeling or painting company might go farther and commit to meticulously cleaning up its work area each day.

Another good approach is to regularly ask for feedback from customers or clients. For example, if you run a bookkeeping service, a copy shop or a janitorial service that does regular business with larger accounts, ask your customers from time to time if your high standards—and the customer's needs—are being met. I was favorably impressed when the landlord who owns the building where my law firm prac-

tices asked me to evaluate the interior and exterior maintenance services we were receiving. There's currently a glut of office space in my town. When my lease is up I'll have a choice of many new buildings. But I'll remember that my current landlord seemed sincerely concerned about keeping this building spic and span.

You may think that a business offering a service as intangible as a seminar would have a hard time developing an effective customer-satisfaction policy—but you'd be wrong. Here's a guarantee from the American Management Association that serves as an excellent model:

A SIMPLE GUARANTEE FOR A COMPLEX BUSINESS WORLD

At AMA, we guarantee the quality of our seminars. It's that simple. More than 98% of our seminar attendees say they would recommend the course they have taken to their colleagues. But if for any reason you are not satisfied with a seminar for which you have paid, AMA will give you credit toward another course of comparable price or will simply refund your fee. That's it! No hassles. No loopholes. Just excellent service. That's what AMA is all about.

Here are some other examples of service businesses that use guarantees as a way of building a customer base:

- If you're unhappy with your hotel room, Hampton Inn will refund your money.

- If you get transferred from phone to phone while seeking an answer to an insurance question, Delta Dental Plan of Massachusetts will send you a $50 check.

- If your mini-pizza takes more than five minutes to be served, Pizza Hut gives you a free one.

- If you're not satisfied with a lawn treatment applied by Green Valley Lawn Care, the company will reapply the treatment at no cost—or, if you prefer, refund the cost of the treatment.

Elements of an Effective Customer Satisfaction Policy

The following ideas for developing your customer satisfaction policy come from *Marketing Without Advertising* by Michael Phillips and Salli Rasberry (Nolo Press):

- Customers should be encouraged to tell you about any problems.

- Customers should know their rights and responsibilities from the beginning.

- Customers should know the circumstances under which they are entitled to get their money back and how to take advantage of other rights.

- Customers—not you—should feel in control. It's far better to provide a full refund if the customer is dissatisfied than to demand that the customer come up with a "good reason" for the refund.

- A refund, or any other recourse you offer, should be prompt.

B. Telling Customers About Your Policies

Every communication between you and your customers is an opportunity to let them know that you're sincerely interested in their complaints and comments. Show your concern through signs in your business place, questionnaires and surveys mailed to them, and by simply inquiring from time to time if their needs are being met. Use your imagination. Labels, receipts, catalogs and packaging afford you the chance to let people know what their rights are and exactly how you'll deal with any problems. And don't use small print. Although it's sometimes hard to accept, you want your customers to know that you welcome the chance to fix problems.

And now, a few words on how not to communicate with customers. We've all seen stores that have negative signs next to the cash register, with unfriendly messages like:

NO RETURNS WITHOUT RECEIPT

NO CASH REFUNDS

NO OUT-OF-TOWN CHECKS

Often, the owner has then added a few Scotch-taped signs with more negative messages such as "$10 is charged for every returned check—no exceptions" or "If you break it, you own it." Not only is this offensive—it's stupid. Your statement of a customer's responsibilities doesn't have to be put in confrontational language. To take one example, even if you decide not to give cash refunds (a policy you may want to re-think), there are friendlier ways to state your policy, such as:

WE ARE PLEASED TO ACCEPT ALL RETURNS WITHIN 30 DAYS FOR FULL STORE CREDIT.

This statement has a positive tone but makes the customer responsible for returning the goods within 30 days to receive credit.

The law in many cities and a few states requires that you post your policies on returns and other customer recourse. In many of those locations, if you don't post your policy, your customers have the right to a full cash refund. But even if the law doesn't require you to post your policy, it makes excellent business and legal sense.

Get Help To Solve Customer Disputes

Sometimes, despite your best efforts to treat customers fairly, a dispute starts to get out of hand. At that point, consider bringing the Better Business Bureau or other respected third party into the picture. I recommend the BBB because according to various national polls, it's usually the first agency that consumers turn to for help when they're trying to solve a problem with a business.

Your local government may also offer mediation as a means of resolving consumer-business disputes without going to court. This is true, for example, in many counties in California. Also, many communities have neighborhood dispute programs that may be helpful for some types of small business disputes.

For more on dispute resolution techniques, including negotiation, mediation, arbitration and litigation, see Chapter 18.

LEGAL REQUIREMENTS FOR DEALING WITH CUSTOMERS

14

Many legal problems can be avoided by adopting enlightened policies for dealing with your customers. Customer-friendly policies, however, can't anticipate every problem. Consequently, you must understand the legal rules that apply. This chapter covers advertising, retail pricing and return practices, warranties and consumer protection laws.

A. Advertising

Before we get into the legal rules for advertising, consider a more fundamental question: Do you really need to advertise?

1. Is Advertising Necessary?

People starting a small business often assume they must advertise to attract customers. This always made good sense to me—until I read and thought about some eye-opening ideas in *Marketing Without Advertising*, by Michael Phillips and Salli Rasberry (Nolo Press). Phillips and Rasberry argue convincingly that for small businesses, most money spent on conventional advertising—radio and TV spots and display ads in newspapers—is wasted. You're competing with thousands of other advertisers, and your message is unlikely to be noticed by enough potential customers to produce a profitable level of sales.

Here's more from *Marketing Without Advertising*:

> The best and most economical way to attract and hold customers is through personal recommendation. A customer who is pre-screened and prepared for what you have to offer is far more likely to appreciate you and use your business than is someone responding to an ad offering a low price. The essence of marketing without advertising is to encourage personal recommendation. How do you do this? Lots of ways, all of which start with creating an atmosphere of trust. Central to doing this is to run an honest business.

Phillips and Rasberry recommend marketing strategies that don't rely on traditional advertising. For example, they discuss the importance of the physical appearance of your business (insist on scrupulous cleanliness and avoid clutter and unpleasant smells). They point out that listing your products or services where customers expect to find them—such as the Yellow Pages, local business directories, trade publications and, depending on the business, the classifieds—is often extremely cost-effective. Interestingly, Phillips and Rasberry distinguish between advertising and listings not on the basis of cost (although advertising does usually cost considerably more), but on whether customers are pre-screened to see your message. For example, someone who checks the Yellow Pages or a local free classified newspaper for a drain cleaning service needs that type of business. By contrast, someone who reads a display ad or hears a radio spot for the same business is unlikely to need that service immediately or to remember the ad months or years later when the need does arise.

2. Legal Standards for Advertising

Advertising is regulated by both federal and state law. Under the law, your ad is unlawful if it tends to mislead or deceive. This means the government doesn't have to prove at an administrative hearing or in court that the ad actually fooled anyone—only that it had a deceptive quality. Your intentions don't matter either. If your ad is deceptive, you'll face legal problems even if you have the best intentions in the world. What counts is the overall impression created by the ad—not the technical truthfulness of the individual parts. Taken as a whole, your ad must fairly inform the ordinary consumer.

In addition, if your ad contains a false statement, you have violated the law. The fact that you didn't know the information was false is irrelevant.

The Federal Trade Commission (FTC) is the main federal agency that takes action against unlawful advertising. State and local governments also go after businesses that violate advertising laws; usually this is the responsibility of the state Attorney General, Consumer Protection agency and local District Attorney. Consumers and competitors may also be able to proceed directly against the advertiser.

Over the years, the FTC has taken action against many businesses accused of engaging in false and deceptive advertising. A significant number of those administrative actions have been tested in court. By and large, courts have upheld even the most stringent FTC policies. For the most part, the FTC relies on consumers and competitors to report unlawful advertising. (See Appendix B for addresses and phone numbers of FTC offices.) If FTC investigators are convinced that an ad violates the law, they usually try to bring the violator into voluntary compliance through informal means. If that doesn't work, the FTC can issue a cease-and-desist order and bring a civil lawsuit on behalf of people who have been harmed. The FTC can also seek a court order (injunction) to stop a questionable ad while an investigation is in progress. In addition, the FTC can require an advertiser to run corrective ads—ads that state the correct facts and admit that an earlier ad was deceptive.

Most states have laws—usually in the form of consumer fraud or deceptive practices statutes—that regulate advertising. Under these laws, state or local officials can seek injunctions against unlawful ads and take legal action to get restitution to consumers. Some laws provide for criminal penalties—fines and jail—but criminal proceedings for false advertising are rare unless fraud is involved.

Consumers often have the right to sue advertisers under state consumer protection laws. (See Section D.) For example, someone who purchases a product or services in reliance on a false or deceptive ad might sue in small claims court for a refund or join with others (sometimes ten of thousands of others) to sue for a huge sum in another court.

A competitor harmed by unlawful advertising, or faced with the likelihood of such harm, generally has the right to seek an injunction and possibly an award of money (damages) as well, although damages are often difficult to prove. Such cases usually are based on one of two legal theories: unfair competition or commercial disparagement.

3. How To Stay Out of Trouble

The following rules will help keep your ads within safe, legal limits.

Rule 1—Be Accurate

Make sure your ads are factually correct and that they don't tend to deceive or mislead the buying public. Don't show a picture of this year's model of a product if what you're selling is last year's model, even if they look almost the same.

Be truthful about what consumers can expect from your product. Don't say ABC pills will cure headaches if the pills offer only temporary pain relief. Don't claim a rug shampooer is a wizard at removing all kinds of stains when in fact there are some it won't budge.

Waterproof or fireproof means just that—not water resistant or fire resistant under some circumstances. The term Polar, when attached to winter gear, suggests that it will keep people warm in extreme cold, not that it's just adequate when the temperature drops near freezing.

Rule 2—Get Permission

Does your ad feature someone's picture or endorsement? Does it quote material written by someone not on your staff or employed by your advertising agency? Does it use the name of a national organization such as the Boy Scouts or Red Cross? If so, get written permission.

Under U.S. copyright law, the "fair use" doctrine allows limited quotations from copyrighted works without specific authorization from the copyright owner. In some circumstances, this doctrine provides legal justification for the widespread practice of quoting from favorable reviews in ads for books, movies and plays—and even vacuum cleaners. However, with the exception of brief quotes from product or service reviews, you should always seek permission to quote protected material. For more on the fair use doctrine and many other aspects of copyright law and practice, see *The Copyright Handbook: How To Protect and Use Written Works*, by Stephen Fishman (Nolo Press).

Rule 3—Treat Competitors Fairly

Don't knock the goods, services or reputation of others by giving false or misleading information. If you compare your goods and services with those of other companies, double-check your information to make sure that every statement in your ad is accurate. Then check again.

Rule 4—Have Sufficient Quantities on Hand

When you advertise goods for sale, make every effort to have enough on hand to supply the demand that it's reasonable to expect. If you don't think you can meet the demand, state in your ad that quantities are limited. You may even want to state the number of units on hand.

State law may require merchants to stock an advertised product in quantities large enough to meet reasonably expected demand, unless the ad states that stock is limited. California, for example, has such a law. In other states, merchants may have to give a rain check if they run out of advertised goods in certain circumstances. Make sure you know what your state requires.

Rule 5—Watch Out for the Word "Free"

If you say that goods or services are "free" or "without charge," be sure there are no unstated terms or conditions that qualify the offer. If there are any limits, state them clearly and conspicuously.

Let's assume that you offer a free paintbrush to anyone who buys a can of paint for $8.95 and that you describe the kind of brush. Because you're disclosing the terms and conditions of your offer, you're in good shape so far. But there are pitfalls to avoid.

- If the $8.95 is more than you usually charge for this kind of paint, the brush clearly isn't free.

- Don't reduce quality of the paint that the customer must purchase or the quantity of any services (such as free delivery) you normally provide. If you provide a lesser product or service, you're exacting a hidden cost for the brush.

- Disclose any other terms, conditions or limitations.

For more information on the use of the word "free," see Section B.1 below.

Rule 6—Be Careful When You Describe Sales and Savings

You should be absolutely truthful in all claims about pricing. Because this point is so important, I discuss it in more detail in Section B.1 below.

Rule 7—Observe Limitations on Offers of Credit

Don't advertise that you offer easy credit unless it's true. A business that's not careful in this area can be charged with engaging in an unfair or deceptive practice that violates the FTC law. You don't offer easy credit if:

- You don't extend credit to people who don't have a good credit rating.

- You offer credit to people with marginal or poor credit ratings but you require a higher down payment or shorter repayment period than is ordinarily required for creditworthy people.

- You offer credit to poor risks, but once all the fine print is deciphered, the true cost of credit you charge exceeds the average charged by others in your retail market.

- You offer credit to poor risks at favorable terms but employ draconian (although legal) collection practices against buyers who fall behind.

If you advertise specific credit terms, you must provide all relevant details, including the down payment, the terms of repayment and the annual interest rate. For further details, order the FTC booklet, *How To Advertise Consumer Credit*, available for $2 from the Superintendent of Documents, U.S. Government Printing Office, Washington, DC 20401.

B. Retail Pricing and Return Practices

In addition to regulating advertising, the federal government and most state governments have laws and rules that address several types of retail practices.

1. Deceptive Pricing

The Federal Trade Commission (FTC) has jurisdiction over deceptive pricing practices. At the state level, usually the Attorney General's office or, in bigger cities, the District Attorney's Consumer Fraud Unit enforces laws dealing with deceptive trade practices. The two biggest problems they encounter concern retailers who (1) make incorrect price comparisons with other merchants or with their own "regular" prices, and (2) those who offer something

that is supposedly "free" but in fact has a cost. (See Section A.)

Offering a reduction from your usual selling price is a common and powerful sales technique. But to satisfy legal requirements, it's essential that the former price be the actual, bona fide price at which you offered the article. Otherwise, the pricing is misleading.

> **Example:** WizWare Inc. produces computer software and announces a new product for $129. But the company sells the product to wholesalers as if it were a $79 product and similarly discounts it to direct customers. The $129 price has never really existed, except to mislead customers into thinking they were receiving a discount.

Price comparisons often use words such as "Regularly," "Usually" or "Reduced." For example, it's common to see a price tag that says, "Regularly $200, Now $150." Or sometimes a sign says "1/3 off our regular price." These comparisons are fine legally—if you in fact offered the sale merchandise at the old price for a reasonable length of time. They're not okay if you've brought a special batch of merchandise especially for the sale and created a fictional "regular" price or one you adhered to for only a day or two.

If your ad compares your price with what other merchants are charging for the same product, be sure of two things:

- The other merchants are selling the identical product; and

- There were a sufficient number of sales at the higher price by merchants in your area so that you're offering a legitimate bargain.

In other words, make sure that the higher comparison price isn't an isolated or unrepresentative price.

Regarding offers of "free" products or services, you can offer gifts only if there are no strings attached. (See the discussion of "free" offers in Section A.)

2. Sales Away From Your Place of Business

A customer has three days—a "cooling off period"—to cancel any sale not made at a normal business place. For details, see the FTC's trade regulation rule called "Cooling Off Period for Door-to-Door Sales," 16 CFR § 429. Here's how the FTC defines a door-to-door sale:

> The sale, lease or rental of consumer goods or services with a purchase price of $25 or more, whether under single or multiple contracts, in which the seller or his representative personally solicits the sale, including those in response to or following an invitation by the buyer, and the buyer's agreement or offer to purchase is made at a place other than the place of business of the seller.

Pay attention to the words "other than the place of business of the seller." They cover a lot of ground. Legally, a door-to-door sale is one made at a customer's home, but it's also one made at a sales presentation at a friend's home, a computer fair, hotel, restaurant, convention or similar site.

If you do any selling covered by the FTC definition, you must do two things. First, give the buyer a fully completed receipt or a copy of the sales contract. These documents must contain everything that you promised orally, as well as the date of the transaction and your name and address. Also, you must have the following words in large boldface type near the signature on the contract or the front of the receipt:

> You, the buyer, may cancel this transaction at any time prior to midnight of the third business day after the date of this transaction. See the attached notice of cancellation form for an explanation of this right.

LAW IN THE REAL WORLD

Selling at Trade Shows

Do you sell consumer goods at trade shows or fairs? If so, you should give customers notices about their right to cancel their purchases. Otherwise, you may be violating the FTC's three-day cooling-off rule.

The FTC devised the rule to protect homebound, unsophisticated consumers from fast-talking door-to-door sales people. (If you've seen the movie *Tin Men,* you know what I mean.) At the time, most transactions at trade shows and fairs were business-to-business; the cooling-off period didn't apply. Over the years, however, trade shows and fairs have expanded considerably. In fact, many shows—featuring everything from computer software to outdoor equipment and housewares—are geared primarily toward consumer sales.

The FTC has "prosecutorial discretion" in pursuing merchants who sell at trade shows and fairs without giving customers a notice of cancellation rights. In most instances, the FTC doesn't stroll the halls of convention centers to shut down non-complying businesses. But it has that power. And an unhappy (and savvy) customer could report you to the agency, which would investigate and could take action against you.

Second, you must give the buyer at the same time a completed form, in duplicate, labelled "NOTICE OF CANCELLATION." It must be attached to the receipt or contract and easily detachable. Here's what the notice must say:

NOTICE OF CANCELLATION

(Enter date of transaction)

You may cancel this transaction, without any penalty or obligation, within three business days from the above date.

If you cancel, any property traded in, any payments made by you under the contract or sale, and any negotiable instrument executed by you will be returned within 10 business days following receipt by the seller of your cancellation notice, and any security interest arising out of the transaction will be canceled.

If you cancel, you must make available to the seller at your residence, in substantially as good condition as when received, any goods delivered to you under this contract or sale; or you may if you wish, comply with the instructions of the seller regarding the return shipment of the goods at the seller's expense and risk.

If you do make the goods available to the seller and the seller does not pick them up within 20 days of the date of your notice of cancellation, you may retain or dispose of the goods without any further obligation. If you fail to make the goods available to the seller, or if you agree to return the goods to the seller and fail to do so, then you remain liable for performance of all obligations under the contract.

To cancel this transaction, mail or deliver a signed and dated copy of this cancellation, notice or any other written notice, or send a telegram to [name of seller], at [address of seller's place of business] not later than midnight of _____.

I hereby cancel this transaction.

_____   _____
            Date   Buyer's Signature

State laws and regulations. Most states also have laws and regulations dealing with door-to-door sales. Some of them go beyond the federal requirements. For example, in some states, the cooling off period is five days. Also, some states require that the notice of cancellation and contract be in the same language as the oral presentation.

3. Refunds

Strictly speaking, once a sale (other than a door-to-door sale) is complete, you don't have to give a refund to a customer who changes his or her mind. This is based on traditional contract law, which says that a sale is a completed contract. In short, unless there's been a significant breach of the contract (for example, the goods or services you sold were seriously flawed) or some provision allows one of the parties to cancel, you're both stuck. So a customer who buys a product from you doesn't have the legal right to cancel the "contract" later and automatically get a refund. By the same token, if you discover that you could have charged a higher price, you can't cancel the sale either.

So much for the legalities. In real life, most retailers give customers the option of returning merchandise for either a cash refund or at least a store credit. Sometimes retailers impose conditions. For example, the customer must return the merchandise within a certain number of days; the merchandise must be unused; the customer must show a receipt or other proof of purchase.

A liberal refund policy can give your customers confidence in your business and can be an effective marketing technique. (See Chapter 13.) Whatever you decide to do about a customer recourse policy, word your rules as positively as possible and post them conspicuously in your store.

California's Refund Statute

In what appears to be the beginning of a trend, California (which is often a legal leader) has adopted a statute about refunds. New York, Virginia and Florida also have refund posting laws.

Under California Civil Code § 1723, a business is not required to give a cash refund or even a store credit to a customer who wants to return a product. You must, however, conspicuously post your policies if you don't meet the following minimum standards for merchandise returned within seven days after the sale:

- You don't give either a cash refund or credit refund; and

- You don't allow an equal exchange for such merchandise.

The California law doesn't apply to sales of food, plants, flowers or other perishable goods. And it doesn't apply to merchandise marked "as is," "no returns accepted" or "all sales final," or goods used or damaged after purchase, special goods received as ordered, goods not returned in their original package and goods which can't be resold due to health reasons.

---

4. Mail Orders

If you take orders through the mail, you need to become familiar with the Federal Trade Commission's "Rule Concerning Mail Order Merchandise," 16 CFR § 435. The rule is explained in an easy-to-read booklet, *A Business Guide to the*

Federal Trade Commission's Mail Order Rule, published by the FTC. Here are some basic features of that rule:

- You must ship the merchandise within 30 days after you receive a properly completed order and payment, unless your ad clearly states that it will take longer.

- If there's going to be a delay, you must notify the customer in writing. You must give the customer the option of a new shipment date (if known) or the opportunity to cancel the order and receive a full refund. You must give the customer a postage-free way to reply. You may assume that a customer who doesn't reply has agreed to the delay.

- If the customer cancels, you must refund the customer's money within seven days after you receive the canceled order. If the customer used a credit card, you must issue the credit within one billing cycle.

- A customer who consents to an indefinite delay can still cancel the order any time before it's shipped.

- A customer who cancels or never receives the ordered merchandise doesn't have to accept a store credit in place of a refund, but is entitled to a cash refund or credit on the charge card.

The mail order rule doesn't cover mail order photo finishing; spaced deliveries such as magazines (except for the first shipment); sales of seeds and growing plants; COD orders; or orders made by telephone and charged to a credit card account.

5. Unordered Merchandise

With only two exceptions, federal law (and the law in most states) makes it illegal to mail unordered merchandise. The exceptions:

- Free samples that you clearly and conspicuously mark as such.

- Merchandise mailed by a charitable organization to solicit contributions.

It's illegal to send the recipient a bill or dunning letter for any unordered merchandise. The FTC applies this law as well to unordered merchandise delivered by means other than the mail. A person receiving unordered merchandise can treat it as a gift.

C. Warranties

Basically, a warranty is a guarantee. It's a commitment that the manufacturer and retailer will stand behind a product. Sometimes a warranty is made through an oral or written statement of the seller. This is called an express warranty.

Even if you don't make an express warranty, however, a warranty may be imposed by law; this is called an implied warranty. In other words, the law holds the manufacturer or retailer responsible for some warranties even if they've said nothing on the subject. Sometimes you can get rid of an implied warranty by making a disclaimer.

The law of warranties comes from two main sources. The first is a law called the Uniform Commercial Code (UCC), which has been adopted in every state. The second is the Magnuson-Moss Warranty Act, a federal law designed to protect consumers. In addition, some states have laws that go beyond the provisions of the UCC or Magnuson-Moss.

Although I focus on the sale of goods, it's also possible for services to be warranted. For example, a TV fix-it service may warrant that a repair job will be good for at least six months; an auto mechanic may warrant the repairs on a car's electrical system for one year; and a lawn maintenance company may warrant that certain weeds won't re-appear during the current season. Warranties for services are almost always express and not implied, and they're not widely regulated by statute.

Plan Ahead To Avoid Warranty Problems

If you're a retailer who sells big-ticket items, try to work out a procedure with manufacturers for handling repair and replacement of defective products and making refunds. Obviously, you'll have better customer relationships if you deal quickly and smoothly with warranty problems.

If you're a retailer and you help customers select, assemble or install products, or give advice or instructions about their use, carry products liability insurance. (See Chapter 9.)

---

1. Express Warranties

Express warranties are statements and promises that a manufacturer or retailer makes about a product or about a commitment to remedy defects and malfunctions in the product. If the statements are untrue or if the stated commitments are not honored, the manufacturer or retailer may be legally liable to the buyer for breach of warranty.

Express warranties take a variety of forms, from advertising claims to a printed certificate that accompanies the product and specifically guarantees it. Express warranties can be made either orally or in writing.

a. ORAL WARRANTIES

If a seller makes an oral promise to a buyer, that is an express warranty.

Examples: A seller says, "This TV set is new" or "This oven heats to over 600 degrees." If the TV set is used, or if the oven heats only to 500 degrees, the seller will be liable for breach of warranty, whether or not the seller knew that the claims were false.

If the seller shows a customer a sample or a model of goods being sold, there's an express warranty that the goods will conform. For example, if a salesperson shows a customer some samples of fax paper and the customer orders a dozen packages based on the sample, the entire order must conform to that sample. And if a dealer shows a customer a small scale model of a garage door, the door the customer receives must look like and be constructed like the model.

But not everything that a seller says as part of a sales transaction is a warranty. Merely giving an opinion about the goods or praising them doesn't create a warranty.

- Martha is at a drugstore looking at hair coloring products. The clerk says: "I recommend this brand. It works very well, and I believe you'll be satisfied with it." Martha uses the product and develops a severe allergic reaction on her scalp.

- Phillip tries on a new suit. The store owner says: "It looks good on you. You'll be wearing it for a long time." In fact, the suit is a size too big and wears out after a year.

These statements would be considered opinions, not promises or statements of fact. They wouldn't constitute express warranties.

b.   WRITTEN WARRANTIES

A statement doesn't have to be called a warranty or guarantee to be legally treated as such. And warranties needn't be part of a formal written contract. Statements made in product literature distributed by the manufacturer or retail store, in advertisements or orally by salespeople can constitute binding warranties.

If a sales contract or order form contains a description of the goods, that constitutes an express warranty by the seller that the goods will be as described. So if the product is described as an Ear Play Model 400 stereo receiver and it turns out to be a different brand or model, the seller has breached an express warranty.

Written warranties on consumer products are covered by state laws and a federal law, the Magnuson-Moss Warranty Act.[1] That law is designed to make it easier for consumers to understand and deal with warranties. It doesn't replace state warranty laws but does add certain requirements.

The Magnuson-Moss Warranty Act covers consumer products normally used for personal, family or household purposes. It doesn't require a manufacturer or seller to give any written warranty at all. But if a written warranty is given, it must comply with the statute and with rules of the Federal Trade Commission.

For a product costing the consumer $15 or more, the written warranty must be in simple, understandable language. Also, the seller must make the terms of the warranty available to the buyer before the sale occurs. There are four ways you can comply with this requirement:

- Clearly and conspicuously display the warranty "in close conjunction to" the warranted product.

- Keep copies of warranties in readily available loose-leaf binders in each department of your store.

- Display packages so that the warranty is clearly visible to customers at the point of sale.

- Place a notice containing the warranty near the product in a way that clearly tells prospective buyers the product to which the warranty applies.

If a product costs $10 or more, the written warranty must state either that it's a full warranty or limited warranty. Naturally, a consumer who sees the words "full warranty" believes that he or she is getting a large measure of protection. To qualify as a full warranty, a written warranty must include at least the following coverage:

- A defective product will be repaired or replaced for free (including removal and installation, if necessary) during the warranty period.

---

[1] 15 USCA § 2301. For official interpretations and implementing regulations, see 16 CFR § 700.

- The product will be repaired within a reasonable time.

- The consumer won't have to do anything unreasonable to get warranty service (such as return a heavy product to a store or service center).

- The warranty is good for anyone who owns the product during the warranty period.

- If the product hasn't been repaired after a reasonable number of tries, the customer gets a replacement or a refund.

- The customer doesn't have to return a warranty card for the warranty to be valid.

- Implied warranties can't be disclaimed or denied or limited to any specific length of time.

Any written warranty that doesn't qualify as a full warranty must be labeled as a limited warranty. You can restrict the duration of implied warranties, as long as the restrictions are not unconscionable (that is, shockingly unfair). Restrictions must be stated clearly, and the implied warranties must last for a reasonable time.

The Magnuson-Moss Warranty Act doesn't supersede state laws that give consumers even greater rights and laws that permit people to recover damages for injuries caused by defective products, despite a disclaimer of liability. For example, in California the Song-Beverly Consumer Warranty Act contains more stringent warranty provisions than the Magnuson-Moss Warranty Act. Among other things, the California statute provides that a manufacturer who provides a written warranty (full or limited) must maintain service and repair facilities in California reasonably close to all areas where its products are sold. The manufacturer can delegate repair and service facilities to retailers or independent repair shops. Repairs must be completed within 30 days, except in unusual circumstances.

RECOMMENDED READING

For an excellent review of the Magnuson-Moss Warranty Act, see the booklet *A Business Person's Guide to Federal Warranty Law* published by the FTC and available from the Superintendent of Documents, U.S. Government Printing Office, Washington, DC 20401, (202) 783-3238. Also see *Consumer Action Guide*, by Barbara Kaufman (Nolo Press); although written specifically for California consumers, it includes an incisive overview of warranties and federal warranty legislation useful to businesses everywhere.

2. Warranties Imposed by Law

Implied warranties don't come from anything a seller says or does. They arise automatically when a product is sold. Under the Uniform Commercial Code, there are two kinds of implied warranties:

- that the product is fit for its ordinary use, and

- that the product is fit for any special use the seller knows about.

Each of these is explained below.

a. FITNESS IN GENERAL

A seller automatically makes an implied warranty that new (not used) goods sold "are fit for the ordinary purposes for which such goods are used"—in other words, that the product will work the way similar products ordinarily work. This implied warranty is also called a warranty of merchantability.

Here are some examples:

- A lawnmower will cut grass that is four inches tall.

- A stepladder will support a 275-pound person.

- A toaster will make both dark and light toast.

- A bicycle's brakes will work in a light rain.
- A bottle of ginger ale won't have loose glass in it.

The manufacturer and retailer of a product that's not fit for ordinary purposes are liable to the purchaser for breach of the implied warranty.

b. FITNESS FOR A PARTICULAR PURPOSE

There's a special implied warranty if the seller has reason to know that (1) the goods are required for a particular purpose, and (2) the buyer is relying on the seller's skill or judgment to select suitable goods. In that situation, the seller is bound by an implied warranty that the goods will be fit for that purpose.

- Joanne goes to a paint store and asks for two gallons of white paint that will work well on plaster walls. The store owner selects paint for her. Unfortunately, it's intended solely for metallic surfaces and ruins her walls.

- Morton asks an air conditioning contractor to pick out and install an air conditioning unit for a part of his plant. He explains that the room contains extensive electronic equipment and must be kept at 55 degrees or cooler at all times. The air conditioner is installed but leads to costly problems, because in hot weather it can't keep the temperature below 62 degrees.

- Wilma goes to a sports retailer and asks for a sleeping bag that will be adequate to 10 degrees Fahrenheit. The retailer selects a certain model for Wilma, and she buys it, but it won't keep a normal person warm below freezing.

In these examples, each seller is liable to the buyer for breach of the implied warranty of fitness for a particular purpose. That's because each seller knew the buyer needed the goods for a particular purpose and that the buyer was relying on the seller's skill or judgment to furnish suitable goods.

This is different from the implied warranty of general fitness discussed in the preceding section. An air conditioner that cooled a room to 62 degrees in hot weather would be fit for the ordinary purposes for which an air conditioner is used. It wouldn't violate the implied warranty of general fitness. But because the seller in the second example knew the buyer had special requirements and was relying on the seller to meet them, this special implied warranty took effect.

c. DISCLAIMERS OF IMPLIED WARRANTIES

The Uniform Commercial Code allows sellers, in many cases, to disclaim implied warranties through a conspicuous written notice. Typically, to disclaim implied warranties, you must inform consumers in a conspicuous manner, and generally in writing, that you won't be responsible if the product malfunctions or is defective and that the entire product risk falls on them. To do this, you must specifically state that you don't warrant "merchantability," or use a phrase such as "with all faults" or "as is."

There are, however, major exceptions to the general rule, which may make it impossible to make a disclaimer.

Exception 1: State Law Restrictions. In some states, you may not be able to avoid implied warranties. Despite its name, the Uniform Commercial Code isn't completely uniform; several state legislatures have tinkered with parts of it, including the part about disclaiming implied warranties. Some states (including Connecticut, Massachusetts and Kansas) don't let you sell consumer products "as is."

Exception 2: Injuries. A disclaimer of implied warranties won't shield you from legal liability if your product is so defective it injures someone. Courts consider such a disclaimer "unconscionable."

Exception 3: Federal Law Restrictions. If you offer a written warranty for a consumer product or offer a service contract on it, you can't disclaim any implied warranty. (This restriction is imposed by the Magnuson-Moss Warranty Act.)

 Implied warranties are difficult to disclaim. If you're going to enter this legal thicket, you'll likely need a lawyer's advice on whether you can disclaim implied warranties in your situation and, if so, how best to do it. Even if the law permits a disclaimer of warranties, if you and a customer slug it out in court, you'll find that judges often tend to be pro-consumer—that is, to rule that unless a seller is absolutely clear, this warranty disclaimer will be disallowed.

Sometimes a seller is interested not in getting rid of implied warranties entirely but only in limiting the remedies in case of a breach. For example, the seller may want to say that in case of a product defect, the buyer can either (1) return the goods and get a refund, or (2) have any defective parts replaced or repaired—but not collect monetary damages. But while a limitation on damages is normally effective, this isn't always true, especially where the limitation is found to be highly unreasonable. Suppose the seller of a $2,000 stereo set puts this language in the warranty: "Seller is obligated only to replace defective parts." After Mildred buys a stereo, a protective circuit fails, causing it to overheat. This destroys several key parts and ruins the stereo. Will a court allow the seller merely to replace the $5 part that didn't work? Perhaps not. The buyer may be able to convince the court that the limitation shouldn't be enforced because (under these circumstances) the limitation deprived her of the "substantial value of her bargain" or because the limitation is unconscionable (that is, shockingly unfair). And remember that a disclaimer can't shield you from liability for personal injury to a consumer hurt by a defective product.

3. What Happens If a Warranty Is Breached

Federal and state laws give consumers certain rights when an express or implied warranty is breached.

a. THE BUYER'S OPTIONS

Under the Uniform Commercial Code, if there's a breach of warranty, the customer usually can return the merchandise and get a full refund. The manufacturer or retailer bound by the warranty, however, has the right to cure the breach by fixing the merchandise or replacing it with non-defective merchandise.

A customer who prefers to keep the merchandise can do so and sue for the direct economic loss—generally, the reduced value of the product because it's defective.

In addition to damages for the reduced value of a defective product, a buyer is also entitled to damages for:

- Consequential economic losses (such as lost profits) resulting from the product's failure to meet requirements and needs that were foreseeable at the time of sale.

  Example: Meadowbrook Golf Course buys 12 golf carts, all of which are defective. As a result, Meadowbrook loses $20,000 in profits over the eight-week period it takes to get the carts fixed. (It proves impractical to get substitute carts on short notice.) It can successfully recover these losses.

- Injury to people and damage to property caused by the defective product.

  Example: Millie buys a CutAbove power lawnmower. One day when her teenage son Reggie is mowing the lawn, the mower propels a small stone into one of his eyes. Reggie loses his sight in that eye. Because the mower doesn't contain normal safety features, Reggie is entitled to collect damages for his injury.

b. WHO IS LIABLE?

Who is liable if a customer buys a product from a retailer and the product fails to live up to the warranty? Sometimes the manufacturer, sometimes the retailer and sometimes both. Although liability depends on the circumstances, here are some general rules:

- *Manufacturer's Express Warranty.* If an express warranty made by the manufacturer was breached, the manufacturer is responsible for making good on the promise. The retailer usually isn't liable, unless it "adopts" the manufacturer's warranty by its conduct at the time of sale.

  Example: Maria goes to Pete's Fitness Mart and looks at HomeBody, a $3,000 set of exercise machines manufactured by Health Horizons Inc. She's interested, but wants to be sure it's backed by a broad warranty. To clinch the sale, Pete calls the president of Health Horizons and has the company send an extensive written warranty.

Nine months after Maria buys the HomeBody, it fails; meanwhile, Health Horizons has gone out of business. Pete's Fitness Mart is bound by the warranty, because it was part of the inducement that Pete used to convince Maria to buy HomeBody.

- *Retailer's Express Warranty.* If the warranty was made independently by a retailer, the retailer is liable. The manufacturer isn't bound unless the retailer was acting under the authority (in legal lingo, as an agent) of the manufacturer in making the warranty.

- *Breach of Implied Warranty of General Fitness.* If there is a breach of the implied warranty that the goods are fit for ordinary purposes, both the manufacturer and the retailer are liable—but if the customer sues the retailer, the retailer in turn will usually have the right to recover against the manufacturer for supplying a defective product.

- *Breach of Implied Warranty of Fitness for a Particular Purpose.* If the customer relied on the retailer to select the goods for a particular purpose and the goods aren't satisfactory for that purpose, the retailer is liable.

- *Personal Injury.* A buyer who's injured by an unfit product can usually sue the manufacturer, even though the injured person didn't deal directly with the manufacturer. What's more, not only the buyer can sue for personal injuries from a defective product. In most states, members of the buyer's family or household, or house guests who are injured, can also sue the manufacturer if it's reasonable to expect that these persons would use or be affected by the product.

Whether or not an injured person can sue the retailer as well as the manufacturer depends on court decisions in your state and the extent of the retailer's involvement in the sale. In many states, a retailer who simply sells an unopened box and makes no statements about the product is immune from liability if the product later injures someone. But some states hold the retailer liable even under these circumstances.

 Get legal advice. Liability for breach of warranties is one of the most complex areas of commercial law. Because liability depends on many factors and because the law is somewhat unsettled, use this book for general background only. Also, it's important to understand that in a lawsuit, a person who has suffered a serious injury or significant economic loss because of a defective product will probably assert additional theories of legal liability (such as negligence and strict liability) besides breach of warranty. See a lawyer for specific legal advice.

D. Consumer Protection Statutes

Remember "caveat emptor"—let the buyer beware? That used to be the law of the marketplace. Not anymore. Today, consumers have clout.

Case 1. In Florida, a Chevrolet dealer promised a "free four-day, three-night vacation to Acapulco" to anyone who bought a car or van. Relying on this special promotion, Peter bought a van from the dealer. When the vacation voucher arrived, Peter found that the so-called free vacation was really a time-share sales promotion. The vacation trip was loaded down with conditions, restrictions and obligations. Believing he'd been cheated, Peter sued the dealer. The jury awarded Peter $1,768 in compensatory damages (the value of the trip) plus $667,000 in punitive damages.

Case 2. In New Jersey, Kenneth ordered some furniture from a store. When it arrived, Kenneth noticed numerous defects. He rejected the order and demanded a return of his deposit. The furniture store refused, and Kenneth sued. The jury awarded him three times the amount of his deposit and ordered the furniture store to pay his attorney fees.

Both cases were brought under state consumer protection statutes. These statutes are meant to protect consumers from unfair or deceptive practices and often go beyond the traditional legal remedies available for breach of warranty. Laws like these are on the books in nearly every state, although the details vary.

Consumer protection laws place a potent weapon in the hands of buyers. In an ordinary lawsuit, a plaintiff can recover only his or her actual losses. For example, without the benefit of a consumer protection law, the man who sued to get back his furniture deposit would be entitled to no more than his $600 deposit. But under the statute in his state, he received triple damages plus attorney fees. Similarly the man who sued the car dealer about the free vacation won punitive damages amounting to many times the value of his trip. The potential for large verdicts gives buyers and their lawyers an incentive to sue if it looks like a law has been violated.

"Big deal," you may say. "I'm an honest and ethical business person. None of this affects me." Well, that may not be so. For one thing, you need to know the details of your state's consumer protection laws so that you can tell your employees about practices that could get you in trouble. Furthermore, these state laws often allow a customer to sue even if the violation was not intentional. If you sell a product manufactured by a U.S.-based company (say, a Schwinn bike) and mistakenly advertise that the product was made in the U.S. when in fact it was made in Taiwan, you may be liable under the statute.

Hundreds of cases have been brought under consumer protection laws, including these:

- A man sued a department store that ran out of an advertised waffle iron and didn't give him a rain check—a violation of the consumer protection law in his state.

- A homeowner sued a roofing contractor who falsely advertised that it could arrange financing for roof repair jobs.

- A woman sued a health spa that reneged on its promise to return her deposit and cancel her contract if she changed her mind within three days.

Health spas, incidentally, have been singled out for special regulation; if you're going to start one, get the FTC pamphlet on this subject.

Most consumer protection laws contain a broad prohibition on "unfair or deceptive practices." In addition, many statutes list specific practices that are forbidden such as bait-and-switch and deceptive pricing, discussed above in Sections A2 and B1.

Cash, Checks and Credit Cards **15**

This chapter considers the three most common ways that businesses get paid for the goods and services they sell: cash, credit cards and checks. If you extend credit directly to customers, clients or patients, you should also read Chapter 16, which explains how to avoid collection problems.

A. Cash

Cash includes not only currency but also equivalents that are as good as cash—certified checks, cashier's checks, traveler's checks and (less common these days) money orders. Personal and business checks are quite another matter. (See Section C.)

If you have very large cash transactions, you may have to report them to the IRS. The reporting requirements are intended primarily to deter money-laundering schemes by customers (often drug dealers) who want to conceal income.

If you receive more than $10,000 in cash, traveler's checks or money orders (but not certified, cashier's, or business or personal checks) in one transaction or two or more related transactions, you're required to provide information about the transaction to the IRS—including the name, address and Social Security number of the buyer. In addition, if you're a retail merchant, you must report:

- cash transactions in which you receive more than $10,000 in installment payments in one year

- transactions of more than $10,000 in which part of the payment is in cash, traveler's checks or money orders; and

- Any "suspicious transaction," no matter what the amount.

Use IRS Form 8300 (*Report of Cash Payments Over $10,000 Received in a Trade or Business*). You must also provide a copy of the completed form to the customer.

B. Credit Cards

Depending on the business you're in, your customers or clients may want to pay with plastic—the familiar Visa, MasterCard, Discover, American Express and other cards. Technically, there's a distinction between "credit cards" (such as Visa or MasterCard) and "travel and entertainment cards" (such as American Express and Diners Club) also called "charge cards." Credit cards are administered through banks; charge cards are usually administered through the issuing company. For most practical purposes, the same legal concepts apply, so I'll simply use "credit card" to cover both types.

In deciding which credit cards to recognize, take into account the preferences of your customers and clients, as well as the size of the discount exacted by the credit card issuer and how quickly you get paid.

When a customer charges goods or services using a bank-administered credit card, the bank credits your account with the amount of the sale less a discount—usually 3% to 5%—which is the bank's fee for handling the transaction and accepting the risk that the customer doesn't pay. In addition, the bank may charge you a start-up fee and an annual rental fee for the imprinting machine you use to record credit card information on sales slips.

If you're in a retail or other business where customers or clients expect to pay on credit, credit cards are often more cost-effective than directly extending credit. In general, if you follow the bank's rules—such as checking the credit card to make sure it hasn't expired and getting approval for all or or at least larger transactions—the credit card issuer (not you) absorbs the loss if the customer doesn't pay up. Some of the newer electronic systems used by credit card issuers do most or all of the checking for you and get the money into your bank account almost immediately.

But whether you check credit cards the old-fashioned phone-in way or rely on the new systems, there are still a few exceptions to this general rule that if you follow the bank's procedures, you're sure to get your money. For example, if the goods are defective and the customer refuses to pay the bank, you may have to bear the loss. This will be spelled out in your contract with the bank. Read it carefully.

About a dozen states restrict your ability to record personal identification information about a credit card holder. The laws on this subject differ from state to state, but the California statute provides a good illustration of the kinds of restrictions that may apply to you. In California, in most circumstances you can't require the cardholder to give you personal identification information such as an address or phone number. There are, however, a few exceptions. You can require the cardholder to provide this information if:

- The bank or other agency that issued the credit card requires it to complete the transaction; or

- You need the information for a special purpose related to the transaction, for example, shipping, delivery, servicing or installation of the merchandise, or for special orders.

There can be hefty penalties for violating these statutes, so learn the rules in your state and make sure that your employees know them.

But even if your state does permit you to record this information, ask yourself if you really need it. After all, if the customer doesn't pay the bill, it's a problem for the bank that issued the credit card, not for you. And because some customers regard the request for personal information as an invasion of their privacy, doing so may be poor marketing. If your main reason to gather this information is to build a mailing list, it's better simply to ask your customers if they'd like to be added to your list.

C. Checks

In any business—and especially in a service or wholesale business—you're likely to find that many customers or clients want to pay for goods and services using personal or business checks. Obviously, accepting payment by check is riskier than accepting

payment by cash or credit card. Approximately 450 million bad checks are written each year.

1. Avoiding Bad Check Problems

Checks can be no good for a number of reasons. Here are the main ones:

- There are insufficient funds in the account to cover the amount of the purchase. Unless the check writer has overdraft protection, the check will be returned to you unpaid.

- The account has been closed—or perhaps it's a fictitious account that never existed.

- The signature of the person who signed the check is a forgery, in which case the bank will refuse payment.

- In the case of a third-party check (such as a paycheck) names or dollar amounts on the check have been altered, or the endorsement is a forgery.

- A person signing or endorsing a check on behalf of a partnership or corporation doesn't have legal authority to sign for the business.

Faced with these many possibilities for losses, some retail businesses adopt a simple policy: No checks. But such a policy often carries its own risks— mainly that you may lose perfectly solvent customers or clients who like the convenience of writing checks. After all, it's customary for most retail, wholesale, service and manufacturing industries to accept checks. And because with checks the bank doesn't keep a percentage of each transaction (as is the case with credit cards), you may actually want to encourage regular customers to pay by check rather than credit card.

No matter what type of business you're in, the best way to approach the potential bad check problem is to adopt sensible rules and stick to them. How stringent you want to be depends on the nature of your business, and how well rules will be accepted by your customers and clients. It boils down to a business decision about how much risk you're willing to accept.

If yours is a retail business, here are some policies to consider:

- Require that checks be written and signed in your presence.

- Accept checks drawn on local banks only.

- Be sure the checks have the customer's name, local address and phone number pre-printed on them.

- Don't accept checks written for more than the purchase price; in other words, don't give change for a check. (Some small businesses, such as grocers, build customer loyalty with minimal losses by issuing check-cashing cards allowing regular customers to write a check for up to $20 more than the price of goods purchased.)

- Wait until the check has cleared before giving a cash refund for returned goods.

- Don't accept third-party checks—paychecks, Social Security checks and other checks that someone else has made out to the customer who then endorses them.

   Example: Laurie offers you a check made out to her from her employer, Amalgamated Products. She endorses it on the back. The check may be a forgery, or maybe the company doesn't have funds in the account to cover the check.

- Don't accept post-dated checks.

- Set a limit on the check amount you will accept. Or at least call the bank and verify that larger checks are good.

- Require a manager's approval for checks over a certain amount. Better yet, hire clerks whose judgment you trust.

- Write the customer's phone number on the check, if the law in your state allows it.

- Ask to see ID—including something that contains a photo and signature. A driver's license is a good choice. Record key information (such as the driver's license number) on the check; it will help you locate the customer if the check is no good.

 Restrictions on ID requirements. Find out if your state has a law restricting the kind of ID you can require. In some states, for example, you can't require a customer to show you a credit card as condition of accepting a check. However, if a customer voluntarily shows you a credit card as ID, state law may permit you to record the type of card, the issuer and the expiration date—but you can't write down the card number. If you violate laws of this type, you may face a fine, a civil lawsuit or both. No matter what your state law is, avoid using credit cards as a form of ID. For one thing, you can't charge the client's credit card account if the check bounces. For another, bank personnel or others seeing a credit card number may use this information improperly. Why subject your customers to this risk?

If you're presented with a check drawn on a business account, be sure that the person signing it has authority to do so. If a check is signed by someone other than the owner, a partner or a corporate officer, call the bank to see if the person presenting the check is an authorized signer.

Some businesses post a sign saying that they charge a specified fee for any check that bounces. The legal reasoning is that in many states you can't collect such fees without advance warning to customers. And some business owners think that such notices deter bad check writers. Still, I generally recommend against posting signs. It's insulting to the customer, and there's no evidence that it will cut down the bad checks you receive. And remember, your main goal is to avoid getting bad checks in the first place—not to try to collect them later plus a $10 fee. But if you do post such a sign or charge such a fee, check the law in your state to see how much you can legally charge.

RECOMMENDED READING

Money Troubles: Legal Strategies To Cope With Your Debts, by Robin Leonard (Nolo Press) is addressed primarily to people who owe money, but the information on bad check laws is also helpful to businesses receiving money.

Once you accept a check, stamp it with an endorsement stamp (available from your bank) and deposit it in your business account the same day. Every day you wait increases the chances that the check-writer will have emptied or closed the account. Under the Uniform Commercial Code, a statute adopted in every state and which governs most banking transactions, there's a presumption that a check becomes "stale" six months after the date it's signed. The bank may refuse to honor it after that period—although in actual practice, they'll usually honor older checks as long as the account is solvent.

2. Dealing With Bad Checks

Even though you take all reasonable precautions, a bad check will occasionally slip through your system. A bank may return a check to you with the notation "insufficient funds" or "NSF," which means the same thing: the customer has an active account but there's not enough in it to cover the check. Or a bank may inform you that the account has been closed.

Here are some steps you can take—many of which apply primarily to bad checks from individuals. Other techniques may be more appropriate when the bad check comes from another business. (See Chapter 16.)

Step 1. Call the Customer

Call the customer and ask that he or she make the check good or pay you in cash. (This is one reason it's good to write down the customer's phone number when you take a check, if permitted by state law.) But be careful about when you call the customer—and how often. Laws in several states limit what you can do to collect debts. (See Chapter 16, Section D.) To avoid problems, call only between 8 a.m. and 9 p.m., don't discuss the debt with the customer's employer and make sure your request for payment is polite. Threatening a debtor that you'll publicize his or her name or notify his or her employer is illegal.

Step 2. Write a Letter

Send a certified letter—return receipt requested—making the same demand. This sets the stage for a possible criminal prosecution if the check-writer intentionally attempted to defraud you. Also, 35 states (including Arizona, California, Colorado, Florida, Illinois, Montana, New York and Washington) have bad-check laws that are particularly favorable to businesses. In such states, if you send a written demand for payment, you may be able to collect extra damages in court (often two or three times the value of the check) if the check-writer doesn't come through.

> **Example:** Monica, the owner of a Florida gift shop, receives a bad check from Norbert. She sends Norbert a notice demanding payment in full plus a service charge of $15 or 5% of the check, whichever is greater. If Norbert doesn't pay within seven days, Monica can sue him under Florida law for the amount of the check plus additional damages of three times the amount of the check (at least $50). This is in addition to court costs, reasonable attorney fees and any bank fees that she incurs.

The sample notice and demand for payment shown below here is derived from the Florida bad-check statute *(Crimes, Sec. 832.07)*. Because the law in each state is different, find out the specific requirements where you do business. (See Chapter 20, Section D, for information on doing legal research.)

SAMPLE BAD CHECK NOTICE (Florida)

You are hereby notified that a check, numbered _____, issued by you on _____,199_, drawn upon ___(name of bank)___, and payable to , has been dishonored. Pursuant to Florida law, you have 7 days from receipt of this notice to tender payment of full amount of such check plus a service charge of $15 or an amount of up to 5 % of the face amount of the check, whichever is greater, the total amount due being $_____ and _____cents. Unless this amount is paid in full within the time specified above, the holder of such check may turn over the dishonored check and all other available information relating to the incident to the state attorney for criminal prosecution. You may be additionally liable in a civil action for triple the amount of the check, but in no case less than $50, together with the amount of the check, a service charge, court costs, reasonable attorney fees, and incurred bank fees, as provided in §68.065.

STATE BAD CHECK LAWS

State	Code Section	Maximum Damages Under State Bad Check Laws
Alabama	6-5-285	Actual and punitive damages (meant to punish), and reasonable attorney fees.
Alaska	09.65.115	$100 or three times the amount of the check, whichever is greater, not to exceed the amount of the check by more than $1,000. If you pay before trial but after suit filed, creditor is entitled to amount of check plus $150.
Arizona	12-671	Twice the amount of the check or $50, whichever is greater, plus costs and reasonable attorney fees.
California	CC 1719	Three times the amount of the check, not less than $100 nor more than $500, plus costs.
Colorado	13-21-109	Three times the amount of the check, not less than $100 nor more than $500, plus costs.
Connecticut	52-565a	Damages set by the court. If check written for which there was no account, damages not to exceed the face amount of the check or $750. If check written on account with insufficient funds, damages not to exceed the face amount of the check or $400.
Florida	68.065	Three times the amount of the check or $50, whichever is greater, plus costs and reasonable attorney fees.
Georgia	13-6-15	Two times the amount of the check, but in no case more than $500.
Hawaii	490:3-505.5	Three times the amount of the check or $100, whichever is greater, but not more than $500.
Illinois	Ch. 17 ¶ 1-a	Three times the amount of the check or $100, whichever is greater, but not more than $500.
Indiana	34-4-30-1	Three times the amount of the check or $100, whichever is greater, but not more than $500.
Iowa	554.3806	Three times the amount of the check, but not more than $500.
Kansas	60-2610	Three times the amount of the check or $100, whichever is greater, but not more than $500.
Louisiana	2782	Twice the amount of the check or $100, whichever is greater, plus reasonable attorney fees and costs.
Maine	14-6071	Face value of check, or court costs, service costs, collection and processing costs not to exceed $40, whichever is less, plus interest at 12% per year.
Maryland	CL 3-512	Twice the amount of the check, not to exceed $1,000.
Massachusetts	93:40A	Damages determined by court, not less than $100 and not more than $500.
Minnesota	332.50	$100 plus interest and reasonable attorney fees.
Mississippi	11-7-12	For checks up to $25, the face amount of the check; for checks between $26 and $200, 50% of face amount, not to exceed $50 nor to be less than $25; if check is over $200, 25% of face amount.
Missouri	570.123	Three times the amount of the check or $100, whichever is greater, but not more than $500.
Montana	27-1-717	Three times the amount of the check or $100, whichever is greater, but not more than $500.
Nevada	41-620	Three times the amount of the check, not less than $100 nor more than $500, plus costs.

State	Code Section	Maximum Damages Under State Bad Check Laws
New Hampshire	544-B:1	Court, service and collection costs; if you fail to pay judgment, you may be fined $10 per business day up to $500, from date of judgement until debt paid.
New Mexico	56-14-1	Three times the amount of the check or $100, whichever is greater, but not more than $500.
New York	GOL 11-104	If check written for which there was no account, two times the amount of the check or $750, whichever is less. If check written on account with insufficient funds, two times the amount of the check or $400, whichever is less.
North Carolina	6-21.3	Three times the amount of the check or $500, whichever is less, but not less than $100.
North Dakota	6-08-16	Three times the amount of the check or $100, whichever is less.
Oregon	20.090, 30.700	Three times the amount of the check or $100, whichever is greater, but not more than $500; attorney fees.
Pennsylvania	42-8304	Three times the amount of the check or $100, whichever is greater, but not more than $500.
Rhode Island	6-42-3	Three times the amount of the check, no less than $200, no more than $1,000.
Tennessee	39-14-121	Three times the amount of the check, not to exceed $500.
Vermont	9-2311	Costs of servicing returned check, the amount of the check, bank fees, interest, attorney fees and damages to $50.
Virginia	6.1-118.1	$10 to cover the returned check fee, the amount of the check and lost wages, to a total of $250.
Washington	62A.3-515	Three times the amount of the check or $100.
Wisconsin	943.245	Actual damages; three times the amount of the check and attorney fees, not to exceed $300.
Wyoming	1-1-115	Two times the amount of the check, not less than $50, and for interest, costs and attorney fees.

Step 3. Contact the Bank

If the customer's bank account is still active, wait a few days and then inquire to see if the check is now good (the customer may have deposited a paycheck after the check was dishonored). You can normally check the status of an account by calling the bank and saying you hold a check for a certain dollar amount and asking if there is enough in the account to cover it. If so, take the returned check to the bank and draw out the cash. Another alternative is to ask the customer's bank for "enforced collection." If the bank offers this service, the bad check will be held in a special category. The next money deposited in the customer's account will go to you. Procedures and costs vary; get details from the bank.

Step 4. Request Prosecution

Intentionally writing a bad check is a crime. As noted above, before you contact the local district attorney's or prosecuting attorney's office to request prosecution, you may have to give the check-writer a written notice. After all, the bad check may have been an innocent mistake. The police department or district attorney can tell you if you must send a notice as a prelude to a prosecution (generally you must) and what the notice must contain. But again, in any oral or written communication with the customer who passed the bad check, avoid the temptation to threaten prosecution. Such a threat may constitute harassment or extortion under some state statutes.

What are the chances of law enforcement officials taking action? Some police departments and prosecuting officials drag their feet on these kinds of cases, saying that they don't want to be used as a collection agency. Others are far more cooperative. Some of the best have bad-check programs under which the person who has written the check is contacted and given a chance to avoid being prosecuted by making the check good and, in some counties, by attending special classes under a "diversion" program.

Step 5. Use Small Claims Court

If you still haven't been paid, consider suing in small claims court, as long as the check is less than the maximum amount you can sue for in small claims—or close enough that you don't mind waiving the excess. Most states have limits of $2,000 to $5,000. (See Chapter 19 on how to represent yourself in small claims court.) As noted in Step 2, if you've followed the bad-check procedures in your state, you may be entitled to two or even three times the amount of the check as damages as well as your court-filing and service-of-process costs. And if the check-writer has a job, you'll generally be able to use post-judgment proceedings to get paid out of the worker's wages—although it's difficult to collect from the wages of low-income people. You might also be able to collect from bank or other deposit accounts. In most states, you can also cheaply and easily put a lien against the debtor's real estate. Chances are you'll ultimately be paid when the property is voluntarily sold or refinanced.

Step 6. Use a Collection Agency

Turning a bad check over to a collection agency is often worth considering. For smaller checks, going to small claims court may not be worthwhile. Or perhaps, despite the huge cut a collection agency takes, you might want to put your time and energy elsewhere. And while some states make small claims court fairly friendly to businesses (for example, you may be able to send an employee to court with business records), other states make the business owner appear to testify in person. That may make suing the check writer more trouble than it's worth. So if you want to keep to a minimum your personal involvement in the collection process, keep open the possibility of letting a collection agency do most of the work.

When the Customer Stops Payment

Sometimes a customer stops payment on a check, claiming that the goods you sold were defective. If there's a legitimate dispute, the customer's good faith will be a valid defense to a prosecution or a civil lawsuit for multiple damages. And if it turns out that the goods were in fact defective, the customer will be entitled to a reduction of the amount owed—or even, in extreme cases, a cancellation of the debt. But if the customer's allegations are a trumped-up excuse to get something for nothing, you'll be entitled to your full legal remedies in court. Often, however, in dealing with a customer who is unhappy with the merchandise purchased, the best policy is simply to have the customer return the goods and to call it a day.

Payment in Full

Be careful about accepting and depositing checks that say "Payment in Full" or something similar. If the check writer owes more, you may be barred from collecting the additional amount.

Where there's a good faith dispute about how much the check writer owes you, depositing a full-payment check usually means that you accept the check in complete satisfaction of the debt. Crossing out the words "Payment in Full" generally won't help you. You'll still be cut off from suing for the balance.

However, a number of states have changed this rule to help creditors. In those states, if you cash a full payment check and explicitly reserve your right to sue for the balance, you can go after the check writer in court. States that have this modified rule include Alabama, Delaware, Massachusetts, Minnesota, Missouri, New Hampshire, New York, Ohio, Rhode Island, South Carolina, South Dakota, West Virginia and Wisconsin.

If your state has modified the rule, you normally can preserve your right to sue for the balance by writing the words "Under Protest" or "Without Prejudice" with your endorsement. California simply lets you cross out the full-payment language, cash the check and sue for the balance—but the check writer may be able to get around this by following certain procedures specified in the statute (California Civil Code § 1526). The statute was created to protect creditors, not debtors, however, so in most instances you can defeat a "Payment in Full" check.

EXTENDING CREDIT AND GETTING PAID

16

In this chapter, you'll find out how to establish credit practices that help ensure that you get paid when you should. You'll also learn how to comply with federal and state credit laws and what to do if customers, clients or patients don't pay when they're supposed to.

A. The Practical Side of Extending Credit

Some businesses give customers 30 or 60 days to pay for goods and services. They may even let customers make installment payments over a longer period. For example, a small wholesaler of children's music products might require retail customers to pay at the time of sale, but extend 30 days' credit to wholesale customers. Similarly, many professionals and other service providers extend short-term credit to clients and customers, who are expected to pay after receiving a monthly invoice.

If you extend credit, you need to set up a well-organized, accurate, easy-to-use system of accounts, send out bills periodically and keep after those who pay slowly or not at all—all of which takes time, money and effort. Many small business people fantasize about avoiding the whole mess by requiring customers to pay cash. Unfortunately, this sort of day-dreaming is normally just that; in many businesses and professional practices it's almost impossible to operate if you don't extend credit.

1. Professional and Personal Service Businesses

In many professional or consulting practices, it used to be considered unusual to require a client or patient to complete a formal credit application. No longer. Today, credit applications are becoming routine, because businesses simply can't afford to work for deadbeats. But if you shy away from a formal application, you can still gather much pertinent information from your new client or patient intake sheet. Ask

where the person works and banks. Ask for the name of the "nearest relative not living with you"—useful information if the client or patient skips out.

Health care professionals will, of course, want to inquire about insurance or Medicaid/Medicare coverage. Consider offering a modest discount (say, 5%) for payment at the time services are rendered—it usually leads to prompt payment. And think about posting a dignified sign saying: "If it's convenient, payment is appreciated when the bill is presented." If you accept credit cards, there's really no reason for the patient not to pay on the spot.

Lawyers, accountants, appraisers, engineers, dentists and other professionals may appropriately ask for advance payment to be applied against the first batch of services, especially if a new client or patient needs extensive services. One way to do this is to present a fee letter to each new client. The letter might state that new clients are asked to pay a retainer and that future payments are due ten days from billing. (See "Putting Professional Relationships on a Sound Financial Footing," below.)

Another positive thing a professional or consultant can do is to routinely record bank account data about the client or patient as payment is received. Then, if you have to sue the client or patient, you have one more place to turn to try to satisfy your judgment.

If you're worried that someone isn't creditworthy—particularly if the bill is likely to mount rapidly—you can run a quick credit check with a credit reporting agency. Credit checks are so routine these days that this won't drive away business. However, you should notify the client or patient beforehand. Also, before using credit reports, familiarize yourself with the Fair Credit Reporting Act and similar state laws. (See Section B.) For example, if you reject credit for a client or patient based on a credit report, you need to disclose this to the person, as well as the name, address and phone number of the credit reporting agency that gave you the negative information.

Putting Professional Relationships on a Sound Financial Footing

If you have a professional practice or run a consulting or personal service business, consider giving each client or patient a written statement of your billing procedures, so that they know what to expect.

It is also businesslike and inoffensive to prepare a letter of retention spelling out the services you'll be performing, how much you'll be charging, when you'll be billing and when payment is due. Such letters may even be legally required. In California, for example, lawyers and clients must sign a fee agreement if the expected fee is more than $1,000 or the fee is contingent on the outcome of a lawsuit.

You could even take the retention letter one step further by providing payment envelopes for the patients to use in sending their monthly checks. This approach works for professionals where fairly predictable services are delivered over a defined time period.

Your letter should state when you expect to be paid—usually within ten days of the statement date. Also, list the amount of any interest or finance charges you'll assess (as permitted by state law) if payment is late, and reserve your right to stop rendering services. (In a few professions, rules of professional ethics may affect how and when you can terminate the relationship.) Have the client or patient acknowledge in writing that he or she has received your letter and agrees to its terms.

To find out legal limits on interest or finance charges, check the index to the annotated statutes (sometimes called a "code") for your state—available in any good law library. Look under the terms interest, usury or finance charges. Also, your professional or trade organization should have helpful information.

2. Wholesale and Manufacturing Businesses

If you're a shoe wholesaler, software company or clothing manufacturer—or if you're in any other wholesale or service business—you should have a credit policy, and you should insist that customers complete a formal application for credit. The details of your credit policy will depend on the kind of business you're in and the type of customers you serve. Here are some issues to think about:

- How many days after billing is payment due?

- Is there a discount for early payment?

- Do you require pre-payment or COD terms for certain classes of customers?

- Do you add interest or finance charges? If so, how much?

- When are credit checks required? (For example, you obviously wouldn't require a credit check if the customer is the government, and probably wouldn't for a major, well-established company. On the other hand, you likely would want to check on the credit of a new small business or an individual making a large purchase.)

- How are credit limits determined?

- When and how often do you send past due notices and follow up with phone calls?

- Do you keep selling to a customer whose account is overdue?

- At what point will you begin aggressive credit efforts?

When you approve credit for new trade accounts, let them know the maximum credit you're allowing and when they're expected to pay—as well as other relevant features of your credit policy.

Should You Charge Interest?

Most businesses don't charge interest or impose finance charges in exchange for granting credit. More typically, interest is charged when bills aren't paid within the agreed time, often between 10 and 30 days. If you decide to impose these charges, you must inform the customer how the charges will be computed. The Truth in Lending Act (see Section B), which applies primarily to sales to consumers, prescribes the disclosures you must make—but not the rates you can charge. That's done by state law.

One reason to consider adding interest or finance charges after a certain date is that customers who are short of cash tend to pay first the bills that carry such charges. Other incentives for early payment include:

- Discounts for prompt payment—for example, 5% off if the customer pays his or her bill on the spot or within 10 days.

- Free shipping and handling (a big item these days) for customers who pre-pay.

- Making the customer responsible for paying for court costs and reasonable attorney fees required to enforce collection if the customer doesn't pay as agreed. The customer must agree to this, either in a credit application or a separate contract.

A sample credit application form designed for trade accounts is shown below.

SAMPLE CREDIT APPLICATION

CREDIT APPLICATION

The undersigned company is applying for credit with ABC ELECTRICAL INC. and agrees to abide by the standard terms and conditions of ABC ELECTRICAL INC. as printed on the reverse side.

Company Name _____

DBA (if different) _____

Contact Person _____

Address _____

Phone (   ) _____   Fax (   ) _____

Federal Tax ID or Social Security No. _____

Type of Business _____ No. of Employees_____

Date Business Established _____

Types of Products You Will Purchase _____

Amount of Credit Requested $_____

Are You a:

☐ CORPORATION

State of Incorporation _____

Names, Titles and Addresses of Your Three Chief Corporate Officers _____

_____

_____

_____

Name and Address of Your Resident Agent

_____

☐ PARTNERSHIP

Names and Addresses of the Partners

_____

_____

_____

☐ SOLE PROPRIETORSHIP

Are you sales tax exempt? Yes ___ No ___

Have you ever had credit with us before? Yes ___ No ___

If yes, under what name? _____

Authorized Purchasers _____

_____

Purchase Order Required? Yes ___ No ___

SAMPLE CREDIT APPLICATION (continued)

TRADE REFERENCES

Reference #1 Name _____

Address _____

Phone (   ) _____

Reference #2 Name _____

Address _____

Phone (   ) _____

Reference #3 Name _____

Address _____

Phone (   ) _____

BANK REFERENCES

Bank #1 Account # _____ Phone (   ) _____

Contact Person _____

Name of Bank _____

Address _____

Bank #2 Account # _____ Phone (   ) _____

Contact Person _____

Name of Bank _____

Address _____

I represent that the above information is true and is given to induce ABC ELECTRICAL INC. to extend credit to the applicant. My company and I authorize ABC ELECTRICAL INC. to make such credit investigation as ABC ELECTRICAL INC. sees fit, including contacting the above trade references and banks and obtaining credit reports. My company and I authorize all trade references, banks and credit reporting agencies to disclose to ABC ELECTRICAL INC. any and all information concerning the financial and credit history of my company and myself.

I have read the terms and conditions stated below and agree to all of those terms and conditions.

Authorized Signature: _____

Printed Name: _____

Title: _____   Date: _____

GENERAL TERMS AND CONDITIONS AND PERSONAL GUARANTEE

1. Bills are sent on the first day of each month. You may take the 5% discount as indicated on the bill if you pay the invoice by the 10th of the month.

2. All bills become payable in full on the 11th day of the month and, if not paid by the end of the month, are considered past due.

3. A service charge of 2% per month will be added to all amounts billed if not paid by the end of the month.

4. No additional credit will be extended to past due accounts unless satisfactory arrangements are made with our credit department.

5. PERSONAL GUARANTEE: If the credit customer is a corporation, then those signing this application, whether signing as an officer or not, personally guarantee payment for all items purchased on credit by the corporation.

Personal guarantees can be a problem. See the discussion in Section 3, below.

3. Extending Credit to Businesses

When the customer is another business, it's wise to get information about who you're really dealing with—especially if the business wants a substantial amount of credit. Is the customer a sole proprietor? A partnership? A corporation? The answer determines who's liable for the debt. If the business is owned by an individual (for example, Bill Jones doing business as Jones Products), the owner's own assets—as well as those of the business—are available to satisfy the debt. With a general partnership, you can go after the assets of the individual partners, if necessary, so it's a good idea to have the names of all the partners listed on the credit application. A limited partnership, on the other hand, consists of general partners and limited partners; only the assets of the general partners are available to satisfy the debts of a limited partnership. (See Chapter 1, Section C.)

With a corporation, you usually are limited to collecting from the business assets. Because you can't collect from the personal bank accounts of the officers and shareholders, there's good reason to seek personal guarantees when dealing with a new or small corporation that wants substantial credit. In some businesses, however, it's completely against trade practices to ask for a personal guarantee. It's your job to learn the practices in your industry before using a clause like number 5, above. If you do decide to seek personal guarantees, check out whether or not a signature on a credit application is sufficient in your state. The law may require that you obtain a new guarantee each time you extend credit to a company.

You may also want to ask for the personal guarantees of others if someone who applies for personal credit has a weak financial status. Maybe a friend or family member will agree to be responsible if the customer doesn't pay on time. This is often called co-signing. You can obtain the personal guarantee or co-

signature on the credit application form or on a separate document called "Guarantee of Payment." As noted above, in some states, a personal guarantee on an application form or a one-time separate document may not suffice. You may need to get a signature from the guarantor each time you extend credit.

4. References and Credit Checks

Your credit application should provide space for the applicant to list several other businesses who will vouch for the fact that the applicant pays on time. Check these references carefully, even though the credit applicant is sure to list people who will say positive things. Your job is to try to penetrate the facade many credit applicants are sure to present that everything is just fine. One way to do this is to ask off beat questions such as, "You mean ABC's credit is so good you'll take me to lunch if they stiff me?"

If the amount of credit you're extending is large, don't stop with checking a few references. Purchase a credit report on an individual from a national credit reporting agency such as Trans Union, TRW or Equifax or, on a business, from Dun & Bradstreet. You'll find them listed under "Credit Reporting Agencies" in the Yellow Pages.

To get a report on an individual, most agencies want the name, address, phone number, Social Security number and date of birth, if possible, of the person you're asking them to search—information you should get on your credit application form.

Be wary of negative information in credit reports, which may be inaccurate or out of date. If an individual seems to be otherwise well-qualified for credit, consider giving him or her a chance to explain the negative stuff before you deny credit.

5. Signatures for Receipt of Goods

Have customers sign receipts when they receive merchandise on credit. If you provide services, have customers sign an acknowledgment of services performed. This avoids arguments about whether or not the customer actually received the goods or services.

B. Laws That Regulate Consumer Credit

Many small businesses don't extend credit directly to consumers. With the widespread availability of credit cards, this is often the safest and most cost-effective way to go. However, if yours if a business where credit must be granted, you must comply with federal laws affecting credit sales to consumers for personal, family or household purposes. States are also beginning to adopt consumer credit laws that mirror many provisions of federal law.

Here's an introduction to the major federal laws that affect consumer credit:

1. The Truth in Lending Act

This statute requires you to disclose your exact credit terms to people who apply for credit, so they'll know what they're expected to pay. It also regulates how you advertise consumer credit. Among the items you must disclose to a consumer who buys on credit are the following:

- The monthly finance charge.
- The annual interest rate.
- When payments are due.
- The total sale price—cash price of the item or service plus all other charges.
- The amount of any late payment charges and when they'll be imposed.

2. The Fair Credit Billing Act

This law dictates what you must do if a customer claims you made a mistake in your billing. The customer must notify you within 60 days after you mailed the first bill containing the claimed error. You must respond within 30 days after you receive the letter unless the dispute has already been resolved. You must also conduct a reasonable investigation and, within 90 days after getting the customer's letter, explain why the bill is correct or correct the error. If you don't follow this procedure, you must give the customer a $50 credit toward the disputed amount—even if your bill was correct. Until the dispute is resolved, you can't report to a credit bureau that the customer is delinquent.

Example: Ron notifies CompuCo that he wasn't properly credited for a payment he sent in on his computer system. Under the Fair Credit Billing Act, CompuCo must acknowledge Ron's notice within 30 days. And within 90 days, CompuCo must either agree with Ron and correct his account or, after conducting a reasonable investigation, send Ron a letter explaining why the company feels his bill was correct. While this is happening, Ron doesn't have to pay the disputed amount. And he can't be penalized for withholding payment. During this period, CompuCo can't tell a credit reporting agency that this is a delinquent bill. CompuCo can charge interest on the disputed bill, but if Ron turns out to be right, the interest must be dropped.

State laws may be even tougher. In California, for example, if you don't comply with the 90-day limit for completing your investigation and responding to the customer, the customer doesn't have to pay any amount—even if the bill was correct. Under federal and state laws, you may be subject to other penalties as well for failing to comply with the required procedures.

In addition to telling you how to handle billing disputes, the Fair Credit Billing Act requires you, in periodic mailings, to tell consumers what their rights are.

3. The Equal Credit Opportunity Act

You may not discriminate against an applicant on the basis of race, color, religion, national origin, age, sex or marital status. The Act does leave you free to consider legitimate factors in granting credit, such as the applicant's financial status (earnings and savings) and credit record. Despite the prohibition on age discrimination, you can reject a consumer who hasn't reached the legal age in your state for entering into contracts.

4. The Fair Credit Reporting Act

This law deals primarily with credit reports issued by credit reporting agencies. It's intended to protect consumers from having their eligibility for credit thwarted by inaccurate or obsolete credit report information. The law gives consumers the right to a copy of their credit reports. If they feel something is inaccurate, they can ask that it be corrected or removed. If the business reporting the credit problem doesn't agree to a change or deletion or if the credit bureau refuses to make it, the consumer can add a 100-word statement to the file explaining his or her side of the story. This becomes a part of any future credit report.

5. The Fair Debt Collection Practices Act

This statute addresses abusive methods used by third-party collectors—bill collectors you hire to collect overdue bills. Small businesses are more directly affected by state laws that apply directly to collection methods used by a creditor. (See Section D.3.)

RECOMMENDED READING

An excellent resource regarding consumer credit is *Consumer Law: Sales Practices and Credit Regulation*, by Howard J. Alperin and Roland J. Alperin (West Publishing Co.). It should be available at most law libraries. Also helpful is *Credit Manual of Commercial Laws*, by Lester Nelson (National Association of Credit Management).

Two fine Nolo Press books discuss these issues from the perspective of the consumer: *Money Troubles: Legal Strategies to Cope with Your Debts*, by Robin Leonard, and *Consumer Action Guide—Your Rights from A to Z* (California Edition), by Barbara Kaufman.

Also very helpful are two booklets published by the Federal Trade Commission:

- *How to Advertise Consumer Credit: Complying With the Law*

- *How To Write Readable Credit Forms*

See Appendix B for FTC addresses and phone numbers.

Finally, you may find helpful information in *Debtor-Creditor Relations in a Nutshell*, by David B. Epstein (West Publishing Co.).

You may be able to get information from a local trade association (such as a contractors', restaurant or tax preparers' association) or Chamber of Commerce.

C. Becoming a Secured Creditor

If you sell major amounts of merchandise or equipment to a customer on credit, look into becoming a secured creditor. If the debt is secured by property of the customer, you can seize that property if the customer doesn't pay the debt as promised. A common arrangement is for a business to take a security interest in the goods it sells on credit. For example, a store that sells furniture on credit keeps a security interest in the furniture. If the buyer gets behind on payments, the store can take the furniture back.

1. Sales of Merchandise or Equipment

The Uniform Commercial Code (UCC), which has been adopted by all states, provides a method for you to acquire a legal (security) interest in the property that you sell to the customer—or in other property of the customer—that will let you sell or take back the property if the customer doesn't pay. Typically, you have the customer sign a financing agreement and a UCC Financing Statement. You then file the UCC Financing Statement with the appropriate public office, such as the county clerk or the secretary of state (it varies from state to state).

Also, if the customer files for bankruptcy, you'll have a big advantage over general (unsecured) creditors—those who didn't take a security interest in the customer's property. The property in which you have a security interest will be earmarked for your benefit. Unsecured creditors get only a share of the bankrupt's unsecured assets—which may repay only a tiny portion of what's owed or (often) nothing at all.

Obviously, it takes time and requires some paperwork and expense to create a security interest. It may not be worth it if you sell someone a $500 washing machine (it's a lot easier to take credit cards and require full payment)—but definitely worth doing when the product is a $10,000 computer system. Banks routinely obtain a security interest when they loan money to a customer to purchase equipment.

Incidentally, as an alternative to extending credit on larger purchases, one option is to refer the customer to a bank or leasing company—particularly one with whom you've established a working relationship. These organizations are in business to take credit risks and can absorb losses better than you can.

2. Special Rights for Those in the Construction Business

A lien is a legal claim on someone's property. Under state law, you may have a mechanic's, materialman's or construction lien on real estate if you provided materials or labor on a construction or renovation project—for example, if you supplied the lighting fixtures or installed the roofing for a new house. If your bill isn't paid, you can foreclose on your lien. This means the real estate can be sold to pay your bill.

Unfortunately, in many states to take advantage of this powerful weapon to protect your rights, you have to file certain legal documents claiming (perfecting) a lien within a short time after you complete your work or supply the materials. Speak to a construction industry trade association or, if necessary, a lawyer about how to do this.

D. Collection Problems

Despite your best efforts to screen your customers, if you extend credit, sooner or later you're going to run into people or businesses who are slow in paying. It can be one of the most frustrating aspects of running a business. Part of the reason is that you may be pursuing several objectives that are not compatible. Here's what I mean:

- You want to be paid in full, of course, but—
- You'd also like to continue doing business with the customer, if possible. What's more—
- You don't want to run afoul of laws that restrict or prohibit aggressive collection tactics, and
- You don't want waste your resources on a wild goose chase.

It's not an easy problem, but a number of techniques can help keep your losses to a minimum.

1. Strategies for Avoiding or Reducing Losses

Following these suggestions should help you hold down your losses on credit transactions:

- Send bills promptly and re-bill at least monthly. There's no need to wait for the end of the month.

- Make sure your bills clearly state the goods sold or the services provided. It's a great idea to include on the bill a request to the customer to contact you if there are problems with the goods or services. If the customer fails to do so and later tries to excuse the failure to pay by claiming the goods or services were unsatisfactory, you have a good argument that the customer is fabricating a phony excuse. Another benefit is that if your goods or services are in fact prone to problems, you open up lines of communication and usually can keep the customer happy.

- Enclose a self-addressed envelope (preferably stamped) to facilitate payment.

- Keep a record of the checking account that the customer uses to pay you.

- Send past due notices promptly when an account is overdue. Ask clearly for payment. Many people worry that the word "pay" sounds too blunt. Here are a few alternate phrases, courtesy of collection expert Leonard Sklar, author of *The Check Is NOT in the Mail* (Baroque Publishing):

  "We'd appreciate it if you would *clear your account*."

  "You can *take care of this* by cash or check, whichever you prefer."

  "Please *bring your account current*."

- If this doesn't work, promptly telephone to ask what's wrong. The customer needs to know that you follow these matters closely. Do not extend more credit, no matter what the hard luck story. This is particularly important. Lots of businesses facing tight finances pay only when they need more merchandise. If you let them have it without payment, you're teaching them that you're a push-over.

- Have a series of letters to use in routine cases. These letters should escalate in intensity as time goes by. (See the discussion of collection letters later in this section.)

- If the customer has genuine financial problems, find out what the customer realistically can afford. Consider extending the time for payment if the customer agrees in writing to a new payment schedule. Call the day before the next scheduled payment is due to be sure the customer plans to respect the agreement.

- Save copies of all correspondence with the customer and keep notes of all telephone conversations.

- Watch out for checks for less than the full amount that say "Payment in Full." In some states, if you deposit the check—especially if the amount owed is in dispute—you may have wiped out the balance owing. (See Chapter 15, Section C.2.) Learn the law in your state before you deposit such a check.

- Continue to keep in contact with the customer— but don't harass him or her. (See Section D.3.)

- If an account is unpaid for an extended period and you're doubtful about ever collecting, consider offering in writing a time-limited, deep discount to resolve the matter. This way, the customer has the incentive to borrow money to take advantage of your one-time, never-again offer to settle.

- When collection starts to put heavy demands on your time, and your chances of recovery are slim because you know the customer is on the skids, consider turning the debt over to a collection agency so you can get on with more productive activities. (But first consider the collection alternatives described in Section E.)

2. Collection Letters

You may find it useful to develop a set of past due notices to use when customers fall behind. Although these are form letters, it's easy to customize them using your computer and wordprocessing software. In writing to an individual customer, use the customer's name. In writing to a company, address your letter to the owner or chief operating office. It's less effective to start out with "Dear Customer" or "Dear Accounts Payable Supervisor."

Your first letter may suggest that perhaps the bill was overlooked, and that payment should be sent now so that the customer can maintain a good credit rating. Your second and third letters should be polite but increasingly firm. Vary the format of your letters. Each one should look a little different. Samples are shown below.

Letter 1

```
              Account No. _____

 Dear _____:

     Our records show that you have an outstanding balance with our company
 of $450.00. This is for  (describe the goods or services) .

     Is there a problem with this bill? If so, please call me so that we
 can resolve the matter. Otherwise, please send your payment at this time
 to bring your account current. I'm enclosing a business reply envelope
 for you to use.

     Until you bring your account current, it's our policy to put further
 purchases on a cash basis.

 Sincerely,




     P.S. Paying your bill at this time will help you to maintain your good
 credit rating.
```

Letter 2

Re: Overdue Bill ($_____)

Account No. _____

Dear _____:

Your bill for $450.00 is seriously overdue. This is for the (describe the goods or services furnished) we supplied to you last (state the month) More than 60 days have gone by since we sent you our invoice. You did not respond to the letter I sent you last month.

We value your patronage but must insist that you bring your account up to date. Doing so will help you protect your reputation for prompt payment.

Please send your check today for the full balance. If this is not feasible, please call me to discuss a possible payment plan. I need to hear from you as soon as possible.

Sincerely,

Letter 3

Re: Collection Action on

Overdue Bill ($_____)

Account No.

_____

Dear _____:

We show an unpaid balance of $450 on your account that is over 90 days old. This is for the _____ that we supplied you over _____ days ago.

I have repeatedly tried to contact you, but my calls and letters have gone unheeded.

You must send full payment by (date) or contact me by that date to discuss your intentions. If I do not hear from you, I plan to turn over the account for collection.

As you know, collection action can only have an adverse effect on your credit rating, and, according to our credit agreement, you will be responsible for collection costs. I hope to hear from you immediately so that the matter can be resolved without taking that step.

Sincerely,

3. Prohibited Collection Practices

Because of abuses, Congress passed the Fair Debt Collection Practices Act to regulate the activities of collection agencies. The federal law doesn't cover small businesses that collect their own bills. Many state laws, however, do crack down on the aggressive collection techniques of such businesses. And in states where the legislature hasn't yet acted, court decisions often penalize businesses that harass debtors or use unfair collection tactics.

Most business owners know intuitively the kind of behavior that's out of bounds. Here are some debt collection practices specifically outlawed by California's Fair Debt Collection Practices statute:

- Using or threatening to use physical force to collect a debt.

- Falsely threatening that the failure to pay a consumer debt will result in an accusation that the debtor has committed a crime.

- Using obscene or profane language.

- Causing expense to the debtor for long distance calls.

- Causing a phone to ring repeatedly or continuously to annoy the debtor.

- Communicating with the debtor so often as to be unreasonable and to constitute harassment.

- Communicating with the debtor's employer regarding a consumer debt unless the communication is necessary or the debtor has consented in writing. (A communication is necessary, according to the statute, only to verify the debtor's employment, to locate the debtor or to carry out a garnishment of wages after you have sued and won a judgment.)

The list goes on and on. If there's a similar statute in your state, get a copy and read it carefully. Like California's, most state laws in this field are modeled on the federal law. Some statutes, however, are more specific than others; for example, some list specific hours during which you can call the debtor.

E. Collection Options

Suppose you can't get the customer to pay up voluntarily. What next? If you're not willing to write off the debt (which is sometimes the wisest thing to do), you have three collection options:

- sue in small claims court

- hire a lawyer

- turn the account over to a collection agency.

Each choice has pros and cons.

Small claims court (see Chapter 19) is inexpensive and speedy. The downside is that it can take a good chunk of your time. Furthermore, any judgment that you receive may be worthless if the debtor lacks a job or bank account.

Lawyers can be effective, but they're expensive. Consider using a lawyer to write dunning letters. Many lawyers are willing to do this for a nominal charge.

Collection agencies are good at tracing elusive debtors, but they take a big percentage of what they collect for you.

PUT IT IN WRITING: SMALL BUSINESS CONTRACTS 17

As the owner of a small business, it's likely that you'll often encounter both written and oral contracts. The most important piece of advice about contracts is obvious: put all important agreements in writing. This chapter shows you how, and tells you what to do if something goes wrong.

A. What Makes a Valid Contract

A valid contract requires two and sometimes three elements:

- An agreement (meeting of the minds) between the parties.

- "Consideration"—a legal term meaning the exchange of things of value.

- Something in writing, if the contract covers certain matters, such as the sale of real estate and tasks that can't be completed in one year. (See Section D.)

For example, suppose you're opening a new store. You meet with Joe, a sign maker, to discuss the construction and installation of a five-foot by three-foot sign. Joe offers to do the work for $450 and to have the sign ready for your grand opening on June 15. "It's a deal," you say. You now have a legally binding contract, enforceable in court or by arbitration. All the necessary elements are present:

- *An Agreement.* Joe offered to build and install the sign at a certain price by a certain date. You accepted the offer by telling Joe, "It's a deal."

- *Consideration.* The two of you are exchanging something of value. You're giving your promise to pay $450. Joe is giving his promise to build and install the sign.

- *Written Agreement Not Required Here.* Normal business contracts that can be performed in less than a year don't have to be in writing to be enforceable.

To understand why "consideration" is important, let's explore the difference between a contract and a gift. Assume that Joe installs the sign on time and

you pay him $450 as agreed. Impressed by the high quality of his work, you say: "Joe, to thank you for the great job you did, I'm going to send you a $100 bonus next week." Can Joe enforce your promise to pay the bonus? No. He got what he bargained for— the $450 payment. He didn't promise you anything (consideration) for the extra $100 payment. If you pay it, fine. If not, Joe can't force you to.

1. Negotiations

Negotiations, which may or may not lead to an agreement, do not constitute a contract. So if instead of meeting face to face with Joe, you call him and describe the job, and he says he can probably do it for about $450, you don't have a contract.

2. Offer and Acceptance

If after negotiations, two people reach an agreement, a contract is formed. Say that after discussing the job with you by phone, Joe promptly sends you a letter in which he says: "I can build and install the sign shown on the enclosed sketch for $450. I'll have it in place by June 15 when you open. You can pay me then." You send back a fax saying: "Sounds good. Go ahead." This is a valid contract. Joe has made a clear offer. You've just as clearly accepted that offer. The fact that you and Joe didn't meet face-to-face and didn't even use the same type of communication medium doesn't alter this conclusion.

In this example, you accepted Joe's offer promptly. But what if you'd waited two weeks or two months to accept? The legal rule is that an offer without a stated expiration date remains open for a reasonable time. What's reasonable depends on the type of business and the facts of the situation. If you're offered a truckload of fish or flowers, it might be unreasonable to delay your acceptance more than a few hours or even minutes, while an offer to sell surplus wood chips at a time when the market is glutted might reasonably be assumed to be good for a month or more. But there's really no need to tolerate any uncertainty in this regard. Include a clear deadline for acceptance when you present an offer. If you want to accept an offer, do it as promptly as possible.

3. Counter-Offers

In the real world, negotiations aren't usually as simple as making an offer and having it accepted. And until an agreement is reached, there's no contract.

For example, say Joe sends you the letter offering to provide your sign for $450. You call his office and leave a message on his voice mail saying: "Go ahead, but I can only pay $400." So far, there's no contract. By changing the terms of Joe's offer, you've rejected it and made a counter-offer. The two of you are still negotiating. If Joe calls back and says, "Okay, I'll do it for $400," you now have a binding contract. Joe has accepted your counter-offer. Again, the fact that and you and Joe weren't in the same room or never spoke to each other isn't significant. What is key is that one of you made an offer (in this case, in the form of a counter-offer), and the other accepted it.

4. Revoking an Offer

Until an offer is accepted, it can be revoked by the person who made it. So if you're about to write Joe a letter accepting his offer, and Joe calls to revoke his offer because he's decided $450 isn't enough, you're out of luck. Joe revoked his offer before you accepted it, so there's no contract. (See "How an Offer To Contract Ends," below.)

How an Offer To Contract Ends

- The person who made the offer revokes it before it's accepted.

- The offer expires.

  Example: "This offer will expire automatically if I don't receive your acceptance by noon on May 10." But unless you've been paid something to keep the offer open (as is common for an option to buy real property—see next section), you (the offeror) can still revoke the unaccepted offer before the period for acceptance expires.

- A reasonable time elapses. As discussed in Section 2, above, there are no hard and fast rules as to what's reasonable. It all depends on circumstances and the practices in your industry.

- The offer is rejected. If you reject an offer and then change your mind, it's too late. To get the deal going again, you'll need to make an offer to the other party.

- Either party dies before the offer is accepted.

---

5. Option To Keep Offer Open

If you want someone to keep an offer open while you think about it, you may have to pay for the privilege. If you do, and the person who made the offer agrees to keep it open, your agreement (which is itself a contract) is called an "option." Options are commonly used when real estate or businesses are sold.

To stay with our sign example, say that when Joe sends you the letter offering to provide your sign, you tell him you're not ready to respond yet, but you want to be sure the offer will stay open while you think about it. Joe responds that if you pay $100 now, he'll keep his offer open for two more weeks. You pay the $100 and accept the offer within the two-week period. The resulting contract would be valid even if Joe tried to withdraw his offer before the end of the two-week period. You and Joe already have a contract (an option), which consists of your right to purchase his services at the $450 price if you act within the two-week period. He received something of value (your $100) in return for granting you this option.

6. How Offers Are Accepted

Usually, offers are accepted either in writing or orally. But that's not always necessary. It is an area of considerable legal complexity, but generally an offer can be accepted by a prompt action that conforms with the terms of the offer. For example, you might leave the sign builder Joe a note at his workshop, saying "Please add a red border to this sign today; I'll pay you an extra $100." Joe comes back that afternoon and adds the red border. You're obligated to pay him.

7. An Advertisement As an Offer

Under traditional contract law, ads are considered only invitations to negotiate or to make an offer; you have no obligation to go through with the deal just because someone offers to meet your advertised price. So if a customer appears and says she wants to buy the house, land or business that you advertised in the classifieds for $200,000, there's no binding contract. One major exception to this rule involves rewards. Generally, an ad offering to pay a reward is binding if someone performs the requested act.

Consumer protection laws have also changed this traditional rule. For example, the law in many states requires merchants to stock advertised items in quantities large enough to meet reasonably expected demand, unless the ad states that stock is limited. And some states require the merchant to give a rain check allowing the consumer to purchase the same merchandise at the same price at a later date. (See Chapter 14 for more on consumer transactions.)

B. Unfair or Illegal Contracts

What if a person makes a bad bargain? Suppose you agree to pay $800 for a used laser printer that's worth only $200. Can you call off the deal on the ground that the contract was grossly unfair? Probably not. As long as there's a valid contract, it doesn't usually matter whether or not the item is objectively worth the price paid for it.

Sometimes, however, a court sets aside a contract if the terms are unconscionable—that is, shockingly unfair. For example, a judge or arbitrator may release an unsophisticated consumer (say a recent immigrant with a language problem) from a grossly unfair contract extracted by a sophisticated, high-pressure salesperson. Applying this principle of law, a contract to sell a $500 television for $5,000 might be set aside. But even though a judge might cite contract law, the decision would probably be based more on the doctrine of fraud or misrepresentation. Or the decision might be based on a state consumer protection statute that prohibits taking advantage of someone who can't protect his or her interests because of disability, illiteracy or a language problem. (See Chapter 14, Section D, for more on this type of statute.)

When it comes to reasonably experienced business people working out contracts with each other, however, unfairness is rarely if ever a legal ground for setting aside a contract. Usually, a party who negotiates a bad deal is stuck with it.

If a contract clause is illegal or against public policy, a judge or arbitrator won't enforce it. For example, a remodeling contract stating that neither party will obtain a legally required building permit would be void as a violation of public policy, as would a similar contract obligating a party to bribe a building inspector.

C. Misrepresentation, Duress or Mistake

If before you sign a contract the other person tells you a false statement about something important, and you rely on that statement in signing the contract, you can go to court and have the contract rescinded (canceled). This is so even if the other person doesn't realize that the fact is untrue. For example, say you buy a pickup truck for your business, relying on the seller's assertion that the truck can carry loads up to two tons. It turns out that the seller got the numbers wrong, and the truck can only carry one-ton loads. You can have the contract rescinded. If you have a contract rescinded, you must return any benefits you already received. In this example, you'd have to return the pickup truck to the seller to get your money back.

If you accept "an offer you can't refuse"—because, for example, the offer is made at gunpoint—the contract isn't legally enforceable. The same is true of any other contract made as a result of unlawful threats. For example, if one party threatens to report the other party to the IRS or a state agency if a one-sided contract isn't signed, the contract isn't enforceable.

A mistake is the other ground for rescission of a contract. You thought you were buying a two-year-old computer. The seller thought you were buying her five-year-old computer. If you were both acting in good faith and simply miscommunicated, a judge or arbitrator would probably set aside the contract. But you can't avoid liability if you simply used bad judgment and paid too much for a five-year-old computer that doesn't provide the quality or speed you need.

Breach of Warranty

Sometimes a buyer can return goods to the seller and get a refund based on a breach of warranty. While the practical result in such cases may be the same as setting aside a contract for the reasons mentioned in this section, a different legal concept is at work.

An action for breach of warranty assumes that there's a valid contract. When a buyer seeks a refund based on breach of warranty, he or she is saying: "I acknowledge that we have a binding contract. I want to enforce my rights under that contract for breach of warranty." (See Chapter 14.)

D. Must a Contract Be in Writing?

Unless a contract falls into one of several specific categories, it is binding even if it's not in writing. You should put all important contracts in writing anyway. Otherwise, you run the risk of a dispute as to exactly what was promised, how much was to be paid, when the contract was to be performed, and on and on and on. And if you argue so long that you end up in court, it can be somewhere between difficult and impossible (not to mention expensive) to prove the existence and terms of an oral contract.

1. Contracts That Must Be in Writing

Each state has a statute (usually called the Statute of Frauds) listing the types of contracts that must be written to be valid. A typical list includes:

a. CONTRACTS INVOLVING THE SALE OF REAL ESTATE OR AN INTEREST IN REAL ESTATE

Examples are a contract to purchase a building or parking lot or a contract to sell someone the right to use part of your land for a certain purpose (an easement).

b. LEASES OF REAL ESTATE LASTING LONGER THAN ONE YEAR

An example is a three-year lease for retail space in a neighborhood shopping plaza.

c. A PROMISE TO PAY SOMEONE ELSE'S DEBT

This generally involves guarantees of payment.

Examples: The president of a corporation personally guarantees to pay for any goods you sell to the corporation; or an uncle guarantees to pay the rent for his nephew's new store.

d. CONTRACTS THAT WILL TAKE MORE THAN ONE YEAR TO PERFORM

This provision of the statute of frauds applies only to contracts that cannot be performed within one year; for example, a contract to provide landscaping services to a hotel for a two-year period.

If performance of a contract is possible within one year, the contract doesn't have to be in writing. How about a contract to plant three maple trees within the next two years? Since the trees could be planted right away, the contract doesn't have to be writing to be enforceable. Here are several more examples of oral contracts performable within one year (and therefore enforceable):

- A contract to teach four new employees within the next 18 months how to use a software program.

- A contract to cater a total of ten sales banquets for a corporation at dates to be selected by the corporation during the next three years.

- A contract to remove debris from the sites of five new homes to be completed within the next two years.

e. CONTRACTS FOR THE SALE OF GOODS (TANGIBLE PERSONAL PROPERTY) WORTH $500 OR MORE

A contract to sell you a notebook computer for $2,000, for example, must be in writing to be enforceable. If you call a computer store and they agree over the phone to sell you the computer for $2,000 but raise the price to $2,500 when you get there, you don't have an enforceable contract.

Under the Uniform Commercial Code (UCC), however, the written contract doesn't have to state the price or time of delivery—only that the parties agree on the sale of goods and the quantity of goods being sold. And in some cases, if the seller simply sends a written confirmation of an oral order and the buyer doesn't promptly object, a contract has been formed. These UCC exceptions are very important; be sure to read Section 3, below, which explains them in more detail.

There's an important exception to the rule that contracts for the sale of goods worth $500 must be in writing. If an oral contract is partially performed, the whole contract becomes binding. For example, say a salesperson offers to sell you a notebook computer for $2,000 and to throw in a modem when the store gets its next shipment in a week. You pay the $2,000 and take the computer home. When you return to the store the next week to pick up your modem, the store denies that it owes you one. You could sue successfully for breach of contract even though you don't have a written contract for a sale of goods over $500. The reason is that partial performance of the oral contract (your payment and the store's partial delivery of the merchandise) removes the transaction from the written contract (Statute of Frauds) requirements. Of course, as a practical matter, it would have been better to get the whole deal in writing.

2. What Constitutes a Written Contract

When state law does require a contract to be in writing, it doesn't mean you need a long-winded document labeled "contract" or "agreement" and signed by both parties. Especially in a business context, judges recognize and enforce writings that contain few details. All that's typically required is a letter, memo or any other writing signed by the party against whom the contract is being enforced. The writing must identify the parties and generally describe the subject and the main terms and conditions of the agreement. That's all. The rules for what the writing must contain are even more relaxed for transactions covered by the Uniform Commercial Code, which automatically fills in many missing details. (See Section 3, below.)

I don't recommend that you settle for the bare-bones legal requirements. Because business people's memories—like everyone else's—are imperfect, and because putting a contract in writing tends to highlight erroneous assumptions, and because not everyone you deal with is completely trustworthy, you want important contracts to contain a reasonable amount of detail.

Example: Arnie, a fish shop operator, meets Phyllis, a phone equipment salesperson, at a trade show. Arnie becomes enthusiastic about purchasing a new telephone system for $3,000, which he believes covers the installation, including all wiring and control panels. Phyllis, the sales rep for FoneTek, thinks her company is providing just the phones themselves. If they go ahead on the basis of an oral contract, disaster clearly looms. If, however, Arnie and Phyllis sit down to write up a contract, the issues that haven't really been agreed on are sure to come out, and Arnie and Phyllis will have ample opportunity to make necessary adjustments or call the deal off.

See Section E, below, for suggestions on writing a business contract.

3. The Sale of Goods: Special Uniform Commercial Code Rules

The Uniform Commercial Code (UCC) contains special rules affecting contracts for the sale of goods. It loosens up the requirements for creating a binding contract when goods are being sold.

The UCC requires you to produce something in writing if you want to enforce a contract for a sale of goods and the price is $500 or more. However, the UCC says that this writing can be very brief—briefer than a normal written contract. Under the UCC, the writing need only:

- indicate that the parties have agreed on the sale of the goods, and

- state the quantity of goods being sold.

If items such as price, time and place of delivery, or quality of the goods are missing, the UCC fills them in based on customs and practices in the particular industry.

 Don't rely on sketchy contracts. Just because the UCC makes legal some very sketchy contracts for the sale of goods doesn't mean it's a good idea to routinely use such contracts. It's far better to follow the outline in Section E, below, to put together a good written contract.

Remember, if a customer comes to a store, pays for merchandise and takes it away, there's no need for a formal written contract—the deal is done. (For larger purchases, it makes sense for the retailer to have the customer sign a receipt acknowledging delivery of the goods.) Under the UCC, having some writing is important when the seller merely promises to deliver the goods.

In most situations, the UCC requires that when a contract must be in writing to be enforceable, it must be signed by the person against whom the other party is seeking to enforce the contract. Stated another way, if A wants to sue B for breach of contract and a writing is required, A must show that B signed something showing an intent to be contractually bound.

But when merchants—people who sell goods— are involved, there doesn't always have to be a signed document. If a seller sends a confirmation of an order and the buyer doesn't object in writing within ten days after receiving it, nothing more is required to satisfy the written contract requirement.

Example: Mindy owns a retail store that sells shoes. Runner's Choice Inc., a manufacturer, sends Mindy a notice saying: "This is to confirm that you agreed to buy 1,000 pairs of men's jogging shoes from this Company." Under normal written contract rules (see Section B above), this wouldn't be enough to permit Runner's Choice to enforce a contract against Mindy, because she's signed nothing. But under the UCC, if Mindy doesn't object in writing within ten days after receiving the notice, she can't complain about the lack of a written document bearing her signature.

In this example, the notice from Runner's Choice satisfies the requirement that the contract be evidenced by a writing. However, if Runner's Choice sues Mindy for rejecting the shipment of shoes, it will still have to convince the judge or arbitrator that before Runner's Choice sent Mindy the notice, the parties actually reached an oral agreement regarding the shoes. In short, the notice, by itself, is not conclusive evidence that the parties reached a meeting of the minds. A contract signed by both sides is always preferable.

Where the UCC Came From

In 1940, someone came up with a brilliant idea: Why not put together a comprehensive code (statute) covering all the branches of commercial law and get it adopted in all states? That way, businesses in Michigan, Illinois, Georgia and Oregon would all follow the same rules.

It took 11 years to carry out this proposal, which resulted in a set of model statutes called the Uniform Commercial Code, or UCC. Every state except Louisiana has adopted it; Louisiana has adopted key portions of it. It covers these areas of law:

- Sales (including Warranties; see Chapter 14, Section C)
- Commercial Paper (drafts, checks, certificates of deposit, promissory notes)
- Bank Deposits and Collections
- Letters of Credit
- Bulk Transfers
- Warehouse Receipts, Bills of Lading and Other Documents of Title
- Investment Securities
- Secured Transactions.

Valid Contracts With No Writing at All. Where specially manufactured goods are ordered, the UCC says you don't need something in writing to enforce a sales contract if the seller has already made a significant effort toward completing the terms of the contract.

Example: A restaurant calls and orders 500 sets of dishes from a restaurant supply company. The dishes are to feature the restaurant's logo. If the supply company makes a substantial beginning on manufacturing the dishes and applying the logo, the restaurant can't avoid liability on the contract simply because it was oral.

Checking Out the UCC

Your state laws (statutes) should be available in any law library in your state, as well as in the reference section of many public libraries. The librarian can help you find the volume containing the Uniform Commercial Code, which is probably indexed under Uniform, Commercial or Commerce. For most small businesses, the section on Sales (Article 2) is the most helpful part of the UCC. The UCC changes fairly often; be sure you have the latest version that's been adopted in your state.

Another way to get the UCC (or specific portions of it) is to call the publisher of the statutes. They may sell the UCC portion separately.

E. Writing Business-to-Business Contracts

Whatever your business, you'll need to write contracts from time to time. You'll probably need a written contract if you want to:

- buy or sell goods
- perform services as an independent contractor or consultant
- lease real estate or equipment
- manufacture, distribute or license products
- enter into joint ventures
- grant credit
- advertise.

1. Checklist of Contract Clauses

The content of a contract depends, of course, on the type of transaction you're getting into. This checklist includes items to consider when you draft a contract:

- Names and addresses of the parties.

- Date that the contract is signed. (See Section F for suggestions about signing a contract.)

- A short preamble ("recitals"). This provides some of the background of the agreement. For example, a contract might recite that Discs Unlimited is a retailer of compact discs and has three stores in the metropolitan area; that Stewart has an inventory management business; and that Discs Unlimited wishes to retain Stewart as an independent contractor to establish and maintain the company's computerized inventory control system.

- What each party is promising to do: Pay money, provide a service, sell something, build something or so on. Often this section of the contract—particularly if it involves a product or a construction project—is labeled "specifications." In many situations, such as designing software, constructing a building or providing consulting services, the specifications require an attachment that can run on for pages and may include drawings, formulas or charts. (See Section 3, below, for how-to information.)

- When the work will be done or the product delivered. If strict compliance with contract deadlines is important, be sure to include the words, "Time is of the essence." Otherwise, a judge would probably allow reasonable leeway in enforcing the deadlines.

- How long the contract will remain in effect.

- The price—or how it will be determined.

- When payment is due. Will there be installments, and will interest be charged? In contracts for consulting and other services, it's common to have a payment schedule tied to interim completion deadlines. For example, a contract for architectural services might provide for payment of one-third of the architect's fees when drawings and specifications are finished and approved; one-third after bids have been received on the construction project and a contract signed with the general contractor; and one-third when the project is completed and a certificate of occupancy is issued by the building department.

- Warranties. If one party guarantees labor and materials for a certain period of time, what steps will be taken to correct warranty problems?

- Conditions under which either party can terminate the agreement.

- "Liquidated damages" if performance is delayed or defective. In cases where actual damages for breach of contract would be difficult to compute, the parties can establish in advance a fixed dollar amount (called liquidated damages) to be paid by a party who fails to perform its contractual obligations properly. (See Section H, below.)

- Whether or not either party can transfer (assign) the contract to another person or company. A contract that allows assignment of contract rights may be okay if it involves just the right to receive money, but not if it means that some other, unknown party will wind up performing skilled services called for by the contract.

- Arbitration or mediation of disputes.

- Whether or not a party who breaches the contract is responsible for the other party's attorney fees and legal costs.

- Where notices of default or other communications concerning the contract can be sent. Typically, the notices are sent to the business headquarters of the contracting parties.

- What state law applies if questions about the contract arise. If the parties have operations in different states or the contract is to be performed in more than one state, you may avoid potentially knotty legal issues if you specify in advance which state law applies.

2. Additional Requirements for Specialized Contracts

Many states require specific provisions in contracts that cover certain types of transactions. Areas where special requirements are likely include:

- sales of new and used vehicles and mobile homes
- home improvement services
- motor vehicle repairs
- apartment and home rentals
- door-to-door sales
- funerals, burials and cremations

If you're in one of these regulated businesses, you not only need to use a written contract; you also need to make sure it conforms to your state's legal rules. Among other things, you may have to put certain information or warnings in type of a certain size, including a statement about the customer's right to cancel the deal under certain conditions. In some states, you may have to print the contract in Spanish as well as English.

> **Example:** In Michigan, a statute requires a funeral director to insert the following language in bold-faced tape in every prepaid funeral contract:
>
> "This contract may be canceled either before death or after death by the buyer or, if the buyer is deceased, by the person or persons legally authorized to make funeral arrangements. If the contract is canceled, the buyer or the buyer's estate is entitled to receive a refund of __% of the contract price and any income earned from investment of the principal less administrative or escrow fees."

3. How To Design Your Contracts

You need contract forms that reflect the specialized nature of what you do, be it creating software, selling produce, publishing books or cleaning buildings. This is especially true if your business is subject to consumer laws that require specific contract language. Typically, you'll need several basic types of contract for your business, each with spaces to fill in the details of the specific transaction.

> **Example:** Brian is setting up a direct mail consulting business. He plans to work with local businesses to show them how to stay in better contact with customers by announcing sales, new merchandise and seasonally

extended hours. Brian needs a contract that covers what he'll do, when he'll do it, what he expects his small business clients to provide, warranties, responsibilities for proofreading and signing off on mailings, and payment.

Brian will also need to hire independent contractors, graphic designers, artists and computer wizards to help him carry out his contracts, so he'll also need a basic "work-for-hire" contract. Finally, Brian plans to use his experience to develop customized software for sale to similar businesses and so will need a basic software licensing agreement.

If you're new to your business, start by gathering copies of contracts used by other people in your field. Some kinds of contracts, such as commercial leases, are widely available. For other kinds, you may have to dig a bit. Trade associations, which commonly publish material containing sample contracts, are one good source. Other people in your line of work may be willing to share their contracts with you. Form books published for lawyers are an excellent starting point for developing your own specialized contract. Talk to the librarian at any major law library to find some suitable books. (See Chapter 20 for tips on finding and using a law library.)

Once you find a simple contract that's more or less suitable, make sure that you understand every word. Obviously, contracts written in plain English are better than those filled with legalese—but if the latter type is all you can find, it may not be too diffi-cult to re-write it. Next, write a rough draft of any additions you may need.

 Professional help. If you plan to use a form contract for major transactions, consider reviewing it with a lawyer who has small business experience—ideally, one who knows something about your field. It can help you see whether or not the contract does what you want it to do and includes everything you need. Because you have done most of the work, your advisor's advice should be reasonably priced. (See Chapter 20 for how to hire and work with a lawyer.)

4. Attachments to Contracts

It's common to use attachments (often called exhibits) to your contract to list lengthy details that don't fit neatly into the main body of the contract. For example, in drawing up a contract with a sign maker, you could attach a sketch of the sign and a list of detailed specifications, including materials to be used. Simply refer in the main contract to Attachment A or Exhibit A and note that you "hereby incorporate it into your contract." By refer-ring to the attachment in the contract itself, you make it a part of the contract.

If you're a consultant or routinely contract for your services, consider using a short basic contract and then adding your performance specs in an attachment. That way you can use the same basic contract form over and over with only slight modifications.

RECOMMENDED READING

Materials Written Primarily for Individuals

- *Simple Contracts for Personal Use*, by Stephen Elias and Marcia Stewart (Nolo Press). This book, which includes promissory notes and agreements to sell, lease and store property, also contains contracts for service providers (child care, planting contractors) that are of use to small business people in these fields.

Materials Written Primarily for Business People

- *The Complete Book of Small Business Legal Forms*, by Daniel Sitarz (Nova Publishing Company). This book covers a variety of small business transactions, including agreements for sale of a business or business assets, agreements not to compete, leases and collection documents.

- *The Complete Legal Guide for Your Small Business*, by Paul Adams (John Wiley & Sons Inc.). Includes agreements for consultants, sales representatives, distributors and employees.

Materials Written Primarily for Lawyers and Law Students

- *Contracts in a Nutshell*, by Gordon D. Schaber and Claude D. Rohwer (West Publishing Co.). An overview of contract law.

- *Sales in a Nutshell*, by John M. Stockton (West Publishing Co.). Legal analysis of the Uniform Commercial Code sections dealing with sales.

- *Basic Legal Forms*, by Marvin Hayman (Warren, Gorham & Lamont). Clear and comprehensive forms. This one-volume work is found in many law offices. It's more expensive than the other books on the list, but well worth the price if you draft a lot of contracts.

- *Business Contract Forms*, by Robert J. English (John Wiley & Sons Inc.). A helpful resource written for both lawyers and non-lawyers.

F. The Formalities of Getting a Contract Signed

Many contracts take the form of a single document containing a series of numbered clauses. Both parties sign in duplicate, and each keeps a copy. But as discussed throughout this chapter, some written contracts are much less formal. Commonly they're in two—or more—parts. For example, A sends B an offer; B accepts by a separate letter or fax. Or A sends B an offer; B sends back a counter-offer; A accepts the counter-offer by letter or fax. As pointed out in Section A, as long as there's a genuine meeting of the minds, a contract contained in several documents is valid.

Another form of contract is a letter that pulls together the details of your deal and is accepted by the other person by a signature at the bottom. This is typical when you and the other party (perhaps someone you've worked with often) have worked out the deal over lunch or through a series of phone calls and don't feel the need for a formal contract. An example is shown below.

```
September 10, 1992

Dear Mary:

    I'd like to summarize our agreement for you to redecorate our store
at 123 Main Street. We agreed that for $2,000 you'll apply wall
covering to the south wall of our sales areas and apply two coats of
paint to the remaining walls. The paint will be XYZ brand latex semi-
gloss, and the wall covering will be ABC brand vinyl, pattern #66.

    In addition to the $2,000 payment, I'll promptly reimburse you for
the paint and wall covering at your cost (when you present invoices
from RacaFrax Wall Coverings), but you'll be responsible for the cost
of all other tools, equipment and supplies.

    I'll pay you $1,000 before you start work and the balance within 7
days after the work is completed. You'll do the work on the next two
Sundays so that our business isn't interrupted. The quality of your
work will meet or exceed the job you recently completed for the Ski
Shoppe next door.

    We also agreed that if any problems come up about this job and we
can't resolve them ourselves, we'll submit our dispute to Metro
Mediators Inc. for mediation and, if that doesn't resolve the problem,
to binding arbitration--and we'll split the cost 50/50.

    If I've accurately stated our agreement, please sign the enclosed
copy of this letter and return it to me by noon Wednesday.

Sincerely,


Jim Dalton
d/b/a Jim's Fitness Shop



    The above terms are acceptable to me.
    Date:_____    _____
                                        Mary Walz
```

 Be sure to read Section D.3, above, for special rules affecting contracts governed by the Uniform Commercial Code.

1. Revising a Contract Before You Sign

In negotiating a contract, it's common for the parties to go back and forth through several drafts, refining the language. If you have access to a computer with word-processing software, it's simple to crank out a fresh version of the contract each time revisions are made. But that's not to only way to handle changes in wording. For minor changes, you can simply cross out the old wording and write in the new, using a typewriter or pen. If you use this method, each party should initial each change when the contract is signed to establish that the changes were properly consented to and not illegally added later.

Still another way to handle changes—particularly if the changes are extensive—is to put them in an addendum. If you use an addendum, state that in case of a conflict between the addendum and the main contract, the wording in the addendum prevails. Both parties should sign the addendum and the main contract.

If a contract has gone through several revisions, it's a good idea to have both parties initial each page so that you're sure everyone has a correct copy of the final draft.

2. Signatures

Business people are sometimes confused as to how best to sign a contract. It depends on the legal form of your business.

- A *sole proprietor* can simply sign his or name, because a sole proprietorship isn't a separate legal entity. But there are two other ways to do it, either of which is just as legal.

Method 1:

Jim Dalton

D/B/A Jim's Fitness Shop

(D/B/A means "doing business as.")

Method 2:

Jim's Fitness Shop

By:_____
            Jim Dalton

- For a *partnership*, the following format is commonly used:

ARGUS ELECTRONICS,

A Michigan Partnership

By: _____

            Randy Argus, a General Partner

Only one partner needs to sign on behalf of a partnership.

 Chapter 2, Section B, contains a discussion of the authority of a single partner to bind the partnership and each of the individual partners.

- For a *corporation*, use this format:

KIDDIE KRAFTS INC.,

A California Corporation

By: _____

            Madeline Arshak, President

A person signing as a corporate officer doesn't assume personal liability for meeting contractual obligations. (See Chapter 9, Section 9, for a discussion of how using the corporate form of doing business can limit the personal liability of people operating the corporation.) If the other party to a contract is a corporation, you may (particularly in a major transaction) want to see a board of directors' resolution or corporate bylaws authorizing the particular officer to sign contracts on behalf of the corporation. You can omit this step if the contract is signed by the corporate president; a president is presumed to have authority to sign contracts for a corporation.

If you're entering into a contract with a corporation and want someone (such as a corporate officer or major shareholder) to sign a personal guarantee, you can use a clause like this one at the end of the contract:

In consideration of Seller entering into the above contract with Starlight Corporation, I personally guarantee the performance of all of the above contractual obligations undertaken by Starlight Corporation.

_____

            Liz Star

3. Witnesses and Notaries

Notarization means that a notary public certifies in writing that:

- You're the person you claim to be, and

- You've acknowledged under oath signing the document.

Very few contracts need to be notarized or signed by witnesses. The major exceptions to this rule are documents that are going to be recorded at a public office charged with keeping such records (usually called the county recorder or register of deeds). These documents are described in the next section. Occasionally—but very rarely—state laws require witnesses or notaries to sign other types of documents.

4. Recording

The great majority of business contracts don't have to be publicly recorded—and, in fact, are usually ineligible for recording. Here are the exceptions:

- Documents that affect title to or rights in real estate. This includes deeds, mortgages, trust deeds

(a form of mortgage used in many states) and easement agreements.

- Long-term real estate leases, or memoranda summarizing them.

- Some documents dealing with tangible personal property, such as UCC financing statements or chattel mortgages, when the seller or a third party is financing part of the purchase price and receiving a security (contingent ownership) interest in the property. Banks, for example, routinely record security interests when making equipment loans.

5. Dates

When you sign a contract, offer, counter-offer or acceptance, include the date—and make sure the other person does too. This helps to establish that there was agreement (remember, a meeting of the minds is an essential element of any valid contract). A simple way to do this is to always put a date line (Date: _____, 199_) next to the place where each person will sign. Don't worry if the dates of signing differ by a few days or even a week, as is common when the parties exchange documents by mail.

> **Example:** If you sign on Monday and the other party signs a week later, you have a valid contract unless (1) you revoked your signature before the other person signed, or (2) you stated in the contract or offer that the other person must accept the offer before that date.

6. Originals and Photocopies

A contract is an "original" as long as the signatures are originals. So a photocopied document which both parties then sign is an original. So is a carbon copy or computer-printed copy which both parties sign.

If you enter into a traditional written contract—one document that contains the full agreement of the parties and is signed by both of them, it's best if each party has a copy of the contract with the origi-

at the same session; simply sign two originals, so each party can keep a fully signed one.

A photocopy or faxed copy of a signed contract can still be enforced as long as the judge or arbitrator is convinced that what you have is an accurate reproduction of the original.

Storing Contracts

Store your contracts and other important documents in a fire-proof safe or file cabinet. Another precaution is to keep photocopies of all important documents at another location. This may seem like overkill—but not if you have to prove what's in a contract and all copies have been destroyed, stolen or lost.

---

7. Revising a Contract After Both Parties Sign

Once a contract has been signed, both parties must agree to change it. In essence this means they're forming a new contract. The simplest way to make fairly minor revisions to a signed contract is through an addendum—or a second or third addendum if necessary. When you write an addendum, follow these steps:

- Refer to the earlier contract by date, names of the parties and subject matter.

- State all of the changes.

- State that in case of a conflict between the terms of the original contract and the addendum, the terms of the addendum prevail.

- Make it clear that all terms of the original contract, except those that you're changing, remain in effect.

- Sign and date the addendum and keep it with the original.

LAW IN THE REAL WORLD
Writing Contracts the Simple Way

Galen owns a small publishing company that specializes in local guide books. Henry, one of Galen's long-time authors, is late in delivering a manuscript for a book on 50 off-beat family adventures in the Northern Rocky Mountains. When he finally turns it in, the computer-printed manuscript is full of nearly incomprehensible handwritten additions.

Galen calls Henry and points out that their contract requires Henry to submit the manuscript neatly typed. Henry is furious. "You told me to get it done fast, no matter what," he says. "I stayed up half the night for two weeks to make the deadline and this is the thanks I get."

Galen prudently waits a few days and then invites Henry to lunch. Once both men look at the plain language of the contract, "Author shall submit all manuscript material neatly typed," Henry has to agree that Galen is right. Galen then offers to have someone on his staff do the typing work and subtract the cost from Henry's future royalties. They scribble the contract addendum on a paper placemat and both sign it. Later, Galen photocopies the placemat and mails it to Henry.

G. Enforcing Contracts in Court

Often, if there's a dispute about a claimed breach of contract, you can resolve it through negotiation. If that doesn't work, you'll need to use one of the other methods of resolving legal disputes: mediation, arbitration or litigation. (See Chapter 18 for an overview on how each works.)

Here is how a contract dispute is likely to be resolved if mediation doesn't work and you resort to more formal proceedings—arbitration or a lawsuit.

Most lawsuits and arbitrations involving contracts focus on two basic questions:

- Was there a breach of contract?

- If so, what relief should be awarded to the non-breaching party?

We'll tackle the first question here, and the second one in Section H.

Suppose your business sues or is sued for an alleged breach of contract or such a claim is taken to arbitration. What defenses can the defendant assert? Here are the main ones:

- *No valid contract was formed.* If there was no meeting of the minds (no legally binding offer and acceptance) in the first place, or no consideration was given in exchange for one party's promise, no contract even exists. (See Section A.) It's a lot easier to establish such a claim if neither side has begun to follow and rely on the so-called contract.

- *There's no written contract, and because of the subject of the contract, one is required by law.* (See Section D.)

- *The contract is void because it's illegal or against public policy.* Contracts that call for criminal or immoral conduct may be unenforceable. (See Section B.)

- *The contract should be rescinded (canceled) because the other side misrepresented the facts in inducing you to sign it.* (See Section C.)

- *The contract was induced by duress.* (See Section C.)

- *There was a mutual mistake.* (See Section C.)

- *There was no breach of contract.* The defendant admits entering into a valid contract with the plaintiff, but fully complied with its terms.

- *The other party suffered no damages.* The breach of the contract was minor or technical and didn't cause the plaintiff any actual loss or damage. For example, if your store delivered a conference table and six chairs to a lawyer's new office a week later than promised, there's likely been minor inconvenience but no real damage—nothing serious enough to make you liable for breach of contract.

- *The plaintiff failed to limit (mitigate) the damages.* All parties to a contract have a legal duty to act

reasonably and keep any damages to a minimum (called "mitigation of damages" in legalese). Or, put another way, it's not legally permissible to sit back and let damages add up when reasonable steps could be taken to stop or limit them. For example, suppose your company services refrigerators, and you signed a two-year contract with a butcher. While you're on vacation, the butcher calls your company and requests that you immediately repair a breakdown in his refrigerator. Your chief assistant is sick, so the job doesn't get done until you return ten days later. The butcher sues for damages, claiming he lost $5,000 worth of meat due to lack of refrigeration. You can point out that the butcher could have mitigated his damages by calling another company to fix his refrigerator. Had he done this promptly, his loss might have been limited to $500 of particularly temperature-sensitive meat plus $300 for the extra service charged. You should be responsible for $800 in damages and not the full $5,000.

 Chapter 10, Section I, explains how the concept of mitigation of damages applies where a lease is involved. This information is generally applicable to all contracts.

Enforcing Lost Contracts

What if a party wants to legally enforce a written contract, but neither party can find a signed copy? The contract is still legally enforceable if you can prove to the satisfaction of an arbitrator or judge that:

- A written agreement was actually signed, and

- It contained the specific terms you're seeking to enforce.

You may be able to reconstruct the terms from an unsigned photocopy or from a final draft stored on your computer's hard drive or a floppy disk.

H. What Can You Sue For?

In a breach-of-contract case, the court may award the plaintiff money damages and may also, in some cases, order the defendant to do—or stop doing—something.

1. Compensatory Damages

If a plaintiff proves that a defendant breached a contract, the usual approach is for the judge or arbitrator to award the plaintiff "compensatory damages." The goal is to put the parties in the same position as they would have been in if the contract had been performed—or to come as close to that as possible.

Let's return to the contract with Joe, the sign maker we discussed in Section A. If Joe failed to build the sign for your business, and it cost you $750 to have someone else do it, you'd be entitled to recover $300 from Joe for breach of contract. This is the difference between the contract price you and Joe agreed on ($450) and what you had to pay to get the job done ($750). This assumes that you made a reasonable effort to limit or mitigate your damages. In this situation, you'd have to show that you made a reasonable attempt to find a second sign maker to do the job at a fair price. You couldn't just go to the

most expensive sign maker in the state and expect Joe to reimburse you for the top dollar. (Mitigation of damages is discussed in Section G, above.)

2. Consequential Damages

A plaintiff may also be entitled to "consequential damages." These are damages that arise out of circumstances that the breaching party knew about or should have foreseen when the contract was made.

For example, what if Joe built your sign for you but didn't get around to installing it until a month after your business's grand opening? Can you sue for the profits you lost because potential customers didn't know your store was there? The usual rule is that you can recover for lost profits only if this issue is covered by your contract or if it was foreseeable to both parties when you signed the contract that you'd lose profits if the other person didn't carry out the contact. Whether or not a judge will award you damages for Joe's failure to install your sign on time is anybody's guess—unless you specifically dealt with the issue in the contract.

If the contract did provide for lost profits, there's another problem: The amount of lost profits you claim must be ascertainable with reasonable certainty. With a new store, you have no earnings history. This makes it difficult to prove and recover lost profits. But you may able to show how much similar stores at similar locations earned when they first started and get a judge to accept this as a reasonable estimate of your losses.

Let's look at one more example. Say that the sign you ordered from Joe was to contain your store name plus the name of a major manufacturer of merchandise you planned to carry. You had a deal with the manufacturer that entitled you to a 10% discount if you put the manufacturer's name on your sign. Because Joe put up the sign a month after the store opened, you didn't receive the discount on the first batch of merchandise, which cost you an extra $1,000. Can you collect this money from Joe? Only if Joe knew about your deal with the manufacturer when you and he entered into your contract. Otherwise, Joe would have no reason to expect you to suffer this additional loss if he installed the sign late.

3. Liquidated Damages

In addition to or in place of compensatory and consequential damages, a plaintiff may be able to recover "liquidated damages." These are damages that the parties agree in the contract will be paid if there's a breach. That is, instead of trying to determine the money damages for a breach of contract after the fact, you do it in advance.

For example, because actual losses caused by late installation of your sign would be difficult to determine, you and Joe could agree in your contract that for each day of delay, Joe would owe you a $25 late fee. If the liquidated damages are a reasonable attempt to estimate the losses you'd suffer and are not intended as a penalty, a judge or arbitrator will enforce this clause.

Contracts for the purchase of real estate commonly contain a liquidated damages clause. For example, if you put down $5,000 in "earnest money" when you sign a contract to purchase a building, the contract will likely allow the seller to retain the $5,000 as liquidated damages if you later back out for no good reason.

4. Injunctions and Other Equitable Relief

In addition to monetary damages, a judge may order "equitable" relief in some circumstances. This can come in a variety of forms, depending on the facts of the case and the ingenuity of the judge. The idea is to reach a fair result and do justice in a way that can't be done simply by an award of money. Here are some equitable remedies that a judge may order:

- *Injunctions.* An injunction is an order issued by a judge prohibiting a person from performing specified activities. Occasionally, a judge issues an

injunction to prevent a party from violating a contract. When time is of the essence, a judge may issue an emergency injunction (sometimes called a temporary restraining order) without a hearing to freeze matters until a court hearing can be held.

Example 1: Aggie accepts a job as the accounts manager for DDS Innovations, a dental supply house. As part of her employment contract, she signs a covenant not to compete in the same business in a four-county area for two years after leaving the company. After 18 months on the job, Aggie quits and starts a business in the same city, competing directly with DDS Innovations. The company sues Aggie for breach of her covenant not to compete. The judge, after conducting a trial, finds that the covenant not to compete is reasonable and legally valid, and enjoins Aggie from continuing in that business for two years.

Example 2: Maurice and Albert are business partners who have a falling out. Unable to resolve the dispute, Maurice sues Albert, claiming a breach of the partnership agreement. Albert counter-sues. The judge holds a preliminary hearing and issues a preliminary injunction—in force while the lawsuit is pending—prohibiting both partners from removing any property from the offices of the partnership and from taking any money from the partnership bank account.

Example 3: Gilda and her landlord Archie have a dispute over who is to pay for electricity to Gilda's restaurant. On Friday afternoon, Archie threatens to shut off the power to Gilda's restaurant, which would ruin a private banquet for 200 guests that night. Based on Gilda's affidavit (sworn statement) showing the likelihood of immediate damage, the judge issues a temporary restraining order (TRO) prohibiting Archie from shutting off Gilda's power. The judge schedules a hearing for 9 a.m. Monday, at which time the TRO may be dissolved or continued. Because a TRO is usually issued based on the statements of one party only ("ex parte" in legal lingo), such an order is signed only if there's an emergency. A court hearing is always scheduled promptly.

- *Specific Performance.* If a contract concerns a unique or special asset—such as a piece of real estate, a work of art or a uniquely valuable item of jewelry—the judge may order the losing party to deliver the property to the other party to carry out the agreement. This remedy is rarely used in any other type of commercial transaction.

- *Rescission*. In an appropriate case a judge may rescind (cancel) a contract and order restitution of any money already paid. This unusual remedy is generally reserved for situations where one party's breach has completely frustrated the objectives of the other party, making enforcement of the contract unfair. To obtain rescission, the party getting a refund must give up any benefits already received. (Grounds for rescission of a contract are discussed in Sections B and C.)

If a judge orders you to perform a contract or stop doing something that violates a contract, you can find yourself in deep trouble if you don't obey the order. You can be held in contempt of court, which is punishable by fines and even time in jail.

RESOLVING LEGAL DISPUTES   18

Legal disputes—actual and potential—come in all shapes and sizes when you run a small business. Consider these examples:

- The phone company puts your Yellow Pages ad in the wrong classification and refuses to do anything about it.

- A former employee claims that you wrongfully fired her.

- Your landlord puts off repairing a leaky roof. As a result, valuable merchandise is ruined in a rain storm.

- Your insurance company offers a ridiculously low settlement when one of your trucks is totalled.

- You refuse to accept a dozen custom-built display cases because they don't meet your specifications. The shop that constructed them threatens to sue.

- You want to stop a former employee from opening a competing business two blocks away and soliciting customers using a copy of your customer list.

- Just when your business begins to do well, your partners claim that you're not doing everything you promised to do in the partnership agreement. They want to terminate the agreement and continue the business without you.

How you handle such disputes can have a profound effect on your bottom line, not to mention your mental health and the morale of your employees. Fortunately, you usually have a number of options available, giving you some control over the time, energy and money that you spend on resolving legal problems.

We live in a litigious society. Often, the first reaction to a business dispute is, "I'll see you in court!" But rarely is litigation the only method for resolving a dispute. Litigation is enormously expensive and almost always results in hard feelings that prevent the contending parties from ever doing business with one another again, so it's always smart to think about alternatives. Commonly available options include negotiation, mediation and arbitration. These non-courtroom approaches to handling legal disputes are often referred to as Alternative

Dispute Resolution or ADR. This chapter explores the various types of dispute resolution so that, whether or not you work with a lawyer, you'll be better able to take charge of tactical and settlement decisions.

A. Negotiating a Settlement

In most situations, a negotiated solution is far better and cheaper than one imposed by an arbitrator or a judge. A settlement often can be reached speedily and at minimum expense. Litigation (and, to some extent, arbitration) can not only empty your wallet—they can also eat up an amazing amount of your time and that of your employees.

Always seek a negotiated settlement before you sue, even if you're so angry you don't want to speak to the other party. Try to evaluate the legal and financial realities objectively. Your goal should be to achieve the best result at the lowest cost. If instead you act on the conviction (whether it's right or wrong makes no difference) that you're being victimized by the other side, chances are you'll end up fighting for the last dollar because of the principle involved. A business person who is controlled by this sort of emotional reaction is almost sure to get ensnared in a lawsuit that will take too long and cost too much.

Here are some helpful pointers for negotiations:

- Listen closely to what your opponent says. Acknowledge that you hear the points your opponent is making even if you disagree with them.

- Avoid personal attacks. This only raises the level of hostility and makes settlement more difficult. Equally important, don't react impulsively to the emotional outbursts of your opponent.

- Try to structure the negotiation as a mutual attempt to solve a problem. Jointly seek solutions that recognize the interests of both parties.

- Learn your opponent's priorities. Maybe dollars are less important than a formula for future business relations. You may not be as far apart as you think.

- Put yourself in your opponent's shoes. What can you offer to make the settlement more palatable? The best settlements are those in which both sides feel they've won (or at least not given up anything fundamental).

- When you propose a specific settlement, make it clear that you're attempting to compromise. Offers of settlement (clearly labeled as such) can't be introduced against you if you ever go to trial.

- If a settlement is reached, promptly write it down and have all parties sign it. You or your lawyer should volunteer to prepare the first draft. That way, you can include protective language that, once included, your opponent may see as too minor to quibble about.

- Money is a powerful incentive to settlement. If your business is going to have to pay something eventually, come to the negotiating table with your checkbook or a wad of $100 bills. The other side may settle at a surprisingly low figure if they can walk away from the bargaining table with payment in hand. Of course, if you pay with cash, be sure to get a receipt.

 RECOMMENDED READING

Getting To Yes by Roger Fisher and William Ury (Penguin Books).

Getting Past No: Negotiating With Difficult People by William Ury (Bantam Books).

B. Understanding Mediation

Many people confuse mediation with arbitration (discussed in Section C). While both are non-judicial ways to resolve disputes, there's a huge difference: arbitration is binding; mediation isn't. The mediator simply helps the parties work out a solution to their dispute. Neither side is committed in advance to accept the mediator's advice.

Where To Find a Mediator

You and the other party can choose anyone you both respect to act as mediator. Local small business or community groups may provide trained mediators, as do the arbitration services listed in Section C.

"Turbo-charged negotiation" is how one lawyer describes mediation. In mediation, you ask the mediator, as a neutral expert, to help both sides negotiate. If you follow the classic model—used by big business for, say, a labor-management dispute—the mediator typically meets separately with each side. Everything said in those meetings is confidential. The mediator helps each party analyze its needs. When both sides get close to a settlement, everyone meets together to work out the details.

Mediators in small business disputes often prefer a much less formal approach. More likely than not, the mediator will have everyone sit down together from the very beginning and allow both parties to express all their issues—even emotional ones. Often this works because the people are mad at each other for reasons that go well beyond the legal issues that are supposed to define the dispute. Once everything is on the table, a good mediator helps the parties find a mutually acceptable solution.

LAW IN THE REAL WORLD

Getting at the Real Problems

Doug rents a store front from Tom for five years. Although they occasionally have their differences over Tom's duty to keep the building in good repair and Doug's to maintain the grounds, they get along reasonably well. Then Doug has a bad financial month and is late with the rent. Tom, who has given Doug an extension several times in the past, threatens to begin eviction proceedings immediately. Doug responds by pointing out that Tom failed to fix a roof leak that damaged some of his inventory. Clearly, the stage is set for a nasty court fight. To head this off, a neighboring business owner suggests that Tom and Doug mediate their dispute under a program co-sponsored by the Chamber of Commerce.

At the mediation, Doug wants to know why Tom is being so unreasonable. The answer, it turns out, is simple. Doug has repeatedly left the gate open in the yard behind the building letting Tom's beloved dog run into the street. Tom finds it hard to forgive such carelessness and is ready to punish Doug by using whatever legal leverage is available. When Doug and Tom work out the dog problem (Tom will put in a better gate, Doug absolutely guarantees to keep it closed), the rest of the issues are quickly resolved, and a lawsuit is avoided.

---

1. The parties will promptly meet to attempt in good faith to negotiate a resolution of the dispute.

2. If, within 30 days after that meeting, the parties have not resolved the dispute, they will submit the dispute to good faith mediation in accordance with the rules of the (name of organization such as American Arbitration Association) to bear equally the costs of the mediation.

3. After a mediator is appointed, the parties will participate in good faith in the mediation. If the dispute is not resolved within 30 days, it will be settled by arbitration in accordance with the rules of (name of organization), and judgment upon the award rendered by the arbitrator may be entered in any court having jurisdiction.

Sample Mediation Clause 2

If a dispute arises between the parties to this contract, the parties agree to participate in at least four hours of mediation in accordance with the mediation procedures of United States Arbitration & Mediation, Inc. The parties agree to split equally the costs of mediation. The mediation will be administered by *[designate either the specific USA&M office or a local USA&M office designated by the USA&M National Headquarters]*.

If your original contract is silent on the subject of mediation or arbitration, you and the other party still can agree to use either or both of these methods to resolve a dispute. Chances are good that your adversary (if a business person) will be as receptive as you are to some method of avoiding the expense and delay of litigation. Even if a negotiating impasse has led to a lawsuit, you can change horses in mid-stream; you can agree to mediation or arbitration, and cancel the lawsuit when you reach a settlement.

But does mediation work? Perhaps surprisingly, given the fact there's no one to impose a solution, the answer is yes, in as many as 80% of mediations. One reason is apparently that by agreeing to mediate a dispute in the first place, you and the other side must cooperate to establish the rules which, in turn, sets the stage for cooperating to find a solution to the dispute.

Sample mediation clauses that you can include in your business contracts are shown below.

Sample Mediation Clause 1

If a dispute arises relating to this agreement, the parties will follow this procedure before pursuing any other remedy:

C. Arbitration

With arbitration, you get a relatively quick, relatively inexpensive solution to a business dispute without going to court. Like a judge, the arbitrator—or arbitration panel—has power to hear the dispute and make a final, binding decision. Where does this power come from? From you and the other party. You agree to submit to arbitration and to be bound by the arbitrator's decision.

Almost any commercial dispute that can be litigated can be arbitrated. Disputes with employees can be arbitrated, as can disagreements with a landlord, supplier, business partner, franchisor, architect, builder, customer or equipment rental company.

Arbitration clauses are becoming a part of most commercial contracts. Insurance contracts, for example, frequently provide that any dispute over the amount of benefits to be paid by the insurance company will be decided by arbitration rather than litigation. The same goes for construction contracts: there's often a clause that requires arbitration for any contractual disputes. Through such clauses, you can provide in advance for arbitration to be used. You and the other party can also decide to use arbitration after a dispute arises.

If the losing party doesn't pay the money required by an arbitration award, the winner can easily convert the award to a court judgment, which can be enforced like any other court judgment. Unlike a judgment based on litigation, however, you generally can't take an appeal from an arbitration-based judgment. (An exception is when there was some element of fraud in the procedures leading to the arbitration award.)

Here are the chief advantages of arbitration:

- Arbitration is usually much less expensive than litigation. The American Arbitration Association, for example, charges on a sliding scale, based on the amount of the claim:

Amount of Claim	Fee
Up to $10,000	$300
$10,000 to $25,000	3% of claim
$25,000 to $50,000	$750 + 2% of amount over $25,000
$50,000 to $100,000	$1,250 + 1% of amount over $50,000

- You're likely to receive an arbitrator's decision within six months after the demand for arbitration is submitted. And when the dispute involves $50,000 or less, the American Arbitration Association has expedited procedures leading to a final decision within 60 to 90 days. Lawsuits, on the other hand, usually aren't decided for a year or often much more—and an appeal may add several more years of delay.

- Unlike a trial, arbitration proceedings are private. There's no need for your competitors or the general public to know your business.

- The rules of evidence are relaxed in an arbitration proceeding. This makes it easier to get to the heart of the matter. Courtroom trials often get bogged down in evidentiary arguments that obscure rather than clarify the facts.

- Arbitration often avoids the bitter acrimony that can affect the parties in a lawsuit. It's not unusual for parties to resume their normal business relationship after their dispute has been arbitrated.

How Arbitration Works: An Example

Smooth Shift Transmission hires Better Builders to add two service bays to its transmission shop for a total of $60,000. The contract calls for a $30,000 down payment. The balance is due when the job is completed. However, after the work is done, Smooth Shift isn't satisfied with the job. There are several large cracks in the concrete floor installed by Better Builders. On the advice of its architect, Smooth Shift delays making the final payment.

A few weeks later the floor begins to settle, creating several gaps where it meets an outside wall. Better Builders claims that these problems are minor and threatens to sue Smooth Shift for the final payment of $30,000. But Smooth Shift points to a clause in the construction contract: "All disputes concerning this project will be submitted to arbitration."

Better Builders sends a "demand for arbitration" to the American Arbitration Association (AAA), a nationwide organization that administers many of the arbitration proceedings in this country. In response, the AAA sends a list of five proposed arbitrators to each side. The parties agree on one of the listed people to serve as their arbitrator. (If parties can't agree, the AAA makes the selection.) A hearing is scheduled a month later.

During the hearing, which takes only three hours, each side makes a brief opening statement describing the controversy. Smooth Shift's owner then shows the arbitrator the construction contract, the plans and specs for the job, and photographs of the floor. The architect hired by Smooth Shift testifies that the floor problems are serious, and that the floor must be replaced.

Now it's Better Builders' turn. The president of Better Builders testifies that the floor problems are minor and can be fixed with $1,000 worth of patching material. A week later, the arbitrator sends the parties his findings and his decision: The floor needs to be replaced at a cost of $18,000. That amount is to be deducted from the $30,000 final payment owed to Better Builders, meaning Smooth Shift owes Better Builders only $12,000. End of case.

How To Find An Arbitrator

- **The American Arbitration Association.** The oldest and largest organization of its kind, with regional offices in 36 U.S. cities. The main office is in New York City. (212) 484-4000.

- **Judicate.** This Philadelphia-based firm handles cases in all 50 states. It emphasizes mediation. (800) 631-9900.

- **Judicial Arbitration and Mediation Services.** This California-based firm specializes in construction, banking and wrongful termination disputes. It has offices in California, Texas and Washington; more are planned. (800) 350-5267.

- **U.S. Arbitration and Mediation.** This Seattle-based firm specializes in insurance and auto disputes, but is prepared to handle a full range of other dispute as well. It has offices in 48 cities and mediators in every state. (800) 933-6348.

- **The American Bar Association** offers a directory of ADR organizations called *Dispute Resolution Program Directory*. The full directory costs $38.99 (which includes shipping and handling), but the ABA will send you the pages for your city free of charge. American Bar Association Standing Committee on Dispute Resolution, 1800 M Street NW, Suite 290N, Washington, DC 20036. (202) 331-2258.

Keep in mind that you are not required to use an organization for arbitration. You and the other party are free to choose your own arbitrator or arbitration panel, and to set your own procedural rules. Just remember that for arbitration to be binding and legally enforceable, you need to follow the simple guidelines set down in your state's arbitration statute. You can usually find the statute by looking in the statutory index under arbitration or checking the table of contents for the civil procedure sections.

Here's a sample clause you can use in a contract to provide for the arbitration of disputes:

Sample Arbitration Clause 1

Any controversy or claim rising out of or relating to this contract, or the breach of this contract, shall be settled by arbitration in accordance with the rules of the American Arbitration Association. A judgment of a court having jurisdiction may be entered upon the arbitrator's award.

Here's an example of an agreement you and the other party should sign if you want to go to arbitration with a dispute that has already arisen and that isn't covered by an arbitration agreement in an existing contract:

Sample Arbitration Clause 2

We agree to submit the following controversy to arbitration under the rules of the American Arbitration Association: (describe the controversy)

We further agree that a judgment of a court having jurisdiction may be entered upon the arbitrator's award.

If you and the other party want to choose an arbitrator on your own to act outside the administrative framework of an organization, use a clause like this one:

Sample Arbitration Clause 3

We agree to submit the following controversy to arbitration by (name of arbitrator): (describe the controversy) .

We further agree that the arbitration procedures shall be as prescribed by the arbitrator and the costs of arbitration shall be as apportioned by the arbitrator.

D. Going to Court

If your attempts at settling a dispute fail and you end up in a lawsuit, you'll need more help than this book can offer. Unless you go to small claims court, in fact, you'll probably need to hire a lawyer to represent you.

Despite its ample drawbacks, litigation may offer advantages in some situations. For example, you may decide you want a jury trial if you're the underdog. If you're a small franchisee going toe to toe with a multi-national corporation, and the questions of fact are pretty evenly balanced, the jury's sympathy may tip the scales of justice in your direction.

Another reason for considering litigation is that the rules of evidence and other procedural safeguards can help ensure that only trustworthy evidence is presented. In addition, using various methods of pre-trial discovery, such as depositions, you can force the other side to disclose the evidence it plans to offer at trial and can also uncover evidence helpful to you. Of course, discovery is a two-way street. The other side can force you to disclose information you'd rather keep to yourself.

1. The Federal and State Court Systems

In the United States, two court systems operate side by side: the federal and state courts. Most business lawsuits (in fact, most lawsuits of every kind) are handled in state courts.

Broadly, federal courts have jurisdiction over only two types of cases. The first type involves what lawyers call federal questions: cases based on provisions in the United States Constitution, treaties and federal laws. This includes such things as discrimination cases arising under federal civil rights laws, and bankruptcy, patent, copyright and trademark cases arising under specific federal statutes.

The second type of case heard by federal district courts involves controversies between citizens of two different states; in these cases, the amount in controversy must exceed $50,000 before a federal court can get involved. This authority of the federal courts is called diversity jurisdiction because the litigants come from different (diverse) states. When a federal court exercises diversity jurisdiction, it's not necessary for a federal question to be involved. The court applies the law of the state in which the case arose.

Example: A truck owned by an Arizona corporation is in an accident on a California freeway with a truck owned by a California corporation. Valuable computer equipment in the Arizona company's truck is ruined. If the ruined equipment was worth more than $50,000, the Arizona corporation can sue the California corporation in either the California state courts or in a federal district court located in California. If the Arizona company sues in federal court, the judge will apply California law relating to vehicle accidents.

In handling cases based on diversity of citizenship, a corporation—a fictional legal person—is treated as a "citizen" of the state where it's incorporated.

As a practical matter, it often doesn't make much difference whether a business case proceeds in federal court or state court. When there's a choice between going to state or federal court, the decision is usually a tactical one based on comparisons between the caliber and philosophy of the state and federal judges, as well as comparisons between the likely composition of the juries in the two courts. Delay may also be a consideration; sometimes one court may have less of a backlog than another.

2. The Litigation Process

In a typical commercial case, the plaintiff (the person or company who sues) asks the judge to issue a judgment against the defendant (the person or company being sued). In many business cases, the plaintiff wants a money judgment—or, in legal parlance, damages.

But judges have power to grant many other kinds of relief to the plaintiff. For example, in a civil (that is, non-criminal) case, a judge may:

- Order a building official to issue a permit allowing the plaintiff company to expand its office building.

- Issue an injunction (order) prohibiting a former corporate officer from improperly disclosing or benefitting from trade secrets.

- Require a seller to transfer legal title to real estate in accordance with a purchase agreement.

- Have the sheriff remove a tenant from business premises and restore possession to the landlord.

- Place business assets in the hands of a receiver for short-term management.

- Order a business to stop infringing on a patent owned by another business.

- Require a partner to make an accounting to other partners.

- Order a state administrative board to issue a license.

- Interpret the meaning of a contract or declare a contract void.

- Force a corporation to open its books and records to all shareholders.

This is just a partial list; the point is that judges have broad powers. The powers of a small claims court (and some other local courts) are more limited. For example, in small claims court, you're generally limited to seeking a judgment for money damages—although the judge may have some additional limited authority such as requiring one of the parties to return goods to the other party as a condition of receiving payment. (For more on small claims court, see Chapter 19.)

It may surprise you to learn that most commercial lawsuits never go to trial. Frequently, a business starts a lawsuit mainly to get the attention of an adversary after attempts at a negotiated settlement have broken down. The message is, "We're serious. This thing can't drag on forever. We've got to resolve it on realistic terms." As costs mount and both parties gain a clearer picture of what they'll be able—or unable—to prove in court, and judges make rulings in preliminary courtroom skirmishes (known as "motions"), the parties often decide to compromise and settle the case.

Never lose sight of the fact that you can reach a negotiated settlement at any time. Any experienced lawyer can recite examples of cases settled "on the courthouse steps" just before the trial was to begin. And many cases have been settled after the evidence was presented and the jurors were in the jury room discussing what the verdict should be.

The High Cost of Justice

We all know lawsuits are expensive. But did you know just how expensive? The business lawyer's meter typically runs at $150 to $250 an hour for a long list of legal chores, including:

- conferences and telephone calls with you, witnesses and other lawyers

- legal research

- drafting documents such as a complaint, answer, counter-complaint, motions, requests for production of documents, briefs and jury instructions

- taking the depositions of witnesses or potential witnesses

- arguing motions in court (including many that affect only the litigation process and not the merits of the case)

- attending conferences in the judge's chambers

- driving to the courthouse and waiting for his or her turn to argue pre-trial motions

- conducting the trial.

Other costs include paying the public stenographer to take down depositions and type up the transcripts, jury fees, investigator costs and expert witness fees.

In most situations, each party pays its own attorney fees, although you can provide in a contract (such as a lease) that if a contract-related dispute goes to court, the losing party pays the fees of the winner's lawyer. If you don't have such a clause, the cost of winning may be so high that it's a hollow victory.

3. Getting Speedy Relief Through an Injunction

With clogged dockets and rules that allow extensive pre-trial discovery (depositions, interrogatories and other devices aimed at learning the facts of the other party's case), it's not always easy to get a speedy hearing in a commercial case. A case may be tied up in court for months or even years before it's decided.

These built-in delays generally work to the advantage of the defendant and the disadvantage of the plaintiff. (It's the plaintiff who's taken the case to court and wants some action.)

In some instances, however, a plaintiff can go to court and get prompt attention. Two key elements must be present:

- The defendant must be causing irreparable harm to plaintiff's business—harm that can't be rectified by monetary damages; and

- There must be a need for immediate relief.

Example: The grand opening of Trudy's new store in a neighborhood shopping plaza is scheduled for Saturday. Trudy's lease gives her the right to use the adjoining parking lot for customer parking. On the Monday before the grand opening, Trudy is stunned to see that a contractor, who is about to build an addition to the plaza, has occupied 16 of the plaza's 20 parking spaces with trucks and a large construction shed. Unable to convince her landlord or the contractor to move the equipment, Trudy goes to court for an injunction.

The judge orders a quick hearing (scheduled for the following day) to hear arguments on whether a preliminary injunction should be issued immediately to prevent harm to Trudy's business, pending a full-scale hearing.

In a case that involves an urgent threat to health or safety, or imminent damage to property, a judge also has the power to issue a temporary restraining order (TRO) to keep any harm from occurring or continuing until a hearing on a preliminary injunction can be scheduled. Because a TRO is issued without a hearing at which both sides can be heard (ex parte), it's a radical remedy. So, before issuing a TRO, the judge has to be convinced that the circumstances are extreme; even then, the restraining order will be in effect only for a day or two—just long enough to make arrangements to bring both sides to court.

To go back to Trudy's situation, if earth movers were about to dig up the pavement of the parking spaces, a judge might issue a TRO for a day based mostly on Trudy's sworn statement (affidavit) that

she was about to suffer irreparable harm (once the pavement was gone, it would be difficult to use the parking spaces). The TRO would last until a hearing was held, at which point the court would decide whether or not to issue an injunction.

4. Testifying in Court

Especially if you're not paying the bill, a lawsuit can be a fascinating experience. Our system of trying cases has evolved and been tested for many hundreds of years. And, although some of the conventions of a trial can seem quaint, litigation remains a largely effective (although not necessarily cost-effective) way to ferret out the truth and reach a just result.

Even if you hire a lawyer to handle your lawsuit, you still need to understand some of the nuts and bolts of the system to make it work for you. You may well be called on to testify in a legal proceeding—either as a plaintiff, a defendant or a witness. Here are some suggestions to help you do it effectively.

- Treat pre-trial discovery—especially depositions—seriously. At a deposition, a party or witness is put under oath and cross-examined by the opponent's lawyer in the presence of a public stenographer. A transcript is typed up. Cases are frequently settled on the basis of deposition testimony. The other lawyer will not only be listening carefully to your testimony but will be sizing you up as a witness. What will the jury think about you? Will you get flustered easily? Can you be baited into an argument? Do you project confidence or fear? In addition, if the case does go to trial, you'll have a lot of explaining to do if your testimony at trial differs from what you said at your deposition. Be accurate.

- Watch what you wear. Your clothing at a deposition or in court should indicate that you treat the case seriously. It should be conservative—not sporty, flashy or obviously expensive.

- In court, you're always "on stage"—not just when you're on the witness stand. If there's a jury, you'll be studied continually, at the counsel table or relaxing in the corridor. So maintain a serious demeanor, and be careful about conversations that the judge or jury may overhear.

- Before testifying, carefully review the typed transcript of your deposition as well as any written statements you've given about your case. You'll be embarrassed on cross-examination if you say something on the witness stand that differs from your earlier statements.

- If your business is incorporated, go to extra lengths to let the jury know that you're a small business—not General Motors. This is particularly important if your opposition is not a corporation. You don't want the jury to think of this as a battle between David and Goliath, with you cast as Goliath.

- On the witness stand, give the lawyer time to complete the question before you attempt to answer. If you're unsure or didn't hear the question, ask the lawyer to repeat it. If you still don't understand what he or she is seeking, ask for clarification.

- Keep your emotions under control during cross-examination. If you get angry, lose your temper or try to meet a lawyer's sarcasm with sarcasm of your own, you'll hurt your case. Be courteous even if the lawyer isn't.

- If possible, answer with a simple yes or no. This is particularly important on cross-examination. If more than a yes or no answer is needed, give only the requested facts. Then stop. Be careful about volunteering information just because you think it will be helpful. Such information may suggest whole new areas of questioning to the cross-examiner.

- Conversely, if the lawyer cross-examining tries to limit you to answering yes or no to a question that you feel you can't properly answer in a single word, say that you're unable to give a yes or no answer. The judge probably will let you explain.

- Unless you're testifying as an expert witness (someone with specialized knowledge who can give opinions in court), limit your testimony to facts—things you've personally seen or heard or done or said. Your opinions and conclusions usually aren't admissible.

- A definite answer is desirable. For example, "It was 10 p.m." is better than "I think it was about 10 p.m." But if you can't speak with such assurance, it's perfectly acceptable—and advisable—to qualify your answer. And there will be times when the only honest answer is "I don't know," or "I don't remember."

- Watch out for words like "always" and "never." Sometimes in cross-examination a lawyer will try to get you to agree with an overly broad statement. For example: "Is it your testimony that your company never extends credit to first-time customers?" "Are you saying that you always send confirming letters?" Chances are the lawyer is setting the stage for further questions that will require you to back off from such an absolute statement. This can undermine your testimony. So your answer might be: "Our general policy is to not extend credit to first-time customers, but we have made some exceptions." Or, "We almost always send confirming letters but I can remember a few times when we did not."

RECOMMENDED READING

- *Trial Advocacy in a Nutshell,* by Paul Bergman (West Publishing Co.). It very readably goes into the details of handling a trial, including techniques for direct and cross examination of witnesses.

- *Everybody's Guide to Municipal Court,* by Judge Roderic Duncan (Nolo Press). This book shows Californians how to take a case, start to finish, through California Municipal Court, which handles claims of up to $25,000.

Representing Yourself in Small Claims Court

19

You might think that paying a lawyer is unavoidable when you file a lawsuit. But that's not necessarily so. There are many times when you, as a business owner, can represent yourself in court. Of course, you wouldn't want to be your own lawyer in defending a $100,000 contract case or a $1 million personal injury suit. But how about suing customers for unpaid bills or a supplier for $5,000 for a breach of contract?

In cases like those, consider using a court designed for non-lawyers: small claims court. In a few states, other names are used, but the purpose is the same: to provide a speedy, inexpensive resolution of disputes that involve relatively small amounts of money. The jurisdictional limits (the amount for which you can sue) in these courts are rising fairly quickly. You may be surprised to learn that in a number of states you can sue for $5,000 or more. (A chart listing each state's small claims court limit is in Section C.)

A business person can use small claims court to collect bills, to obtain a judgment for breach of contract or to seek money for minor property damage claims—for example, suing someone who broke a sign in your parking lot. Small claims court offers a great opportunity to collect money that would otherwise be lost because it would be too expensive to sue in regular court. True, for very small cases, it's not always cost-effective, and occasionally you'll have problems collecting your judgment. But small claims should still be part of the collection strategies of many businesses.

Before you start a lawsuit in small claims court, investigate alternatives. If your case involves a written contract, check to see if the contract requires mediation or arbitration of disputes. (See Chapter 18, Sections B and C.) If so, this may limit or cut off your right to go to any court, including small claims court. Second, consider other cost-effective options such as free or low-cost publicly operated mediation programs. If you're in a dispute with a customer, or perhaps another business, and you still have hopes of preserving some aspect of the relationship, mediation—even if not provided for in a contract—is often a better alternative than small claims court. Any litigation tends to harden peoples' feelings. (See Chapter 18.)

RECOMMENDED READING

Everybody's Guide to Small Claims Court, by Ralph Warner (Nolo Press), goes into great depth on all of the topics covered in this chapter. It will be especially valuable in helping you prepare evidence and present your case to the judge.

A. Deciding Whether To Represent Yourself

Most people who go to small claims court handle their own cases. In fact, in some states, lawyers aren't allowed to represent clients in small claims court. In any case, representing yourself is almost always the best choice—after all, the main reason to use the small claims court is because the size of the case doesn't justify the cost of hiring a lawyer. (The second benefit of using small claims court may be to satisfy any courtroom fantasies inspired by "L.A. Law"—although this one wears out pretty quickly.)

If you're doing business as a corporation and wish to proceed on your own, check the law in your state. In a few states, even if you're the president and sole shareholder of your corporation, you aren't allowed to represent the corporation. The reasoning is that the corporation legally is a separate entity and, therefore, appearing in court for a corporation amounts to practicing law without a license. Most states, however, allow a corporation to designate an officer or employee to appear for the corporation in small claims court. Even better, in some states, you can send your bookkeeper to testify in a small claims matter involving unpaid debts—the most common type of case. The clerk of the court can tell you what the rules are in your state.

Viewed strictly in terms of dollars and cents, if you can spare time away from your business, it's almost always better to represent yourself in small claims court than to hire a lawyer. To see just how great the savings can be, let's value your time at $30 an hour and assume that a typical small claims case takes 15 hours from filing to collection.

Lawyer's Time at $150 an hour x 15 hours = $2,250

Lawyer's Time at $250 an hour x 15 hours = $3,750

Your Time at $30 an hour x 15 hours = $ 450

Clearly, we're looking at more than pennies here. And several studies show that people who represent themselves in small claims court do just as well as those represented by a lawyer. So it's hardly surprising that many business people who regularly use small claims court swear by it.

On the other hand, if your business is keeping you so busy that you can't easily afford the time to deal with a small claims case (chances are you'll still have to show up in court), you may have no choice but to hire a lawyer. In some states, this can be done in small claims court; in others, such as California, Michigan and New York, lawyers can't appear in small claims. The case will have to go to formal court, where chances are that more complicated procedures will add considerably to the time it takes. In that situation, you might want to seek a lawyer willing to take the case on a contingent fee basis. This

means the lawyer gets a percentage of your recovery if you win and nothing if you lose. A lawyer who takes a $5,000 case on a contingent basis calling for a legal fee of one-third will receive $1,667 if there's a verdict for the full amount of the claim and if (sometimes a big if) the full amount is actually collected. This is substantially less than the $2,250 or $3,750 you'd be obligated to pay the lawyer—win or lose—under a straight hourly arrangement.

Another alternative is a partial contingent fee arrangement. Following this approach, you might find a lawyer who would charge you $100 an hour plus 15% or 20% of the amount actually recovered. Under such an arrangement, you spread between yourself and the lawyer some of the risks of not recovering the full amount of your claim. (For more on lawyers and fee arrangements, see Chapter 20, Section B.)

A far less costly approach is to represent yourself but have a lawyer occasionally give advice on legal points or help with strategy.

LAW IN THE REAL WORLD

Using a Lawyer Wisely

George is a skillful, honest and hard-working real estate appraiser. While most of his customers pay their bills promptly, each year a dozen or so drag their feet. It drives George up the wall to think that people are ripping him off by not paying their bills. Several years ago, he decided to pursue every non-paying customer if the amount involved was significant and there was a reasonable chance of collection.

Initially, he spent some time with his lawyer to become familiar with court procedures and to discuss pre-court strategies such as sending an effective collection letter. He also spent $15 for a complete copy of the court rules that apply in all courts of the state. (George is more ambitious than most business people and sometimes ventures into the regular courts, where legal matters can get a bit more complicated.)

Over the years, George has done very well in collecting unpaid accounts. Occasionally, if matters get complicated, he calls or visits his lawyer. Phone calls rarely last longer than 15 minutes, and visits rarely last longer than a half-hour. Wisely, George groups together several problems so he can discuss them at the same time. Occasionally, George has his lawyer draft a legal pleading or a notice or letter.

(See Chapter 20 for more on effective ways to work with a lawyer.)

B. Learning the Rules

Small claims court procedures are simple and easy to master. Basically, you pay a small fee, file your lawsuit with the court clerk, see to it that the papers are served on your opponent, show up on the appointed day and tell your story. Check with the court clerk for the specifics. The court rules are usually published in a booklet or information sheet.

In addition, clerks in small claims court are expected to explain procedures to you. They may even help you fill out the necessary forms, which are quite simple anyhow. If necessary, be persistent. If you ask enough questions, you'll get the answers you need to handle your own case comfortably. Also, in some states such as California, you can consult a small claims court advisor for free.

C. Meeting the Jurisdictional Limits

How much can you sue for in small claims court? The maximum amount varies from state to state. Generally, the limit is $2,000 to $2,500. But in a few states, the limits are as high as $5,000. Check your state's limit on the chart below, but also ask the court clerk to see if the limit has been increased since the chart was prepared; state legislatures regularly increase these limits.

Don't assume that your case can't be brought in small claims court if it's for slightly more than the limit. You may want to ask for the jurisdictional limit and forget about the rest. For example, suppose you're in the wholesale lighting fixture business, and a local retailer owes you $3,650 for some lamps. If the jurisdictional limit in your state's small claims court is $3,000, in the long run, it may be less expensive for you to forget about the $650 excess. Hiring a lawyer and going to regular court would be even more expensive.

SMALL CLAIMS COURT LIMITS

State	Amount	State	Amount
Alabama	$1,500	Montana	$3,000
Alaska	$5,000	Nebraska	$1,800
Arizona	$1,500	Nevada	$2,500
Arkansas	$3,000	New Hampshire	$2,500
California	$5,000	New Jersey	$1,500
Colorado	$3,500	New Mexico	$5,000
Connecticut	$2,000	New York	$2,000
Delaware	$5,000	North Carolina	$2,000
District of Columbia	$2,000	North Dakota	$3,000
Florida	$2,500	Ohio	$2,000
Georgia	$5,000	Oklahoma	$2,500
Hawaii	$3,500	Oregon	$2,500
Idaho	$3,000	Pennsylvania	$5,000
Illinois	$2,500	Puerto Rico	$500
Indiana	$6,000**	Rhode Island	$1,500
Iowa	$2,000	South Carolina	$2,500
Kansas	$1,000	South Dakota	$4,000
Kentucky	$1,500	Tennessee	$10,000*
Louisiana	$2,000	Texas	$5,000
Maine	$1,400	Utah	$2,000
Maryland	$2,500	Vermont	$2,000
Massachusetts	$1,500	Virginia	$10,000
Michigan	$1,750	Washington	$2,500
Minnesota	$6,000	West Virginia	$3,000
Mississippi	$1,000	Wisconsin	$2,000
Missouri	$1,500	Wyoming	$2,000

*$15,000 if county population over 700,000.
**$6,000 in Marion and Lake Counties.

D. Before You File Your Lawsuit

Before you start your lawsuit by filing papers in small claims court, ask yourself some questions to figure out if a small claims court suit is right for you.

1. Do You Have a Good Case?

First, you want to be relatively sure of your legal position. You must have a valid legal basis for a lawsuit. Do you have a decent chance of proving in court that the defendant refused to pay a fair and just bill, or broke a contract, or negligently damaged your property? If not, any talk about going to small claims court is just an idle threat that will hurt your credibility. *Everybody's Guide to Small Claims Court*, by Ralph Warner (Nolo Press), has a good chapter on how to analyze common types of cases, including breach of contract, personal injury, property damage and breach of warranty.

2. Can You Sue the Defendant in Your State?

If you conclude that your case is legally sound, next determine whether or not you can sue the defendant in your state. In legal terms, you must find out whether or not your state courts have jurisdiction over the defendant. Generally, you can sue in your state if the defendant resides there or regularly does business there.

If all your contacts with an out-of-state defendant have been by mail and telephone, and the defendant doesn't have an office, warehouse or sales staff in your state, you may not be able to sue that defendant in your local courts. You could sue in the defendant's home state, but unless it's right next door, it's probably more trouble than a small claims case is worth.

3. Can You Settle Out of Court?

Your next step is to call the other side to see if the matter can be settled without going to court. Mention that you're planning to go to court if the matter can't be resolved. The other side may decide to pay the claim or suggest terms for a fair settlement.

If the response to your call is negative, follow up with a demand letter in which you state your claim, demand payment and again inform the other side that you'll go to court if the matter isn't promptly settled. In your letter, restate the facts in the dispute even though the other side knows them. That way, if you do go to court later, you can use the demand letter to show the judge that you made every reasonable effort to collect the bill. In some states, a demand letter is required before you can sue. In any state, it's a good idea. A sample letter is shown below.

SAMPLE DEMAND LETTER

December 25, 1993

Sonya Renaud
Chez Posh
54 Lakeshore Ave.
Seattle, WA

Dear Sonya:

It's been three months since I finished installing the sound system at your new restaurant, Chez Posh. As you know, our deal was that you'd pay me $1,000 before I started work, with the balance ($3,500) to be paid when the job was done. All I've received so far is the down payment.

You've told me several times that the sound system works perfectly. But when I press you for payment, you keep putting me off. As the owner of a small business, I need a steady flow of cash to keep going. I'm making this final request for payment before I take this matter to small claims court. Please bring me your check for $3,500 by Thursday. If I don't receive it by then, I will file a lawsuit.

I think it's in your best interest to pay voluntarily. If I have to sue, I'm sure the judge will order you to pay my court costs, as well as interest. Also, a lawsuit may hurt your credit--something a new business can't afford. So please bring your check to me by Thursday.

Sincerely,

Bill Presley
Owner, King Sound Company

4. Could You Collect If You Win?

Before you actually file your papers, determine if you're likely to collect if you win. If you won't be able to collect, there's no point in throwing good money after bad in a small claims court lawsuit. If you think the defendant might not pay a small claims court judgment voluntarily, ask yourself this questions:

- Is the defendant employed? If so, usually it is fairly easy to collect from (garnish) the defendant's paycheck unless he or she has a very low income job or lots of other judgment creditors are already in line. However, you can't collect from a welfare, Social Security, unemployment, pension or disability check.

- Does he or she have a bank account? Do you know where? And are you confident that it will stay open? If so, you'll be able to collect the judgment from funds in the account.

- Does the defendant own a home or other real estate? If so, you can place a lien (legal claim) on the property. The lien must be paid off when the property is sold. And if you want to go to a lot of trouble, you can force the sale of the property to pay the judgment if the defendant's equity exceeds prior debts (such as mortgages) and protected amounts called "statutory exemptions."

- Is the defendant a solvent business, or at least one with a positive cash flow? If so, you can probably collect a judgment.

If the defendant is unlikely to pay a judgment voluntarily and lacks a job, a bank account or other assets that you can go after to satisfy the judgment, you should probably forget about suing—unless you're reasonably sure the defendant will be solvent soon, as might be the case with a college student or someone who stands to inherit money. Although judgments can usually be collected for five to ten years, depending on the state (and can sometimes be renewed), a significant number of small claims judgments are never collected.

E. Figuring Out Who To Sue

Normally, it makes sense to sue all defendants who are reasonably likely to be legally liable to you. This increases the chances of getting a collectible judgment from at least one person or business. For example, if a husband and wife purchased some merchandise for their house and owe you money, sue both of them—that is, name both of them as defendants in your lawsuit. Similarly, if an employee of a computer repair company damaged your equipment while repairing it, sue both the employee and the company.

When suing a business, check to see if it's a sole proprietorship, a partnership or a corporation.

- If it's a sole proprietorship, the defendant would be "John Smith doing business as Smith Furniture Company."

- In a partnership, name all of the individual partners and also give the name of the partnership. For example: "Smith-Jones Software Specialists, an Indiana partnership, John Smith and Ida Jones, jointly and severally."

- In the case of a corporation, name the corporation as the defendant: "Rackafrax Inc., a California corporation." The lawsuit papers can be served on the resident agent—the person designated by the corporation as the official recipient of lawsuit papers—or on one of several officers of the corporation.

You may need to do a little research to find out who owns a business or what its correct legal name is. Check the county office that accepts filings of assumed or fictitious names. They'll tell you the owner or owners of a sole proprietorship. Corporate names and corporate assumed names are usually on file with the a state office such as the secretary of state's office.

Don't worry if you're not 100% accurate when you name a business or the owners in a lawsuit. In most states if you name a business defendant incorrectly (you sue Joe's Bar, which is owned by Abdul Irani), you can correct it in court. And in some states, such as Michigan, you can sue a business in small claims court in any name used in an advertisement, sign, invoice, sales slip, register tape, business card, contract or other communication or document used by the business.

F. Handling Your Small Claims Court Lawsuit

Small claims court is designed to be used without lawyers—that's one of its best features. You shouldn't have any trouble going it alone.

1. File Your Complaint

The first formal step in starting your small claims case is to fill out a form known as a "complaint" or "statement of claim" or "affidavit and claim." These forms are available from the court clerk. You'll write a brief statement (perhaps one or two sentences) describing your claim and why the defendant is liable. You'll also state how much money you're asking for. If you're suing on a written contract—as would be common if the defendant failed to pay a bill—you may be asked to attach a photocopy of the contract to the court papers. The court clerk will issue a document called a "summons," which informs the defendant that the suit has been filed and where and when to appear for the hearing.

2. Serve Your Papers

Every state has rules on how the defendant must be notified of a lawsuit. If you don't follow the rules carefully, the court cannot rule against the defendant. In many states, papers can be served on (delivered to) the defendant by registered or certified mail. Also in many states, the clerk's office takes care of sending the papers to the defendant, often by certified mail with a return receipt requested. If state law requires that the papers be given to the defendant in person (or if he or she refuses to accept certified mail), this can be done at modest cost by a private process server or by a public officer, such as a sheriff or marshal. Depending on the law in your state, you may be able to recover the costs of doing this only if you first try to serve the papers by mail.

About half of defendants refuse to accept registered or certified mail, so you'll probably have to turn to personal service a good deal of the time.

3. Prepare for Court

Many small claims cases involve only an unpaid bill, and there's no dispute about the amount owed. You may win such a case by default because the defendant doesn't bother to show up for the hearing. In more complicated cases, your success in court may turn on how well you prepare. You need to think carefully about how you're going to convince that judge that you're right.

Since there's lots of truth to the old saying that a picture is worth at least 1,000 words, bring pictures to court whenever possible.

> **Example**: Rosalie, suing ABC Contractors for damage they did to her roof, brings photos showing the condition of her building before and after ABC workers damaged it.

You may be able to make a point effectively by preparing a drawing or chart. For a few dollars, you can pick up a huge piece of poster board on which you can create a chart or diagram with a felt tip pen. You can use a drawing to show how a room is laid out or how a complicated piece of machinery works. Judges, like everybody else, focus their attention on pictures, graphs and charts.

Incidentally, if your business provides custom goods or services, consider routinely taking pictures of your completed jobs and products. If you later must sue for an unpaid bill, this will make it more difficult for the customer to concoct a bogus claim that he or she failed to pay because the job was badly done. Another good technique is to include a request on every invoice that the customer notify you immediately if there is any problem with the goods or services. Then, if you have to sue to collect on an unpaid bill and the defendant shows up and says that there were problems with the goods or services, you can argue convincingly that the customer never complained before you pressed for payment.

It's almost always helpful to have an eyewitness testify on your behalf. In an undisputed case involving the collection of a bill, you or your bookkeeper can testify about past billings and how much the customer or supplier still owes. Be sure to have copies of the bills. In a contested case, you may want to line up appropriate witnesses. For example, if the unpaid bill is for your company's installation of a telephone system, you might arrange for the person who actually installed the system to come to court. You're entitled to subpoena witnesses, but usually you won't want to use that power to compel a reluctant witness to appear. A person who is hostile can do you more harm than good. A subpoena is useful, however, so that a friendly witness can show it to his or her employer and not have any problems getting off work to come to court.

You may want to present an expert opinion, such as an appraisal of a car repair. As long as it can easily be presented in written form, many states allow this type of evidence in the form of a letter even though technically it's hearsay—a type of evidence that's not admissible in most other courts. This special treatment recognizes that it's not economic to have expert witnesses standing by in small claims court. If you're in doubt as to the rules in your state ask the court clerk.

> **Example**: Cyril pays $3,000 to have Roxanne build some laminated counter tops for his kitchenware shop. He later has to pay someone else $2,000 to repair the job because Roxanne botched it. Cyril sues Roxanne in small claims court to recover the extra $2,000 he had to pay. He contacts another counter top contractor to testify, as an expert witness, that the original job was well below usual standards.

Business records (including letters you sent the defendant) can be very useful at the hearing. Be prepared with all contracts and other records and papers that relate to the transaction involved in the lawsuit. It's better to come with too many papers than too few.

4. Present Your Case at the Court Hearing

Many small claims court defendants simply fail to show up for the trial. Normally, that means the plaintiff can probably get a judgment (by default) after briefly stating his or her case. A default judgment that grants you the relief you want is as valid as any other. But if the properly served defendant comes into court a few days later with a good reason for not showing up (illness, emergency business trip, transportation problems), the judge may be willing to set aside the default judgment and hold a new hearing. However, if the defendant waits more than a month to ask for relief, the judge probably won't grant the request.

In small claims court, the rules of evidence and procedure are informal. Especially if no lawyer is involved, each side simply stands and tells the judge its story and presents its witnesses and other evidence.

Begin your presentation by telling the judge in a sentence or two what the case is about, for example: "My company sells and installs telephone systems. We installed a system for Dr. Jones, a veterinarian. He owes us $2,800 and refuses to pay." Or: "We have a video rental store. Superior Decorating Service signed a contract to paint our store for $2,500. They didn't show up and we had to hire somebody else. It cost us $4,000 to complete the job."

After the short summary of the case, be prepared to lay out the important facts in chronological order. This will be much more helpful than a long rambling presentation that skips back and forth. During the hearing, you can present your photographs and drawings. Usually you do this by showing them to the other party and then handing them to the court clerk or bailiff to give to the judge. Most courts have blackboards if you need to improvise during the hearing.

Be sure to bring to court a copy of the demand letter you sent to the defendant and present it to the judge. This not only shows that you made a reasonable effort to resolve the dispute without a hearing in court, but is another way to present the facts as you see them.

Address your testimony to the judge, not to the other side. Avoid arguing with the other side. Often small claims judges interrupt and ask questions. Always respond directly to the point the judge is inquiring about; then go back to making your points. If the judge keeps interrupting and throws you off balance, politely ask for a moment to review your notes to be sure you've covered all key points. At the end of the case, it's appropriate to point out inconsistencies or fallacies in your opponent's testimony. But stick to the facts and never put your argument on a personal basis.

As you conclude your presentation, ask the judge to award you the amount you're suing for plus court costs. If you win, you're normally entitled to have the other side pay your filing fee, any fees for service of papers and any fees that you paid to witnesses you had to subpoena.

Judges sometimes give their decisions at the end of the hearing. It's also common for the judge to mail out a written decision a few days after the case has been heard. If the case goes against you, check out your appeal rights. (See Section H, below.)

G. Representing Yourself If You're the Defendant

If you receive small claims papers naming you as the defendant, read the papers carefully. In most states, a written answer is not required. You just show up in court and tell your story. When in doubt, call the court clerk or check the local rules. Also, based on your time and energy constraints, decide whether you want to hire a lawyer (lawyers are prohibited in a few states) or perhaps exercise your option to transfer the case to regular court where formal rules of evidence and procedure apply and you always have the right to be represented by a lawyer.

Consider calling the plaintiff with an offer to settle. Often the person suing will accept far less than the amount claimed in the complaint. If you do arrange for a compromise, be sure to get the lawsuit formally dismissed and get a written release from any further liability. Local practice varies, but a common phrase is that the lawsuit is "dismissed with prejudice." This means that the plaintiff can't sue you again over the same transaction.

If the case can't be compromised, think about filing a counterclaim. Suppose the Acme Rug Cleaning Company sues you for $500 for failing to pay them for cleaning the carpets in your office. Let's assume you had two reasons for not paying their bill. First, they did a terrible job of cleaning the rug, and, in your judgment, aren't entitled to any payment. Second, they destroyed an antique chair valued at $1,000. In addition to denying liability for the $500 cleaning bill, you may want to file a counterclaim for $1,000 for the ruined chair. If your counterclaim is over the limits of the small claims court, the case will be transferred from small claims to the regular court.

Even if you don't have much of a defense, it may pay you to show up in court if you wish to pay a judgment in installments. In a number of states, a judge can order a small claims judgment to be paid over time if you so request.

If you don't show up for a hearing, the plaintiff can get a default judgment. And if you, as a defendant, show up at a hearing but the plaintiff doesn't, you're entitled to have the case dismissed. If this happens, ask the judge to dismiss the case "with prejudice." As noted above, this means that the plaintiff can't start up the case against you later on. However, if the plaintiff had a good reason for not showing up in court, the judge may set a new hearing date and keep the case alive.

H. Appealing Small Claims Decisions

In a few states, one price you pay for going to small claims court is the loss of your right to appeal. In most, though, you can appeal a decision of a small claims court to a higher court. In some states, such as California and Massachusetts, only the defendant is permitted to appeal. Where an appeal is allowed, check with the court rules to see whether you're entitled to a complete new trial on the facts of what happened or whether the higher court simply reviews the small claims judgment to see if the judge applied the correct legal rules.

As a practical matter, the right to take an appeal may not be all that important. Especially in smaller cases, spending time on an appeal is usually not cost-effective.

I. Collecting Your Judgment

Winning a judgment in small claims court will make you feel good. But you haven't really won your case until the other side pays up. Fortunately, many individuals and most reputable businesses pay voluntarily after a judge renders a decision. People recognize that they've had their day in court and that an outsider (the judge) has determined they truly owe the money.

When the losing party does pay you, you must give that person a "satisfaction of judgment" form. This form is usually available from the court clerk and simply acknowledges that you've been paid. It helps the losing party maintain good credit. One

word of caution: Don't sign a satisfaction of judgment form until you're sure you've been paid in full. Because the person who pays you may be tempted to stop payment on a personal check, wait until the check clears or insist on cash, a certified or cashier's check, or a money order.

Unfortunately, a significant number of debtors refuse to pay even after a court enters a judgment against them. There are many ways that debtors can protect themselves and, in effect, become "judgment-proof." Many people who are not completely without assets are still beyond the reach of your efforts to collect from them. For example, a creditor can't legally take the food from a debtor's table, or the TV from his living room, or even (in many cases) the car from his driveway.

If the defendant (now called a "judgment debtor") has a job and a bank account, garnishment may be the answer if the defendant refuses to pay you. By filing certain forms with the court where you obtained your judgment, you can require the debtor's employer to pay the judgment out of wages, or the debtor's bank to pay it out of a bank account. If you garnish wages, you'll be able to obtain only a portion of the person's paycheck. You may have to go through repeated garnishments.

Judgments can also be collected from other sources. For example, you may be able to use the debtor's motor vehicles and real estate as a collection source. The procedure is called "attachment." But many types of property are exempt from attachment. For example, in many states a portion, or all, of the equity in a debtor's home is exempt under a "homestead" exemption. In Arizona this amount is $50,000; in Massachusetts, it's $100,000.

If the judgment debtor is a going business, you may be able to impose a "till tap"—that is, a right to collect a certain part of the daily receipts of the business. You'll have to check the procedures in your state.

If you don't know where a judgment debtor works or has assets, you can file forms requiring the person to come back into court and disclose these things to you. After being put under oath, the judgment debtor will have to reveal information that may lead to collection of the judgment, including:

- where he or she works and the amount of wages he or she receives

- the location and extent of bank accounts

- any personal property, such as stocks and bonds or cars

- real estate holdings

- business assets.

Then, through garnishment and other proceedings, you may be able to obtain enough money to satisfy your judgment. Most of the time, however, if you have to force the judgment debtor into court to disclose assets, you'll find yourself wasting a lot of valuable time with very little likelihood of ever getting full payment.

For more on debt collection, see Chapter 16.

LAWYERS AND LEGAL RESEARCH   **20**

When you own or run a small business, you need lots of legal information. Lawyers, of course, are prime sources of this information, but if you bought all the needed information at their rates—$150 to $250 an hour—you'd quickly empty your bank account. Fortunately, as an intelligent business person, there are a number of efficient ways you can acquire on your own a good working knowledge of the legal principles and procedures necessary to start and run a small business.

But can you run your business without ever consulting a lawyer? Probably not. Lawyers do more than dispense legal information. They also offer strategic advice and apply sophisticated technical skills. How frequently you'll need professional help is hard to say. It depends on the nature of your business, the number of employees you hire, how many locations you have, and the kinds of problems you run into with customers, suppliers, landlords, contractors, the government, the media, insurance companies and a host of other people and entities. Your challenge isn't to avoid lawyers altogether but rather to use them on a cost-effective basis.

Ideally, you should find a lawyer who's willing to serve as a legal coach and help you educate yourself. Then you can often negotiate legal transactions on your own and prepare preliminary drafts of documents, turning to your lawyer from time to time for advice, review and fine-tuning.

In working with a lawyer, remember that you're the boss. A lawyer, of course, has specialized training, knowledge, skill and experience in dealing with legal matters. But that's no reason for you to abdicate control over legal decision-making and how much time and money should be spent on a particular legal problem. Because you almost surely can't afford all the legal services that you'd benefit from, you need to set priorities. When thinking about a legal problem, ask yourself: "Can I do this myself?" "Can I do this myself with some help from a lawyer?" "Should I simply put this in my lawyer's hands?"

How a Business Lawyer Can Help You

Here's a brief checklist of ways that a lawyer can help you:

- Assist with the start-up of your business (review a partnership agreement or incorporation documents, for example).

- Look over a proposed lease.

- Analyze land use regulations in zoning ordinances and private title documents.

- Review employment agreements and sensitive employee terminations.

- Represent you before governmental bodies and helping to cut through bureaucratic red tape.

- Assist you with "intellectual property" issues—patents, copyrights, trademarks, trade secrets and business names.

- Coach or representing you in lawsuits or arbitrations where the stakes are high or the legal issues particularly complex.

- Review or drafting documents for the purchase or sale of a business or real estate.

- Check or drafting estate planning documents—wills, trusts and powers of attorney.

- Advise on public offerings of corporate stock (compliance with Blue Sky laws).

A. How To Find the Right Lawyer

Locating a good lawyer for your small business may not be as easy as you think. The fact is that most lawyers lack in-depth experience in working for small businesses. Of the close to 800,000 lawyers in America today, probably fewer than 50,000 possess sufficient training and experience in small business law to be of real help to you.

1. Compile a List of Prospects

Don't expect to locate a good business lawyer by simply looking in the phone book, consulting a law directory or reading an advertisement. There's not enough information in these sources to help you make a valid judgment. Almost as useless are lawyer referral services operated by bar associations. Generally, these services make little attempt to evaluate a lawyer's skill and experience. They simply supply the names of lawyers who have listed with the service, often accepting the lawyer's own word for what types of skills he or she has.

A better approach is to talk to people in your community who own or operate truly excellent businesses. These people obviously understand quality in other ways, so why not in lawyers? Ask them who their lawyer is and what they think of that person. Ask them about other lawyers they've used and what led them to make a change. If you talk to half a dozen business people, chances are you'll come away with several good leads.

Other people who provide services to the business community can also help you identify lawyers you should consider. For example, speak to your banker, accountant, insurance agent and real estate broker. These people come into frequent contact with lawyers who represent business clients and are in a position to make informed judgments. Friends, relatives and business associates within your own company can also provide names of possible lawyers. But ask them specifically about lawyers who have had experience working for business clients and consider carefully whether they really know enough about business and human nature to know what they're talking about.

In some types of specialized businesses—software design, restaurants, plant nurseries—it can pay to work with a lawyer who already knows the field. That way you can take advantage of the fact that the lawyer is already fairly far up the learning curve. Besides having knowledge about a certain type of business, a specialist may have experience with specific types of legal problems; for example, a lawyer may have special expertise in zoning law, liquor

licenses or intellectual property matters. Sometimes specialists charge a little more, but if their specialized information is truly valuable, it can be money well spent. Trade associations are often a good place to get referrals to specialists.

Here are a few other sources you can turn to for possible candidates in your search for a lawyer:

- The director of your state or local chamber of commerce may know of several business lawyers who have the kind of experience that you're looking for.

- A law librarian can help identify authors in your state who have written books or articles on business law.

- The director of your state's continuing legal education (CLE) program—usually run by a bar association, a law school or both—can identify lawyers who have lectured or written on business law for other lawyers. Someone who's a "lawyer's lawyer" presumably has the extra depth of knowledge and experience to do a superior job for you—but may charge more.

- The chairperson of a state or county bar committee for business lawyers may be able to point out some well-qualified practitioners in your vicinity.

Once you have the names of several lawyers, a good source of more information about them is the *Martindale-Hubbell Law Directory*, available at most law libraries and some local public libraries. This resource contains biographical sketches of most practicing lawyers and information about their experience, specialties, education and the professional organizations they belong to. Many firms also list their major clients in the directory—an excellent indication of the types of practice the firm is engaged in. In addition, almost every lawyer listed in the directory, whether or not he or she purchased space for a biographical sketch, is rated "AV," "BV" or "CV." These ratings come from confidential opinions that Martindale-Hubbell solicits from lawyers and judges. The first letter is for "Legal Ability," which is rated as follows:

"A"—Very High to Preeminent

"B"—High to Very High

"C"—Fair to High

The "V" part stands for "Very High General Recommendation," meaning that the rated lawyer adheres to professional standards of conduct and ethics. But it's practically meaningless because lawyers who don't qualify for it aren't rated at all. (*Martindale-Hubbell* prudently cautions that the absence of a rating shouldn't be construed as a reflection on the lawyer; some lawyers ask that their rating not be published, and there may be other reasons for the absence of a rating.)

I believe that the rating system works remarkably well. Don't make it your sole criterion for deciding on a potential lawyer for your business, but be reasonably confident that a lawyer who gets high marks from other business clients and an "AV" rating from *Martindale-Hubbell* knows what he or she is doing.

2. Shop Around

After you get the names of several good prospects, shop around. If you announce your intentions in advance, most lawyers will be willing to speak to you for a half hour or so at no charge so that you can size them up and make an informed decision. Look for experience, personal rapport and accessibility. Some of these characteristics will be apparent almost immediately. Others may take longer to discover. So even after you've hired a lawyer who seems right for you, keep open the possibility that you may have to make a change later.

Pay particular attention to the rapport between you and your lawyer. No matter how experienced and well-recommended a lawyer is, if you feel uncomfortable with that person during your first meeting or two, you may never achieve an ideal lawyer-client relationship. Trust your instincts and seek a lawyer whose personality is compatible with your own.

Your lawyer should be accessible when you need legal services. Unfortunately, the complaint logs of all law regulatory groups indicate that many lawyers are not. If every time you have a problem there's a delay of several days before you can talk to your lawyer on the phone or get an appointment, you'll lose precious time, not to mention sleep. And almost nothing is more aggravating to a client than to leave a legal project in a lawyer's hands and then have weeks or even months go by without anything happening. You want a lawyer who will work hard on your behalf and follow through promptly on all assignments.

Try to find a lawyer who seems interested in your business and either already knows a lot about your field or who seems genuinely eager to learn more about it. Avoid the lawyer who's aloof and doesn't want to get involved in learning the nitty-gritty details of what you do.

Some lawyers are nitpickers who get unnecessarily bogged down in legal technicalities. They point out a million reasons why something can't be done. Meanwhile, a valuable business opportunity slips away. You want a lawyer who blends legal technicalities with a practical approach—someone who figures out a way to do something, not one who offers reasons why it can't be done.

B. Fees and Bills

When you hire a lawyer, have a clear understanding about how fees will be computed. And as new jobs are brought to the lawyer, ask specifically about charges for each. Many lawyers initiate fee discussions, but others forget or are shy about doing so. Bring up the subject yourself. Insist that the ground rules be clearly established. In California, all fee agreements between lawyers and clients must be in writing if the expected fee is $1,000 or more, or is contingent on the outcome of a lawsuit. Perhaps this will be common everywhere soon.

1. How Lawyers Charge

There are four basic ways that lawyers charge. The first is by the hour. In most parts of the United States, you can get competent services for your small business for $150 to $250 an hour.

Sometimes a lawyer quotes a flat fee for a specific job. For example, the lawyer may offer to draw a real estate purchase agreement for $300. Or to represent you before a state licensing board for $3,000. You pay the same amount regardless of how much time the lawyer spends.

In some cases, a lawyer may charge a contingent fee. This is a percentage (such as 33 1/3 %) of the amount the lawyer obtains for you in a negotiated settlement or through a trial. If the lawyer recovers nothing for you, there's no fee. However, the lawyer does generally expect reimbursement for out-of-pocket expenses, such as filing fees, long distance phone calls and transcripts of testimony. Contingent fees are common in personal injury lawsuits but relatively unusual in small business cases.

Finally, you may be able to hire a lawyer for a flat annual fee (retainer) to handle all of your routine legal business. You'll usually pay in equal monthly installments and, normally, the lawyer will bill you an additional amount for extraordinary services— such as representing you in a major lawsuit.

Obviously, the key to making this arrangement work is to have a written agreement clearly defining what's routine and what's extraordinary.

Comparison shopping among lawyers will help you avoid overpaying. But the cheapest hourly rate isn't necessarily the best. A novice who charges only $80 an hour may take three hours to review a consultant's work-for-hire contract. A more experienced lawyer who charges $200 an hour may do the same job in half an hour and make better suggestions. Take into account the lawyer's knowledge in your field, his or her reputation and personal rapport.

2. Ways To Save on Legal Fees

There are many ways to hold down the cost of legal services. Here's a summary.

- **Group together your legal affairs.** You'll save money if you consult with your lawyer on several matters at one time. For example, in a one-hour conference, you may be able to review the annual updating of your corporate record book, renewing your lease, and a non-competition agreement you've drafted for new employees to sign.

- **Help out.** You or your employees can do a lot of work yourselves. Help gather documents needed for a real estate transaction. Line up witnesses for a trial. Write the first couple of drafts of a contract; give your lawyer the relatively inexpensive task of reviewing and polishing the document.

- **Ask the lawyer to be your coach.** Make it clear that you're eager to do as much work as possible yourself with the lawyer coaching you from the sidelines. Many lawyers find it gratifying to impart their knowledge and experience to others, but they're used to clients who simply drop their problems on the lawyer's desk to solve. Unless you specifically ask for coaching, you may never tap into your lawyer's ability to help you in that way.

- **Read trade journals in your field.** They'll help you keep up with specific legal developments that your lawyer may have missed. Send pertinent clippings to your lawyer—this can dramatically reduce legal research time—and encourage your lawyer to do the same for you.

- **Show that you're an important client.** The single most important thing you can do to tell your lawyer how much you value the relationship is to pay your bills on time. Also, let your lawyer know about plans for expansion and your company's possible future legal needs. And if your business wins an award or otherwise is recognized as being a leader in its field, let your lawyer know about it—everyone feels good when an enterprise they're associated with prospers. Also, let your lawyer know when you recommend him or her to your business colleagues.

- **Use non-lawyer professionals.** Often, non-lawyer professionals perform some tasks better and at less cost than lawyers. For example, look to management consultants for strategic business planning; real estate brokers or appraisers for valuation of properties; accountants for preparation of financial proposals; insurance agents for advice on insurance protection; and CPAs for the preparation of tax returns. Each of these concerns is likely to have a legal aspect, and you may eventually want to consult your lawyer, but normally you won't need to until you've gathered information on your own.

A Tax Tip

If you visit your lawyer on a personal legal matter (such as reviewing a contract for the purchase of a house) and you also discuss a business problem (such as a commercial lawsuit you've been threatened with), ask your lawyer to allocate the time spent and send you separate bills. At tax time, you can easily list the business portion as a tax-deductible business expense.

C. Problems With Your Lawyer

Relations between lawyers and clients are not always perfect. If you see a problem emerging, nip it in the bud. Don't just sit back and fume; call, visit or write to your lawyer. The problem won't get resolved if your lawyer doesn't even know there's a problem. Sure, it's hard to confront someone who you may need to rely on for future help and advice—but an open exchange is essential for a healthy lawyer-client relationship.

Whatever it is that rankles, have an honest discussion about your feelings. Maybe you're upset because your lawyer hasn't kept you informed about what's going on in your case or has failed to meet a promised deadline. Or maybe last month's bill was shockingly high or lacked any breakdown of how your lawyer's time was spent.

One good test of whether a lawyer-client relationship is a good one is to ask yourself if you feel able to talk freely with your lawyer about your degree of participation in any legal matter and your control over how the lawyer carries out a legal assignment. If you can't frankly discuss these sometimes sensitive matters with your lawyer, get another lawyer. Otherwise, you'll surely waste money on unnecessary legal fees and risk having legal matters turn out badly. Remember that you're always free to change lawyers and to get all important documents back from a lawyer you no longer employ.

YOUR RIGHTS AS A CLIENT

As a client, you have the following rights:

1. to be treated courteously by your lawyer and the members of his or her staff

2. to receive an itemized statement of services rendered and a full explanation of billing practices

3. to be charged reasonable fees

4. To receive a prompt response to phone calls and letters

5. to have confidential legal conferences, free from unwarranted interruptions

6. to be kept informed of the status of your case

7. to have your legal matters handled diligently and competently

8. to receive clear answers to all questions.

D. Do-It-Yourself Legal Research

Law libraries are chock full of valuable information—information that you can easily ferret out on your own. All you need is a rudimentary knowledge of how the information is organized.

1. Finding a Law Library

Your first step is to find a law library that's open to the public. You may find such a library in your county courthouse or at your state capitol. Public law schools generally permit the public to use their libraries, and some private law schools grant access to their libraries—sometimes for a modest user fee. The reference department of a major public library may have a fairly decent legal research collection. If you're lucky enough to have access to several law

libraries, select one that has a reference librarian to assist you.

Finally, don't overlook the law library in your own lawyer's office. Most lawyers, on request, will gladly share their books with their clients.

RECOMMENDED READING

- *Legal Research: How To Find and Understand the Law*, by Stephen Elias and Susan Levinkind (Nolo Press). A nontechnical book written for the average person and covering basic legal materials. Among other things, it explains how to use all major legal research tools and helps you frame your research questions.

- *Legal Research Made Easy: A Roadmap Through the Law Library Maze*, by Robert C. Berring (Legal Star/Nolo Press). An entertaining videotape with a six-step strategy for legal research. If you really plan to do your own legal research, this is a must-see. It's available from many public and law library video collections.

- *The Plain-Language Law Dictionary for Home and Office*, edited by Robert S. Rothenberg (Penguin Books). The more familiar *Black's Law Dictionary* frequently uses jargon to define jargon.

---

2. Federal and State Law

Every business is governed by both federal law and state law. If yours is a typical small business, you'll be concerned primarily with state law. For example, the law dealing with how you form a sole proprietorship, partnership or corporation is almost entirely based on state sources, as is the law controlling buying a business, leasing space, hiring employees, forming contracts and resolving disputes through arbitration or small claims court. Federal law deals with federal taxes, trademarks, consumer protection and equal opportunity standards. In some areas of business (such as consumer protection and equal opportunity legislation) federal and state laws may overlap.

3.   Primary and Secondary Sources

In doing legal research, you'll refer to both primary and secondary sources. Primary sources are statements of the law itself, including:

- Constitutions (federal and state)

- Legislation (laws—also called statutes or ordinances—passed by Congress, your state legislature and local governments)

- Administrative Rules and Regulations (issued by federal and state administrative agencies charged with implementing statutes)

- Case Law (decisions of federal and state courts interpreting statutes—and sometimes making law, known as "common law," if the subject isn't covered by a statute)

A small business rarely gets involved in questions of constitutional law. You're far more likely to be concerned with law created by a federal or state statute, or by an administrative rule or regulation. At the federal level, that includes the Internal Revenue Code and regulations adopted by the Internal Revenue Service; regulations dealing with advertising, warranties and other consumer matters adopted by the Federal Trade Commission; and equal opportunity statutes such as Title VII of the Civil Rights Act administered by the Justice Department and Equal Employment Opportunities Commission. At the state level, you'll likely be interested in statutes dealing with licensing, partnership law, corporate law, commercial transactions (your state's version of the Uniform Commercial Code), employment matters and court procedures. You may also need to get into local laws dealing with zoning, health and building and safety regulations.

Depending on the type of business you have, you may also want to research statutes and regulations dealing with other legal topics such as the environment, labor relations, product liability, real estate, copyrights and so on.

4.   How To Begin

Obviously, primary sources—statements of the "raw law"—are important. But most legal research begin with secondary sources—books that comment on, organize or describe primary materials.

It often makes sense to start with one of the two national encyclopedias, *American Jurisprudence 2d* (cited as *AmJur2d*) or *Corpus Juris Secundum* (cited as *CJS*). If your state has its own encyclopedia, check that too. These encyclopedias organize the case law and some statutes into a narrative statements organized alphabetically by subject. Through citations in footnotes, you can locate the cases and statutes themselves.

It's also helpful if you can find a treatise on the subject you're researching. A treatise is simply a book (or series of books) that covers a specific area of law. I've always been impressed by the Nutshell Series published by the West Publishing Co. You may want to look at *Contracts in a Nutshell* by Gordon A. Schaber and Claude D. Rohwer and *Corporations in a Nutshell* by Robert W. Hamilton.

Law reviews published by law schools and other legal periodicals may also contain useful summaries of the law. The *American Bar Association Journal* as well as the journal published by your state bar association should be available in the law library that you use. In these journals, you'll often find well-written and timely articles on legal issues that affect small businesses. You can locate law review and bar journal articles through *The Index to Legal Periodicals*. Be warned, however, that law school reviews contain articles by law professors and students, and are of more academic than practical interest.

I highly recommend *The Practical Lawyer* published by the Joint Committee on Continuing Legal Education of the American Law Institute and American Bar Association (ALI-ABA). Each edition contains half a dozen clear and practical articles— many of which address topics of interest to small businesses. The checklists and forms are superb. This resource is virtually unknown outside the legal profession. If you get hooked on the law, consider subscribing.

Finally, practically every state has an organization that provides continuing legal education to practicing lawyers. Especially in the more populous states, these organizations publish excellent books on business law subjects which, unlike nationally-published treatises, focus on the law in your state and contain state-specific forms and checklists. You can also find a wealth of relevant information in the course materials prepared for continuing legal education seminars.

Tips for Researching Business Law

- When looking up statutes, use an annotated version. It comes in a multi-volume set and contains the laws themselves plus references to court and administrative decisions interpreting the statutes and often to treatises and articles that discuss the law.

- Statutes are frequently amended. Always check the pocket-part supplement at the back of statute (code) books to make sure you have the latest edition.

- When you look up a state court decision (case), use the regional reporter published by West Publishing Co. if it's available. Before the text of the case begins, an ingenious system of notes (called the "key number" system) helps you tap into other similar cases. Ask the reference librarian to explain, or consult one of the books on legal research referred to earlier.

- Use the Shepard Citation system to see if and where the court case you're looking at has been relied on, discounted or overruled by a later court. *Legal Research: How to Find and Understand the Law,* by Stephen Elias and Susan Levinkind (Nolo Press) has a good, easy-to-follow explanation of how to use the Shepard's system.

- A relatively unknown resource for quickly locating state business laws is the United States Law Digest volume of the *Martindale-Hubbell Law Directory*. There's a handy summary of laws, including statutory citations, for each state. Dozens of business law topics are covered, including Commercial Code, Consumer Protection, Corporations, Employer and Employee, Insurance, Landlord and Tenant, Leases, Partnership, Principal and Agent, Real Property, Statute of Frauds and Trademarks, Tradenames and Service Marks. But you may need a magnifying glass: the print is minuscule.

APPENDIX A

STATE OFFICES THAT PROVIDE SMALL BUSINESS HELP

Alabama
Alabama Development Office
State Capitol
Montgomery, AL 36130
(800) 248-0033*   (205) 263-0048

Alaska
Division of Economic Development
Department of Commerce and Economic
    Development
PO Box D
Juneau, AK 99811
(907) 465-2017

Arizona
Office of Business Finance
Department of Commerce
3800 North Central Avenue
Suite 1500
Phoenix, AZ 85012
(602) 280-1341

Arkansas
Small Business Information Center
Industrial Development Commission
State Capitol Mall
Room 4C-300
Little Rock, AR 72201
(501) 682-5275

California
Office of Small Business
Department of Commerce
801 K Street, Suite 1700
Sacramento, CA 95814
(916) 327-4357 (916) 445-6545

Colorado
One-Stop Assistance Center
1560 Broadway, Suite 1530
Denver, CO 80202
(800) 333-7798 (303) 592-5920

Connecticut
Small Business Services
Department of Economic Development
865 Brook Street
Rocky Hill, CN 06067
(203) 258-4269

Delaware
Development Office
PO Box 1401
99 Kings Highway
Dover, DE 19903
(302) 739-4271

District of Columbia
Office of Business and Economic
    Development
Tenth Floor
717 14th Street NW
Washington, DC 20005
(202) 727-6600

Florida
Bureau of Business Assistance
Department of Commerce
107 West Gaines Street, Room 443
Tallahassee, FL 32399-2000
(800) 342-0771*

Georgia
Department of Community Affairs
100 Peachtree Street, Suite 1200
Atlanta, GA 30303
(404) 656-6200

Hawaii
Small Business Information Service
737 Bishop Street, Suite 1900
Honolulu, HI 96813
(808) 548-7645 (808) 543-6691

Idaho
Economic Development Division
Department of Commerce
700 State Street
Boise, ID 83720-2700
(208) 334-2470

Illinois
Small Business Assistance Bureau
Department of Commerce and
    Community Affairs
620 East Adams Street
Springfield, IL 62701
(800) 252-2923*

Indiana
Ombudsman's Office
Business Development Division
Department of Commerce
One North Capitol, Suite 700
Indianapolis, IN 46204-2288
(800) 824-2476* (317) 232-7304

Iowa
Bureau of Small Business Development
Department of Economic Development
200 East Grand Avenue
Des Moines, IA 50309
(800) 532-1216* (515) 242-4899

Kansas
Division of Existing Industry Development
400 SW Eighth Street
Topeka, KN 66603
(913) 296-5298

Kentucky
Division of Small Business
Capitol Plaza Tower
Frankfort, KY 40601
(800) 626-2250* (502) 564-4252

Louisiana
Development Division
Office of Commerce and Industry
PO Box 94185
Baton Rouge, LA 70804-9185
(504) 342-5365

Maine
Business Development Division
State Development Office
State House
Augusta, ME 04333
(800) 872-3838* (207) 289-3153

Maryland
Division of Business Development
Department of Economic and Employment
    Development
217 East Redwood Street
Baltimore, MD 21202
(800) 873-7232 (301) 333-6996

Massachusetts
Office of Business Development
100 Cambridge Street
13th Floor
Boston, MA 02202
(617) 727-3206

Michigan
Michigan Business Ombudsman
Department of Commerce
PO Box 30107
Lansing, MI 48909
(800) 232-2727* (517) 373-6241

Minnesota
Small Business Assistance Office
Department of Trade and Economic
    Development
900 American Center Building
150 East Kellogg Boulevard
St. Paul, MN 55101
(800) 652-9747 (612) 296-3871

Mississippi
Small Business Bureau
Research and Development Center
PO Box 849
Jackson, MS 39205
(601) 359-3552

Missouri
Small Business Development Office
Department of Economic Development
PO Box 118
Jefferson City, MO 65102
(314) 751-4982 (314) 751-8411

Montana
Business Assistance Division
Department of Commerce
1424 Ninth Avenue
Helena, MT 59620
(800) 221-8015* (406) 444-2801

Nebraska
Existing Business Division
Department of Economic Development
PO Box 94666
301 Centennial Mall South
Lincoln, NE 68509-4666
(402) 471-3782

Nevada
Nevada Commission on Economic
    Development
Capitol Complex
Carson City, NV 89710
(702) 687-4325

New Hampshire
Small Business Development Center
University Center
400 Commercial Street, Room 311
Manchester, NH 03101
(603) 625-4522

New Jersey
Office of Small Business Assistance
Department of Commerce and Economic
    Development
20 West State Street, CN 835
Trenton, NJ 08625
(609) 984-4442

New Mexico
Economic Development Division
Department of Economic Development
1100 St. Francis Drive
Santa Fe, NM 87503
(505) 827-0300

New York
Division for Small Business
Department of Economic Development
1515 Broadway
51st Floor
New York, NY 10036
(212) 827-6150

North Carolina
Small Business Development Division
Department of Economic and Community
    Development
Dobbs Building, Room 2019
430 North Salisbury Street
Raleigh, NC 27611
(919) 733-7980

North Dakota
Small Business Coordinator
Economic Development Commission
Liberty Memorial Building
604 East Boulevard
Bismark, ND 58505
(701) 224-2810

Ohio
Small and Developing Business Division
Department of Development
PO Box 1001
Columbus, OH 43266-0101
(800) 248-4040* (614) 466-4232

Oklahoma
Oklahoma Department of Commerce
PO Box 26980
6601 N. Broadway Extension
Oklahoma City, OK 73126-0980
(800) 477-6552* (405) 843-9770

Oregon
Economic Development Department
775 Summer Street NE
Salem, OR 97310
(800) 233-3306* (503) 373-1200

Pennsylvania
Bureau of Small Business and Appalachian
    Development
Department of Commerce
461 Forum Building
Harrisburg, PA 17120
(717) 783-5700

Puerto Rico
Commonwealth Department of Commerce,
Box S
4275 Old San Juan Station
San Juan, PR 00905
(809) 721-3290

Rhode Island
Business Development Division
Department of Economic Development
Seven Jackson Walkway
Providence, RI 02903
(401) 277-2601

South Carolina
Enterprise Development
PO Box 1149
Columbia, SC 29202
(800) 922-6684* (803) 737-0888

South Dakota
Governor's Office of Economic
    Development
Capital Lake Plaza
711 Wells Avenue
Pierre, SD 57501
(800) 872-6190* (605) 773-5032

Tennessee
Small Business Office
Department of Economic and Community
    Development
320 Sixth Avenue North
Seventh Floor
Rachel Jackson Building
Nashville, TN 37219
(800) 872-7201* (615) 741-2626

Texas
Small Business Division
Department of Commerce
Economic Development Commission
PO Box 12728
Capitol Station
410 East Fifth Street
Austin, TX 78711
(800) 888-0511 (512) 472-5059

Utah
Small Business Development Center
102 West 500 South, Suite 315
Salt Lake City, UT 84101
(801) 581-7905

Vermont
Agency of Development and Community
    Affairs
The Pavillion
109 State Street
Montpelier, VT 05609
(800) 622-4553* (802) 828-3221

Virginia
Small Business and Financial Services
Department of Economic Development
PO Box 798
1000 Washington Building
Richmond, VA 23206
(804) 371-8252

Washington
Small Business Development Center
245 Todd Hall
Washington State University
Pullman, WA 99164-4727
(509) 335-1576

West Virginia
Small Business Development Center
    Division
1115 Virginia Street East
Charleston, WV 25301
(304) 348-2960

Wisconsin
Public Information Bureau
Department of Development
PO Box 7970
123 West Washington Avenue
Madison, WI 53707
(800) 435-7287* (608) 266-1018

Wyoming
Economic Development and Stabilization
    Board
Herschler Building
Cheyenne, WY 82002
(307) 777-7287

---

*In-state calling only.

Source: National Association for the Self-
    Employed,
    USA TODAY research.

APPENDIX B

FEDERAL TRADE COMMISSION OFFICES

Headquarters

Federal Trade Commission
6th and Pennsylvania Avenue, NW
Washington, DC 20580
(202) 326-3175

Regional Offices

11000 Wilshire Boulevard
Los Angeles, CA 90024
(213) 209-7890

901 Market Street
San Francisco, CA 94103
(415) 744-7920

1405 Curtis Street
Denver, CO 80202-2393
(303) 844-2271

1718 Peachtree Street, NW
Atlanta, GA 30367
(404) 347-4836

55 East Monroe Street
Chicago IL 60603
(312) 353-4423

10 Causeway Street
Boston, MA 02222-1073
(617) 565-7240

150 William Street
New York, NY 10038
(212) 264-1207

668 Euclid Avenue
Cleveland, OH 44114
(216) 522-4210

100 North Central Expressway
Dallas, TX 75201
(214) 767-5501

915 Second Avenue
Seattle, WA 98174
(206) 442-4656

Index

SELF-HELP LAW BOOKS & SOFTWARE

ESTATE PLANNING & PROBATE

Plan Your Estate With a Living Trust
Attorney Denis Clifford
National 2nd Edition
This book covers every significant aspect of estate planning and gives detailed specific, instructions for preparing a living trust, a document that lets your family avoid expensive and lengthy probate court proceedings after your death. *Plan Your Estate* includes all the tear-out forms and step-by-step instructions to let you prepare an estate plan designed for your special needs.
$19.95/NEST

Nolo's Simple Will Book
Attorney Denis Clifford
National 2nd Edition
It's easy to write a legally valid will using this book. The instructions and forms enable people to draft a will for all needs, including naming a personal guardian for minor children, leaving property to minor children or young adults and updating a will when necessary. Good in all states except Louisiana.
$17.95/SWIL

Who Will Handle Your Finances If You Can't?
Attorneys Denis Clifford and Mary Randolph
National 1st Edition
If illness or old age makes it impossible for you to handle your own day-to-day financial affairs, someone must step in to take care of matters. Usually, a family member must go to court and ask a judge to appoint a conservator—a painful and intrusive process.
But by using this book to create a **durable power of attorney for finances** you can avoid court involvement altogether. In a durable power of attorney you appoint a trusted person to take care of your finances if it becomes necessary. This book contains tear-out durable power of attorney forms and all the instructions necessary.
$19.95 FINA

The Conservatorship Book
Lisa Goldoftas & Attorney Carolyn Farren
California 1st Edition
When someone becomes incapacitated due to illness or age, a conservator may need to take charge of their medical and financial affairs. *The Conservatorship Book* comes with complete instructions and all the forms necessary to file conservatorship documents, appear in court, be appointed conservator and end a conservatorship.
$24.95/CNSV

How to Probate an Estate
Julia Nissley
California 7th Edition
If you find yourself responsible for winding up the legal and financial affairs of a deceased family member or friend, you can often save costly attorneys' fees by handling the probate process yourself. This book also explains the simple procedures you can use to transfer assets that don't require probate, including property held in joint tenancy or living trusts or as community property.
$34.95/PAE

software

WillMaker
Nolo Press
Version 4.0
This easy-to-use software program lets you prepare and update a legal will—safely, privately and without the expense of a lawyer. Leading you step-by-step in a question-and-answer format, *WillMaker* builds a will around your answers, taking into account your state of residence. *WillMaker* comes with a 200-page legal manual which provides the legal background necessary to make sound choices. Good in all states except Louisiana.
IBM PC
(3-1/2 & 5-1/4 disks included) $69.95/WI4
MACINTOSH $69.95/WM4

Nolo's Personal RecordKeeper
(formerly For the Record)
Carol Pladsen & Attorney Ralph Warner
Version 3.0
Nolo's Personal RecordKeeper lets you record the location of personal, financial and legal information in over 200 categories and subcategories. It also allows you to create lists of insured property, compute net worth, consolidate emergency information into one place and export to *Quicken®* home inventory and net worth reports. Includes a 320-page manual filled with practical and legal advice.
IBM PC
(3-1/2 & 5-1/4 disks included) $49.95/FRI3
MACINTOSH $49.95/FRM3

Nolo's Living Trust
Attorney Mary Randolph
Version 1.0
A will is an indispensable part of any estate plan, but many people need a living trust as well. By putting certain assets into a trust, you save your heirs the headache, time and expense of probate. *Nolo's Living Trust* lets you set up an individual or shared marital trust, make your trust document legal, transfer your property to the trust, and change or revoke the trust at any time. The 380-page manual guides you through the process step-by-step, and over 100 legal help screens and an on-line glossary explain key legal terms and concepts. Good in all states except Louisiana.
MACINTOSH $79.95/LTM1

GOING TO COURT

Everybody's Guide to Municipal Court
Judge Roderic Duncan
California 1st Edition
Everybody's Guide to Municipal Court explains how to prepare and defend the most common types of contract and personal injury law suits in California Municipal Court. Written by a California judge, the book provides step-by-step instructions for preparing and filing all necessary forms, gathering evidence and appearing in court.
$29.95/MUNI

Everybody's Guide to Small Claims Court
Attorney Ralph Warner
National 5th Edition
California 10th Edition
These books will help you decide if you should sue in Small Claims Court, show you how to file and serve papers, tell you what to bring to court and how to collect a judgment.
National $15.95/NSCC
California $15.95/ CSCC

Fight Your Ticket
Attorney David Brown
California 5th Edition
This book shows you how to fight an unfair traffic ticket—when you're stopped, at arraignment, at trial and on appeal.
$17.95/FYT

Collect Your Court Judgment
Gini Graham Scott, Attorney Stephen Elias & Lisa Goldoftas
California 2nd Edition
This book contains step-by-step instructions and all the forms you need to collect a court judgment from the debtor's bank accounts, wages, business receipts, real estate or other assets.
$19.95/JUDG

How to Change Your Name
Attorneys David Loeb & David Brown
California 5th Edition
This book explains how to change your name legally and provides all the necessary court forms with detailed instructions on how to fill them out.
$19.95/NAME

BUSINESS/WORKPLACE

The Legal Guide for Starting & Running a Small Business
Attorney Fred S. Steingold
National 1st Edition
This book is an essential resource for every small business owner, whether you are just starting out or are already established. Find out everything you need to know about how to form a sole proprietorship, partnership or corporation, negotiate a favorable lease, hire and fire employees, write contracts and resolve disputes.
$19.95 / RUNS

Sexual Harassment on the Job
Attorneys William Petrocelli & Barbara Kate Repa
National 1st Edition
This is the first comprehensive book dealing with sexual harassment in the workplace. It describes what harassment is, what the laws are that make it illegal and how to put a stop to it. This guide is invaluable both for employees experiencing harassment and for employers interested in creating a policy against sexual harassment and a procedure for handling complaints.
$14.95/HARS

Your Rights in the Workplace
Dan Lacey
National 1st Edition
Your Rights in the Workplace, the first comprehensive guide to workplace rights —from hiring to firing—explains the latest sweeping changes in laws passed to protect workers. Learning about these legal protections can help all workers be sure they're paid fairly and on time, get all employment benefits, and know how to take action if fired or laid off illegally.
$15.95/YRW

How to Write a Business Plan
Mike McKeever
National 4th Edition
If you're thinking of starting a business or raising money to expand an existing one, this book will show you how to write the business plan and loan package necessary to finance your business and make it work.
$19.95/SBS

Marketing Without Advertising
Michael Phillips & Salli Rasberry
National 1st Edition
This book outlines practical steps for building and expanding a small business without spending a lot of money on advertising.
$14.00/MWAD

The Partnership Book
Attorneys Denis Clifford & Ralph Warner
National 4th Edition
This book shows you step-by-step how to write a solid partnership agreement that meets your needs. It covers initial contributions to the business, wages, profit-sharing, buy-outs, death or retirement of a partner and disputes.
$24.95/PART

How to Form Your Own New York Corporation & How to Form Your Own Texas Corporation

(computer editions)
Attorney Anthony Mancuso

These book/software packages contain the instructions and tax information and forms you need to incorporate a small business and save hundreds of dollars in lawyers' fees. All organizational forms are on disk. Both come with a 250-page manual.

New York 1st Edition
IBM PC 5-1/4 $69.95/ NYCI
IBM PC 3-1/2 $69.95/ NYC3I
MACINTOSH $69.95/ NYCM

Texas 1st Edition
IBM PC 5-1/4 $69.95/ TCI
IBM PC 3-1/2 $69.95/ TC3I
MACINTOSH $69.95/ TCM

MONEY MATTERS

Stand Up to the IRS

Attorney Fred Daily
National 1st Edition

Stand Up to the IRS gives detailed stategies on surviving an audit with the minimum amount of damage, appealing an audit decision, going to Tax Court and dealing with IRS collectors. It also discusses filing tax returns when you haven't done so in a while, tax crimes, concerns of small business people and getting help from the IRS ombudsman. This book also includes confidential forms, unavailable to taxpayers, used by the IRS during audits and collection interviewers.
$19.95 / SUIRS

Money Troubles:
Legal Strategies to Cope With Your Debts

Attorney Robin Leonard
National 1st Edition

Are you behind on your credit card bills or loan payments? If you are, then *Money Troubles* is exactly what you need. It covers everything from knowing what your rights are, and asserting them, to helping you evaluate your individual situation. This practical, straightforward book is for anyone who needs help understanding and dealing with the complex and often scary topic of debts.
$16.95/MT

How to File for Bankruptcy

Attorneys Stephen Elias, Albin Renauer & Robin Leonard
National 4th Edition

Trying to decide whether or not filing for bankruptcy makes sense? *How to File for Bankruptcy* contains an overview of the process and all the forms plus step-by-step instructions on the procedures to follow.
$24.95/HFB

Simple Contracts for Personal Use

Attorney Stephen Elias & Marcia Stewart
National 2nd Edition

This book contains clearly written legal form contracts to buy and sell property, borrow and lend money, store and lend personal property, release others from personal liability, or pay a contractor to do home repairs. Includes agreements to arrange childcare and other household help.
$16.95/CONT

PATENT, COPYRIGHT & TRADEMARK

Trademark: How to Name Your Business & Product

Attorneys Kate McGrath and Stephen Elias, With Trademark Attorney Sarah Shena
National 1st Edition

This is by far the best comprehensive do-it-yourself trademark book designed for small businesses. It explains step-by-step how to protect names used to market services and products, and shows how to: choose a name or logo that others can't copy, conduct a trademark search, register a trademark with the U.S. Patent and Trademark Office and protect and maintain the trademark.
$29.95 / TRD

Patent It Yourself

Attorney David Pressman
National 3rd Edition

From the patent search to the actual application, this book covers everything including the use and licensing of patents, successful marketing and how to deal with infringement.
$34.95/PAT

How to Copyright Software

Attorney M.J. Salone
National 3rd Edition

This book tells you how to register your copyright for maximum protection and discusses who owns a copyright on software developed by more than one person.
$39.95/COPY

The Inventor's Notebook

Fred Grissom & Attorney David Pressman
National 1st Edition

This book helps you document the process of successful independent inventing by providing forms, instructions, references to relevant areas of patent law, a bibliography of legal and non-legal aids and more.
$19.95/INOT

The Copyright Handbook

Attorney Stephen Fishman
National 1st Edition

Writers, editors, publishers, scholars, educators, librarians and others who work with words all need to know about copyright laws. This book provides forms and step-by-step instructions for protecting all types of written expression under U.S. and international copyright law. It contains detailed reference chapters on such major copyright-related topics as copyright infringement, fair use, works for hire and transfers of copyright ownership.
$24.95/COHA

CONSUMER/REFERENCE

How to Win Your Personal Injury Claim

Attorney Joseph Matthews
National 1st Edition

If you face an insurance company without the information in this book, you may receive a settlement that is only a fraction of what you deserve. If you hire a lawyer, the lawyer will take up to 50% of the settlement in fees and costs. However, settling an injury claim on your own can be simple. All you need is some basic information about how the insurance claims process works.
This book will show you how to:
• protect your rights after an accident
• understand what your claim is worth
• prepare a claim for compensation
• negotiate a fair settlement.
$24.95/PICL

Nolo's Pocket Guide to California Law

Attorney Lisa Guerin and Nolo Press Editors
California 1st Edition

The only plain English guide to the laws that affect you everyday. Get quick clear answers to questions about child support, custody, consumer rights, employee rights, government benefits, divorce, bankruptcy, adoption, wills and much more.
$10.95/CLAW

Barbara Kaufman's
Consumer Action Guide

Barbara Kaufman
California 1st Edition

This practical handbook is filled with information on hundreds of consumer topics. Barbara Kaufman, the Bay Area's award-winning consumer reporter and producer of KCBS Radio's *Call for Action*, gives consumers access to their legal rights, providing addresses and phone numbers of where to complain when things go wrong, and providing resources if more help is necessary.
$14.95/CAG

VISIT OUR STORE

If you live in the Bay Area, be sure to visit the Nolo Press Bookstore on the corner of 9th & Parker Streets in west Berkeley. You'll find our complete line of books and software—new and "damaged"—all at a discount. We also have t-shirts, posters and a selection of business and legal self-help books from other publishers.

Monday to Friday	10 A.M. to 5 P.M.
Thursdays	10 A.M. to 6 P.M.
Saturdays	10 A.M. to 4:30 P.M.
Sundays	11 A.M. to 4 P.M.

NOLO PRESS / 950 PARKER STREET / BERKELEY CA 94710

ORDER FORM

Name

Address (UPS to street address, Priority Mail to P.O. boxes)

Catalog Code	Quantity	Item	Unit price	Total

Subtotal		
Sales tax (California residents only)		
Shipping & handling		
2nd day UPS		
TOTAL		
PRICES SUBJECT TO CHANGE		

SALES TAX
California residents add your local tax

SHIPPING & HANDLING
$4.00   1 item
$5.00   2-3 items
+$.50   each additional item
Allow 2-3 weeks for delivery

IN A HURRY?
UPS 2nd day delivery is available:
Add $5.00 (contiguous states) or
$8.00 (Alaska & Hawaii) to your regular shipping and handling charges

FOR FASTER SERVICE, USE YOUR CREDIT CARD AND OUR TOLL-FREE NUMBERS:
Monday-Friday, 7 a.m. to 5 p.m. Pacific Time
Order line	1 (800) 992-6656
General Information	1 (510) 549-1976
Fax us your order	1 (800) 645-0895

METHOD OF PAYMENT
☐ Check enclosed
☐ VISA ☐ Mastercard ☐ Discover Card ☐ American Express

Account #   Expiration Date

Signature Authorizing

Phone   RUNS

When you register, we'll send you our quarterly newspaper, the *Nolo News,* free for two years. (U.S. addresses only.) Here's what you'll get in every issue:

INFORMATIVE ARTICLES

Written by Nolo editors, articles provide practical legal information on issues you encounter in everyday life: family law, wills, debts, consumer rights, and much more.

UPDATE SERVICE

The *Nolo News* keeps you informed of legal changes that affect any Nolo book and software program.

BOOK AND SOFTWARE REVIEWS

We're always looking for good legal and consumer books and software from other publishers. When we find them, we review them and offer them in our mail order catalog.

ANSWERS TO YOUR LEGAL QUESTIONS

Our readers are always challenging us with good questions on a variety of legal issues. So in each issue, "Auntie Nolo" gives sage advice and sound information.

COMPLETE NOLO PRESS CATALOG

The *Nolo News* contains an up-to-the-minute catalog of all Nolo books and software, which you can order using our toll-free "800" order line. And you can see at a glance if you're using an out-of-date version of a Nolo product.

LAWYER JOKES

Nolo's famous lawyer joke column continually gets the goat of the legal establishment. If we print a joke you send in, you'll get a $20 Nolo gift certificate.

We promise *never* to give your name and address to any other organization.

Your Registration Card

Complete and Mail Today

The Legal Guide for Starting & Running a Small Business — Registration Card

We'd like to know what you think! Please take a moment to fill out and return this postage paid card for a free two-year subscription to the *Nolo News.* If you already receive the *Nolo News,* we'll extend your subscription.

Name _____ Ph.(   ) _____

Address _____

City _____ State _____ Zip _____

Where did you hear about this book? _____

For what purpose did you use this book? _____

Did you consult a lawyer?	Yes	No	Not Applicable			
Was it easy for you to use this book?	(very easy) 5	4	3	2	1	(very difficult)
Did you find this book helpful?	(very) 5	4	3	2	1	(not at all)

Comments _____
_____
_____
_____
_____

THANK YOU   **RUNS**

[Nolo books are]..."written in plain language, free of legal mumbo jumbo, and spiced with witty personal observations."

—ASSOCIATED PRESS

"Well-produced and slickly written, the [Nolo] books are designed to take the mystery out of seemingly involved procedures, carefully avoiding legalese and leading the reader step-by-step through such everyday legal problems as filling out forms, making up contracts, and even how to behave in court."

—SAN FRANCISCO EXAMINER

"...Nolo publications...guide people simply through the how, when, where and why of law."

—WASHINGTON POST

"Increasingly, people who are not lawyers are performing tasks usually regarded as legal work... And consumers, using books like Nolo's, do routine legal work themselves."

—NEW YORK TIMES

"...All of [Nolo's] books are easy-to-understand, are updated regularly, provide pull-out forms...and are often quite moving in their sense of compassion for the struggles of the lay reader."

—SAN FRANCISCO CHRONICLE

NO POSTAGE
NECESSARY
IF MAILED
IN THE
UNITED STATES

BUSINESS REPLY MAIL
FIRST-CLASS MAIL PERMIT NO 3283 BERKELEY CA

POSTAGE WILL BE PAID BY ADDRESSEE

NOLO PRESS
950 Parker Street
Berkeley CA 94710-9867